prism

Volume 16 / Issue 2 / October 2019

THEORY AND MODERN CHINESE LITERATURE

Method as Method

CARLOS ROJAS, *Special issue editor*

CARLOS ROJAS

Method as Method

In 1960 Japanese scholar of Chinese literature Takeuchi Yoshimi gave a pair of lectures titled "Asia as Method," in which he considered how one might engage with Western theory from an East Asian perspective. In this intervention Takeuchi was particularly interested in Western universal values of freedom and equality, noting the manifest tension between these ideals themselves and the imperial legacies with which they are linked. Takeuchi suggested that one response to this tension would be to simply reject these Western ideals out of hand, but he instead proposed that a more productive response would be for Asia to "re-embrace the West" and attempt to improve the West's own ideals by reassessing them from an outside perspective. In order for this to be possible, he concluded, Asia must have "[its] own cultural values." Noting the possibility that "these values do not already exist, in substantive form," Takeuchi concluded that they may nevertheless still be possible "as method"—which is to say, "as the process of the subject's self-formation." He called this process "'Asia as method'" and added that it was "impossible to definitively state what this might mean."[1]

Subsequently published in essay form, Takeuchi's lectures have inspired a wide range of critical interventions, including ones that take as their starting point Asia or Asian regions and others that engage with different objects or phenomena. These studies include Mizoguchi Yūzō's "China as Method" (1989), Kuan-hsing Chen's *Asia as Method* (2004), Yu-lin Lee's "Taiwan as Method" (2009), Stephen Yiu Wai Chu's edited volume *Hong Kong (Studies) as Method* (2016), and Brian Bernards's "Malaysia as Method" (2016). More generally, Takeuchi's approach has been applied to an array of other topics and fields. For instance, from the year 2013 alone, we find Neilson and Mezzadra's *Border as Method*, Ruth Levitas's *Utopia as Method*, and Catherine McKinnon's essay for *Signs*, "Intersectionality as Method." In each case the emphasis on method is both programmatic and oppositional, in that each study proposes an alternative methodological approach while also critically interrogating an existing set of analytical practices.

Taking inspiration from these sorts of interventions, this special issue features essays that focus not on specific objects, phenomena, or theoretical frameworks

PRISM: THEORY AND MODERN CHINESE LITERATURE • 16:2 • OCTOBER 2019
DOI 10.1215/25783491-7978475 • © 2019 LINGNAN UNIVERSITY

in their own right, but rather on an underlying set of methodological processes. This attention to method treats analysis as a type of praxis that produces knowledge through a dialectical engagement with its object rather than assuming that knowledge is either intrinsic to the object itself or is generated solely by the corresponding theoretical framework. Our objective, accordingly, is to propose methodologies that can be delinked from the objects or phenomena that inspired them and can be productively applied to a broader array of issues.

Beyond this attention to methodology itself, we are specifically interested in how these methodological concerns take inspiration from—and may be applied to—a set of Chinese topics. The reasons for this focus on China are twofold. First, to the extent that Western critical theory has often tended to view China as occupying a space of radical alterity, by taking China as our starting point we hope to reveal some of the underlying assumptions on which these Western paradigms are predicated. Second, like the concept of *the West* itself, *China* is a fundamentally heterogeneous category composed of countless differentiable elements that each rely on different sets of assumptions and presuppositions, and one of our objectives is to help reassess how these conceptual categories are constituted in the first place.

The essays in this issue can be divided into three groups that address a set of translational processes, ecological paradigms, and mapping regimes, respectively. In the first group, four essays examine processes by which social realities are figuratively translated into cultural representations—and just as discussions of linguistic translation focus not only on what is able to be translated but also on what is left untranslatable, each of the essays in this first group similarly attend, in different ways, to the inevitable gaps that emerge between social realities and corresponding cultural representations. The essays in the second group, meanwhile, all revolve around a set of ecological concerns, in the sense of an interest in the relationships between different elements within a larger ecosystem (either literal or metaphorical)—including relationships that range from being nominally harmonious to parasitic to self-consumptive. Finally, the essays in the third group all engage with questions of mapping, including not only the assignation of geopolitical borders but also processes of conceptual categorization and differentiation—and particularly how we may understand the categories of *China* and *Asia* themselves.

The first group of essays attend to the translational nexus between interpretive frameworks and their corresponding objects. First, in my own essay, I use translation as a prism through which to consider how literary works negotiate their relationship to a set of embedded voices that they seek to represent. Just as translation studies often zero in on the figure of the untranslatable as a limit point of translatability, what is particularly interesting about this focus on processes of translation between various voices within and outside the text is not necessarily what gets translated but rather what inevitably gets left out of this translational process. More broadly, translation (both literal and metaphorical) functions not merely as the object of analysis; it also becomes a model for understanding the analytical process itself. Next, Christopher Rea turns to fictional works about tricks or hoaxes. If translation, in the abstract, gestures toward the possibility of effectively transposing meaning from one medium to another, the figure of the hoax aspires to the precise opposite—of using one medium to *misrepresent* the contents of another. Through a survey of a wide variety of Chinese literary and cinematic works, Rea proposes eight different categories of hoaxes, and in the process opens up a broader reflection on the nature of creativity and cultural representation itself. To the extent that fiction itself may be viewed as a kind of hoax—an attempt to convince readers to accept (even if only provisionally) a set of counterfactual propositions—literary and cinematic portrayals of hoaxes may therefore be viewed as a microcosm of cultural representation itself, and by focusing representations of misrepresentation, Rae offers a more nuanced inquiry into our understanding of representation.

The other two essays in this first group both take as their starting point phenomena that are closely linked to processes of urbanization in contemporary China, and they use these phenomena to offer a broader reflection on issues of social structure and processes of representation. First Margaret Hillenbrand considers a subgenre of cultural production featuring images of urban waste or refuse. Hillenbrand considers not only how artists take urban waste and transform it into art, but also the striking absence, in many of the works in question, of the people who live in and around these urban waste dumps and struggle to eke out a living by collecting discarded items and putting them back into circulation. From this point Hillenbrand develops a critical reflection on the structural relationship between concepts of waste and precarity. Borrowing Walter Benjamin's figure of the ragpicker, Hillenbrand uses rag picking to describe the methodological approach not only of the contemporary artists seeking to represent urban waste as well as the precariat forced to make a living collecting that same waste, but also of the analysts, like Hillenbrand herself, who attempt to interpret this phenomenon in the first place. In the next essay Yomi Braester turns to a different dimension of urbanization in contemporary China, which is the tendency—found across a wide array of different media—to produce images featuring broad urban vistas. Braester considers the underlying forces and tendencies responsible for producing this phenomenon, which he dubs a panoramic imaginary in contemporary Chinese urbanism. Just as Hillenbrand focuses on rag picking to draw attention to conditions of precarity in contemporary urban China, Braester is similarly interested in using a panoramic methodology to offer insight into how social relations and the possibility of civic engagement are being reimagined and reconfigured in contemporary China.

The second group of essays consider a set of concerns that could be characterized as ecological, in the sense that they are about the interrelationship between different entities and forces within a larger environment. This focus on ecology, however, does not necessarily emphasize a harmonious relationship among the various elements that make up a certain ecosystem, and instead it may emphasize the internal tensions and contestations within that same system.

First Robin Visser considers a collection of Sinophone eco-fiction from or about Inner Mongolia—including works either by ethnic Mongol authors or by an ethnically Han author who lived in Inner Mongolia. In different ways each of these works gestures to the possibility of an indigenous ontology that might present a radical alternative to the agrarian, industrialized logic associated with the majority Han culture, or what Visser calls *Hanspace*. At points these indigenous perspectives suggest the possibility of a radically non-anthropocentric ecological ontology, wherein humanity is simply one element among many.

Next Lorraine Wong turns to a rather different form of anti-anthropomorphism, in the form of cannibalism. In particular Wong considers a recent Hong Kong television series that explores the aftermath of an incident in which three young members of a band consumed the flesh of a fourth bandmate after the group lost their way in a blizzard. The majority of the series is then set eighteen years later, in 2010, and traces the attempts by the surviving bandmates to come to terms with the traumatic legacy of the earlier cannibalistic incident. Treating cannibalism not only as a cultural trope but also as a methodological approach in its own right, Wong suggests that the series uses this act of self-consumption to comment on the threat that China poses to contemporary Hong Kong and also to deconstruct a set of binary oppositions between colonizer and colonized, inside and outside, self and other.

Finally Belinda Kong examines the concept of pandemic, which she suggests is most productively understood not as an autonomous category but rather as a set of discursive relations. In particular Kong notes that US discourses of infection and contagion often tend to target Asian bodies and regions, reflecting a logic that Kong calls bio-orientalism. In this way Kong uses the discursive nexus of pandemic to examine some of the ways in which logics of biosecurity, geopolitics, and neo-orientalism are intricately intertwined with one another.

Although all of the preceding essays focus on topics relating to Chinese society and culture, it is in the final group that we find the most explicit reflections on the categories of China and Asia themselves. Collectively these final four essays ask how we might understand China's relationship to the West and to other Asian regions, as well as the relationship between various different Chinese regions themselves.

The first two essays in this final grouping each take a specific text as their starting point. Shuang Shen looks at the 2013 novel *Crazy Rich Asians* by Singapore-born and US-based author Kevin Kwan, while Petrus Liu focuses on the 1992 martial arts film *Swordsman II: Asia the Invincible*, directed by Hong Kong director Ching Siu-tung and produced by the Vietnam-born Hong Kong filmmaker Tsui Hark. Shen takes Kwan's novel as a provocation to think beyond a set of conventional East-West boundaries and to rethink the concept of borders in the context of a global Chinese diaspora. Liu takes Ching's film as an invitation to reexamine the significance and ramifications of the Cold War, arguing that the concept (and its corresponding methodologies) should be expanded to include not only tensions within Asia itself, but also phenomena following the 1991 collapse of the Soviet Union.

In their coauthored essay "Script as Method," Laikwan Pang and Ko Chun-kit use the Chinese writing system as a lens through which to examine the post-1949 split between Communist China, on the one hand, and Taiwan, Hong Kong, and other Sinophone regions, on the other. Pang and Ko are specifically interested in the ramifications of China's decision in the 1950s to adapt simplified versions of many Chinese characters. Although in principle this simplification process was carried out in order to help increase literacy levels in China, in practice, when combined with the strict censorship policies that China began implementing around the same period, it yielded a system wherein many texts can only be published in one version of the Chinese script and not the other. Pang and Ko focus specifically on works that can currently only be published in the "complicated" script (*fantizi* 繁體字) used in Taiwan, Hong Kong, and elsewhere and not in the "simplified" script (*jiantizi* 簡體字) used in Mainland China.

Finally Hsiao-hung Chang takes Taiwan's recent legalization of same-sex marriage to reflect on the implications of the claim that Taiwan was the "first in Asia" to reach this important legal-political threshold. Through a dialogue with Takeuchi's "Asia as Method" and related texts, Chang proposes two distinct ways of viewing Asia, which she dubs *Area Asia* (i.e., Asia as a concrete geo-historical region) and *bloc asia* (i.e., Asia as a virtual aggregate), respectively. Taking inspiration from Takeuchi's suggestion, in his 1960 "Asia as Method" lectures, that Asia should attempt to "roll back" the West's ideals of universal equality so as to help realize the unrealized potentiality contained within those ideals themselves, Chang suggests that contemporary debates over same-sex marriage in Taiwan offer a similar opportunity to reassess not only the Western ideals of universal equality on which these debates are grounded but also the category of Asia against which these contemporary debates are being played out.

To the extent that all of these essays share an interest in method, accordingly, this special issue itself could be viewed as a meta-reflection on method as method—which is to say, on the implications of taking methodology as an object of focus in its own right. In contrast to approaches centered on texts or objects, which tend to elide theoretical and methodological considerations, and in contrast to theory-centered approaches, which tend to take for granted the universal applicability of the theoretical paradigm in question, a methodology-based approach attends simultaneously to both objects and theories—including both ways in which objects are constituted by specific sets of theoretical assumptions and the ways in which theoretical paradigms often rely on the objects and localities out of which they emerge. By inviting focus on methodologies rather than on objects or theories, accordingly, we seek to denaturalize both objects and theories, thereby enabling approaches that are more attuned to the ways in which they mutually constitute one another.

The cover image of this special issue illustrates the volume's twin concerns with methodology, on the one hand, and with reexamining a set of transregional and transcultural hermeneutic practices on the other. The image is a reproduction of a 2003 painting titled *Fan Kuan—Cezanne N*, by the New York–based expatriate Chinese artist Hongtu Zhang 張宏圖 (fig. 1). Part of a series of works in which Zhang uses the distinctive painting styles of famous modern European painters to re-create iconic paintings from premodern China, this particular work uses the post-impressionist style of Paul Cézanne to re-create a work attributed to the Northern Song dynasty landscape painter Fan Kuan 范寬 (ca. 950–ca. 1032), who is best known for his painting *Travelers among Mountains and Streams* 谿山行旅圖 (Xishan xinglü tu)—a monumental mountain-scape with a tiny mule train in the foreground (fig. 2). This iconic work is widely regarded as a classic in the Chinese landscape tradition and has been endlessly reproduced and imitated. The painting that inspired the work used as the cover image of this issue, however, is not *Travelers among Mountains and Streams* but rather *Sitting Alone by a Stream* 臨流獨坐圖 (Linliu duzuo tu) (fig. 3). Although traditionally attributed to Fan Kuan, the work in question does not bear his seal or signature (though it does feature a large array of collector's seals and inscriptions, documenting the subsequent circulation of the painting itself), and furthermore some of the work's stylistic features suggest that it was produced by some later artist working in the Fan Kuan style. In particular, while *Sitting Alone by a Stream* shares compositional elements with *Travelers among Mountains and Streams*, other elements, such as the brushwork used for the rocks and for the human figure in the foreground, are incompatible with the style found in Fan Kuan's known paintings or other works from his period.

In his own contemporary painting, however, Zhang takes these specific points of stylistic divergence between an authentic Fan Kuan painting like *Travelers among Mountains and Streams* and a historically and stylistically proximate work like the extant version of *Sitting Alone by a Stream* and turns them on their head. Instead Zhang has created a work that hews quite closely to the compositional model of the earlier work but radically diverges from it in stylistic terms—in that nearly all the stylistic elements of the original (e.g., brushwork,

FIGURE 1. Hongtu Zhang 張宏圖, *Fan Kuan—Cézanne N.* Oil on canvas, 70×48 in., 2003. Reproduced with permission of the artist.

texture, and coloration) have been replaced with elements inspired by the work of Cézanne (the work may be compared, for instance, to Cézanne's *Mont Sainte-Victoire*, which has a rather different compositional arrangement but similar stylistic features as Zhang's contemporary work) (fig. 4).

On the surface, Zhang's work may be viewed as an allegorical commentary on a process of Western appropriation of non-Western cultural elements, particularly in the modern period (for instance, it is well known that the Impressionist movement took inspiration in part from Japanese ukioyo-e woodblock prints). In context, however, the situation is somewhat more complicated, insofar as Zhang, throughout his career, has explicitly positioned himself at the interstices of Chinese and Western art, using a strategic dialogue between these two traditions as a site of artistic creativity and social critique. Moreover, in using a later artistic style (Cézanne's) to reimagine an earlier one (Fan Kuan's, or that of the

FIGURE 2. Fan Kuan 範寬, *Travelers among Mountains and Streams* 谿山行旅圖. Hanging scroll, ink and light color on silk, 206.3×103.3cm., tenth to eleventh century National Palace Museum, Taipei. Public domain.

FIGURE 3. Artist unknown (sometimes attributed to Fan Kuan 范寬), *Sitting Alone by a Stream* 臨流獨坐圖. Hanging scroll, ink and light color on silk, 156.1×106.3cm, eleventh century. National Palace Museum, Taipei. Public domain.

unidentified later Song dynasty artist working in the Fan Kuan tradition), Zhang is invoking an artistic practice with deep roots in Chinese art history. That is to say, whereas imitations in the context of Western art are often viewed as either a form of apprenticeship (part of an artist's training) or a form of deception (plagiarism), in a traditional Chinese context this is viewed as a highly valorized form of artistic creativity in its own right—wherein artists simultaneously pay tribute to earlier masters while at the same time using the process of imitation (or imitation with difference) to develop their own distinctive stylistic attributes.

Known as *fang* 放, or "imitation," the Chinese artistic practice Hongtu Zhang is imitating in his contemporary work can be seen as an exercise in pure method, wherein the painting's artistry lies precisely in its performance of a multiple overlapping processes of imitation—an imitation of Cézanne's style, an imitation of

FIGURE 4. Paul Cézanne, *Mont Sainte-Victoire (La Montagne Sainte-Victoire).* Oil on canvas, 57.2×97.2cm, circa 1902–6. Metropolitan Museum of Art. Public domain.

Fan Kuan's compositional qualities, an imitation of the unidentified Song artist's imitation of Fan Kuan's work, as well as an imitation of the Chinese artistic practice of *fang* itself. In this way Zhang offers a reflection on the complicated interplay between tradition and modernity, Chinese and Western practices, form and content, creativity and reproduction. In deploying imitation as a method, he simultaneously makes it an object in its own right while also positioning it as the potential basis for a theory of artistic practice and cultural negotiation.

CARLOS ROJAS is professor of Chinese cultural studies; gender, sexuality, and feminist studies; and arts of the moving image at Duke University. He is the author, editor, and translator of numerous books, including *Homesickness: Culture, Contagion, and National Transformation* (2015).

Note

1 Takeuchi, "Asia as Method," 165.

Reference

Takeuchi, Yoshimi. "Asia as Method." In *What Is Modernity? Writings of Takeuchi Yoshimi*, edited and translated by Richard F. Calichman, 149–65. New York: Columbia University Press, 2005.

CARLOS ROJAS

Translation as Method

ABSTRACT Taking Lu Xun's work as its starting point, this essay examines translation as a methodology for negotiating not between different languages or dialects but rather between different voices. To the extent that some fiction attempts to manifest the voices of socially marginalized figures, this translational approach offers a way of examining the possibilities and limits of this sort of negotiation. By extension, a similar translational framework may also be used to understand the attempts by critics to assess fiction's own attempts to render these marginalized voices.

KEYWORDS translation, voice, Lu Xun, Yan Lianke, subaltern

> A translation issues from the original—not so much from its life as from its afterlife.
>
> —Walter Benjamin

At first glance, the English title of Leo Ou-fan Lee's 李歐梵 1987 study of Lu Xun 魯迅 (1881–1936), *Voices from the Iron House*, might appear to be a close approximation of the title of Yi Huimin's 尹慧珉 1991 Chinese-language version of the work, *Tiewu zhong de nahan* 鐵屋中的吶喊.[1] The Chinese title of Lee's study references a pair of terms Lu Xun famously used in an early discussion of his own work, and Lee's original 1987 title would appear to feature straightforward renderings of those same terms into English. Upon closer inspection, however, it turns out that several crucial differences intervene within this translational process from Chinese into English and back into Chinese—with the result being that not only are the two versions of Lee's title *not* precisely equivalent to one another; they actually express exactly opposite meanings.

Of course, there is no requirement that the title of a book published in translation must necessarily be an exact rendering of the work's original title, and it is certainly the case that the titles of each version of Lee's study resonate well with one another. At the same time, however, it is worth examining the specific points where the meanings of two titles diverge, because these divergences underscore an important tension within Lu Xun's own fictional project—a tension, moreover, that relates to a broader set questions of translation pertaining to literature in general.

PRISM: THEORY AND MODERN CHINESE LITERATURE • 16:2 • OCTOBER 2019
DOI 10.1215/25783491-7978483 •

In *Voices from the Iron House*, Lee notes that Lu Xun was active as a translator from the beginning of his career. In fact, as early as 1903, his first year in Japan, Lu Xun translated into Chinese Jules Verne's novels *From the Earth to the Moon* and *Journey to the Center of the Earth*, for which he relied primarily on Japanese retranslations of English translations of Verne's original French texts. Not only are the resulting translations of each of these texts several orders removed from the French originals, but Lu Xun also took considerable liberties in editing and adapting the source texts, resulting in a process of free translation that subsequently came to be called "heroic translation" (*haojieyi* 豪傑譯).[2] Moreover, Lu Xun maintained a commitment to translation throughout his career, though his perspective on the process underwent significant transformations over time. In particular, whereas many of Lu Xun's early translations were loose adaptations that were often based on retranslations, in his later years he turned instead to a hyper-literal approach he called "hard translation" (*yingyi* 硬譯), which involved producing a virtually unintelligible word-for-word rendering of the source text. Focusing on Russian-language literature and Marxist theoretical works, Lu Xun produced translations that attempted to preserve the syntax and word order of the original, despite the fact that the result was often difficult to parse in Chinese.

In this trajectory from his early exercise in heroic translation to his later advocacy of hard translation, Lu Xun straddled the two dominant approaches that Friedrich Schleiermacher calls reader-friendly and author-friendly translation, respectively. As Lawrence Venuti explains, "Schleiermacher allowed the translator to choose between a *domesticating* method, an ethnocentric reduction of the foreign text to target-language cultural values, bringing the author back home, and a *foreignizing* method, an ethnodeviant pressure on those values to register the linguistic and cultural difference of the foreign text, sending the reader abroad."[3] In Lu Xun's case, his early translations were attempts to introduce foreign ideas in a form that would be easy for Chinese readers to digest, and he pursued them at a moment when there was considerable interest in such widely accessible Chinese translations.[4] His later efforts, meanwhile, deliberately sought to preserve the foreignness of the source text and, in the process, help transform the Chinese language from within.[5]

In the following discussion, however, I am interested not in Lu Xun's translations between different *languages* but rather in his approach to the problem of how to figuratively translate between different *voices*. In particular, I examine the relationship between Lu Xun's own literary voice and those of the fictional characters who populate his works, together with the extratextual voices of the individuals whom he is representing and addressing in his fiction. I argue that, in mediating between these two sets of voices (namely, Lu Xun's own and those of others), Lu Xun alternately draws on what we might call domesticating and foreignizing approaches, and the true significance of his works lies in the interplay between these two different methodological approaches. More generally, I am interested in how this sort of attention to the process of translating between voices can be applied to a broader range of literary works, particularly works about subjects that have tended to be marginalized or silenced within mainstream discourse.

In using translation to examine the relationship between literary representation and silenced voices, I am also proposing that translation may serve as a useful model for the way in which literary critique seeks to transpose its object of analysis into the language of criticism. Moreover, just as a translational method may ultimately be most interested in moments of translational failure, an approach that views analysis as itself a form of translation will be similarly attuned to the possibility of analytical failure, including the potential inability of analysis to engage with the marginalized voices with which the literary works in question are in potential dialogue.

Voices and Shouts

Both versions of Lee's title trope on Lu Xun's iron house allegory from the preface to his first collection of short stories, *Nahan* 吶喊 (Call to Arms, 1923). In this essay Lu Xun describes how in 1918 his colleague Qian Xuantong 錢玄同 (1887–1939) tried to encourage him to contribute to the literary journal *Xin qingnian* 新青年 (New Youth). Feeling pessimistic about the possibility of implementing sociopolitical reform, Lu Xun initially responded by comparing contemporary China to an iron house full of sleepers unaware that they are in a death trap. Lu Xun asked Qian whether it would be ethical to try to rouse the sleepers, if in doing so one would probably only increase the agony they would experience during their resulting death. Qian responded by observing that if, upon awakening, there was even a slight possibility that the sleepers might be able to save themselves, then one should certainly attempt to rouse them and grant them that option. Acknowledging Qian's point, Lu Xun proceeded to compose and publish several stories offering a critique of the problems plaguing contemporary China—explaining that he was using these stories to attempt to give his readers a sense of hope that he himself was not able to share. A few years later, in 1923, Lu Xun republished several of these early texts as a single volume, for which he wrote the preface containing his iron house allegory.

Lu Xun titled his first short story collection *Nahan*, and in the corresponding preface he included four separate instances of this binome—which in Chinese can be used either as a noun ("a shout") or as a verb ("to shout").[6] In its first and last appearances in the preface, the binome is used to cite the title of the short story collection itself, while in the other two instances it refers to Lu Xun's hypothetical efforts to figuratively awaken his slumbering compatriots. Whether used to refer to the title of Lu Xun's volume or to the act of shouting, however, all four of these instances of the binome in the preface clearly refer to the author's *own* attempts use his literary writings to elicit a productive response from his compatriots and thereby help promote sociopolitical reform—suggesting that these figurative shouts ultimately function as a metonym for Lu Xun's literary project itself.

Although at first glance the use of *nahan* in the 1991 Chinese-language title of Lee's book might appear to be a direct transposition of the use of *voices* in the 1987 English-language title, which in turn seems to invoke a key term from Lu Xun's preface to his 1923 collection of short stories, in actuality the meaning of this term diverges at each step in this translational process. To begin with, in English the word *voices* fails to capture the specific connotations of "shouting" present in the Chinese term, and instead the word refers more generally to utterances of various sorts. Second, although *nahan*, if used as a noun, could in principle be either singular or plural, the corresponding term in Lee's English-language title is plural and, furthermore, is used in a way that would almost always refer to utterances of multiple different individuals. Accordingly, whereas the *nahan* in Lee's Chinese title clearly refers to Lu Xun's own utterances, the corresponding reference to *voices* in the English-language title presumably refers to the voices of the people trapped inside the proverbial iron house.

In sum, while Lee's 1995 Chinese-language title could be translated back into English as "[Lu Xun's] shouts *to* [those sleeping inside] the iron house," his original 1987 English-language title appears to refer instead to the "voices *from* [those sleeping inside] the iron house." That is to say, whereas the Chinese title follows the spirit of Lu Xun's preface and emphasizes the author's self-described attempt to awaken his sleeping compatriots, the English title instead refers to the voices of those compatriots themselves. In context, accordingly, the meanings of these versions of Lee's book title are precisely opposed to one another—insofar as one refers to Lu Xun's own writings and the other refers instead to the voices of those with whom he is in dialogue. My point, however, is not that it is necessary to choose between one approach and the other (i.e., a textual versus contextual reading of Lu Xun's works) but rather that it would be useful to examine the interpretive gaps that open between the two versions of Lee's title.

Here I am interested in the relationship between Lu Xun's shouts and the other voices with which he is implicitly in dialogue, and specifically the ways in which remediated versions of these other voices are incorporated into Lu Xun's fiction (i.e., his figurative shouts). These remediated voices can be divided into three categories, of which the first two follow directly from Lu Xun's iron house allegory, while the third represents an interesting lacuna within his work. That is to say, while some of Lu Xun's fictional characters correspond to the sociopolitically awakened state that Lu Xun seeks to bring about through his fiction, others are instead reminiscent of the allegory's "sound sleepers." A paradigmatic example of the former would be the protagonist of Lu Xun's short story "Kuangren riji" 狂人日記 (Diary of a Madman)—initially published in 1918 and subsequently reprinted as the first story in *Nahan*. In this work, the titular diarist has managed to gain some awareness of contemporary Chinese society's self-destructive nature, which he articulates through his insistence that everyone around him has cannibalistic tendencies. Although the fictional diarist is not necessarily aware that he is advancing a sociopolitical critique, his vision of a cannibalistic society is conventionally viewed as a powerful indictment of contemporary Chinese society's regressive tendencies. Conversely, in Lu Xun's short story "Kong Yiji" 孔乙己—initially published in 1919 and reprinted as the second story in *Nahan*—the protagonist is an aspiring scholar known as Kong Yiji[7] who has spent decades studying for the imperial civil service examinations but has never succeeded in passing the exams and consequently was never able to find employment. In the story's diegetic present, Kong Yiji has been reduced to begging and stealing in order to try to cover his growing debt at the local tavern, even as he continues to promote ideas and attitudes associated with the Confucian worldview contained in the texts he was studying for the exams.

Although these two categories of remediated voices—namely, those of society's proverbial sleepers and those of the figuratively awakened—might appear to be diametrically opposed, in many of Lu Xun's stories they are in fact interwoven with one another in complex ways. For example, in "Diary of a Madman," the diarist's voice is contrasted with those of his family and neighbors, who not only remain oblivious to society's self-destructive condition but are even unwittingly complicit in helping to perpetuate it. Consequently, while the diarist's critical insight into the problems plaguing contemporary society is manifested through his conviction that his family and neighbors are all cannibals, others around him discount his words as merely the ravings of a madman. Similarly, although none of the other characters in "Kong Yiji" shares the titular character's reliance on traditional Confucian scholarship and ideology, it is also true that none of them appears particularly enlightened either—and instead of recognizing the degree to which Kong Yiji is a victim of a social system that is largely beyond his control, these other characters instead settle for mocking and belittling him. In both stories, accordingly, the voice of the protagonist is presented as being in dialogic interaction with the voices of other characters, and underlying these different voices are markedly different understandings of the sociopolitical status of contemporary China.

Another layer of complexity involves the relationship between Lu Xun's nominal protagonists and their respective narrators. In some cases, the narrator appears to be significantly less enlightened than the protagonist—as is the case, for instance, in "Diary of a Madman," which opens with a short preface in which the first-person narrator explains that the journal in question was written by an old friend who, at the time he wrote the journal, was suffering from an acute case of "persecution complex" (*pohuaikuang* 迫害狂). The narrator adds that he has decided to preserve the journal as a service to the medical profession, in the hope that it might be useful to researchers working on mental illness. The implication, accordingly, is that the diarist is profoundly misunderstood not only by his own family and the other members of his community, but also by the fictional narrator, who decides to preserve and publish the diary in question. Conversely, in other works the narrator may appear to be somewhat *more* awakened than the nominal protagonist. For instance, "Kong Yiji" is narrated by a young boy who at the age of twelve began working at a local tavern, where he encountered the man known as Kong Yiji. More so than the tavern's other patrons, however, the young narrator appears to retain a certain degree of sympathy for the failed scholar and seems to intuit that he is a victim of circumstances largely beyond his control. In the end, however, the narrator settles for merely describing what he observes at the tavern and makes little effort to actually help Kong Yiji, even as his circumstances between increasingly dire.

A particularly good example of the intertwining of different voices can be found in Lu Xun's story "Yao" 藥 (Medicine)—initially published in 1919 and reprinted as the third story in *Nahan*. The story describes how the parents of a tubercular boy attempt to cure their son by feeding him a steamed bun soaked in human blood, but as the story develops it becomes increasingly clear that the central concern of the work is not so much the sick boy and the folk remedy that fails to save his life but rather the executed man from whom the blood for the remedy is taken. It turns out that the man was a revolutionary who had been turned in to the authorities by his own relatives and was subsequently executed on account of his political activities—though we as readers only learn all of this information indirectly, via the accounts of other characters who clearly do not understand the significance of the stories they are telling. In other words, embedded within Lu Xun's story—in his figurative shouts—we find the voices of the allegory's "sound sleepers," while embedded within the voices of those same sleepers we find remediated traces of the voice of an "awakened" revolutionary. The story, accordingly, features two sets of translational processes—whereby the revolutionary's words are first recounted (or translated) by the other work's other characters and then are incorporated (or retranslated) into Lu Xun's story itself. Moreover, it is precisely the failure of the first set of translations (in that none of the story's other characters appear to have any real appreciation of what the revolutionary stood for or even any clear understanding of what he was saying) that sets the groundwork for the potential success of the second set of translations (in that Lu Xun attempts to use the characters' inability to understand the revolutionary's message in order to communicate that same message, together with the circumstances of its marginalization, to his readers). By dramatizing these multiple processes of translation and transmediation, in other words, Lu Xun presents his story as a figurative shout that might thereby help to awaken his somnolent compatriots.

In addition to these two categories of dormant and awakened characters, Lu Xun's works also feature a third set of characters who are radically disempowered and are effectively silent. In some cases these disempowered characters (who may include peasants, servants, and women) are literally voiceless, in that they have no speaking roles within the text itself, while in other cases they are figuratively voiceless, insofar as no one (including the story's protagonists and perhaps even the author himself) appears capable of understanding them.

One example of this latter sort of voiceless character is the peasant servant woman in Lu Xun's story "Zhufu" 祝福 (Benediction, also translated as "New Year's Sacrifice"), initially published in 1924 and reprinted as the first story in his second collection of stories, *Panghuang* 徬徨 (Wandering, 1926). The work begins with the narrator's description of his lunar New Year's trip visit to see some relatives, the Lu clan, where he encounters a woman known simply as Xiang Lin's wife (Xiang Lin *sao* 祥林嫂). The woman had previously worked for the Lu clan, but by this point she is living on the streets as a beggar. She asks the narrator whether people become ghosts after they die, and he is deeply troubled by his inability to give her a satisfactory answer. The narrator worries that the woman's question might have been some sort of premonition, and that evening he is further disconcerted to learn that Xiang Lin's wife passed away shortly after he saw her. After this short opening account, the story then offers a retrospective overview of the woman's bleak life, whereby "fragments of her life, seen or heard before, now combined to form one whole" 先前所見所聞的她的半生事跡的斷片，至此也聯成一片了.[8] In particular, we are told that Xiang Lin's wife was first brought in to work for the Lu clan after having recently been widowed, and a few months later her former mother-in-law sent some men to retrieve her so that she could be remarried. Despite her desperate attempts to resist the remarriage, Xiang Lin's wife was forcibly married and soon after became pregnant. She had a son, but within three years of the marriage her husband died of illness and her son was killed by a wolf, after which the Lu clan agreed to take her in again. The story concludes with the narrator waking up on the morning of the New Year's festival and finding that the doubts that had plagued him as a result of his encounter with Xiang Lin's wife the previous day have been washed away by the tumult of the New Year's celebrations.

Although Xiang Lin's wife is not exactly silent, the story repeatedly focuses on the ways in which her voice is systematically elided. For instance, after returning to the Lu clan, she repeatedly recounts how her son was eaten by a wolf, and while those around her initially find her tragic story to be a source of amusement, they soon grow bored with her routine. In fact, eventually even the narrator shifts his attention from the news of her death to the family's New Year's celebrations.

In her 1983 article "Can the Subaltern Speak?," Gayatri Spivak asks whether subalterns—which is to say, individuals who are radically disempowered along multiple different axes—can ever truly make their voices heard within the discursive spheres from which they are structurally excluded. Spivak argues that in attempting to recuperate subaltern voices previously excluded from the historical record, even progressive scholars like the Subaltern Studies Group run the risk of simply appropriating those voices for their own purposes. Part of Spivak's argument relies on a consideration of the relationship between two distinct concepts that are both contained within the English verb *to represent* but are distinguishable in German. She explains that *to represent* can be rendered in German either as *darstellen* or as *vertreten*—with the first referring to a process of aesthetically re-presenting someone and the second referring to the process of politically standing in for someone. Spivak argues that it is ultimately impossible to disaggregate these two processes, in that the act of aesthetic re-presentation inevitably involves a process of political representation. Contending that it is impossible to reproduce someone else's words without at the same time standing in for them (and, by extension, using them for one's own purposes), she concluded at the time that "the subaltern cannot speak."

In this context, the fact that subaltern figures in Lu Xun's stories are comparatively silent may be viewed as a constructive response to the type of conundrum that Spivak posits. That is to say, rather than attempting to speak on behalf of those who are structurally voiceless, Lu Xun's works instead tend to let those silences speak for themselves, thereby permitting the possibility that the characters' silence—which is to say, the strategic erasure of their voices—may become a powerful social commentary in its own right. The works' primary significance, accordingly, lies not so much in the stories they tell but rather in the ways in which they illustrate how subaltern voices may be systematically undermined and elided or appropriated for other purposes.

Of course, Spivak's point in the article in question is that, even if the subaltern's silencing is easily diagnosable, there is no obvious solution to it, since any attempt to speak on behalf of the subaltern (which is to say, to translate their language into one that is legible by the power/knowledge systems from which they are structurally excluded) necessarily entails the possibility of speaking *for* them and thereby appropriating their voices to further someone else's objectives.[9] In other words, to the extent that the act of critical intervention may be compared to a process of translation, it is invariably haunted by the specter of mistranslation.

The Blind Man and the Lamp

Lu Xun's concept of "hard translation" is similar to what the celebrated author and translator Yang Jiang 楊絳 (1911–2016) calls "dead translation" (*siyi* 死譯), by which Yang means a clause-by-clause mapping of the original text into the target language. More specifically, in a 1986 essay, Yang (who translated *Don Quixote* and other works into Chinese) characterizes her translational practice as a progression from "dead translation" to what she calls "hard translation" (*yingyi* 硬譯), meaning a translation that is technically accurate but comparatively rigid, and finally to a process of "direct translation" (*zhiyi* 直譯), by which she means an optimal melding of meaning and form.[10] Although Yang Jiang's terminology here is slightly different from Lu Xun's, they both use the term "hard translation" to emphasize the way in which a highly literal translation may produce a profound sense of defamiliarization that, in turn, is essential to the translational process.

Walter Benjamin (1892–1940), in his celebrated 1923 essay "The Task of the Translator," uses a similar concept of what he calls *Wörtlichkeit*, or literally "word-by-word-ness," to argue that it is only by means of a hyper-literal rendering of the primary text that translation may thereby remain completely faithful to the original: "A real translation is transparent, it does not cover the original, does not block its light, but allows the pure language, as though reinforced by its own medium, to shine upon the original all the more fully. This may be achieved, above all, by a literal rendering of the syntax which proves words rather than sentences to be the primary element of the translator."[11] Benjamin's emphasis on the importance of letting the light of the original shine through in the translation, however, is in productive dialogue with another key metaphor for translation that he introduces in this essay: namely, the metaphor of translation as a kind of "afterlife" of the original.[12] Whereas Benjamin's concept of "word-by-word-ness" emphasizes a close fidelity to the original, he invokes the metaphor of translation as afterlife to argue that "one can demonstrate that no translation would be possible if in its ultimate essence it strove for likeness to the original. For in its afterlife—which could not be called that if it were not a transformation and a renewal of something living—the original undergoes a change. Even words with fixed meaning can undergo a maturing process."[13] In likening translation to a form of afterlife, in other words, Benjamin implies that the translational process is predicated on the figurative death of the original—suggesting that translation involves a process of speaking through death.

A contemporary author who engages in a particularly compelling manner with issues of translation, death, and the remediation of marginalized voices is Yan Lianke 閻連科 (1958–). Born in 1958 in rural Henan, Yan joined the People's Liberation Army (PLA) in 1978, the same year Deng Xiaoping 鄧小平 (1904–97) launched the Reform and Opening Up campaign, and he published his first story the following year. Yan Lianke proceeded to work as a professional author for the PLA for over a quarter century, and while his early work was written in a social-realist tradition, in the late 1990s he began to develop a more experimental approach that used dark humor to explore a set of social concerns. One of the distinguishing characteristics of these latter works is that they incorporate an array of different voices, including voices of children, peasants, bureaucrats, and intellectuals, and a wide array of discursive styles, including Biblical discourse, mythological discourse, historiographic discourse, revolutionary discourse, and a form of "Mao-speak" that tropes on Chairman Mao's distinctive blend of slogans, poetry, and Marxist theory.

Underlying this cacophony of disparate voices and discourses, meanwhile, is a focus on a set of marginalized individuals and communities. For instance, the novel *Riguang liunian* 日光流年 (Streams of Time, 1998) features a cancer village whose residents are poisoned by excessive chlorine in the water supply, leading them to suffer afflictions that include darkened teeth, joint disease, skeletal deformities, and paralysis;[14] *Shouhuo* 受活 (Lenin's Kisses, 2004) revolves around a similarly remote village in which virtually all of the residents are handicapped; *Dingzhuang meng* 丁莊夢 (Dream of Ding Village, 2006) features a so-called AIDS village (*aizibing cun* 艾滋病村) where most of the residents become infected with the AIDS virus as a result of contaminated blood-selling equipment; and *Sishu* 四書 (The Four Books, 2010) features a reeducation camp for accused rightists during the Great Leap Forward and the ensuing Great Famine. While the fictional communities featured in these works represent social formations that have been systematically erased from the historical record, Yan Lianke makes a concerted attempt to recreate their voices and to dramatize the predicaments that they face.

Paralleling Yan's attention to marginalized communities, meanwhile, is a focus on death. In *Streams of Time*, for instance, all of the village's residents are fated to die before they reach the age of forty—with death sometimes coming just moments before what would have been the victim's fortieth birthday. The result is that all of the villagers live their entire lives under the immediate shadow of death—a fact that is dramatized by the novel's unusual structure, whereby the narrative begins with the protagonist's death, and then works its way backward to his birth. In *Lenin's Kisses,* meanwhile, the novel's focus on the handicapped residents of the remote community of Liven—which, for most of its history, was so marginalized that it didn't even appear on the maps of the three closest counties—is paralleled by the work's focus on the afterlife of Lenin's embalmed corpse, which a local bureaucrat decides to purchase from Moscow in order to install it in a new Lenin Mausoleum in the Chinese county under his jurisdiction. In *Dream of Ding Village*, the narrator is a twelve-year-old boy who, before the beginning of the main narrative, is poisoned by another villager in retribution for the role that the boy's father had (unwittingly) played in contributing to the village's blood-borne HIV/AIDS epidemic. Roughly half of the novel is narrated in the voice of the dead boy, from beyond the grave. Finally, in *The Four Books*, one of the protagonists—a mysterious politically powerful character known simply as "The Child"—oversees a political reeducation compound that is plagued by an epidemic of death during China's Great Famine, and who at the end of the novel commits suicide through a public act of self-crucifixion.

In these works, death is presented not only as a limit-point of speech, but also as a powerful form of expression in its own right. Just as Spivak devotes the final portion of "Can the Subaltern Speak" to a detailed discussion of how a young Indian woman by the name of Bhuvaneswari Bhaduri attempted to use her act of suicide in order to make a political statement, and Lu Xun, in stories like "Medicine" and "Benediction," explores the possibility that profoundly marginalized characters may come to acquire a greater significance through a narration of their death,[15] Yan Lianke similarly uses the narration of death to consider ways in which processes of marginalization and figurative silencing may become powerful forms of expression in their own right.

One of the most intriguing examples of this process of speaking though death can be found in Yan's novella *Balou tiange* 耙耧天歌 (Marrow, 2001), which describes a rural family with four mentally impaired adult offspring. It is revealed early on that the father took his own life more than twenty years before the diegetic present in which the story is set, though the mother continues to have conversations with him as though he were still alive. The father's post-mortem presence becomes even more significant at the end of the work, when the mother discovers that the children's illness can be cured by ingesting their parents' flesh. She cures one of her daughters by feeding her a dish made from the father's twenty-year-old bones, and then takes her own life so that her other three children can cure themselves by drinking her blood. In this way, the peasant family's socially marginal status is concretized through the figure of the children's illness, and it is precisely through the parents' suicide that they children are able to be cured and metaphorically regain their voices.

One of the ironies haunting Yan's commitment to engaging with these marginalized voices, meanwhile, is the fact that in recent years the author's own voice has become increasingly suppressed within his home country. While most of Yan's early works were published openly in China, over the past decade his works have increasingly become subjected to a combination of overt political censorship (e.g., *Wei renmin fuwu* 為人民服務 [Serve the People!, 2005]),[16] self-censorship (e.g., *Dream of Ding Village*),[17] and a process of "soft censorship" whereby publishers preemptively decline to accept manuscripts they anticipate might run into problems with the authorities (e.g., *The Four Books*).[18] In fact, not only are almost all of Yan's recent works effectively unpublishable in mainland China, the authorities have also basically banned re-editions of his earlier publications while also placing considerable restrictions on the publication of scholarly studies of his works. As a result, Yan has become increasingly reliant on publishing houses in Taiwan and Hong Kong for Chinese-language editions of his works, together with numerous international presses.[19]

Yan Lianke is sanguine about the relationship between his understanding of his literary project, on one hand, and the practical hurdles that he increasingly faces in his attempt to communicate with his fellow countrymen, on the other. In a formulation that is strikingly evocative of Benjamin's metaphor of how hyper-literal translation may permit the light of the original to shine through in the translation, meanwhile, Yan Lianke has compared his literary project to a blind man using a lamp to help those around him perceive the darkness that he himself cannot see. In his acceptance speech for the Franz Kafka Literary Prize in 2014, Yan Lianke describes how, in the village where he grew up, there was a blind man who always carried a flashlight when he went out at night, so that others wouldn't run into him, and also to help illuminate the world around him. Yan notes that when the blind man died, his fellow villagers commemorated him by filling his coffin with flashlights with fresh batteries. Yan Lianke then compares his own writing project to the act of giving a blindman a lamp, on the grounds that "because this lamp exists, the blind man who is fated to see only darkness can come to believe that in front of him there is light. Moreover, thanks to this light people can therefore perceive the existence of darkness, and consequently will be able to more effectively ward off that same darkness and suffering" 燈在的話，那個注定只能看到黑暗的盲人會相信在他面前有光存在。進一步，由於這光，人們能因此發現黑暗的存在，因而能更有效地抵擋同樣的黑暗和苦難.[20]

In this evocative metaphor, Yan Lianke suggests that his literary mission involves helping others to "see," which can be compared to Lu Xun's own description of his attempt to awaken his countrymen asleep in the figurative iron house. Just as Lu Xun characterized his literary project as an attempt to convey to his readers an optimism that he himself did not share, Yan Lianke's metaphor of the blind man similarly describes an attempt to use his literature to grant his readers a vision of social reality to which he himself does not have access. The difference, however, is that whereas Lu Xun believed his literature could help his readers figuratively see the light, Yan Lianke views his objective as enabling his readers to *see the darkness* around them.

Moreover, the same way that even as Lu Xun attempts to use his figurative shouts to help wake up those sleeping in the iron house, his stories nevertheless attend to the difficulties of fully remediating those voices into his own, Yan Lianke similarly offers a metaphor of trying to use his literature to permit others to see, even as he expresses skepticism as to whether he can ever truly incorporate that resulting vision into his own literary works. Instead, Yan's project could be described as an attempt to use a process of figurative "hard translation" or "dead translation" to transpose a set of social concerns into literary form in a direct and immediate manner—such that the literary work comes to function not as an end in its own right, but rather a starting point for reassessing the state of contemporary society and of the marginalized voices that are buried within it.

By extension, if we apply this same translational lens to the understand the role of the interpreter or critic, it suggests that one key objective of literary interpretation is to render audible (or legible) the voices contained within the text—but with the reminder that this project is haunted by the possibility of its own failure, together with the irony that, in order to analytically retrieve these buried voices, it may first be necessary to translate them into a critical language that would likely be as alien to them as Lu Xun's "hard translation" was to his own readers.

CARLOS ROJAS is professor of Chinese cultural studies; gender, sexuality, and feminist studies; and arts of the moving image at Duke University. He is the author, editor, and translator of numerous books, including *Homesickness: Culture, Contagion, and National Transformation* (2015).

////////////////////////////////

Notes

1 Lee, *Voices from the Iron House*; Li, *Tiewu zhong de nahan.*

2 On this early process of "heroic translation," see Jiang, *Liang Qichao 'Haojie yi' yanjiu.* See also Liu, "'Heroic Translators.'"

3 Venuti, *Translator's Invisibility*, 20. See also Schleiermacher, "From 'On the Different Methods of Translating.'"

4 In fact, one of the most prolific translators during the late nineteenth and early twentieth centuries was Lin Shu, who did not know any foreign languages and who instead collaborated with co-translators to render foreign literary works into a particularly elegant form of classical Chinese.

5 During the May Fourth period, Lu Xun played an active role in developing the new *baihua* 白話 vernacular Chinese writing system, which attempted to more closely model the form of the Chinese language that people used in everyday speech but which also incorporated significant amounts of Westernized grammar and orthographic conventions.

6 The title of Lu Xun's 1923 collection has been rendered in English as *The Outcry* (trans. Marston Anderson), *Call to Arms* (trans. Yang Hsien-yi and Gladys Yang), and *Cheering from the Sidelines* (trans. William Lyell).

7 The narrator explains that no one in the tavern knew the man's full name, but given that his surname was Kong and he used many archaisms when he spoke, they nicknamed him Kong Yiji, which are the first three characters in a children's primer for writing Chinese characters.

8 Lu Xun, "New Year's Sacrifice," 131; Lu Xun, "Zhufu," in *Nahan yu Panghuang*, 112.

9 When Spivak returned to this essay two decades later, in her book *Critique of Postcolonial Reason*, she conceded that her original conclusion might have been overly pessimistic. In this revised and expanded version of the piece, accordingly, she argues instead that through education and political activism, it is in fact possible for the subaltern to acquire a voice.

10 Yang Jiang, "Shibai de jingyan."

11 Benjamin, "Task of the Translator," 260.

12 Ibid., 254. In this same passage, Benjamin also notes that "the idea of life and afterlife in works of art should be regarded with an entirely unmetaphorical objectivity."

13 Ibid., 256.

14 Notably Yan published the novel several years before the term *cancer village* entered the popular discourse (the journalist Deng Fei 鄧飛 helped popularize the term in 2013, when he published a map of several dozen Chinese villages with unusually high cancer rates).

15 While Spivak's central contention is that the significance of Bhuvaneswari's suicide was misinterpreted by everyone around her, including even her own family, and therefore should be deemed to be a communicative failure, Spivak herself appears confident in her ability to correctly interpret the significance of the suicide. Similarly, although in Lu Xun's "Medicine" and "Benediction" the significance of the protagonist's death is not appreciated by the works' other characters, the underlying premise of the stories is clearly that the works themselves may be capable of communicating the significance of these deaths directly to the works' readers.

16 Although *Serve the People!* was initially published in the literary journal *Jiangnan* 江南, the text was subsequently banned and the journal's editor was fired.

17 Yan cites *Dream of Ding Village* as one of his biggest literary disappointments, since he reluctantly self-censored the novel in hopes of helping it get past the censors, only to see it ultimately recalled and banned anyway. (The novel was initially approved and went through a single print run but then was not approved for any additional printings.)

18 Beginning with *The Four Books*, several of Yan's novels have been subjected to this sort of "soft censorship." For a more general discussion of this trend, see Yan, *Chenmo yu chuanxi*. Also, Yan has subsequently indicated that, anticipating that publishers might decline to accept his manuscript for *The Four Books*, he asked them to explain in writing why they were turning it down. He had originally hoped to add a postface to the novel that would include versions of their responses but was disappointed to find that none of them were willing to offer an explanation of their decisions.

19 For several of his recent novels, Yan has self-published limited runs for his friends and colleagues in Mainland China, which end up being the only printed versions of these works available in simplified Chinese characters.

20 Yan, "Finding Light in China's Darkness."

References

Benjamin, Walter. "The Task of the Translator," translated by Howard Zohn. In *Walter Benjamin: Selected Writings*, vol. 1, *1913–1926*, edited by Marcus Bullock and Michael W. Jennings, 253–63. Cambridge, MA: Harvard University Press, 1996.

Jiang Lin 蔣林. *Liang Qichao 'Haojie yi' yanjiu* 梁啟超「豪傑譯」研究 [A Study of Liang Qichao's "Heroic Translation"]. Shanghai: Shanghai yiwen chubanshe, 2009.

Lee, Leo Ou-fan. *Voices from the Iron House: A Study of Lu Xun*. Bloomington: Indiana University Press, 1987.

Li Oufan 李歐梵. *Tiewu zhong de nahan* 鐵屋中的吶喊 [Voices from the Iron House], translated by Yi Huimin 尹慧珉. Hong Kong: Sanlian, 1991.

Liu, Ken. "The 'Heroic Translators' Who Reinvented Classic Science Fiction in China." *Gizmodo*, April 10, 2015. io9.gizmodo.com/the-heroic-translators-who-reinvented-classic-science-1696944844.

Lu Xun 魯迅. *Nahan yu Panghuang* 《吶喊》與《徬徨》 [*Call to Arms* and *Wandering*]. Changchun: Jilin daxue chubanshe, 2008.

Lu Hsun [Lu Xun]. "New Year's Sacrifice." In *Selected Stories of Lu Hsun*, translated by Yang Hsien-yi and Gladys Yang, 126–44. Beijing: Foreign Languages Press, 1960.

Schleiermacher, Friedrich. "From 'On the Different Methods of Translating,'" translated by Waltraud Bartscht. In *Theories of Translation: An Anthology of Essays from Dryden to Derrida*, edited by Rainer Schulte and John Biguenet, 36–54. Chicago: University of Chicago Press, 1992.

Spivak, Gayatri Chakravorty. "Can the Subaltern Speak?" In *Marxism and the Interpretation of Culture*, edited by Cary Nelson and Lawrence Grossberg, 271–313. Urbana: University of Illinois Press, 1988.

Spivak, Gayatri Chakravorty. *Critique of Postcolonial Reason: Toward a History of the Vanishing Present*. Cambridge, MA: Harvard University Press, 1999.

Venuti, Lawrence. *The Translator's Invisibility: A History of Translation*. London and New York: Routledge, 1995.

Yan Lianke 閻連科. *Chenmo yu chuanxi: Wo suo jingli de Zhongguo he wenxue* 沉默與喘息：我所經歷的中國和文學 [Silence and Breath: The China and Literature That I Have Experienced]. Taipei: Ink Publishing House, 2014.

Yan Lianke. "Finding Light in China's Darkness," translated by Carlos Rojas. *New York Times*. October 22, 2014. www.nytimes.com/2014/10/23/opinion/Yan-Lianke-finding-light-in-chinas-darkness.html.

Yang Jiang 楊絳. "Shibai de jingyan: Shitan fanyi" 失敗的經驗：試探翻譯 [The Experience of Failure: Discussing Translation]. In *Yang Jiang zuopinji* 楊絳作品集 [Yang Jiang's Selected Works], vol. 3, 228–44. Beijing: Zhongguo shehui kexue chubanshe, 1993.

CHRISTOPHER REA

Hoax as Method

ABSTRACT The hoax is universally condemned as an underhanded method—a transaction that, while sometimes clever in design or execution, is injurious. Hoaxers act in bad faith, exploiting, and thus diminishing, the social trust society needs to function. Hoaxes harm individuals and undermine institutions, all the more reason to reconsider such deceptions from a functional, rather than purely moral, perspective. The hoax can be a *method to do what*? What are the outcomes of hoaxes, whether intended or unintended? This essay offers eight answers to these questions, drawing evidence from an array of Chinese writings and films. It argues that the hoax is a useful concept to explain certain practices, styles, and trends in Chinese literary history. Further it proposes that the hoax offers a theoretical paradigm for rethinking more venerated categories, such as creativity, art, and value, as well as method itself.

KEYWORDS hoax, fraud, swindle, creativity, ingenuity, China

Have I got a proposition for you!

Method, in Chinese, is *fa* 法. Technique, or skill, is *shu* 術. Put method and technique together and—voilà!—you get *fashu* 法術, or magic.[1] If scholarly talk about method strikes you as so much sleight of hand, you might well be onto something. For, as anyone who knows Chinese will hasten tell you, defining *fa* simply as method is a bit disingenuous; *fa* can also carry meanings as varied as "law," "practice," "remedy," and "magic." Then there is Sun Tzu's 孫子 *bingfa* 兵法, that treatise on how to outmaneuver rival armies, whose title is typically translated as *The Art of War*.

Art, method, law, magic: the term *fa* conjures up a powerful array of seemingly contradictory connotations, from the orderly to the irrational, the predictable to the ineffable. *Fa* encapsulates the tendency among scholars of method to emphasize polysemy.[2] The inclination of the methodologist, who wants to convince readers that they've been doing things the wrong way, is to point out that things are more complicated than they appear to the casual observer, yet that the complexity of individual cases can be distilled into a simpler set of laws, rules, or principles. The theorist's tendency is to oversimplify or to overstate the case for rhetorical effect. Yet to persuade, he or she must also gain an audience's confidence.

Dear reader, I ask you, for the duration of this essay, to suspend any moral qualms you might have about people deliberately deceiving others and to con-

PRISM: THEORY AND MODERN CHINESE LITERATURE • 16:2 • OCTOBER 2019
DOI 10.1215/25783491-7978491

sider why they might do so and what the intended or unintended consequences of that action might be. Lying—which Oscar Wilde called "the proper aim of Art"[3]—is banal, so let us focus on a more elaborate type of deception: the hoax.

A hoax is a premeditated deceptive act of some complexity staged for a putatively unwitting individual or group. It is a transaction considered to have been enacted in bad faith, at the expense of one party and for the benefit of the hoaxer and perhaps also for a broader audience of spectators. That benefit might be amusement, profit, edification, publicity, or accrual of some other type of political, monetary, or cultural capital.[4] Edification, for example: a hoax might be an object lesson in how the world works—a method of conveying information or insight. Unlike lies, which might be reactive or improvised on the spur of the moment, hoaxes involve planning. They take effort to conceive and orchestrate, and they follow an arc from planning through execution to exposure and response. It takes time, and often precision, to write a spurious novel or to paint a forgery. Hoaxers take pains.

The concept of the hoax, in both English and Chinese (in modern Chinese, typically *e'zuoju* 惡作劇 or *pianju* 騙局), exists within a constellation of terms associated with a broader category of human actions labeled deception (fraud, scam, swindle, humbug, imposition, practical joke, stunt, etc.). At risk of playing fast and loose with terminology, let us treat these various words as more or less the same. In fact, let's use the hoax to open up some creative possibilities. Whenever you encounter the word *hoax* in this essay, I ask you to consider which other words—such as *art* or *fiction* or *storytelling*—might profitably be substituted in its place.

We might distill the criteria for defining the hoax to:

1. the intention to deceive;
2. the presumption that the target is unaware of the attempt to deceive; and
3. the staging of a drama to effect the deception.

The first criterion is straightforward enough in principle; however, ascribing intention can be, in practice, extremely problematic. The intentional fallacy warns us that interpreting a work of art based on the purported intentions of the author can distract us from accounting for the work's effects; by the same token, we should not exclude hoaxes from theoretical consideration because we ascribe to them an intention to deceive. The second criterion, presumption of ignorance, is necessary to distinguish the hoax from the magic trick, which is presented to an audience that expects and even seeks to be deceived for entertainment purposes.[5] As for the third, I say more below about the theatricality of the hoax; for now, suffice it to say that the hoax, as I conceive of it, involves misdirection in the form of a show of impersonation and a storytelling arc. This being a journal of literary criticism, I focus on hoaxes relating—if not necessarily confined—to the literary sphere.

Hoax is a method *to do what*?

My speculative answers, which I'll illustrate with a selection of Chinese and comparative examples, are

1. to rewrite cultural history;
2. to manufacture a reputation;
3. to displace one type of value with another;
4. to accrue power;
5. to dramatize vice and virtue;
6. to beguile the time;
7. to challenge perceptions of reality; and
8. to exalt ingenuity.

Note: I am not claiming that people *should* use hoaxes for these reasons. I am claiming that they have and that they do. And I am asking what the implications of these facts are for critical practice. A secondary question, about which I make only a few speculative claims in passing, is whether *Chinese* sources tell us anything different about "hoax as method."[6]

In the December 10, 2018 issue of the *New Yorker*, Louis Menand surveys several Euro-American literary hoaxes to answer an ethical question: If a book has merit as entertainment or information, does it matter if we're misled about the identity of the author? He argues: "Literature is a game with language, and hoaxing alerts us to the fact that the rules are not written down anywhere."[7] Harm, in the case of literary hoaxes, tends to be more symbolic than material. We're embarrassed, but we're not out that much money (at least individually), and no one dies.

The concept of the hoax, Menand says, should provoke us to think about ideas such as authenticity and identity and, above all, to continue reading. I believe that the philosophical and historiographical implications are even broader. I argue below that the notion of the hoax is useful in part because it alerts us to presumptions—our own and others'—about authorial intention, about audience/readerly disposition, about human nature, about the discernibility of truth versus fiction, and about the nature of creativity.

The hoax has been used, for example, as a method . . .

To Rewrite Cultural History

Is deception more endemic in some historical periods than others? If so, why and to what degree? Or are we apt to exaggerate differences? Economic historian Edward J. Balleisen, writing about the United States since the nineteenth century, argues that the "shape-shifting, never-changing world of fraud" is consistent in its basic narratives and varies only in its particulars; in the words of one of Balleisen's sources, we see only "ancient gimmicks in shiny new packages, tailored to the modern age."[8]

Four conspicuous moments in the history of fraud in Chinese literary culture include the Ming-Qing transition, the late Qing to early Republican period, the Mao era (which I'll skip for now), and the post-Mao era. Swindling and other forms of elaborate deception are major themes in the works of Feng Menglong 馮夢龍 (1574–1646), Ling Mengchu 凌濛初 (1580–1644), and their contemporaries, including the obscure writer Zhang Yingyu 張應俞 (fl. 1610s), who wrote *Jianghu lilan dupian xinshu* 江湖歷覽杜騙新書 (A New Book for Foiling Swindlers, Based on Worldly Experience, preface 1617), later known as *Pian jing* 騙經 (The Book of Swindles).[9] These thematics endured into the early Qing period. Robert E. Hegel observes that in the story collection *Doupeng xianhua* 豆棚閒話 (Idle Talk under the Bean Arbor, ca. 1660), "*Pian*, meaning 'trickery' or 'swindling,' is a term that recurs in virtually every story and describes all too many relationships."[10] Scams and impersonations of the sort found in *The Book of Swindles* and *Idle Talk* reappear as real-life court cases in the eighteenth century.[11]

Hoaxes and swindles come to the fore of literary culture again in the late Qing and early Republican periods. Historians have identified the "exposé" (*xianxingji* 現行記), the "black curtain" (*heimu* 黑幕), and the "true record" (*zhenxiang* 真相) as emblems of a publishing market, circa 1900s to 1920s, obsessed with deception. These works anatomized the brazen scams practiced by government officials, as well as by opportunists and pretenders in a variety of modern institutions, from new-style schools to stock exchanges.[12] A scan of book titles from this era indicates that the term "deceptive technique" (*pianshu* 騙術) also became a newly prominent subject matter for literature, especially in the forms of the anecdote and the short story. These story collections routinely marketed themselves as containing a panorama (*daguan* 大觀) of remarkable (*qi* 奇) stories.[13] Their existence thus not only confirms that there was widespread interest in scams as subject matter, but also alerts us to two categorical imperatives: to be astonishing and to be comprehensive.

These collections sometimes astonish for unintended reasons. For example, the second item in Ma Litai's 馬利泰 (fl. 1910s) *Pianshu qi zhong qi* 騙術奇中奇 (Each Scam More Remarkable than the Last, 1911), "Ti xingpian tu" 題行騙圖 (On Patterns of Scamming), begins: "Alas! The world is but a venue for fraud, and history but a hoax" 嗚呼天地一騙場也。古今一騙局也. The passage concludes: "I too am describing this world of hoaxes [*pianju*] from my current dwelling within it so as to warn you about the ingenious scams of swindlers active within this world of fraud" 吾亦日處於騙局之中觀此圖題此語吾將為騙子之行騙機於騙場者告也.[14] As it turns out, *Each Scam More Remarkable than the Last* is a work of literary piracy—a completely plagiarized version of Lei Junyao's 雷君曜 (1871–1941) *Huitu pianshu qitan* 繪圖騙術奇談 (Remarkable Swindle Tales Illustrated, 1909), released two years later by a different publisher and with only the title and the author's name changed.

Fraud, in other words, was not just literary subject matter but also a literary practice. In Eileen Chang's 張愛玲 (Zhang Ailing, 1920–95) novel *Xiao tuanyuan* 小團圓 (Little Reunions, finished 1979, published 2009), a relative tells Julie that in the 1920s Julie's mother once wrote to the celebrity writer T'ang Ku-wu, whom she had never met, proposing to elope with him. The narrator comments: "In those days, it was common for people to write articles pretending to be women. Julie surmised that T'ang Ku-wu didn't reply to Rachel's letter because he assumed it was written by an idle reader impersonating a woman, or perhaps even another writer pulling his leg" 那時候常有人化名某某女士投稿。九莉猜想湯孤鶩收到信一定是當作無聊的讀者冒充女性，甚至於是同人跟他開玩笑，所以沒回信.[15]

Research on late Qing and early Republican literary journals confirms that gender impersonation was endemic in the Chinese literary culture of the early twentieth century, with both professional writers and their readers adopting a feminine prose style and passing themselves off as "Miss" So-and-so. The famous Francophile writer Zeng Pu 曾朴 (1892–1935) is even said to have once proposed marriage to a male reader who wrote to him posing as a Catholic schoolgirl.[16] In Chang's novel, the fictional T'ang Ku-wu (possibly a fictional version of Zhou Shoujuan 周瘦鵑 [1895–1968], the editor who helped Chang get her literary start) is a stand-in for an actual generation of market-oriented writers whose ethos of accessibility to readers and responsiveness to their sentimental appeals also came with the risk of deception and public mortification.

There is much to say about the rhetoric of deception in the Mao era, which began with the imperative that everyone "put on a new face" (*gaitou huanmian* 改頭換面) for New China and a simultaneous paranoia about spies and bogus revolutionaries. There is also a strong case to be made that the institutionalized hypocrisies of state socialism partially explain the climate of low social trust in the Reform era.[17]

This essay will, however, gloss over that history and jump immediately to the post-Tiananmen era, which has seen a crescendo of voices commenting on, lamenting, celebrating, and otherwise exclaiming on the pervasiveness of bad faith. When author Yu Hua 余華 (1960–) summed up "China in ten words," two of those words were "copycat" (*shanzhai* 山寨) and "bamboozle" (*huyou* 忽悠).[18] *Shanzhai* has provoked polar responses from those who view it as simply piracy of intellectual property and those who highlight it as a form of creativity whose practitioners, in their pursuit of profit, also score a victory against the hegemony of a Western-centric intellectual property regime.[19] In post-Mao China, Chinese writers have not only resumed Zhang Yingyu's practice of compiling true-crime swindle stories, they have even juxtaposed today's swindles with those of the late Ming dynasty, as in compilations such as Qi Shoucheng's 齊守城 *Gujin pianshu qiguan* 古今騙術奇觀 (Remarkable Swindles Old and New, 1994) and Zhou Xinhui's 周心慧 *Gujin pianshu daguan* 古今騙術大觀 (Panorama of Swindles Old and New, 2004).

These author-editors are, in effect, using the hoax to rewrite Chinese cultural history. The virtue of such works is to identify patterns in human behavior and storytelling that are not limited to a specific culture or historical period. They identify transhistorical tropes that show that problems of the current moment are not unique. They even encourage comparisons to non-Chinese examples. At the same time, the hoax-as-history method risks a reductive and ahistorical logic about which I will have more to say below.

To Manufacture a Reputation

By some accounts, the modern Chinese literary revolution was propelled, if not actually started, by a hoax. The story goes that in 1918, *Xin qingnian* 新青年 (La Jeunesse), the flagship publication of the New Culture Movement, was generating only a lackluster response to its calls to literary revolution. The magazine had carried essays arguing for classical Chinese to be replaced with a vernacular written language or even, in the most radical proposal, Esperanto. Scholarly polemic, however, was not attracting readers. Editors Qian Xuantong 錢玄同 (1887–1939) and Liu Bannong 劉半農 (Liu Fu 劉復, 1891–1934) were thus delighted to print, in the March 15, 1918 issue, a letter by a certain Wang Jingxuan 王敬軒, who derided vernacular literature and its proponents and upheld the influential ancient-prose stylist Lin Shu 林紓 (also known as Lin Qinnan 林琴南, 1852–1924) as a superior model for the new generation. The letter, written in classical Chinese, punctuated in an archaic literati style, and striking a condescending, hectoring tone, seemed almost designed to get under the skin of *La Jeunesse* readers. The editors made it clear that they would not take such provocation lying down. Immediately following Wang's letter, Liu Bannong appended a rejoinder three times its length in which he rebutted Wang's points one by one and mocked him for being hopelessly behind the times—a relic of the defunct Qing dynasty.

Liu became a celebrity for having "eviscerated" Wang Jingxuan, making Wang and the literary faction he represented seem not just reactionary but laughably so. *La Jeunesse* garnered more readers and also more significant contributions, notably the landmark story "Kuangren riji" 狂人日記 (Diary of a Madman), which appeared in the May 1918 issue and inaugurated Lu Xun's involvement with the journal. When Liu died of illness in 1934, obituary writers remembered the Wang Jingxuan debate as a significant moment in his varied and illustrious career of writing, scholarship, and activism. Section 2 of the *Zhongguo xin wenxue daxi* 中國新文學大系 (Compendium of China's New Literature) volume on literary debates

Wenxue lunzheng ji 文學論爭集, published in 1935, is titled "Cong Wang Jingxuan dao Lin Qinnan" 從王敬軒到林琴南 (From Wang Jingxuan to Lin Qinnan).[20]

Within seventeen years, then, Wang Jingxuan had proved useful in several ways. He enhanced the visibility of a magazine and the prestige of its contributors and the Wang Jingxuan event was enshrined in the new literature canon as a landmark debate, a turning point in the periodization of the movement's history, as told by its participants. Yet no such person existed. Qian Xuantong is said to have been the true author of the Wang Jingxuan letter and to have invented Wang as a foil to the *La Jeunesse* agenda.[21] Wang Jingxuan was a straw man, a speech-act. The editors of the *Compendium* knew this yet apparently saw nothing wrong with treating a pseudo-debate as legitimate. After all, it had an effect.

The rationale of the original Wang Jingxuan hoax chimes with what Menand describes as the "higher-truth defense" of literary impersonation: the person need not be real, and the events described need not have actually happened, so long as the voice is representative of the truth of a group. It is the simulated typicality that matters.[22] Wang Jingxuan need not have existed, so long as the worldview of his ilk could be expressed through ventriloquism.

The canonization of the hoax, however, indicates a different motive: of witting self-consecration. If the best way for an artist to boost the market value of his or her works is to die, giving birth to a fictional nemesis just to kill them off again can also be a rhetorically profitable gambit. The editors of the *Compendium* doubled down on the original hoax by including the letter credited to Wang Jingxuan, the response of Liu Bannong, and eighteen other essays by writers such as Hu Shi 胡適 (1891–1962), Cai Yuanpei 蔡元培 (1868–1940), Yan Fu 嚴復 (1854–1921), Qian Xuantong, Chen Duxiu 陳獨秀 (1879–1942), and Lin Shu. An act of literary imposture was repackaged as a significant historical event to create a myth of self-becoming.

To Displace One Type of Value with Another

Hoax is a putative category. A deceptive action is discovered and is labeled a hoax—only at that point of negative reception is a hoax literally said to exist. Value, too, is in the eye of the beholder. Accusations of hoax occur because one party in a transaction believes that they have been denied value commensurate to their investment of money, time, or attention. To accuse someone of a hoax is to accuse them of misrepresentation, to posit a gap between represented value and actual value. The offended party is also claiming that the right to define and measure value is theirs.

The very concept of the hoax is thus predicated on an awareness of different types of value: if you discover that someone has passed you a counterfeit bill or an ingot of iron painted to look like silver, you realize that its *intrinsic* value is below your expectations but that its *exchange* value might be unchanged—since it could be passed on to someone else. Then there is *use* value: Chen Guangsheng 陳廣

生 and Cui Jiajun 崔家駿's spurious *Lei Feng de gushi* 雷鋒的故事 (The Story of Lei Feng, 1973) and the myth-making biopic *Baiqiu'en daifu* 白求恩大夫 (Doctor Bethune, 1964), however unreliable as history, have use value as propaganda and might yet be an enjoyable read. Lin Shu's (and his translator-collaborators') deliberate modifications of Western novels are misrepresentations by conventional standards of fidelity. Each rendering of *Nicholas Nickleby*, say, or *David Copperfield* could be considered a hoax—an imposition in which the translators arrogate for themselves creative prerogatives ostensibly exclusive to the original author. Yet from a reader's perspective, the use value of Lin Shu, Inc.'s work might be equivalent or even superior to that of the original work.[23]

Hoax is thus a method for reconsidering the boundaries between putatively legitimate and illegitimate or authentic and inauthentic cultural production. One question bedeviling the literary historian working in a language like Chinese is what to do with spurious books (*weishu* 偽書), be they plagiarized works or spurious attributions. Spurious attributions borrow the cultural capital of a celebrity author to increase the market value of their own product. Plagiarists appropriate value created through others' labors to save time and labor of their own.

Like other forgeries (*weizuo* 偽作), such works are so named because they are considered to have been born with the original sin of false pretenses. What value do they possess? *Wei* labels a thing illegitimate; the convention in mainland China is still to refer to "the illegitimate Manchukuo" (*wei Manzhouguo* 偽滿州國) and "the illegitimate Wang Jingwei authority" (*wei Wang Jingwei zhengquan* 偽汪精衛政權), grafting rejection onto the noun.[24] One effect of such moral condemnation—whether intended or not—is to discourage functional analysis.

Wilde famously remarked that "to censure an artist for forgery [is] to confuse an ethical with an aesthetical problem."[25] Xu Bing's 徐冰 (1955–) "fake" Chinese characters, for example, have aesthetic value despite their illegibility or inauthenticity—indeed, part of their claim to high culture status is that they confront audiences with a new type of value. But the question of value turns on context as much as verisimilitude: seeming appearance is very different in the art gallery than it is in the world of political power. How well Wang Jingwei's government governed is a separate issue from whether or not it should have existed in the first place. Arguing for the aesthetic value of a thing widely condemned as illegitimate, of course, is to invite controversy.

The nineteenth-century American entrepreneur P. T. Barnum's response to accusations that he foisted humbugs upon the public was to opine that all comers received good value for their money—even if the value wasn't of the type they expected. The elderly African American woman patrons paid to see at one of his roaming exhibitions, Joice Heth (c. 1756–1836), was not actually George Washington's real wet nurse, as claimed in the advertisements (or an automaton, as claimed in counter-advertisements);[26] but in lieu of witnessing an authentic artifact with their own eyes, audience members came away from their experience a story richer. The hoaxer's stock-in-trade is often referred to as the bait and switch, but what the hoaxer does that keeps suckers coming back for another helping is switching in an alternative type of value that fills in, to a sufficient degree, the loss of the expected type.

What is a perpetrator of a hoax to do if they are exposed, suspected, or accused? To put forward a new value proposition to the public, or to mollify the public's feelings of betrayal by pointing to a value of the stunt that has been overlooked. They face a skeptical audience: having shown bad faith, why should anyone trust them again? Here the hoaxer has to convince the public of two things: that their motives were altruistic and that their ruse was a minor and temporary but necessary evil in the service of a greater good. The hoaxer, in other words, must make it clear that their hoax was to benefit the public and that if the ruse was effective it need not be repeated. Their goal was not self-enrichment, and if any money happened to make its way into their pocket, this was purely incidental to the main goal of righting a great wrong. The hoaxer presents deception as the modest fee the public pays for a major service.

To Accrue Power

Sunzi bingfa and *Sanshiliu ji* 三十六計 (The Thirty-Six Stratagems) tell stories of battles won through cunning rather than force. Hoaxes can be a sign of desperation—for power, attention, money, or survival. Zhuge Liang 諸葛亮 (181–234) invented the "empty-town bluff" (*kongcheng ji* 空城計), the story goes, because he needed to buy time for additional troops to come to raise a siege. Historian Mark McNicholas writes of fraud in the mid-Qing period that "forgery and imposture as the state defined them were quintessentially political acts involving the manipulation of official symbols and identities," and that even the pettiest of fraudsters were aware that they were manipulating political power.[27] Cases from radically different contexts suggest that the hoax is usually a power play. When, in 1970, Clifford Irving (1930–2017) conceived the idea of a forged autobiography of billionaire Howard Hughes, he was a writer desperate for attention from a major publisher. The hoax may be a vehicle for the unknown to gain fame or for the fading to launch a comeback.

The 1918 Wang Jingxuan hoax is one example of the hoax being used as a method to overcome obscurity. The sensation created by a war of words was wind in the sails of *La Jeunesse*, its cultural program, and its fearless leaders, who had shown admirable fighting spirit in the face of oppression. A ghostwritten phantom was conjured into existence to rally others to a struggling cause. The foundational hoax of the modern literary revolution turned the tables on an existing power relationship.

Publicity stunts reappeared with a vengeance in literature of the post-Mao market economy. In Wang Shuo's 王朔 (1958–) novel *Wanzhu* 頑主 (Masters of

Mischief, 1988), a small enterprise calling itself the Three-T Company promises to "tackle problems, terminate boredom, and take the blame" ("tiren jienan, tiren jiemen, tiren shouguo" 替人解難，替人解悶，替人受過) for its customers. On behalf of one no-name writer eager for acclaim, they organize an award ceremony for a "Three-T Literary Prize," attracting an audience with the promise of a free party to follow, awarding first prize to their client, and assigning lesser prizes to several well-known writers. (The prizes are underwritten by the client himself.) The episode casts media spectacles (*chaozuo* 炒作) as a commonplace hoax of the era and cocks a snook at establishment institutions that arrogate the authority to consecrate cultural value.[28]

The hoax in Wang Shuo's novel is conceived and orchestrated by a particular type of intermediary: an independent company. The scrappy enterprise, which is itself struggling for survival in the new market economy, appears as an ironic hero that engineers a way for a writer with limited resources to achieve a symbolic triumph.[29] The drama is a conspiracy of the underdogs. The English title given to the 1988 film version, *The Troubleshooters*, emphasizes resourcefulness (the quintessential quality of fixers, brokers, and other intermediaries) in filling a need or repairing something. Indeed, publicity-seeking hoaxers often present themselves as helping to fix a broken system.[30]

Feng Xiaogang's 馮小剛 (1958–) Lunar New Year film *Dawan* 大腕 (Big Shot's Funeral, 2001) pushes even further the conceits that commerce has run amuck but that its mechanisms can be navigated and exploited with a deft turn of the wrist. Ge You's 葛優 (1957–) character, Youyou, is not a powerful "big wrist" (*dawan*) but a cash-poor intermediary trying to pull bigger economic levers to bring off an audacious stunt: a "comedy funeral" to be held in the Forbidden City. The parable resonates in the internet age, when the barriers to promotion and self-promotion, including through dubious means, have dropped even further.[31]

A hoax dramatizes a type of power that the creator/author has over the audience. This power may be real or symbolic, but in all cases the power dynamic is connected to asymmetry of knowledge: the hoaxer knows of the hoax's existence before the target does. In the cases cited immediately above, the hoax is an attempt by a weaker party to turn the tables in a power relationship with a military adversary, the commercial market, or a neglectful public.

Hoaxes also engage with the power of aesthetic expectations, including genre expectations, narrative expectations, and what might be sympathetically termed the tyranny of cliché. A hoax acknowledges (explicitly or implicitly) the existence of a nominal order even as it disrupts it. The first half of Jiang Wen's 姜文 (1963–) film *Guizi laile* 鬼子來了 (Devils on the Doorstep, 2000) builds up one modal expectation by employing buffoonish acting and slapstick action and, in the climactic party scene, abruptly betrays that expectation by bayonetting a child. Near the end of the film, Jiang Wen surprises the viewer yet again by switching from black-and-white cinematography, reminiscent of historical documentary, to show a decapitated head in lurid color, as it turns to regard the audience, breaking the fourth wall. The abrupt change reveals the creator's attitude vis-à-vis the audience, namely that their expectations can be anticipated and foiled.

To Dramatize Vice and Virtue

The hoax is a form of moral theater involving two integral structural elements: the deception and the reveal.[32] The very term *e'zuoju* 惡作劇 implies a theatrical act staged with malice aforethought; indeed hoaxes often deceive by employing external trappings of costume, script, and character. The *ju* 局 in *pianju* suggests a totalizing situation, be it of a game (of chess, say), of a political situation (*daju* 大局), or of a trend or tendency (*jushi* 局勢). A *ju* might also be a round in a game. These associations resonate with the hoaxer's/dramatist's goal of focusing the mark's attention on the scene before their eyes, to the exclusion of anything else. Hoaxers typically claim to be using deception to expose the deceit or failings of others, and do so by putting on a show.

Consider, for example, how many late imperial Chinese stories dramatize the stereotype that Buddhist monks are swindlers. In the late Ming and early Qing, the term *guanggun* 光棍, or "bare sticks" (nowadays often used to refer to bachelors), was used to denigrate both Buddhist monks and "single males who wandered about the countryside looking for work and getting into trouble."[33] Both were stereotyped as idlers "bare" (*guang* 光) of a productive occupation, shaven monks also sporting a bare pate.

This stereotype is dramatized in session 6 of *Idle Talk from under the Bean Arbor*, which includes a tale set in Henan province during the Tang dynasty about a bogus "exalted monk" who has set up shop in a temple swindling donations from impoverished townspeople. He gets his comeuppance at the hands of Commander Li, who is desperate to feed his troops. Li persuades the swindler-abbot to let out that the abbot will publicly "transcend" (*chaosheng* 超昇) on a funeral pyre on a certain day and to solicit alms from the public in anticipation of this spectacular event. The ruse rakes in donations, but the abbot realizes only as the flames are about to consume him on the platform stage that Commander Li has blocked his escape passage. The bogus monk burns to death. Li, having eliminated this scourge, then builds a pagoda to house bones of the Dead Ash Patriarch (really just white pebbles) and collects another three hundred thousand *yuan* to provide for his troops.[34] This fantasy of revenge against a duplicitous social type has the duped trickster literally dying on stage.

To be an effective hoax, the deception must be perpetrated in secret, or at least hiding in plain sight. P. T. Barnum's come-on to visitors to his American Museum was that the common man should come decide for himself whether the Feejee Mermaid was a real mermaid or not. The hoax comprised a bogus corpse packaged in fraudulent advertising. The reveal may be effected by the perpetrator of the hoax, by its victim, or by a third-party observer looking on with dramatic irony.

In the case of Barnum, the self-reveal was in itself deceptive, a pseudo-event meant to generate publicity and garner admissions. Barnum pandered to populist disdain for experts and authorities and appealed to the average citizen to make the final determination of true versus false based on personal observation. Haiyan Lee, drawing on Claude Lefort and other political philosophers, notes that the politics of the reveal can also be exploited, in the name of fixing democracy, to antidemocratic ends: "When popular sovereignty is 'revealed'—in the paranoid imagination of the disenchanted masses—to be a *mere* fiction and is stripped of its mystique . . . then those who exercise power are 'exposed' as agents of special interests. . . . Great then is the temptation for a party or clique to claim to reverse the descent into realpolitik ('to drain the swamp') by seizing the empty place in the name of the people (the silent majority, the hard-working folk, etc.), by becoming one with the people and exercising authority under the cover of this identification. This, for Lefort, is the first step on the path to totalitarianism."[35] The hoax, I noted above, can be a method to accrue power, a process in which the reveal carries significant narrative and dramatic power.

Since the reveal is *of* the deception, the hoax could be said to include a self-referential element of meta-theater: every hoax draws attention to its own form and structure, turning all participants into spectators while making them self-aware, at the moment of reveal, of their participation and degree of knowledge. In other words, the narrative arc of the hoax leads through deception and *discovery* of deception to a response of surprise and enlightenment (and—depending on the stakes—chagrin, anger, amusement, or admiration). To be clear: as every totalitarian knows, "enlightenment" can itself be a stage-managed delusion, a "formulaic truth"[36] repeated as a ritual incantation by political or commercial actors.

A hoax is yet a *participatory* drama: it engages the reader or audience, wittingly or unwittingly, willingly or unwillingly, in the show, figuratively dragging them up on stage. The audience is not permitted to remain passive spectators; they are conscripted as players. In the early twentieth century, popular writers in Shanghai often used hoaxes as a means of reader engagement. Literary hoaxes make readers more (self-)conscious of the assumptions they bring to consuming a work of literature, such as their invisibility to the authors. Through a literary hoax, the authors reveal that they can not only "see" the readers but even psychologize them—they know readers' minds, anticipate their thought processes and expectations, and are willing to manipulate them.

A literary hoax evinces a market consciousness on the part of the author that is overtly presumptuous. In his famous 1902 oesophagus hoax, Mark Twain inserted a paragraph of nonsensical yet lyrical scenic description featuring a flying esophagus, using a form of literary "passing" to test the complacency or vigilance of his readership. A self-exposé followed in paratexts: an authorial comment about the stunt in which Twain included excerpts from readers' puzzled letters.[37]

Xu Zhuodai 徐卓呆 (1880–1958), a cultural entrepreneur and prolific comic writer of Republican Shanghai, structured many of his plots as hoaxes. A female writer posts an ad in the newspaper claiming to be seeking a husband and, on three dates (at which she never appears), fleeces the hordes of men who reply to the ad. A fixer helps his two impoverished friends make a small windfall by having one of their back-to-back shops sell hair tonic and the other sell a secret head-shaving method and then channeling bald and hairy customers through the back of the shop they entered and out the front door of the other shop, creating the illusion of instant results. Stories like these are presented as stage plays in several acts, witnessed by an urban public, who themselves become actors in the drama. Characters in these stories refer to these stunts as hoaxes (*e'zuoju*). In some stories, such as "Yangzhuang de chaoxijia" 洋裝的抄襲家 (Plagiarist in Western Dress, 1923), Xu Zhuodai goes one step further by challenging his real-world readers to figure out whether his story is an original creation, a translation, or a plagiarism, holding them in suspense before he reveals the truth in the magazine's next installment.[38] The self-congratulatory author-hoaxer presents himself as a stage manager: will the reader be able to decode the stage directions, so as to see through the artifice, or will they—even with fair warning—end up becoming an actor following a prepared script?

Hoaxes are also theatrical in the sense that they seek to garner publicity for their moral lessons through sensational means. Alan Sokal's 1996 *Social Text* hoax—submitting a nonsensical paper to an academic journal and convincing the editors to publish it—evinces the same spirit as Twain's hoax in trying to put one over on a putatively gullible readership; in the triumphant gesture of self-unmasking; and in making hay of "the affair" with a barrage of polemic, self-congratulation, and publicity seeking.[39] One significant trend in the history of hoaxing is perpetrators' not only setting the stage and raising the curtain but also writing the reviews of the show.

To Beguile the Time

Swindlers are consummate storytellers. They make a living by weaving a plausible story around the unworthy product or investment they are peddling. The duped party is then left to decide for themself whether the story they consumed was worth the price of being fleeced. But in a hoax, the story is a means to an end—the aesthetic merits of the story itself tend to be secondary to its functional effectiveness in creating the trust necessary for the dupe to take the plunge. A hoax is a story with utility. "Credible mimicry, charismatic personalization, and persuasive deflection" are the con artist's means for navigating social situations.[40] When the stakes are low, as for the reader of a story known to be fictional, the discovery of a hoax might actually enhance enjoyment or pleasure by enhancing the work's qualities of surprise and delight.

In Wang Xiaobo's 王小波 (1952–97) novella *Huangjin shidai* 黃金時代 (The Golden Age), set mostly in Cultural Revolution–era Yunnan, public security officers coerce Wang Er into writing confessions about his illicit sexual relations with Chen Qingyang. First he simply admits that they "have an indecent relationship" 有不正當的關係, but the officers press for details. He complies and embellishes his narrative with ever-more explicit descriptions.[41] Sensationalism displaces fidelity, as the storyteller and his readers both get caught up in the imaginative thrills of Wang's storytelling. So, reports Wang Er, was his career as a fiction writer born, and looking back as narrator twenty years later, he savors his hoax for both its creative and cathartic pleasures and for its career benefits.

The subtext, of course, is that all coerced confessions are unreliable. (An English-major friend later tells Wang Er that his confessions have "the charm of Victorian underground novels" 有維多利亞時期地下小說的韻味 and that he was right to cut out certain details because "those details destroyed the unity of the story" 那些細節破壞了故事的完整性.)[42] By extension, the Cultural Revolution turned the literary hoax into a new norm by compelling autobiographical insincerity.

The exposé turns the reader or audience into part of the story, as well as the author. It exposes the audience's desires and expectations while revealing an authorial agenda. The reader was a fool for believing that the author was a woman, when he was in fact a man impersonating a woman. The reader had been led to believe that Edgar Allan Poe's narrator was a reliable guide to the forensic process of uncovering a murderer, when in fact the narrator himself was the murderer. At the moment of exposé, the hoax changes from being theme or motif or subject matter within a story to a method of meta-commentary on storytelling itself. The implied author and reader become characters in an extra-fictional exchange.

The exposé, by implication, is not the final stage of the hoax-as-story narrative. The final stage is the reader's reinterpretation of the story following that staged moment of enlightenment and might include the creation of new discourses. In highly politicized literary contexts such as the late Qing and early Republican eras, authors tend to preface their "stories to awaken the world" (*jingshi xiaoshuo* 醒世小說) by explicitly calling for the reader to undertake such work of reflection. They promise a didactic story and invoke self-improvement as a readerly imperative. Hoaxers and moralists share a belief that the audience is malleable and impressionable—responsive to their impositions. A minority acknowledge that hoaxes can turn readers themselves into storytellers. A reader who has fallen for a hoax, after all, has some explaining to do.

To Challenge Perceptions of Reality

When we fall for a hoax, we become aware of our own fallibility. Conspiracy theorists and fabulists often label events "hoaxes" as a tactic to discredit a person, institution, or political position to which they are hostile. Like "fake news," the concept of the hoax presumes that reality is knowable and that sham representations thereof can be definitively identified and rejected. Obviously this claim can be made in bad faith, or by people in thrall to thought leaders with ulterior motives. A hoax is a violation of conventions of trust, belief, or faith in the way the world works; it tests our capacity as individuals and as groups to assess its workings accurately. The target of the hoax makes certain presumptions about the social (or text-mediated) context of the exchange, among them that the counterparty (such as the author) is who they represent themselves to be and that the object in question (the text, the product, the commodity, the event) has the value claimed of it.

The gap between representation and reality has been an obsession in Chinese letters since at least the Confucian Rectification of Names and does not need rehashing here. In the modern period, a few trends stand out. In the late Qing, tabloid writers like Li Boyuan 李伯元 (1867–1906) and Wu Jianren 吳趼人 (1866–1910) presented the reality of officialdom as being a series of transparent hoaxes and scams. The genre of serialized novels conventionally known as "exposés of officialdom" (*guanchang xianxing ji* 官場現形記) used hoaxes and scams as a structural device in an episodic narrative. In these novels the proliferation of hoaxes is presented as evidence of a degraded reality of weak governmental and social control and rampant abuse of power.

New Literature writers of the 1910s and 1920s posited vast swaths of premodern philosophical and other ideological texts as being fundamentally deceptive because they imposed rigid social roles that conflicted with natural human behaviors. Formulaic genres such as "scholar-beauty romance" were sham versions of reality, elitist fantasies disconnected from everyday life. These critics diagnosed unconscious, serial deception as being a debilitating legacy of China's literary heritage. As later scholars have pointed out, such broadsides against the past were colored by self-interest: they were, in part, a space-clearing gesture for the new generation.

Peeling back layers often reveals hoaxes within hoaxes. Lin Shu, one victim of the Wang Jingxuan hoax, was himself a huckster of spurious modern pharmaceuticals such as "Dr. Williams' Pink Pills for Pale People," a participant in what Michael Hill calls "a prodigious network of global quackery."[43] Clifford Irving baited the prospective publisher of his spurious Howard Hughes autobiography by claiming that Hughes had expressed admiration for the biography Irving had written of the art forger Elymr de Hory, *Fake!* (1969)—a critic of a faker became a faker himself.

In *Prince of Tricksters*, Matt Houlbrook traces the transnational career of con man Netley Lucas (c. 1903–40), who impersonated aristocracy, wrote "true crime" confessionals as a "reformed" criminal, penned spurious biographies of European royalty, and wrote an autobiography entitled *My Selves* (1934). The effect of such serial deception—Houlbrook purports to have identified "thirty-eight guises" for Lucas and suggests that "there may be more"[44]—is to undermine the plausibility of all narratives. The historian confesses his own complicity in the swirl of storytelling surrounding a confidence trickster, even including sections in which he addresses his subject directly: "I made you, Netley. You are nothing without me and without the stories that I have told about you."[45] To the reader, Houlbrook says, "all I offer is a gambit, plausible histories and effects of verisimilitude, and something approaching a reveal."[46]

My own limited research suggests that most popular and academic discourse on hoaxes is glib and specious. Even Menand resorts to broadside. His verdict that contemporary public discourse "is almost completely corrupted by mendacity"[47] echoes the sweeping claims of Xiong Zhenji in his 1617 preface to *The Book of Swindles* that "morals degenerate and fraud flourishes with every passing day" and that "the decline in morals has reached such a crisis that a gentleman of conscience cannot help but be alarmed."[48] Yet reflexive skepticism is no more reliable than reflexive credulity. The facts of any particular hoax, much less those of an age, are often less knowable than we might seek to impress upon others.

To Exalt Ingenuity

One resolution to the (un)knowability conundrum is to embrace the hoax for its aesthetic value. The hoax is an expression of ingenuity in that it involves the manipulation of form to novel effect. Ingenuity of the author or creator may be taken as a counterpart to the ingenuousness (faith in the form or inclination to believe others' representations) that self-superior hoaxers tend to presume of their targets. Whatever their attitude toward others, hoaxers often claim of their own handiwork that, besides teaching lessons, it gives pleasure in its own right. Zhang Yingyu, who compiled his *Book of Swindles* in the late Ming dynasty, would seem to agree, as his authorial commentaries often evince admiration for a cleverly laid trap or brilliantly executed swindle.

Patrick Hanan writes of the early-Qing writer Li Yu 李漁 (1611–80):

> Ingenuity (*qiao* [巧]) is another type of novelty that Li Yu's commentators praise, coupling it with *xin* [新] ("new") and *qi* [奇] ("unusual") in discussing his work. A surprising number of his plays and stories depend on the ingenu-

ity of the characters, who may be taken as surrogates for the author. Almost all of these works have some enterprising hero or heroine, and brilliant schemes (*miaofa* 妙法) abound in them. Like Boccaccio's stories, Li Yu's are all full of the joy of an ingenious plan beautifully executed and cunningly revealed to the reader.[49]

Hanan adds: "The commentaries to *Carnal Prayer Mat* and other works liken Li Yu's mind to the Creator's and praise his writing as like the Creator's work, using Li Yu's favorite attributes, remarkable (*qi*) and ingenious (*qiao*). But it is creativity of a particular kind that the analogy leads to—the creativity of the artist as the maker or artificer who has a plan or concept to carry out."[50]

At a fundamental level, then, the hoax provokes us to rethink the terms of creation. To *write*, *author*, *script*, *translate*, *draft*, *film*, *edit*—some verbs come across as functional and morally nonjudgmental. To *plagiarize*, *fake*, *crib*, *impersonate*, *ape*, *sham*, *steal*, *rip off*, *masquerade as*, *pass for*—other verbs imply disapprobation. Yet others, like *imitate*, *copy*, and *parody*, occupy a middle ground. Verbs presume intention, investment, consciousness, motive—or lack thereof.

These distinctions matter in the field of modern Chinese literature insofar as the notion exists that art can be divided into the true (disinterested in anything but truth) and the market-driven (tainted by ulterior motives of money or fame). By definition, a hoax has both witting and unwitting participants. An auteurist philosophy of the hoax both credits hoaxers with (and blames them for) the effects of their hoaxes; a reader-response critic would hold that hoaxes do not actually exist until someone falls for them, thus crediting the reader/audience target with the actual creation of the hoax and casting the hoaxers as at most coauthors.

Theorists tend to overstate their claims so as to make an impression, and this essay is no exception. For the theorist of hoaxes, the professional hazard is to overstate the certitude of the facts of any particular hoax, especially those of the distant past or those learned secondhand. Who knows who *really* wrote that Wang Jingxuan letter? Perhaps it was in fact a collective work (*jiti chuangzuo* 集體創作). Republican Chinese literary culture exalted individual literary celebrities and personalities; in Maoist China, cloaking the identity or identities of actual authors with a collective attribution became the new literary orthodoxy.

Like the magician's sleight of hand, hoaxes alert us to an ongoing contest between the storyteller's or performer's methods of indirection and the audience's methods of perception or detection. Every age makes its own demands on the ingenuity of the artist and the audience, not least an age characterized by "an alternative reality propped up by a vast state apparatus"—a phrase that today could easily apply both to the United States of America and to the People's Republic of China—many of whose citizens, in thrall of an egocrat, "crave evidence-free formulaic truth."[51]

In closing, but not in triumph, we might revisit the old storyteller's truism that "there are no stories without coincidences" (*wu qiao bucheng shu* 無巧不成書) in light of Li Yu's interpretation of *qiao* as ingenious skill. The hoaxer, who excels in inventing methods to get people to suspend disbelief, begs the question: To what extent might deception be necessary, fundamental, or intrinsic to art? For truly, there are no stories without ingenuity.

CHRISTOPHER REA is professor of Asian studies at the University of British Columbia. He is the author of *The Age of Irreverence: A New History of Laughter in China* (2015), the translator of *China's Chaplin: Comic Stories and Farces by Xu Zhuodai* (2019), and the co-translator of *The Book of Swindles: Selections from a Late Ming Collection* (2017).

Acknowledgements
My thanks to Carlos Rojas for inviting me to contribute to this journal issue, and to him and the other participants at the 2018 Duke seminar on method for their comments. My thanks also to the two anonymous reviewers for *Prism*, to Patricia Rea for proofreading this article, and to Haiyan Lee for sharing a draft of her *PMLA* article.

Notes

1 *Lin Yutang's Chinese-English Dictionary of Modern Usage* defines *fashu* 法術 as (1) "magic trick," and (2) "generally, effective means." Online at humanum.arts.cuhk.edu.hk/Lexis/Lindict.

2 Mezzadra and Neilson, *Border as Method*, 4, citing Balibar, *Politics and the Other Scene*, 76.

3 Wilde, "Decay of Lying."

4 Gregory Mackie, for example, notes that "the profit motive . . . is insufficient explanation for th[e] sudden flourishing of Wilde fakes" in the 1920s, which evinces a greater interest in following the writer's stylistic lead, as forgery "occupies a central position in Wilde's aesthetic philosophy and may well be the master Wildean metaphor for artistry and creativity." Mackie, *Beautiful Untrue Things*, 10.

5 The magician is arguably harder pressed to conceal the method of deception than the hoaxer, whose audience is unsuspecting.

6 John H. McWhorter highlights Chinese examples (especially in chapter 4, "Dissing the Chinese") in arguing against the commonplace notion that language shapes worldview. But in my opinion, the title of his book should really be *The Language Delusion* or *The Language Fantasy*, because he never establishes that the Sapir-Whorf hypothesis has gotten traction because of deliberate deception. See McWhorter, *Language Hoax*. In an email on July 27, 2019, McWhorter told me that the title was proposed by the publisher and confirmed that "no, there is no 'hoax,' per se!"

7 Menand, "Faking It," 73. Menand's essay is a review of Christopher L. Miller's *Imposters: Literary Hoaxes and Cultural Authenticity* (2018). Gregory Mackie's *Beautiful Untrue Things* (2019) is a recent study of forgeries related to a single literary celebrity, Oscar Wilde.

8 Balleisen, *Fraud*, 14. For a European example of fraudulence as a "cultural preoccupation" extending beyond literary fiction, see Carpenter, *Aesthetics of Fraudulence*

in Nineteenth-Century France. I mention several examples from nineteenth-century America below.

9 For more on the literary context of this work, see the translators' introduction to Y. Zhang, *Book of Swindles*.

10 Hegel, "Introduction: Gossip and Exaggeration in Aina's Short Stories," in Aina the Layman, *Idle Talk under the Bean Arbor*, xvi.

11 See the discussion of court cases in McNicholas, *Forgery and Impersonation in Imperial China*, especially chaps. 3 and 4.

12 See, for example, Lin, *Xuetang xiaohua, yiming xuetang xianxingji* (1910); the monthly *Zhengxiang huabao* 真相畫報 (True Record, Shanghai, 1912–13); Jinghua guike and Tianchansheng, *Fupi zhi heimu* (1917); and Jiang, *Jiaoyisuo xianxingji* (1922). Bryna Goodman, who translates the latter title as *Exchanges Unmasked*, notes that Jiang Hongjiao's 江紅蕉 (1898–1972) novel was one of a pair of books on the subject of exchanges published in the aftermath of a Shanghai market crash and roughly a decade before Mao Dun's 茅盾 (1896–1981) famous novel, *Ziye* 子夜 (Midnight, 1933). Goodman, "Dubious Figures," 120–21.

13 Sample titles include Lei, *Huitu pianshu qitan*; Ma, *Pianshu qizhongqi*; Bao, *Pianshu daguan*; and Cangya shi zhuren, *Gujin pianshu daguan*.

14 Ma, *Pianshu qi zhong qi*, 1.

15 Zhang A., *Xiao tuanyuan*, 154; Chang, *Little Reunions*, 147.

16 On Zeng, see Hutt, "*Monstre Sacré*." On Chinese male writers impersonating female writers in the early twentieth century, see studies by contributors to the University of Heidelberg–led project on "Chinese women's magazines in the late Qing and early Republican period." The editors note that "a trend among male writers in the early twentieth century was to use female pseudonyms to publish their writings in women's magazines. A prominent example is the young Zhou Zuoren 周作人 (1885–1967). Adopting several female pseudonyms, Zhou regularly contributed his own stories as well as translated ones to the Fiction column in *Nüzi shijie*." See "*Nüzi shijie*."

17 Some threads of this argument are explored in Lee, *Stranger and the Chinese Moral Imagination*.

18 Yu, *Shige cihui li de Zhongguo*, chaps. 9 and 10.

19 Book-length studies of *shanzhai* include Yang, *Faked in China*, and Lin, *Fake Stuff*. Laikwan Pang critiques prevalent foreign discourses about China and piracy/counterfeiting in *Creativity and Its Discontents*.

20 Zheng, *Zhongguo xin wenxue daxi*. Section title: "Cong Wang Jingxuan dao Lin Qinnan" 從王敬軒到林琴南.

21 A full account of the Wang Jingxuan hoax appears in Hill, *Lin Shu, Inc.*, chap. 7, "Becoming Wang Jingxuan." On this and a later likely hoax perpetrated by Qian Xuantong and Liu Bannong in 1926, see Rea, *Age of Irreverence*, 93–95.

22 Menand, "Faking It," 68.

23 On Lin's translation practice, see Michael Gibbs Hill's *Lin Shu, Inc.* (2012) and Qian Zhongshu's 錢鍾書 (1910–1998) "Lin Shu de fanyi" 林紓的翻譯 (Lin Shu's Translation), translated in Qian, *Patchwork*, 139–88. Qian notes that the *Shuowen jiezi* 說文解字 (Explanations of Simple and Compound Characters) glosses *e* 囮 as *yi* 譯 and that *e* is a homophone of *e* 訛, meaning "to misrepresent." Qian further notes that *e* 囮, *e* 訛 (to misrepresent), and *hua* 化 (to transform) are all variants of the same character, as a prelude to arguing that "the highest ideal of literary translation, it may indeed be said, is 'to

transform.'" See Qian, *Patchwork*, 139 and 146–51 on Lin's additions to Charles Dickens's works.

24 I am referring to usage in modern popular and political discourse. One Daoist critique of Confucianism, expressed in the *Zhuangzi*, holds that "the acts of civilization enforced through the imposition of social divisions, ranks, and institutionalized relationship as hailed in the Confucian texts and celebrated by the establishment of exemplary models are acts of *wei* 偽 (*Daodejing* 18)—literally, acts of 'human making.' In other words, they are inherently artificial or, to put it once again in contemporary language, social constructs." Moeller and D'Ambrosio, *Genuine Pretending*, 9.

25 Oscar Wilde, *The Portrait of Mr W.H.* (1899), qtd. in Ruthven, *Faking Literature*, 44.

26 Cook, *Arts of Deception*, 22.

27 McNicholas, *Forgery and Impersonation in Imperial China*, 174.

28 See Wang, *Wanzhu*, chap. 1. Forged literary prizes evince a similar logic to literary forgeries, which, K. K. Ruthven claims, "constitute a powerful indictment of such cultural practices as literary reviewing and the awarding of literary prizes." Ruthven, *Faking Literature*, 4.

29 On this fictional episode as a commentary on reform-era "cultural entrepreneurship," see Rea and Volland, *Business of Culture*, chap. 12.

30 For a recent North American example, see the statements of the academic hoaxers profiled in Schuessler, "Hoaxsters Slip Breastaurants and Dog-Park Sex into Journals."

31 Apps of the multibillion-dollar corporation Meitu, Inc. 美圖, designed to "beautify" selfies through seamless digital manipulation, for example, have made image enhancement so cheap and commonplace that, according to one selfie celebrity, "it is considered a solecism to share a photo of yourself you haven't doctored." Fan, "China's Selfie Obsession." The Meitu regime, which is global, is something of a mass-market, digital-age iteration of the local, artisan-crafted consumer wish-fulfillment fantasies seen in Feng Xiaogang's film *Jiafang yifang* 甲方乙方 (Dream Factory, 1997).

32 I agree with James W. Cook that audiences are not necessarily as gullible as hoaxers, or historians, sometimes believe. As Cook (2001) argues in his study of P. T. Barnum's era, audiences may be well aware that the proposition is dubious and play along with the charade. The reveal or exposé doesn't always come as a surprise.

33 Aina, *Idle Talk under the Bean Arbor*, 259n11. Zhang Jing, quoted here, translates the term *guanggun* as "troublemakers."

34 Apropos of my discussion of hoax as method "to challenge perceptions of reality," translator Zhang Jing provides the kicker of this exposé: "the historical Tang general Li Baozhen died from an overdose of immortality pills, a death by delusion, ironically group[ing] him with the gullible laity deceived by the exalted monks." See Zhang Jing, note on session 6, in Aina, *Idle Talk under the Bean Arbor*, 217. The translation of "Da heshang jiayi chaosheng" 大和尚假意超昇 (The Exalted Monks Who Faked Transcendence) appears on 86–100. Online edition of original: ctext.org/wiki.pl/if=gb&chapter=930428.

35 Lee, "When Nothing Is True, Everything Is Possible," 1158.

36 Ibid. The term is Anthony Giddens's.

37 Here is the incriminating passage from Twain's "A Double Barrelled Detective Story" (1902): "It was a crisp and spicy morning in early October. The lilacs and laburnums, lit with the glory-fires of autumn, hung burning and flashing in the

upper air, a fairy bridge provided by kind Nature for the wingless wild things that have their homes in the tree-tops and would visit together; the larch and the pomegranate flung their purple and yellow flames in brilliant broad splashes along the slanting sweep of the woodland; the sensuous fragrance of innumerable deciduous flowers rose upon the swooning atmosphere; far in the empty sky a solitary oesophagus slept upon motionless wing; everywhere brooded stillness, serenity, and the peace of God." The oesophagus hoax is described in more detail in chap. 5 of Rea, *Age of Irreverence*.

38 A translation of this story appears in Rea, *China's Chaplin*, 67–79.

39 Sokal has archived his paper, "Transgressing the Boundaries," on his personal website: www.physics.nyu.edu/faculty/sokal/transgress_v2/transgress_v2_singlefile.html. He has also created an archive of related material (http://www.physics.nyu.edu/faculty/sokal/index.html) and written a book, *Beyond the Hoax: Science, Philosophy, and Culture* (2008).

40 Balleisen, *Fraud*, 39.

41 Wang X., *Huanjin shidai, Baiyin shidai*, 22, 39, 51; Wang X., *Wang in Love and Bondage*, 82–83, 101, 115. "The leaders always said that I didn't confess thoroughly enough and needed to continue" 領導上總說，交待得不徹底，還要繼續交待.

42 Wang X., *Huangjin shidai, Baiyin shidai*, 42; Wang X., *Wang in Love and Bondage*, 104.

43 Hill, *Lin Shu, Inc.*, 203.

44 Houlbrook, *Prince of Tricksters*, 310.

45 Ibid., 339.

46 Ibid., 346.

47 Menand, "Faking It," 69.

48 Y. Zhang, *Book of Swindles*, 200.

49 Hanan, *Invention of Li Yu*, 51; Chinese characters added. Li Yu propounded his novelty in extreme terms: "In half a lifetime's writing, I have not filched a single word from other people" 不佞半世操觚，不攘他人一字. Hanan, *Invention of Li Yu*, 48.

50 Hanan, *Invention of Li Yu*, 55.

51 Lee, "When Nothing Is True, Everything Is Possible," 1159, 1162.

References

Aina jushi 艾衲居士 [Aina the Layman]. "Da heshang jiayi chaosheng" 大和尚假意超昇 [The Exalted Monks Who Faked Transcendence]. In *Doupeng xianhua* 豆棚閑話 [Idle Talks under the Bean Arbor]. N.d. ctext.org/wiki.pl?if=gb&chapter=930428.

Aina jushi 艾衲居士 [Aina the Layman]. *Idle Talk under the Bean Arbor: A Seventeenth-Century Story Collection*, edited by Robert E. Hegel. Seattle: University of Washington Press, 2018.

Balibar, Étienne. *Politics and the Other Scene*, translated by Christine Jones, James Swenson, and Chris Turner. London: Verso, 2002.

Balleisen, Edward J. *Fraud: An American History from Barnum to Madoff*. Princeton, NJ: Princeton University Press, 2017.

Bao Duxing 包獨醒. *Pianshu daguan* 騙術大觀 [Panorama of Swindles]. Shanghai: Shanghai xiaoshuo she, 1920.

Cangya shi zhuren 蒼崖室主人. *Gujin pianshu daguan* 古今騙術大觀 [Panorama of Swindles Old and New]. Shanghai: [illegible] shuju, 1923.

Carpenter, Scott. *Aesthetics of Fraudulence in Nineteenth-Century France: Frauds, Hoaxes, and Counterfeits*. London: Routledge, 2016.

Chang, Eileen. *Little Reunions*, translated by Jane Weizhen Pan and Martin Merz. New York: New York Review Books, 2018.

Chen Guangsheng 陳廣生 and Cui Jiajun 崔家駿. *Lei Feng de gushi* 雷鋒的故事 [The Story of Lei Feng]. Beijing: Renmin chubanshe, 1973.

Cook, James W. *The Arts of Deception: Playing with Fraud in the Age of Barnum*. Cambridge, MA: Harvard University Press, 2001.

Fan, Jiayang. "China's Selfie Obsession." *New Yorker*, December 11, 2017. www.newyorker.com/magazine/2017/12/18/chinas-selfie-obsession.

Goodman, Bryna. "Dubious Figures: Speculation, Calculation, and Credibility in Early Twentieth-Century Chinese Stock Exchanges." In *The Cultural History of Money and Credit: A Global Perspective*, edited by Chia Yin Hsu, Thomas M. Luckett, and Erika Vause, 111–32. Lanham, MD: Lexington Books, 2016.

Hanan, Patrick. *The Invention of Li Yu*. Cambridge, MA: Harvard University Press, 1988.

Hill, Michael Gibbs. *Lin Shu, Inc.: Translation and the Making of Modern Chinese Culture*. New York: Oxford University Press, 2012.

Houlbrook, Matt. *Prince of Tricksters: The Incredible True Story of Netley Lucas, Gentleman Crook*. Chicago: University of Chicago Press, 2016.

Hutt, Jonathan. "*Monstre Sacré*: The Decadent World of Sinmay Zau 邵洵美." *China Heritage Quarterly*, no. 22 (2010). www.chinaheritagequarterly.org/features.php?issue=022&searchterm=022_monstre.inc.

Jiang Hongjiao 江紅蕉. *Jiaoyisuo xianxingji* 交易所現形記 [Exposé of the Stock Exchange]. Serialized in *Xingqi* 星期 [The Sunday], 1922–23.

Jinghua guike 京華歸客 and Tianchansheng 天懺生. *Fupi zhi heimu* 復辟之黑幕 [Behind the Black Curtain of Yuan Shikai's Imperial Restoration Attempt]. Shanghai: Yiwen bianyishe, 1917.

Lao Lin 老林. *Xuetang xiaohua, yiming xuetang xianxingji* 學堂笑話，一名學堂現形記 [Illustrated Amusing Stories from New-Style Schools; or, An Exposé of New-Style Schools]. Shanghai: Gailiang xiaoshuo she, 1910.

Lee, Haiyan. *The Stranger and the Chinese Moral Imagination*. Stanford, CA: Stanford University Press, 2014.

Lee, Haiyan. "When Nothing Is True, Everything Is Possible: On Truth and Power by Way of Socialist Realism." In "Poetics of Facts, Politics of Facts," special issue of *PMLA*, 134, no. 5 (2019): 1157–64.

Lei Junyao 雷君曜. *Huitu pianshu qitan* 繪圖騙術奇談 [Remarkable Swindle Tales Illustrated]. 4 vols. Shanghai: Saoye shanfang, 1909.

Lin, Yi-chieh Jessica. *Fake Stuff: China and the Rise of Counterfeit Goods*. New York: Routledge, 2011.

Ma Litai 馬利泰. *Pianshu qi zhong qi* 騙術奇中奇 [Each Scam More Remarkable than the Last]. Shanghai: Shanghai zhongxing she, 1911.

Mackie, Gregory. *Beautiful Untrue Things: Forging Oscar Wilde's Extraordinary Afterlife*. Toronto: University of Toronto Press, 2019.

McNicholas, Mark. *Forgery and Impersonation in Imperial China: Popular Deceptions and the High Qing State*. Seattle: University of Washington Press, 2016.

McWhorter, John H. *The Language Hoax: Why the World Looks the Same in Any Language*. New York: Oxford University Press, 2014.

Menand, Louis. "Faking It: Literary Hoaxes and the Ethics of Authorship." *New Yorker*, December 10, 2018. www.newyorker.com/magazine/2018/12/10/literary-hoaxes-and-the-ethics-of-authorship.

Mezzadra, Sandro, and Brett Neilson. *Border as Method; or, The Multiplication of Labor*. Durham, NC: Duke University Press, 2013.

Moeller, Hans-Georg, and Paul J. D'Ambrosio. *Genuine Pretending: On the Philosophy of the Zhuangzi*. New York: Columbia University Press, 2017.

"*Nüzi shijie.*" *Chinese Women's Magazines in the Late Qing and Early Republican Period*. kjc-sv034.kjc.uni-heidelberg.de/frauenzeitschriften/public/nuezi_shijie/the_magazine.php?magazin_id=2 (accessed October 15, 2019).

Pang, Laikwan. *Creativity and Its Discontents: China's Creative Industries and Intellectual Property Rights Offenses*. Durham, NC: Duke University Press, 2012.

Qi Shoucheng 齊守城. *Gujin pianshu qiguan* 古今騙術奇觀 [Remarkable Swindles Old and New]. Shenyang: Liaoshen shushe, 1994.

Qian Zhongshu 錢鍾書. "Lin Shu de fanyi" 林紓的翻譯 [Lin Shu's Translations]. In *Qi zhui ji* 七綴集 [Patchwork], 77–114. Beijing: Sanlian shudian, 2002.

Qian Zhongshu 錢鍾書. *Patchwork: Seven Essays on Art and Literature*, translated by Duncan M. Campbell. Leiden: Brill, 2014.

Rea, Christopher. *The Age of Irreverence: A New History of Laughter in China*. Oakland: University of California Press, 2015.

Rea, Christopher, trans. *China's Chaplin: Comic Stories and Farces by Xu Zhuodai*. Ithaca, NY: Cornell East Asia Center, 2019.

Rea, Christopher, and Nicolai Volland, eds. *The Business of Culture: Cultural Entrepreneurs in China and Southeast Asia, 1900–65*. Vancouver: UBC Press, 2015.

Ruthven, K. K. *Faking Literature*. Cambridge: Cambridge University Press, 2001.

Schuessler, Jennifer. "Hoaxsters Slip Breastaurants and Dog-Park Sex into Journals." *New York Times*, October 4, 2018. www.nytimes.com/2018/10/04/arts/academic-journals-hoax.html.

Sokal, Alan D. "Transgressing the Boundaries: Towards a Transformative Hermeneutics of Quantum Gravity." *Social Text*, nos. 46–47 (1996): 217–52. physics.nyu.edu/faculty/sokal/transgress_v2/transgress_v2_singlefile.html

Sokal, Alan D. *Beyond the Hoax: Science, Philosophy and Culture*. Oxford and New York: Oxford University Press, 2008.

Twain, Mark. "A Double Barrelled Detective Story." www.gutenberg.org/files/3180/3180-0.txt.

Wang Shuo 王朔. *Wanzhu* 頑主 [Masters of Mischief]. Beijing: Beijing shiyue wenyi chubanshe, 2012.

Wang Xiaobo 王小波. *Huangjin shidai, Baiyin shidai* 黃金時代白銀時代 [The Golden Age; The Silver Age]. Beijing: Zhongguo qingnian chubanshe, 2002.

Wang Xiaobo 王小波. *Wang in Love and Bondage: Three Novellas*, translated by Hongling Zhang and Jason Sommer. Albany: State University of New York Press, 2007.

Wilde, Oscar. "The Decay of Lying." 1899. In *The Decay of Lying, and Other Essays*. London: Penguin Classics, 2010. Ebook.

Yang, Fan. *Faked in China: Nation Branding, Counterfeit Culture, and Globalization*. Bloomington: Indiana University Press, 2016.

Yu Hua 余華. *Shige cihui li de Zhongguo* 十個詞彙裡的中國 [China in Ten Words]. Taipei: Maitian, 2011.

Zhang Ailing 張愛玲. *Xiao tuanyuan* 小團圓 [Little Reunions]. Taipei: Huangguan, 2009.

Zhang, Yingyu. *The Book of Swindles: Selections from a Late Ming Collection*, translated by Christopher Rea and Bruce Rusk. New York: Columbia University Press, 2017.
Zheng Zhenduo 鄭振鐸, ed. *Zhongguo xin wenxue daxi—Wenxue lunzheng ji* 中國新文學大系——文學論爭集 [Compendium of China's New Literature—Literary Debates]. Hong Kong: Xianggang wenxue yanjiushe, 1986.
Zhou Xinhui 周心慧, ed. *Gujin pianshu daguan* 古今騙術大觀 [Panorama of Swindles Old and New]. Beijing: Zhongguo zhigong chubanshe, 2004.

MARGARET HILLENBRAND

Ragpicking as Method

ABSTRACT This article explores the relationship between precarity, waste, and the ragpicker in contemporary Chinese visual culture. It asks first why precarity has come so little and so late to the theoretical scene in China, a society in which precarious experience is so rife as to be almost endemic. The essay then goes on to show how some of China's leading artists now work profusely with refuse—as a core theme of the precarious present—while noting the strange anomaly that their works offer up scant if any space for the figure of the waste picker. The artist, instead, has taken over her mantle as the sifter and sorter of garbage. This missing human figure matters, in part because waste is always about people—and their absence from aesthetic space suggests that art is responding to a felt sense that personhood is coming under assault as basic life sureties fray. But this essay also argues that the garbage takeover is part of a sustained practice of appropriation, effacement, even cruelty in the artistic representation of precarity in China. China's wasteworks are art forms born at the tense interface between different class actors, and they disclose fraught fears over where brittle life experience begins and ends in a society that has tried to eliminate class as a category of political action and analysis.

KEYWORDS garbage, waste picker, precarity, artwork, class tension

An eleven-year-old girl, small for her age, cuts out a picture of shiny red ballet flats from a French fashion magazine. She displays them on a grubby cushion at her feet, alongside a dozen other pairs of pink, red, and gingham-checked paper shoes, similarly scissored out of glossy magazines (fig. 1). Her own sandals, made of dirty yellow plastic, are several times the size of the sleek magazine cut-outs. But they don't fit her feet properly anyway. The magazine, with its fashion spread of high-end footwear, is rare bounty for the girl, scavenged from the vast plastic dump in which she lives and works alongside her parents and four siblings.[1] The family are migrants from Sichuan casually employed at a plastics recycling workshop in Shandong, one of hundreds of informal businesses that process the mounds of plastic waste that China imported from Japan, Europe, and the United States up until 2018. They sift through the mass of the identifiable (butter cartons, mineral water bottles, DHL banners, dog food sacks, hospital IV drips and blood bags) and the far vaster mass of the unidentifiable to claim the plastic matter that can be shredded, rendered into slurry, and finally kerneled into small hard pellets that are then sold to local plastics manufacturers. As her special find shows, the girl—whose name is Yi Jie—is both a recycler and a ragpicker. She is a *chiffonier*

PRISM: THEORY AND MODERN CHINESE LITERATURE • 16:2 • OCTOBER 2019
DOI 10.1215/25783491-7978499 •

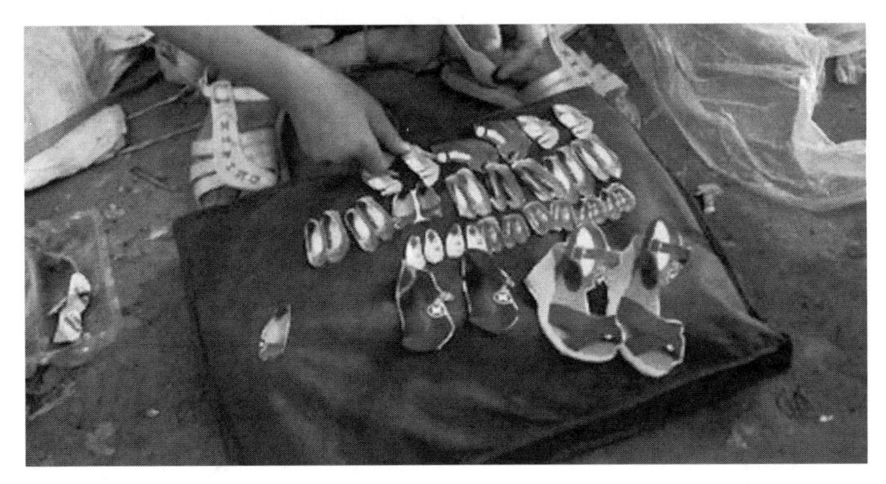

FIGURE 1. Screenshot from *Plastic China*, dir. Wang Jiuliang, 2016. Yi Jie can only experience fashion via paper simulacra.

of the kind that Baudelaire romanced in *Les Fleurs du Mal*, the scavenger who is bent double by "the jumbled vomit of enormous Paris," but is still able to "bring glory to the love-drunk folks at home" with tiny treasures foraged from the mire.[2] More than this, Yi Jie is an artist of the dump. She is just as creatively alive as the activist documentary maker Wang Jiuliang 王久良 (1976–), whose film *Suliao Zhongguo* 塑料中國 (Plastic China, 2016) tells her story.

As Walter Benjamin observed, Baudelaire's poem "The Ragpicker's Wine" is more about the poetic process than nineteenth-century dumpster-diving: it reads the *chiffonier* as a dirty double for the writer, since both spin gold from bits of scrap. Baudelaire writes: "Here we have a man whose job it is to gather the day's refuse in the capital. Everything that the big city has thrown away, everything it has lost, everything it has scorned, everything it has crushed underfoot he catalogues and collects. He collates the annals of intemperance, the capharnaum of waste."[3] To this, Benjamin responds with the following gloss:

> This description is one extended metaphor for the poetic method, as Baudelaire practiced it. Ragpicker and poet: both are concerned with refuse, and both go about their solitary business while other citizens are sleeping; they even move in the same way. . . . This is the gait of the poet who roams the city in search of rhyme-booty; it is also the gait of the ragpicker, who is obliged to come to a halt every few moments to gather up the refuse he encounters.[4]

Benjamin goes on to observe that "there is much evidence that Baudelaire secretly wished to develop this analogy,"[5] but not, it seems, by broadening the metaphoric operation to acknowledge that if the poet is a ragpicker, the ragpicker may also be a poet. Yi Jie illustrates this again later in the documentary, when she fashions a computer monitor from a Japanese advertisement for weight-loss pills and a keyboard from the tiny milk pots served at hotel breakfasts, and then in a stunning scene toward the end, in which she decorates her family's shanty with artisanal wallpaper crafted from taped-together KitKat wrappers (fig. 2). These activities are more than just a diligent reuse of materials, what Susan Strasser calls the appropriate "stewardship of objects."[6] They constitute focused artistic endeavor.

The dump is a slur on all taxonomic systems, a "cemetery for lost objects that never made it to the world of categories," as Michael Taussig puts it.[7] To process garbage is to face down that affront to order through the tactile labor of sorting. So as waste besieges us, hemming in whole cities like ring roads, it is perhaps unsurprising that the arts of assemblage—variants on the sorting impulse—are now in the aesthetic ascendant. Many artists are ragpickers now. So much so, in fact, that some art critics wonder if the use of garbage-as-bricolage has hardened into something canonical, as "rubbish becomes a strange vale of soul making and creativity" now that nature is being forced to evacuate the terrain.[8] Euroamerica may apparently have reached "peak stuff"—the notion that consumption has reached its zenith—but as the dumping ground for so much foreign waste until recently, China is still very much processing the consequences of disposability as a socioeconomic cult. This is partly why the art of waste has also become a surging aesthetic movement in Chinese art in recent years, via the work of artists such as Xing Danwen 邢丹文 (1967–), Han Bing 韓冰 (1974–), Du Zhenjun 杜震君 (1961–), Yang Yongliang 楊泳梁 (1980–), Yao Lu 姚璐 (1967–), Jiang Pengyi 蔣鵬奕 (1977–), Xu Bing 徐冰 (1955–), Wang Zhiyuan 王智遠 (1958–), and others. Their works are often taken as exemplars of eco-art, since they engage directly with issues of contamination and sustainability. Ultimately, though, it is the scavenging impulse—ragpicking as method—which reigns in many works that explore waste in China. And scavenging is nothing if not a precarious practice, a practice of the precariat. Yet precarity remains a near absent, or at best incipient, discourse in the study of contemporary China, with the result that the symbolically dense role of waste in Chinese life and art has not been probed with the same depth that the theme has received in other places.[9]

In this article, I explore the relationship between precarity, waste, and the ragpicker in contemporary Chinese visual culture. My aim in what follows, though, is to think beyond the waste picker as a literalized embodiment of precarity, and I begin instead by considering the ways in which precarity and waste are organically linked. Next I explore why precarity has come so little and so late to the theoretical scene in China, a society in which precarious experience is so rife as to be almost endemic, and in which this pain feels sharper for many as the security blanket provided, for some at least, by socialism has been rolled back or snatched away. I then go on to show how some of China's leading artists now

FIGURE 2. Screenshot from *Plastic China*, dir. Wang Jiuliang, 2016. Improvised décor for the family home.

work profusely with garbage—building-site debris, dumpster trash, e-waste—while noting the strange anomaly that their works offer up scant if any space for the figure of the waste picker. The artist, instead, has taken over his or her mantle as the sifter and sorter of refuse, which itself has assumed a symbolic cast. This missing human figure matters, in part because waste is always about people—and never more so than now, as its rising volume becomes a cipher for precarity as a mode of existence that threatens everyone. As materiality of a grossly abject kind squeezes Anthropos out of aesthetic space, it shows, on one level, that precarity is impacting the forms of art as much as the art form is having any measurable impact on precarity as a state of life. Even more than this, the "thingly turn"[10] as it manifests in Chinese visual culture might seem to suggest that art is responding to a felt sense that personhood is coming under assault as basic life sureties fray. These missing human figures are symbolic victims of a new ontological order, in which waste rules and is arrogating the privileges of subjectivity to itself.

Yet the garbage takeover, I argue here, is also part of a sustained practice of appropriation, effacement, even cruelty in the artistic representation of precarity in China. Over the last couple of decades, art-world treatments of precarious people have proliferated in China, and many have won international recognition. But what many of these works surprisingly lack, despite their sustained focus on the beleaguered body, is a discernible will to realize the subjecthood of fragile lives both in art and through art-making—as *Plastic China* demonstrates via its against-the-grain depiction of the ragpicker as artist. This absence is curious. Surely it should be a clear imperative for artists who publicly identify themselves as *engagé* to create representations that grant maximal agency to precarious people.

So why do so many fail or decline to do so? I conclude by suggesting that the awkwardness of China's dump art, in which artists dabble at waste-picking rather like Marie Antoinette played at being a shepherdess, speaks of more than just appropriation. It also discloses a deeper anxiety over where brittle life experience begins and ends in a social world in which precarity is generating suppressed class strife—as opposed to the overt class struggle of the Maoist period—as much as any sense of common ground in uncertainty. It is in this sense that ragpicking reveals itself not just as an artwork trait or aesthetic practice but also as a method that discloses some of the fraught and ugly contours of the present. China's waste-works are frictive forms born at the tense interface between different class actors, as part of the push and pull of social mobility in a society that has tried to eliminate class as a category of political action and analysis. Such works do not simply register experiences of uncertainty, disposability, and vulnerability as artistic themes. Rather, they are places in which precarity can be felt as an atmospheric trepidation, as a force that can change our social point of origin, and thus as a zone of mounting interclass conflict.

Conditions of Our Time

In *The Mushroom at the End of the World*, her study of what the complex global trade in matsutake mushrooms reveals about ecology, capitalism, and survival amid the ruins, Anna Tsing writes, "We hear about precarity in the news every day. . . . But most of the time we imagine such precarity to be an exception to how the world works. It's what 'drops out' from the system. What if . . . precarity is the condition of our time—or to put it another way, what if our time is ripe for sensing precarity?"[11] Here I am interested in a further connected question: what if we were to substitute the word *waste* for *precarity* in this quotation—or rather better, what if we were to consider the ways in which precarity and waste constitute, in fact, an organically linked method for coming to terms with the present, in China as much as in other places? To consider precarity and waste as indissociable forces in the making of the present is to notice their many zones of overlap. To be precarious is to feel futureless. It is to live at the mercy of other people and greater powers, occupying transient ground and subsisting without a forward direction. This is also the space-time of the dump, whose locations shift arbitrarily and whose temporality is at best cyclical rather than teleological—and often simply stalled. When Nicolas Bourriaud writes that "an object is said to be precarious if it has no definitive status and an uncertain future or final destiny,"[12] he could just as easily have been describing waste. Yi Jie's father makes this same point in *Plastic China* when he describes how he and his family moved from Sichuan, where they lived at the "mercy of nature" (kaotian chifan 靠天吃飯), to Shandong, where they now live at the mercy of refuse, their futures suspended in limbo.

Precarity, just like garbage, is also growing. It encompasses more and more of us in its orbit of uncertainty, just as landfills swell and the oceans clog with non-degradable trash. Relatedly, precarity and waste are yoked in their relation to the natural world. As waste runs wild, it heightens our precariousness as a species. But circling things around, precarity is also the hallmark of a society without decent stewardship of objects, driven by what Zygmunt Bauman calls "the horror of expiry."[13] The contents of the dump are precarious—stuff on the verge, about to crumble, to decay, to turn effluent—just as precarious experience is so often characterized by a sense of waste, as talent and opportunity are kept in a state of abeyance. Precarious labor—work that is casualized, unwaged, informal, irregular—mirrors the lawlessness of the dump and its lack of classificatory order. Yet at the same time, this parallel also works inversely, since waste connotes an excess of materiality, while precarity refers to a brittle thinness in human lifeworlds. Finally, both have imprinted themselves on public consciousness more or less simultaneously as immanent perils. Thus it is that the ragpicker, as a combinant identity in which waste and precarity meet, is a methodological archetype for our age. She or he is not simply an icon of poverty in the Global South but a personage in which "the condition of our time" is crystallized.

Precarious China

In a world rife with precarity, in which "we are all precarious now," China has remained oddly absent from the vast academic literature that has built up around the theme of fragile life and labor since the millennium. China is in many ways prime precarious, yet it has been seldom named as such. Why so? Perhaps the first answer is that precarity—and most particularly its partner political concept, the precariat—has struggled to throw off its origins in the European protest movements of the early 2000s. Thus to apply it to China may seem at first sight historically and politically anachronistic, or worse. Certainly, precarity to date has most commonly been taken to mean "economic and existential experiences of risk and uncertainty" within post-Fordism,[14] most specifically within liberal-democratic experiences of the contracting welfare state, where its pain is perceived as a sharp adjustment against a long backdrop of stability. Precarity, born as a justice movement to battle so-called flexploitation, was rooted in a deep sense of rupture—in the notion that a once-tightly woven social contract was being unpicked and workers were being cast into freefall. The problem here, as Neilson and Rossiter note, is that "precarity appears as an irregular phenomenon only when set against a Fordist or Keynesian norm."[15] They argue further that "if we look at capitalism in a wider historical and geographical scope, it is precarity that is the norm and not Fordist economic organization."[16] This recognition that labor security within the welfare state was just a spatiotemporal blip has gained broad currency as scholars have begun to argue that the precarian is essentially the new subaltern: a broad category encompassing all those whom power excludes and betrays, and whose existence long predates the coining of the term.

Yet this notion of precarity as an ineluctable historical norm often hits the theoretical buffers precisely as researchers seek to apply it in more lateral ways across wide global spaces. As Ronaldo Munck puts it: "Is the term novel or even relevant, for the millions of workers and urban poor in the global South for whom precariousness has always been a seemingly natural condition?"[17] Precarity, for Munck and others, is a term overdetermined and undermined by "a totally Northern sensibility" that is narcissistically blind to the fact that work in the Global South "has always-already been precarious."[18] The ax this argument grinds is about the breathless sense of the new on which discussions of precarity and the precarian seem to rest. Precarity has many asynchronous modes, and for Munck and others the discourse that grabbed attention in the early 2000s was not novel so much as unacceptably belated. For the "global informal working class," which stands a billion people strong, what can this sudden attention to a perennial reality offer?[19] Even when theorists of precarity recognize—as do Neilson and Rossiter, among others—that precarity is the standardized and age-old reality for so many of the world's workers, its discursive roots as a term that articulates nostalgia for an era that the Global South never got to enjoy excludes it from real political consequence.

Does this, though, hold entirely true of China? Here, we might legitimately argue, the notion of precarity does carry at least some palpable novelty power. The rolling back of the socialist-era command economy that occurred during the reform period in China is, of course, not precisely parallel to the passing of Fordism. Yet it was a bonfire of the certainties for many Chinese urban workers nonetheless—even if the ructions of repeated political campaigns meant that not everyone who experienced the Maoist era felt nostalgic at its passing. As free market economics took hold, the iron rice bowl was smashed, factories were decommissioned, and their workers were laid off. This process and its ructions have been researched exhaustively. Yet there has been insufficient space given in the vast literature on this topic to the idea that such conditions make precarity not just a plausible but a necessary conceptual construct through which to read the experiences of significant cohorts in Chinese society. What gave the term *precarity* its critical edge and its rallying power in early millennial Europe was precisely a sense of incinerated sureties, of a security blanket gone up in smoke as one era gave way to another. This mood of epochal change has been felt as pain among city-based workers in China, too, and to an extent it obviates Munck's broadbrush claim that work outside the North has "always-already been precarious."

A key stumbling block here is that this sense of aftermath quickly acquired the name "postsocialism," and as such it has gone on to dominate the theoretical landscape, eclipsing from view the precarity that should arguably be its core partner term. Indeed, if one of the implied arguments of Nancy Fraser's work on postsocialism is that this condition goes far beyond the Soviet Union and other former communist states in its scope—that we are all postsocialist now—then the same is self-evidently true of precarity, which in many ways is as pertinent to China as postsocialism is to the contemporary United States.[20] Precarity and postsocialism are twin conditions: partner plights. Yet for the most part they have been theorized as discrete entities, across a stark spatial divide.[21] A quantity of scholarly work has been produced over the last twenty years to explain China's long goodbye to socialism within multiple domains. But in overlooking the fundamental intersection between this condition and the state of precarity that has been theorized so extensively in Europe and America over the same approximate period, postsocialism as a method for making sense of lifeworlds in contemporary China lacks full intellectual coherence. A two-way conduit is needed, one that not only opens up precarious Euroamerica to its identity as postsocialist, but that also expressly names postsocialist China as precarious. And as part of this process, precarity itself requires theoretical modification—it will need to be decolonized and provincialized—so that the experiences of precarious people in China can feed into and thus reshape how this crucial experience of our present time is understood. Or to put this another way, if modernities are understood to be multiple, then so too are the norms and forms of precarity.

This is by no means to suggest, however, that experiences of so-called aftermath are uniform in China. Against the decisive sense of epochal shift identified by many Euroamerican theorists of precarity stands, most notably, the argument that China's vast migrant workforce, as it has streamed into the cities from the countryside, has simply swapped older forms of uncertainty for newer variants. Rural conditions under Maoism were predicated on systemic risk and poverty, rather than on the iron rice bowl associated with much urban work, with famine an ever-looming hazard. In this sense, migration to the cities promised a measure of relief—even the whisper of deliverance—from the still more acute uncertainties of rural life. At the very least, the risks of relocation may have seemed more bearable since they also contained the kernel of hope. Yet to argue that precarity as a construct for understanding China's floating population is invalid because there was no good life for these migrants to mourn is to assume that precarious experience is always rooted in longings for paradise lost. On the contrary, such fantasies are projected into the future as often as they linger on the past, as Lauren Berlant has argued,[22] and the chimera of the good life may be all the more seductive to those who have never seen and felt it in the flesh.

This chimera has, however, infamously failed to take concrete shape. Under the iniquitous *hukou* 戶口 system, China's new urban workforce has found itself forced to endure exclusion from core benefits—including pension, health care, and education—that those with an urban birthright enjoy, while working in industries that often lack safeguards, contracts, and guaranteed wages. For many migrant workers, therefore, precarity is precisely the nervy apprehension that their hopes are brittle, which is, of course, why oneiric propaganda—the China dream—is plastered all over the building sites on which many of these migrants work. More than this, rural life, however grueling, was a life determined (overdetermined, even) by roots. By contrast, a lack of place-based identity, aggravated by prejudicial outsider status in China's big cities, induces in China's migrants an embodied sense of drift and dislocation, which brings the meaning of the term *precarity* back to its own etymological roots: not securely held in position, liable to fall, unmoored. Indeed, rather than being entirely peripheral to the Euroamerican discourses of precarity that have gained currency across the world since the millennium, Chinese migrant experiences of being and feeling precarious should by rights be at the very core of those discussions. This is because what we see in China is a vast experiment in the strategic incitement of unrealizable desire—"cruel optimism," in Berlant's terminology—within a context of mass territorial-emotional displacement.

A final potential sticking point for "precarious China" relates to precarity's partner concept of the precariat. This is the idea, first set out by Guy Standing, that those who work under conditions of informal, casualized, and piecemeal labor constitute an emergent, and insurgent, political class.[23] The interchangeability with which the terms *precarious* and *precariat* are often invoked is perhaps a problematic slippage in the case of China, most obviously because tight political control, in the form of the stability maintenance (*weiwen* 維穩) apparatus, effectively roadblocks the formation of the kind of insurrectionary groupings that the term *precariat* connotes in the work of Standing, who dubs this class dangerous. Here again, though, we might argue that a precariat without the capacity to mobilize en masse and at scale, possessing only the weapons of the weakest—despite its vast human scale—is a political category that theories of precarity should scrutinize most closely. This, in a sense, is Wang Hui's pertinent question when he asks: "Why in early twentieth-century China, when the working class was small and weak, did proletarian class politics sweep the entire region? And why has China today, the 'world's factory' with almost 300 million workers, been unable to generate a working-class politics of the sort?"[24] His explanation is that class "vagabondage"—in which well-born social actors who had fallen through the cracks during the Republican era linked up with the aspirant poor to foment insurgency—has waned into apathy in twenty-first-century China.[25] Class disunity is the new norm.

Smith and Ngai, in one of the few scholarly studies that tests the workability of precarity as a keyword for understanding contemporary China, go further. As they put it: "The idea central to the precariat thesis, that there is a class divide in terms of the employment conditions of the salariat and precariat, falls at the first hurdle. All workers are insecure in China, and precariousness is not evidence of a separate class, but part of the general condition of waged labor in the country . . . non-standard forms of employment are recognizable across work with different forms of status, from unskilled to more white collar and professional occupations."[26] Their point that precarity is also "white collar" and professional is hardly specific to China, even as the country's vast insecure graduate class gives this notion of cross-caste labor volatility a sharper theoretical edge. But the broader argument here—that precariousness "is part of the general condition of waged labor in the country"—is in many ways a still more essential and evocative one. It alludes, through its sheer scope, to precarity as an ambient, wraparound experience. If all waged labor in China is insecure, and all workers are precarians, then precarity becomes a force profoundly constitutive of Chinese social reality. In particular, as I argue below, it is a force with the capacity not just to disunify but also to sow active class division.

Indeed, this notion that precarity is now a forceful life mode is gathering pace wherever fragile lifeworlds are studied. While it has long been common to argue that precarity signifies "both the multiplication of precarious, unstable, insecure forms of living and, simultaneously, new forms of political struggle and solidarity,"[27] precarity's conceptual reach has expanded as it has become widely normalized as an experiential condition. Precarity as something systemic, as what Isabell Lorey refers to as an entrenched vulnerability, means not just "destabilization through wage labor" but also a "destabilization of ways of living and hence of bodies."[28] Precarity, in short, is a matter of affect. On one level, this is the dissolution of dreams identified by Berlant, and the incorporation of people into an emotional regime that tethers like a dead weight while giving them something deceptively promising on which to cling. But here I also explore the notion that precarity is an invidious thing, a set of affects that pits class actors against one another in a climate of fear and fretfulness. I undertake this exploration within the realm of culture, using waste—a material and abstract force closely tied to brittle life—as a method. More particularly, I use the art of the dump and the notion of the ragpicker as artist to explore the often tense politics of representing precarity in contemporary China.

Animal, Vegetable, Mineral

So what does it mean, then, for the ragpicker to declare him- or herself an artist? To answer this question, we might usefully turn first to some artists who have declared themselves ragpickers. China has seen increasing numbers of these in recent years, as waste has emerged as a major aesthetic topos. A notable example is Xu Bing and his *Fenghuang* 鳳凰 (Phoenix, 2010). This work (fig. 3) consists of a pair of giant birds, each nearly one hundred feet long and weighing sixteen tons between them, welded entirely from debris gleaned from building sites across

FIGURE 3. Xu Bing: *Phoenix* Project, 2010. Vast avian structures protest inhumane working conditions in the Chinese construction industry; but the only visible human presence is the spectators.

Beijing: helmets, shovels, pliers, hammers, rivets, drill bits, broken wheels, corrugated metal, fire extinguishers, hooks, rods, tubes, cogs, and bolts. Originally commissioned as a statement piece that would ornament the atrium of the World Financial Center building, the *Phoenix* project began to diverge from its brief as Xu contemplated the fissures between the low-rent labor of the migrant construction crews and the high-spec corporate steeple that they were building. These disparities, Xu states, made his "skin quiver."[29] Enlisting the help of the laborers, Xu salvaged over a thousand pieces of detritus and used this ragpicker's feast to assemble his phoenixes from the flames, which seem to soar forth from the ashes of hardscrabble toil. The project's backstory is compelling, even more so since the buyers withdrew the commission, finding it too political. But Xu declined to compromise and stuck to his vision of the aestheticized leftovers of neoliberalism. Later the pieces were purchased by Taiwanese art collector Barry Lam, who allowed the birds to be exhibited in both Beijing and New York before adding them to his private collection. They also live on in beautiful book form, via a

Thircuir edition that brings together Xu's sketches, portraits of individual pieces of scrap metal, and photographs of the phoenixes at various sites of display.[30]

Despite their stated humanism, though, the phoenixes are never anything other than birdlike: there are no actual ragpickers in this installation about the intersection of waste and precarity. In fact, even their avian character has something formalistic or even incidental about it, since the force that really defines *Phoenix* is its materiality, both as an effect of the overwhelming size of the sculptures and of their patchwork density. Something similar is at work in another piece that purports to offer an animalistic allegory of waste: Wang Qingsong's 王慶松 (1966–) installation *Du zhizhu* 毒蜘蛛 (Poisonous Spider, 2011). In this work (fig. 4), Wang spins a spider's web of barbed wire, on which are suspended items of banal daily trash: a Styrofoam cup, a scratched disc, a discarded shoe, a bunch of bananas, wilted lettuce, plastic bags, odd socks. Conceptually, the garbage might be both lure and prey and, as such, is already suggestive of unsettled ontological relations. But this point comes over more strongly when the installation is contrasted with an apparent partner piece of 2005, Wang's earlier digital print of the same name (fig. 5). This photograph is well-nigh identical to its three-dimensional successor—except for the worker who lies trapped at the heart of the web, limbs splayed in a pose of helpless capture. As the concept for the piece moves through time, transitioning from one medium to another, it sheds its human presence, seemingly surrendering that space to proxies from the natural world. Just like *Phoenix*, however, it is not the spider's web so much as the gross materiality it ensnares that provides the central logic of the installation. Whether bird or arachnid, the creatures who provide the structural morphology, the exoskeleton, of these works are simply platforms for the artistic display of waste. Both works are instances of scavenger art, in which foul or discarded matter is reclaimed to prove Claes Oldenburg's claim that a "refuse lot in the city is worth all the art stores in the world."[31] In both, a surfeit of gross, abject materiality crowds out the animate subject of representation, and the artist is the only ragpicker whose presence a spectator might directly sense.

On one level, it might seem logical to understand these works as renderings in art of the evolutionary fact that cities are altering species at speed. As Menno Schilthuizen has shown, urban spaces do not simply serve as sites of biological extermination. They are also crucibles for genome development, as "city pigeons develop detox plumage" and the common or garden blackbird becomes the *Turdus urbanicus*, a mildly mutated version of the original creature that is beautifully synced to the megacity habitat.[32] Schilthuizen also references the work of arachnologists, who have shown that the urban spider *Larinioides sclopetarius*, which builds its webs in the spaces between handrails on pedestrian bridges, overwhelmingly gravitates toward spaces near fluorescent lighting, where insect pickings are richer.[33] Schilthuizen does not dwell on refuse in his study, perhaps

FIGURE 4. Wang Qingsong: "Poisonous Spider," 2011. Spinning a web of mixed waste.

a strange omission given that the dump is arguably the most materially volatile zone in urban space and thus a locale likely to catalyze genetic change. Viewed through this lens, Xu Bing's phoenixes have their own kind of "detox plumage," via the red hardhats arrayed like crested feathers atop each bird's head; and Wang Qingsong's light-seeking spider's web magnetizes trash, pulling it by force into its orbit. But rather like Schilthuizen, who spares only a few paragraphs for the idea that urban life is changing *human* biology, both artists eliminate the human subject in their explorations of how waste is producing novel ontological states.

Anything but Human

This tendency is by no means restricted to China. Commentators on the so-called toxic sublime, for example, have noted the routine absence of humans in these landscapes.[34] Art forms such as these, often photographic, acknowledge that the sites they represent are often contaminated beyond salvage, yet cannot help but show their wonderment at iridescent oil slicks and chemical spills. Humans, though, are mostly missing in the work of toxic sublimists such as Edward Burtynsky and Chris Jordan. Viewers understand, of course, that human agency crafted these environments; but Anthropos vanishes from sight amid Jordan's statistical renderings of plastic beverage bottles, for example. To an extent, this might be because the waste picker is so fraught a figure to aestheticize. As Katherine Boo notes in her personalized ethnography of waste pickers in a Mumbai slum, work of this kind "could wreck a body in very short time. Scrapes from

FIGURE 5. Wang Qingsong: "Poisonous Spider," 2005. An earlier iteration of the work entangles a migrant worker at the heart of the web.

dumpster-diving pocked and became infected. Where skin broke, maggots got in. Lice colonized hair, gangrene inched up fingers, calves swelled into tree trunks."[35] Keeping the ragpicker out of art could be construed, then, as a gesture of delicacy.

Certainly it is true that the figure of the waste picker has seemed more graspable within the hardcore documentary mode in China. Productions such as *Tielu yanxian* 鐵路沿線 (Along the Railway, 2000; dir. Du Haibin 杜海濱 [1972–]), *Nanjing lu* 南京路 (Street Life, 2006; dir. Zhao Dayong 趙大勇 [1970–]), *Huxiao de jinshu* 呼嘯的金屬 (Heavy Metal, 2009; dir. Jin Huaqing 金華青 [1984–]), *Shihuangzhe* 拾荒者 (Ragpicker, 2010; dir. Zhong Yanshan 鍾延山), *Laji de cunzi* 垃圾的村子 (Trashy Village, 2013; dir. Zou Xueping 鄒雪平 [1985–]), and *Weichao* 危巢 (When the Bough Breaks, 2011; dir. Ji Dan 季丹 [1963–]) all seek, with greater or lesser success, to realize the lives of waste pickers on screen. They do so, however, in ways rather different from Wang Jiuliang's *Plastic China*. These works adhere for the most part to the now-canonical *xianchang* 現場, or "on-the-spot," style of documentary filmmaking, within which a deliberate kind of deskilling takes place as muddy audio, clunky editing, and handheld camerawork

FIGURES 6–8. Xing Danwen: from *DisCONNEXION*, 2003–3. The thingly turn writ large.

serve as tokens of authenticity. As such, these are works possessed of a certain anti-aesthetic drive; their core currency is informational indexicality. And by showing repeatedly that the waste picker is an acceptable subject for reportage, they obliquely draw attention to the absence of this figure from the less literalized, more evocative spaces of art. Evidently this is a far cry from Yi Jie in *Plastic China*, who amply corroborates Patricia Yaeger's remarks about "the power of waste" in American culture. As Yaeger puts it, "not only does detritus replace nature, but waste managers and garbage haulers are its poets and purveyors, its historians and makers."[36] But what makes this latter point telling is not just the usurpation of the earth by trash but also the idea that garbage haulers are the poets of the contemporary. They are at once the subjects of works about refuse and the purveyors of truth about where and what we are in the present. In this sense, artworks (whatever their provenance) that deanthropomorphize waste in the age of the Anthropocene—and in which refuse becomes the reigning presence—are suggestive of certain realities. They tell oblique stories about humans, almost despite themselves.

This anomaly of the missing human figure in so much dump art from China becomes more politically pressing when we think again about the nexus between precarity and waste, and most especially about the status of the ragpicker as a personage who brings these forces together in ways that constitute a method for our age. To put this another way, waste is always about people. In waste we find out exactly who we are, unfiltered and unperfumed. Waste lives right alongside us, which partly explains, as Maurizia Boscagli puts it, "the disturbing extension of its characteristics to human beings when they themselves have become disposable."[37] What's more, the carelessness with which so many twenty-first-century people continue to discard things belies the intimate secrets that refuse always harbors. Indeed, the very process of waste is predicated on a reckless suspension of disbelief. Even now, many of us remain invested in the idea that there are no comebacks from junking our possessions, otherwise dumpsters would not keep on yielding bank statements, medical records, criminal evidence, plutonium, pets, and even abandoned infants. As Robert Stam puts it, "the truth of a society is in its detritus. The socially peripheral points to the symbolically central."[38] So what does it mean not just when waste becomes a canonical mood in art, but when garbage emerges as a stand-alone pictorial subject, and when the waste picker—a figure crucial to understanding why detritus is so "symbolically central"—is simply an identity slipped on and off at all will by the artist?

Material World

Here it may be instructive to look briefly at the work of Chinese artist Xing Danwen. In her series *Jueyuan* 絕緣 (disCONNEXION, 2002–3), Xing herself effectively assumes the role of ragpicker. Across forty chromogenic color prints, the artist maps a taxonomy of the e-waste that until recently lapped China's southern shores from the United States, Europe, and Japan: telephone wires, circuit boards, shattered casings, silicon chips, computer cables, defunct keyboards, cellphone cases, and obsolete chargers. Each category of e-trash becomes the subject of its own portrait, a point so obvious that critics haven't paid it much attention, focusing instead on what the series says about globalizing China and ugly aesthetics. But the sorting impulse—the gathering, sifting, dismantling, and pigeonholing of miscellaneous waste—constitutes the deep meaning of the series. Xing's prints are the final fruits of extreme labor, the toil of the precarious waste pickers of Guangdong province who tear various electronic devices into their component parts while toxifying their own bodies. The artist's statement about the work posted on Xing's website reads as follows: "In *disCONNEXION*, her critical eye and sharp lens examine the aesthetics of technological waste, reflecting environmental concerns, but more importantly, an anxiety about changes in the lives of workers along the south coast, whose ghosts can be sensed despite their absence from the frames."[39] Perhaps these ghosts are sensed by some viewers. But the classificatory order imposed on the electronic detritus in *disCONNEXION* inevitably ends up looking much more like the handiwork of the artist, whose "sharp lens" beautifies the debris, thus owning it still further. And as part of this artmaking process, the series as a whole comes over more forcefully as hostage to its own charismatic materiality than as a testimony to precarious lives.

The cables in figure 6, for example, are lithe and serpentine: they have a strong agency as they squirm around the frame; the tiny nuts and bolts in figure 7 look like wood lice swarming; while the smashed keyboards in figure 8, concertinaed up against each other, are reminiscent of Bill Brown's point that "we begin to confront the thingness of objects when they stop working for us: when the drill breaks, when the car stalls, when the windows get filthy, when their flow within the circuits of production and distribution, consumption and exhibition, has been arrested, however momentarily."[40] These photographs also share a lineage with Xu Bing's *Phoenix* and Wang Qingsong's *Poisonous Spider*, discussed already in terms of their overt materiality. They resonate closely, too, with the work of Han Bing, whose photographs in his series *Urban Amber* 都市琥珀 (*Dushi hupo*, 2005–11) are all shot from reflections in cesspools, and via this technique turn the scum and detritus that float on the surface into the super-subjects of these images. In figure 9, for example, the discarded bottle and plastic bag enjoy aesthetic subjectivity as they hover in the middle of the frame. Han's camerawork creates a superimposed look, as if he had literally plucked the garbage and pasted it digitally over the landscape, a sense heightened by the dark shadow that trails the objects. Once again the artist becomes waste picker while creating a topography that is populated by trash and emptied of people. This process becomes still more vivid in the wasteworks of Yang Yongliang, famed for his tonally textured digital collages, which arrest the eye initially as reincarnations of the Chinese landscape

FIGURE 9. Han Bing: from *Urban Amber*, 2005–11. Garbage floats as delicate cumulus over the cityscape.

tradition, with mist-clad mountains and cascading waterfalls that undulate across the three grounds of pictorial space and are denuded of humans. But zoom in closer, and it becomes clear that the *shanshui* 山水 aesthetic has been subverted by ruin and garbage: the foreground of Yang's composite photographs emerges as a terrain of demolished structures, effluent waste, tilting pylons, and rebar (fig. 10). Yang's identity as waste picker is, though, even more hygienically removed from the grime of e-waste than that of Xing Danwen, since he uses Google Tilt Brush, a software tool, to sort and sift the detritus with which he composes the image.[41]

This material turn can be detected more broadly elsewhere, too, as precarity increasingly drives new genres of object-oriented aesthetic form in China. An obvious example is Jia Zhangke's 賈樟柯 (1970–) *Sanxia haoren* 三峽好人 (Still Life, 2006) and its fixation with the daily emblems of a hand-to-mouth existence, the glue and grit of precarious living: the hessian sacks, thermos flasks, bottles of liquor, and packets of tea that merge into a shared object ecology for people under duress and thereby acquire an increasingly visible subjectivity. A similar elevation of object to subject is also on show in Jia's next feature film, *Ershisi chengji* 二十四城記 (24 City, 2008), where prosaic items—a portable IV drip, a battered ID card, a tear-off wall calendar, a patched bedspread, a strategically positioned glass on a table—join the film's much-discussed tableaux vivants as subjects for the camera's intent gaze. The IV drip, which character Da Li 大麗 holds above her head as she walks around her residential compound, seems to live again in the early moments of Wang Jiuliang's *Plastic China*, when the camera

FIGURE 10. Yang Yongliang: From *The New World* (Laizi xindalu), 2014. Look closer and rubble reveals itself amid the timeless peaks and rivers.

zeroes in on a similar piece of medical junk, now lying redundant on the dump. Objects, it seems, have come to assume a kind of personhood within Chinese visual culture, challenging Baudrillard's claim that "we have always lived off the splendor of the subject and the poverty of the object."[42] As materiality surges as a theme in art and cinema and then turns steadily to waste, it begs questions about the changing form and praxis of visual culture under the regime of precarity.

The Susceptible Arts of Precarity

To be more precise, the notion that art can intervene in unsteady lives—that art about precarity can provide some sort of fix for situations—needs to be overhauled or, at the very least, supplemented by a closer focus on what uncertainty has done to the nature of aesthetic form. I have already alluded to the ways in which a mood of risk and jeopardy has produced, in pre- and postmillennial China, a huge corpus of what might be called bodyworks. This is art that uses the human form in postures of barely clothed duress to bid for visibility and as an apparent call to political arms. These representations of what Wang Hui calls China's "new workers"—those who engage in *dagong* 打工 (working for the boss) rather than *laodong* 勞動 (the more elevated labor of working for the socialist state)—have oscillated between a range of forms.[43] One category comprises works in which the artist claims close kinship with the urban underclass and presents himself as a precarian, such as in Zhu Fadong's 朱發東 (1960–) work *Ciren chushou jiage mianyi* 此人出售價格面議 (This Person Is for Sale, 1994) and Luo Zidan's 羅子丹 (1971–) *Yiban shi bailing, yiban shi nongmin* 一般是白領，一半是農民 (Half White-Collar/Half Peasant, 1996). Another is a practice of delegated performance, in which the artist enlists the "labor" of semi-naked, often load-bearing, almost clone-like and undifferentiated migrant workers. They are shown

FIGURES 11–14. The life cycle of plastic: screenshots from *Plastic China*. Matter is made grossly vibrant at the dump.

FIGURES 15–18. Screenshots from *Plastic China*. At one with waste.

FIGURES 19–21. Li Jikai: *The Waste Pickers*, 2014. A rare painterly depiction of the Chinese wastepicker suggests the genetic costs of living with trash.

supporting a massive infrastructure (in the work of Wang Jin 王晉), raising the water level in a fishpond (in the work of Zhang Huan 張洹), suspended by their fingertips from a high building (in the work of Chen Chenchen 陳陳陳),[44] or squeezed into suffocating rabbit hutches (in the work of Wang Qingsong).[45] A third typology encompasses the wastescapes I discuss here, in which real-life waste pickers are kept out of sight while the artist sifts junk him- or herself.

Inevitably, perhaps, critics have read these various bodyworks in terms of their interventionist potential. But they can equally be understood as works that show the corporalization of art in China, a remarkable move given the long-standing prudishness over the nude image in Chinese painting. Experiences of precarity—migration, the factory regime, lives suspended in limbo among the so-called low-end population (*diduan renkou* 低端人口)—have turned the endangered body into the subject and medium for art in ways that have little precedent in the Chinese pictorial tradition. This deployment of flesh, bone, blood, and sweat marks how precarity has arguably changed the praxis of contemporary art a good deal more than these works have succeeded in heightening awareness of precarious conditions, let alone actually improving them. Social jeopardy has produced a genre of art in which bodies are squeezed, racked, burdened, and suspended, and whose forms—performance art, participatory art—also incline increasingly toward impermanence. Precarity has made Chinese art more bodily in its substance and more ephemeral in its praxis. It is becoming a method for cultural making itself.

If endangerment is a keynote of precarious experience, then so, as suggested earlier, is waste. Indeed the two may exist dialectically in visual culture. As the human body is stress-tested to the point of physical harm in art, refuse rises to prominence as a parallel aesthetic mode. Again this shift marks a formational change in the substance and practice of art. Just as the naked, imperiled body that toils is barely a feature of the Chinese pictorial tradition,[46] so too does waste register a radical departure from the Chinese nonfigurative tradition, which finds its roots and blossom in landscape painting. The rise of waste as a dominant aesthetic signature reverses many of the conventions of the landscape tradition, which typically took nature as a place of solace rendered via the medium of paint. In wasteworks the external world is more commonly represented in sculpture, composite photography, and installation: modes of art overtly concerned with relations of materiality. And in these highly materialized works, the natural world as a site of calm reflection has been usurped by landscapes of toxicity. Thus these two movements in Chinese visual culture—the strained human subject, the rampant waste object—can be read together as tandem impacts on art by the precarious condition. This resonates with Andrea Muehlebach's point when she notes anthropology's changing relation to precarity: "What we have seen building in the last few years is a radically transforming discipline—or, rather, a discipline being moved into transformation by the very forces it seeks to describe."[47] Precarity, she suggests, "has inserted itself into the very heart of anthropology itself."[48] While art has attempted to take on the condition of the present, often with the intention of "making things right," precarity has more forcefully worked its way into art, bringing forth new methods of making art and being an artist.

Getting Wasted

But garbage is also, of course, political, and the rise of the wastescape needs to be parsed for its ideological meanings too. To an extent, the material turn that Chinese visual culture has taken in recent years can be read as a symptom of the quest for solid bearings that precarious people undertake as life is suspended in a state of deferral and uncertainty. Objects, especially prosaic and comforting ones, can be stitched into an affective safety net that offers a handhold of sorts for those tumbling through the time of the present: in small things shall we trust and have our being. As mentioned above, this process can be seen in Jia Zhangke's cinema, as items of sustenance take on talismanic status, operating as the last stabilizing hope for those excluded from the social safety zone. Wasteworks ramp up this process, but they also push it in new directions. Specifically, their effaced human presence suggests that the enthronement of the defunct object is the corollary of a creeping kind of dehumanization. In this sense, the recent interplay in Chinese visual culture—between the imperiled body and the impermanent artwork, on the one hand, and the exuberance of waste in strongly materialist projects on the other—may also gesture toward a shifting of ontological ground under conditions of precarity. Which is to say, the spaces of art may be responding, intuitively, rhetorically, and perhaps predictively, to a sense of threat. This jeopardy is that the central experiences of precarity in contemporary China—migrancy, the factory regime, subsumption into the "low-end" of the population—are causing definitions of personhood, and who or what can possess it, to fray.

The stress-tested human body and the new resplendence of trash may, therefore, have a consecutive relationship. First comes the objectification of the human body by trials and tests (how much load can it bear, how long can it be suspended midair, how tightly can it be squeezed before its physical integrity collapses), and then as a natural segue to this comes the subjectification of waste, its rise into something close to personhood within the spaces of art. At first sight, the strained human body might appear to be the most eloquent site on which to inscribe this political message. Certainly it is true that China's bodyworks coin a bold visual idiom for the physical toll taken by precarity. But waste may be an even more appropriate method through which to explore the notion of ontological sureties in freefall under the regime of uncertainty. Waste is emerging as a signature in Chinese visual culture because it is a space in which subject/object, human/nonhuman relations exist in a state of suppleness. It is well understood that the dump is a crucible for this kind of symbolic change, which is why so many theorists of new materiality have turned to waste as a core case study. The ontological turnover of recycling, the dump's dematerialization and then rematerialization of the object, the shapelessness of waste, its excessive volume, the way this size and scale can give refuse the power of a live threat, the impact that garbage has on the personhood of the human subject who toils with it: these all make trash crucial to the so-called thingly turn.

Subject/Object, Object/Subject

More than this, in fact, the dump belongs to what Nicholas Bourriaud calls the "realm of the *exformal*: the site where border negotiations unfold between what is rejected and what is admitted," between what is human and what is not. He continues: "*Exform* designates a point of contact, a 'socket' or 'plug,' in the process of exclusion and inclusion—a sign that switches between center and periphery, floating between dissidence and power. Gestures of expulsion and the waste it entails, the point where the exform emerges, constitute an authentically organic link between the aesthetic and the political."[49] In many ways this statement can be read alongside Michel Serres's well-known concept of the quasi-object and the quasi-subject. In its original formulation, Serres sets out this idea via a sporting analogy. He writes:

> The ball isn't there for the body; the exact contrary is true: the body is the object of the ball; the subject moves around this sun. Skill with the ball is recognized in the player who follows the ball and serves it instead of making it follow him and using it. It is the subject of the body, subject of bodies, and like a subject of subjects. Playing is nothing else but making oneself the attribute of the ball as a substance. The laws are written for it, defined relative to it, and we bend to these laws. Skill with the ball supposes a Ptolemaic revolution of which few theoreticians are capable, since they are accustomed to being subjects in a Copernican world where objects are slaves.[50]

Here the scene of a football game becomes a time-space in which the hierarchical rules between players and ball collapse into flattened, fluid relations. Agency shifts and the humans bend so obediently to the physics of the object that Serres calls it a "Ptolemaic revolution." Rather than strict subjects and objects, the actants in the game share a state of intersubjectivity, but one in which the ball arguably calls more of the shots.

Plastic China throws further light on this idea of quasi-subjects and quasi-objects. The camera repeatedly closes in on plastic waste in the process of metamorphosis: rendered down in vats, oozed out of pipes, squeezed into filaments, and shredded into pellets. This is the story of the life cycle of garbage, its matter made vibrant as it moves through solid and liquid states, in ways that feel uncannily like a wildlife documentary (figs. 11–14). This life cycle is mirrored by that of the waste pickers, who are shown in positions of naturalized subservience to trash as they work, forage, eat, rest, play, and, most extraordinarily, give birth amid the waste. In figure 15 they work waist-high amid Sisyphean piles of plastic; in figure 16 they catch a fish for supper from a polluted river; in figure 17 they share a meal at a small outdoor table encircled by sacks brimming over with waste; and in figure 18 the children try to scale the heaps of refuse as part of a game. Yi Jie's mother even gives birth to her sixth child on the premises of the recycling workshop, her cries of labor echoing among the mounds of plastic. This charting of life rhythms, and the way that they proceed at the mercy of garbage, suggests the extent to which the dump, like the football field, is a space of quasi-object, quasi-subject relations in which waste is increasingly calling the shots. Indeed, it is in this sense that Bourriaud's "realm of the *exformal*" becomes telling. As a "site where border negotiations unfold between what is rejected and what is admitted," the dump, and working at the dump, applies pressure to personhood and objecthood. This is a pressure that art can elucidate, and thereby function as "an authentically organic link between the aesthetic and the political."

In her study of *catadores*, or waste pickers, in Rio de Janeiro, Kathleen Millar argues that working with waste generates new forms of being. As she puts it: "Just as the transition to wage labor in industrial capitalism entailed the creation of new worker-subjectivities, the transition to precarious labor in contemporary capitalism is also a process involving the transformation of desires, values, and arts of living. In other words, like wage labor, work on the garbage dump is a site of subject-making, which catadores experience and express as transformative of their inner dispositions."[51] In a sense Millar's point here is precisely that the waste picker is an archetype for our age, whose "desires, values, and arts of living" require exploration in art as much as in anthropology. It might seem logical to expect, therefore, that artwork about the dump would naturally seek to represent it as a "site of subject-making." But Wang Jiuliang's *Plastic China* is unusual—exceptional, even—in its sustained effort to realize the subjectivity of the waste picker in Chinese visual culture. In particular the film's frank yet delicate treatment of quasi-object, quasi-subject relations at the plastics recycling workshop—its self-consciously *ontological* exploration of what it means to live and work with waste—sets it apart from the many other artworks and documentaries whose makers have felt the gravitational pull of garbage.

A further exception may be the artist Li Jikai 李繼開 (1975–), to my knowledge the only contemporary painter to represent waste pickers in his work, who also alludes to deep ontological shift in his *Shihuangzhe* 拾荒者 (The Waste Pickers, 2014). This series of acrylics on canvas represents the dump as a dwelling place where life runs through its cycles. The figures are shown clothed, naked, reading, sleeping, resting, working, thinking, praying, cooking, having a haircut, and, once again, giving birth. Life goes on; but it also shifts at the genome level. Several of the figures have malformed or mutated limbs and disproportionate sizing (some juxtaposed figures are huge, while others are tiny); their faces are blank and puppet-like; and some bodies even show stitch marks to reinforce their identity as quasi-subjects or marionettes (figs. 19–21). Wang goes further than Li, though, in his approach to subjectivity. The methodological shift that *Plastic China* makes, however utopian it may seem, from the artist as ragpicker to the ragpicker as artist marks a singular transition in the Chinese representation of precarious lives.

Hypervisible, Invisible

So far, I have discussed wasteworks first in terms of what they tell us about the impact of precarity on the art form and second as a kind of bellwether about the state of personhood within the regime which Lorey calls "entrenched vulnerability." But these are also works about social relations. They are spaces in which precarity as a structure of feeling—and as a sometimes *ugly* structure of feeling—is made tangible. As such they emerge as a salient method for grasping the contours of the present. Commentators on the bodyworks mentioned earlier have certainly noted that they may veer into indelicate terrain. Thus the close kinship that some artists claim with China's urban poor—as Zhu Fadong put it in 2007, "I am one of them"[52]—has been seen as facile or disingenuous, since many such artists come from affluent homes, have received tertiary education, and pass only briefly through the vale of social endangerment.[53] Similarly, critics have charged that Chinese artists who deploy the strained and stressed bodies of the precariat in delegated performance art are practicing forms of aesthetic exploitation, deliberate or otherwise[54]—not least since they seldom pay workers wages for services that have on occasion catapulted the artist herself or himself into global fame.[55] These are not new arguments, nor is the worry over how best to represent those with little socioeconomic capital a fresh sort of angst. At root it is the hyper-visibility of the poor body in such works that threatens to compromise the ethics of their makers. If precarity is "the condition of our time," not just the plight of those who drop out from the system but that system's actual mechanism—the very rails on which it runs—then the voyeurism that seems an inalienable premise and effect of these bodyworks is both exploitative and out of sync with the present. A political art of precarity that operates via othering, which shows mainly that some people are more precarious than others, or that precarity is someone else's problem, can induce at best a brief and passing pity. It cannot act politically. As Rancière argues of horror as a spectacle: "If horror is banalized, it is not because we see too many images of it. We do not see too many suffering bodies . . . [but] we do see too many nameless bodies, too many bodies incapable of returning the gaze we direct at them, too many bodies that are an object of speech without themselves having a chance to speak."[56]

A parallel problem of (in)visibility is also at work in representations of waste. The human figure that is visualized to voyeuristic excess in the genre of bodyworks that emerged in China in the late 1990s is effaced in many of the works I have referenced in this article. The result is that waste—the effluvium of precarity, in both physical and metaphysical ways—is also partially demobilized as a subject for political art. This is not to say that works such as Xu Bing's *Phoenix* lack political meaning. On the contrary, some aspire to and may well attain the heights of the toxic sublime, in which "trash has become a material for enacting the exultations"[57] once associated with nature and thus offers a narration on the state of late capitalism. But as Yaeger notes, "Our society creates and then disavows rubbish in excess. Detritus is objects—both natural and artificial—that have reached the end of their life of value. Given this opposition, why should the dominant aesthetic response to trash suggest that we need to revalue it, to soak up its numina, its radioactive glow?"[58] The effacement of the human that occurs in work that is hostage to these numina undertakes a transposing move that is ideologically similar to the displacement of precarity onto the urban poor that we see in China's bodyworks. Waste is othered. It is disassociated, via art, from the humans who are fundamentally indissociable from it. These wasteworks, like the bodyworks I discussed earlier, profess to be the arts of the precarious, as evinced by the statements that artists themselves make about them. Yet in many ways their aesthetic strategies are digressive, arguably even hostile.

In Art Shall We Aspire

It is in this broader, global context that a work like Wang Jiuliang's *Plastic China* acquires political value. The documentary commits itself to delineating the subjectivity of Yi Jie, as a ragpicker-cum-artist, in ways that press for her personhood amid the ontological quagmire of the dump. In this sense, *Plastic China* stands in radical contrast to a work such as Zhang Dali's 張大力 (1963–) *Zhongzu* 種族 (Chinese Offspring, 2003), in which the artist made resin casts of the bodies of migrant workers and then strung these life-size casts, each tattooed with an issue number, upside down from warehouse ceilings for the purposes of exhibition. The point and power of the work is, of course, its visual rendering of China's migrant labor force as indecent puppets, as closely identical to one another as clones. Like the resin casts, they exist in strung-up, subject-less suspension. As Wu Hung notes, "this approach entails risks for the artist—not only does the temporary employer-employee relationship created between himself and his migrant laborer models reproduce the social power relations and economic operations he aims to criticize, but the act of producing a model of the subject in plaster also evokes the utility and brutality of these power relations and economic structures."[59] Wu reads Zhang's studied response to this risk positively, arguing that the artist's decision to photograph and publicize his aesthetic process both lays bare these "operations of power" and also reframes "a potential issue of artistic morality into the self-marginalization of avant-garde art."[60] This, though, is an argument made from the perspective of Zhang as subject, which revolves around an artist-based dilemma: namely, is his aesthetic personhood an exploitative one? Can it be redeemed if Zhang is upfront about it? Meanwhile the migrants are voyeurized twice: first during the artistic process of producing the casts when they are suffocatingly swathed in plaster and resin, and second during the exhibitionary process, as their naked, number-stamped casts are dangled from the rafters. Their subjectivity exists in entirely objectified form. As such, they take their place alongside a significant cluster of similar works (such as Liang Shuo 梁碩's *Shishang nongmin ba xiongdi* 時尚農民八兄弟 [Trendy Peasants—Eight Brothers, 2002] and his *Chengshi nongmin* 城市農民 [Urban Peasants, 2007]) that deindividuate or massify migrant workers, casting them—often as statues or molds—in postures that are passive, inert, and hapless.

As Lisa Richaud and Ash Amin note, a core focus for researchers who study precarious lives should be to "reconsider the affective and psychological dimensions of urban stress and uncertainty . . . by exploring the active management of subjectivity by individuals."[61] Against the understandably dominant narrative of Foxconn suicides, PTSD in the aftermath of factory fires, and "travelling psychosis" among those who have to cross a vast continent to see their families for the briefest of annual visits, the role of ritualized resilience and "situated endurance"[62]—how to bear the quotidian across an accumulation of perilous days—is a story that also needs telling, and in art, again, as much as in anthropology. For Richaud and Amin, it is specifically via what might be called the arts of the everyday ("the effervescence of a card game, the laughter exchanged during chitchat, the rituals of living normally") that the "moments of relief" on which an actively managed subjectivity depends can be grasped.[63] These routines are the mechanism through which precarious people go about "rejecting abjection by staying active, purposeful, sane."[64] But *Plastic China* extends this notion of the arts of the everyday into something much more explicitly aesthetic. It is via the making of art—the cut-out shoes, the improvised home computer, the chocolate-wrapper wallpaper—that eleven-year-old Yi Jie not simply manages her subjectivity but arrogates to herself a personhood on a par with that of the documentarist who films her. As such, the film presents what Arjun Appadurai calls the "capacity to aspire"[65] as a specifically aesthetic quantity that enables Yi Jie to assert her personhood within a domain that consistently threatens to reduce her to a quasi-subject.

The artists discussed in this article, I should emphasize, see themselves as political. Their express aim is to undo the us-versus-them distinctions that are so rife in mainstream discourses on the urban poor in China, which typically blame migrant workers for "rising crime rates, moral depravity, public health and hygiene concerns, and many other contemporary social ills."[66] We know this not just from the visual codes via which the works of these artists communicate but also from their own paratextual musings and media interviews.[67] And although I have described their waste-picking practices as borderline exploitative or appropriative, likening them to the faux-milkmaids of Versailles, most of these artists would probably either refute the suggestion that their art crosses the line, or at the very least strategize that step as does Zhang Dali. In a sense, though, this dissensus merely heightens the anomaly of an art practice that says it wants to intervene on behalf of precarious people and yet ends up so visibly effacing their agency. Why does this anomaly happen? Appadurai notes that we need "to ask how the poor may be helped to produce those forms of cultural consensus that may best advance their own collective long-term interests in matters of wealth, equality, and dignity."[68] This strategy does not obviate the role of the artist. But it does very much foreground the importance of training and toning what Appadurai calls the "voice" of the poor as a "cultural capacity." This capacity functions by "those levers of metaphor, rhetoric, organization, and public performance that will work best in their cultural worlds,"[69] and it is a process in which artists, particularly those who have lived among extremely precarious people, can become instrumentally enabling. Yet voice—which represents a transformative shift from looking at precarious people to hearing them—is what is absent from so many of China's bodyworks and wasteworks alike. This aphasia asks for an explanation because, on the surface, it appears counterintuitive within such consciously *engagé* practices of art-making.

Cruel Gazing

The condition of precarity, as many theorists have made clear, is transversal. It cuts across class and race, gender and nation. It has been a driving mission of the European precarity movement to broker alliances between these diverse cohorts: between creatives and factory workers, between artists and migrants, and so on. Theorists of precarity have been keen to show that even as endemic uncertainty smothers life chances, it can "hold the potential to contribute to a political composition of the common"[70] by fostering new ways and means of being political together. The devil, though, lies in the detail. As Gill and Pratt put it,

> The appeal of the notion of precarity is precisely in this potentiality, yet it also produces tensions common to all forms of transversal politics: how to deal with differences, how to find "common cause." how to build solidarity while also respecting the singularity and specificity of the very different experiences of (say) janitors, creatives and office temps. . . . Not least is the question of whether there are *grounds* for such solidarity in a global frame characterized by enormous disparities in wealth and power.[71]

In short, precarity's cross-cutting does not necessarily breed effortless solidarities: this is Angela Mitropoulos's point when she asks if it really favors "the maquiladora worker to ally herself with the fashion designer."[72] Her question meshes with the practices discussed here, in which it is sometimes hard to see what material or even abstract benefits accrue to the waste picker whose anonymized toil makes it into a photographic series by a big-name artist—even if that artist started out as a migrant, has lived in a migrant village and shared in its patterns of sociality, and has long experience of unsteady work with low or no pay.

Yet it seems insufficient simply to critique the relationship between artists and waste pickers, to pull up the former for exploitatively annexing the identity and labor of the latter. Rather, what these artworks require is a closer look at how the tensions of transversal politics actually play out within aesthetic space, at how waste picking reveals itself as a method for navigating the strains of the present. Or why it is, more precisely, that so many practitioners of the arts of precarity create a representational language that aims for solidarity but ends up visually reproducing the "enormous disparities in wealth and power" referred to above. Earlier I suggested that these artistic practices tend toward the digressive. Either arrogating the position of the precarious subject to themselves or presenting precarity as someone else's problem, they effectively decline to take part in the important work of mentoring what Appadurai calls voice among the poor. As mentioned above, a more or less Rancièrian view has prevailed among commentators who have noted this tendency in China's arts of precarity. Lily Chumley summarizes the prevailing take when she argues that such works "appear to viewers as images of others, recruiting viewers to roles of sympathetic objectification rather than empathetic identification."[73] According to this best-case interpretation, artists and their spectators are sometimes misguided but fundamentally benign. They mean well even when they misfire.

But what about a less favorable or even worst-case scenario? What about the possibility that art of this kind manages the threat that precarity now poses to so many constituents of society—effectively boxing it into the rabbit hutches of the urban poor, as in the photography of Wang Qingsong? Even as this art appears to be politically radical, in other words, its strategies of othering may also be socially reassuring. More than this, in fact, when parsed on a structural plane, the visual language of this art arguably displays an investment in keeping the poor silent. In this sense, such practices suggest that the transversal nature of precarity, rather than fostering a natural solidarity, may instead breed fear over fluid social status and the ever-present possibility of a sudden plummet downward. Activists want to believe that precarity is furnishing the grounds for new experiences of the common, and many contemporary people want to believe these arguments. But the closeness of the artist and the precarious worker may also be a space in which anxious processes of social differentiation are staged at the very same moment that allegiance is staked. Precisely because precarity is so big—inducing what Lauren Berlant calls "a notion of systemic crisis or 'crisis ordinariness'"[74] that shrouds so many in its heavy uncertainties—it may well be a condition that is less, not more, likely to incite a new politics of the commons. Moving on from this, perhaps we also need to consider the possibility that artworks that depict precarious people in postures of punishment, degradation, and strain may also call a cruel or disdainful gaze into being, and the related possibility that artworks in which the role of precarian is assumed by the artist may possess a rivalrous or controlling drive alongside the stated urge for solidarity. This, I should note, is not to accuse particular artists, nor their audiences, so much as to drill down into the visual language of these works and parse them for their syntactical meaning.

What used to be called *jieji* 階級—or "class"—in Chinese has become something of an outlawed term in recent years. Society, as Hu Jintao famously declared, is harmonious now (*hexie shehui* 和諧社會), and so a different term—*jieceng* 階層, or stratum—has been coined to indicate differentials in income, equality, and opportunity. These gaps are glossed as gulfs that social mobility can supposedly bridge rather than as the expressions of a caste system that class struggle should violently dismantle. Meanwhile, China's Gini coefficient has shot through the roof, a middle class with clear but anxious wants has emerged, pressure on space and resources in China's cities has intensified, and the media is saturated with stories about vicious verbal and even physical clashes between migrants and permanent urban residents. This tension, moreover, often mingles with an awkward sense of resentment: many urban dwellers rely heavily on the labor of migrant workers even as some evidently begrudge these subalterns' claims on the city. Labor activists such as Shen Mengyu 沈夢雨 (1992–), who graduated from the elite Sun Yat-sen University and went straight to Shenzhen to work at a car parts factory, where she began mobilizing her fellow workers,[75] are the poster people for the power of solidarity between different constituencies within a precarious social world. But the practices of ill-use, imperilment, appropriation, rivalry, and effacement that recur across so many artworks about China's most vulnerable people suggest that art is a zone in which fraught, inadmissible, and ugly feelings also play themselves out. Even if not outright cruel or disdainful, at the very least these bodyworks and wasteworks enable a conflicted gaze. This is a look that can profess, and even feel, a politically correct sympathy for class others but that may also derive an illicit sense of reassurance, even gratification, as these same others are kept visibly in their subaltern place—or are simply wiped from the picture altogether. In this sense, the missing waste picker becomes a disappeared person whose lost voice speaks volumes, and Yi

Jie's on-screen passage to artistic personhood becomes a methodologically significant act.

MARGARET HILLENBRAND is associate professor in modern Chinese literature and culture at the University of Oxford. Her book *Negative Exposures: Knowing What Not to Know in Contemporary China* will be published in 2020.

////////////////////////////////

Acknowledgements
I am very grateful to Carlos Rojas and Xavier Ortells-Nicolau for their help in the preparation of this article.

Notes

1 For a resonantly similar ethnographic narrative of the role played by fashion in the emotional life of waste pickers, see Wu and Zhang, *Feipin shenghuo*, 133–34.
2 Baudelaire, *Flowers of Evil*, 136–37.
3 Quoted in Benjamin, *Selected Writings*, 48.
4 Ibid.
5 Ibid.
6 Strasser, *Waste and Want*, 21.
7 Taussig, *My Cocaine Museum*, 182.
8 Yaeger, "Editor's Column," 325.
9 An exception is Wu and Zhang's illuminating *Feipin shenghuo*.
10 Verbeek, *What Things Do*, 3
11 Tsing, *Mushroom at the End of the World*, 20.
12 Bourriaud, "Precarious Constructions," 32.
13 Bauman, *Liquid Life*, 3.
14 Neilson and Rossiter, "Precarity as a Political Concept," 54.
15 Ibid.
16 Ibid.
17 Munck, "Precariat," 747.
18 Ibid., 752.
19 Davis, *Planet of Slums*, 178.
20 Fraser, *Justice Interruptus*.
21 This is not to suggest that postsocialism should only be understood in its harsher neoliberal dimensions. Rather than marking a sharp caesura with the socialist period, *postsocialism* as a term also signifies the extent to which the legacies of the Maoist era—state interventionism chief among them—have persisted into the reform and post-reform eras.
22 Berlant, *Cruel Optimism*.
23 Standing, *Precariat*.
24 Wang H., *China's Twentieth Century*, 215.
25 Another explanation may be that bitter memories of class struggle between intellectuals and the anointed "workers, peasants, and soldiers" (*gong-nong-bing* 工農兵) during the Maoist period may be inhibiting this kind of vagabondage. I am grateful to Chen Ziru for helpful discussions on this point.

26 Smith and Ngai, "Class and Precarity in China," 47.
27 Gill and Pratt, "In the Social Factory?," 3.
28 Lorey, "Governmental Precarization."
29 Quoted in Vogel, "Phoenixes Rise in China and Float in New York."
30 Xu B., *Phoenix.*
31 Quoted in Rose, *Claes Oldenburg*, 191.
32 Schilthuizen, *Darwin Comes to Town*, 203–16.
33 Ibid., 138–39.
34 See, for example, Peeples, "Toxic Sublime."
35 Boo, *Behind the Beautiful Forevers*, 35.
36 Yaeger, "Editor's Column," 331.
37 Boscagli, *Stuff Theory*, 230.
38 Stam, "Hybridity and the Aesthetics of Garbage."
39 Xing D., "*disCONNEXION*."
40 Brown, "Thing Theory," 4.
41 The work of Wang Zhiyuan, in particular his garbage installation *Longjuanfeng* 龍捲風 (Thrown to the Wind, 2010)—an eleven-meter-tall tornado of entirely depersonalized trash—provides still further examples of the artist as waste picker.
42 Baudrillard, *Fatal Strategies*, 141.
43 Wang H., *China's Twentieth Century*, 193–95.
44 For a detailed discussion of this work by Chen, see Yomi Braester's essay in this special issue.
45 For more on the first two categories, see Eschenburg, "Fixing Identities."
46 During the socialist period, of course, the worker reigned dominant in poster art and official visual culture as a muscular and luminous figure.
47 Muehlebach, "On Precariousness and the Ethical Imagination," 298.
48 Ibid.
49 Bourriaud, *Exform*, x.
50 Serres, *Parasite*, 223–24.
51 Millar, "Precarious Present," 45.
52 Quoted in Parke, "Migrant Workers," 230. Elsewhere Zhu reinforces his claim to subaltern status when he states that his aim was to use "my conditions of existence as the subject of my art" in works such as *This Person Is for Sale* (quoted in Wu, *Contemporary Chinese Art*, 214). Zhang Dali 張大力 makes a similar point in interview. In response to the suggestion that he has now "gradually become estranged from lower-class life, with his Italian nationality, professional artist status, connections with art museums and galleries, and improved material conditions," he states that "because of my past experience, I have not changed in the least, and spiritually still retain memories of life at the bottom" 當時的張大力已經漸漸脫離了底層的生活。意大利國籍，職業藝術家，作品也與美術館和畫廊發生關係，物質生活正在改善。「但是因為我的經歷，我無論怎麼改變，精神上還是有底層的記憶. Quoted in Yang, "Yishujia Zhang Dali."
53 See, for example, Eschenburg, "Fixing Identities," 31. More common, however, are treatments of such work that either ignore the problematic elements of this claim of kinship (Bian, "Zhu Fadong," 74–77) or see nothing troubling in the equivalence of identities. This is Parke's point when she argues that Zhu's "adoption of the identity of a migrant is confirmed by his biography and it is not just an identity he was performing for this piece" (Parke, "Migrant Workers," 231). The difficulty here is the assumption that China's nearly 300 million–strong migrant population is homogeneous in terms of class origin

and class destiny, and that an artist migrant with an international reputation is experientially coterminous with an economic migrant with no escape route from precarious labor.

54 See Parke, "Migrant Workers," 233–34; and Eschenburg, "Fixing Identities," 36.

55 Zhang Huan is the standout example here. As he puts it, "I received the most benefit from the fish pond piece (*To Raise the Water Level in a Fishpond*). This piece changed my situation, my life. Everybody likes this piece" (Borysevicz, "Before and After," 61).

56 Rancière, *Emancipated Spectator*, 96.

57 Yaeger, "Editor's Column," 330.

58 Ibid., 335.

59 Wu, "Instantaneous Copying and Monumentality," 13–14.

60 Ibid., 14.

61 Richaud and Amin, "Life amidst Rubble," 1.

62 Ibid., 2–3.

63 Ibid., 2.

64 Ibid., 1.

65 Appadurai, "Capacity to Aspire."

66 Dooling, "Representing *Dagongmei*," 137.

67 See, for example, Zhang, "Zai huati yu zhengyi zhong xunzhao 'Zhongzu' mima"; and Wang Qingsong's commentary on his work, Wang Q., "Dream of Migrants." In this artist's statement, he writes, "I am empathetic to this 'migrant' population. I think they hold on dearly to their dreams and like to be recognized for their contribution to the constructions of China's cities as they attempt to fulfill their dreams of improving their lives. . . . In 1993, I moved to Beijing, also from a faraway place, from Jinzhou, in Hubei Province. Jinzhou is a very small city. I also had my big dreams despite being surprised by the huge scale of the city of Beijing, a capital city with a population 100 times larger than the population of my hometown. . . . I survived because of the realization that my situation was not special and there were tens of thousands of people just like me pouring into China's cities hoping and trying to realize their dreams."

68 Appadurai, "Capacity to Aspire," 64.

69 Ibid., 67.

70 Neilson and Rossiter, "Precarity as a Political Concept," 55

71 Gill and Pratt, "In the Social Factory?," 12.

72 Mitropoulos, "Precari-us."

73 Chumley, *Creativity Class*, 101.

74 Berlant, *Cruel Optimism*, 10.

75 Xu, "Guangzhou nü shuoshi chengwei gongren weiquan daibiao hou zao kaichu."

References

Appadurai, Arjun. "The Capacity to Aspire: Culture and the Terms of Recognition." In *Culture and Public Action*, edited by Vijayendra Rao and Michael Walton, 59–84. Palo Alto, CA: Stanford University Press, 2004.

Baudelaire, Charles. *The Flowers of Evil*, edited by Marthiel and Jackson Mathews. New York: New Directions, 1989.

Baudrillard, Jean. *Fatal Strategies*, translated by Philip Beitchman. Cambridge, MA: MIT Press, 2008.

Bauman, Zygmunt. *Liquid Life*. Cambridge: Polity, 2005.

Benjamin, Walter. *Selected Writings*, vol. 4, *1938–1940*. Cambridge, MA: Harvard University Press, 2003.

Berlant, Lauren. *Cruel Optimism*. Durham, NC: Duke University Press, 2011.

Bian Jiaojiao 卞皎皎. "Zhu Fadong: Jixu 'chushou'" 朱發東：繼續「出售」[Zhu Fadong: Still for Sale]. *Yishujie* 藝術界 [Leap], no. 1 (2011): 74–77.

Boo, Katherine. *Behind the Beautiful Forevers: Life, Death and Hope in a Mumbai Slum*. London: Portobello Books, 2012.

Bourriaud, Nicolas. *The Exform*, translated by Erik Butler. London: Verso, 2016.

Bourriaud, Nicolas. "Precarious Constructions: Answer to Jacques Rancière on Art and Politics." *Open*, no. 17 (2009): 20–36.

Borysevicz, Mathieu. "Before and After: An Interview with Zhang Huan." *Art Asia Pacific*, no. 30 (2001): 56–61.

Boscagli, Maurizia. *Stuff Theory: Everyday Objects, Radical Materialism*. New York and London: Bloomsbury Academic, 2014.

Brown, Bill. "Thing Theory." *Critical Inquiry* 28, no. 1 (2001): 1–22.

Chumley, Lily. *Creativity Class: Art School and Culture Work in Post-socialist China*. Princeton, NJ: Princeton University Press, 2016.

Davis, Mike. *Planet of Slums*. London: Verso, 2006.

Dooling, Amy. "Representing *Dagongmei* (Female Migrant Workers) in Contemporary China." *Frontiers of Literary Studies in China* 11, no. 1 (2017): 133–56.

Eschenburg, Madeline. "Fixing Identities: The Use of Migrant Workers in Chinese Performance Art." *Yishu: Journal of Contemporary Chinese Art* 16, no. 3 (2017): 26–36.

Fraser, Nancy. *Justice Interruptus: Critical Reflections on the "Postsocialist" Condition*. New York: Routledge, 1997.

Gill, Rosalind, and Andy Pratt. "In the Social Factory? Immaterial Labour, Precariousness and Cultural Work." *Theory, Culture and Society* 25, no. 7–8 (2008): 1–30.

Lorey, Isabell. "Governmental Precarization," translated by Aileen Derieg. *Eipcp*, January, 2011. eipcp.net/transversal/0811/lorey/en/print.html.

Millar, Kathleen. "The Precarious Present: Wageless Labor and Disrupted Life in Rio de Janeiro, Brazil." *Cultural Anthropology* 29, no. 1 (2014): 32–53.

Mitropoulous, Angela. "Precari-us." *Mute: Culture and Politics after the Net* 1, no. 29 (2005). www.metamute.org/editorial/articles/precari-us.

Muehlebach, Andrea. "On Precariousness and the Ethical Imagination: The Year 2012 in Sociocultural Anthropology." *American Anthropologist* 115, no. 2 (2013): 297–311.

Munck, Ronaldo. "The Precariat: A View from the South." *Third World Quarterly* 34, no. 5 (2013): 747–62.

Neilson, Brett, and Ned Rossiter. "Precarity as a Political Concept, or, Fordism as Exception." *Theory, Culture & Society* 25, nos. 7–8 (2008): 51–72.

Parke, Elisabeth. "Migrant Workers and the Imaging of Human Infrastructure in Chinese Contemporary Art." *China Information* 29, no. 2 (2015): 226–52.

Peeples, Jennifer. "Toxic Sublime: Imaging Contaminated Landscapes." *Environmental Communication: A Journal of Nature and Culture* 5, no. 4 (2011): 373–92.

Rancière, Jacques. *The Emancipated Spectator*. London: Verso, 2011.

Richaud, Lisa, and Ash Amin. "Life amidst Rubble: Migrant Mental Health and the Management of Subjectivity in Urban China." Unpublished manuscript, July 25, 2019. www.researchgate.net/profile/Lisa_Richaud/publication/325381537_Richaud_Amin_forthcoming_Public_Culture_Life_amidst_Rubble_Migrant_Mental_Health_and _the_Management_of_Subjectivity_in_Urban_China/links/5b091fdb4585157f87171e94/Richaud-Amin-forthcoming-Public-Culture-Life-amidst-Rubble-Migrant-Mental-Health-and-the-Management-of-Subjectivity-in-Urban-China.pdf.

Rose, Barbara. *Claes Oldenburg*. New York: Museum of Modern Art, 1970.

Schilthuizen, Menno. *Darwin Comes to Town*. New York: Picador, 2018.

Serres, Michel. *The Parasite*, translated by Lawrence R. Schehr. Baltimore: Johns Hopkins University Press, 1982.

Smith, Chris, and Pun Ngai. "Class and Precarity in China: A Contested Relationship." In *Gilded Age: Made in Yearbook 2017*, edited by Ivan Franceschini and Nicholas Loubere, 44–47. Canberra: Australian National University Press, 2017.

Stam, Robert. "Hybridity and the Aesthetics of Garbage: The Case of Brazilian Cinema." *Cultura Visual en América Latina* 9, no. 1 (1998). eial.tau.ac.il/index.php/eial.

Standing, Guy. *The Precariat: The New Dangerous Class*. London: Bloomsbury, 2011.

Strasser, Susan. *Waste and Want: A Social History of Trash*. New York: Holt Paperbacks, 2000.

Taussig, Michael. *My Cocaine Museum*. Chicago: University of Chicago Press, 2004.

Tsing, Anna. *The Mushroom at the End of the World: On the Possibility of Life in Capitalist Ruins*. Princeton, NJ: Princeton University Press, 2015.

Verbeek, Peter Paul. *What Things Do: Philosophical Reflections on Technology, Agency, and Design*, translated by R. P. Crease. University Park: Pennsylvania State University Press, 2005.

Vogel, Carol. "Phoenixes Rise in China and Float in New York. Xu Bing Installs His Sculptures at St. John the Divine." *New York Times*, February 14, 2018. www.nytimes.com/2014/02/15/arts/design/xu-bing-installs-his-sculptures-at-st-john-the-divine.html.

Wang Hui. *China's Twentieth Century: Revolution, Retreat, and the Road to Equality*. London: Verso, 2016.

Wang Qingsong 王慶松. "Dream of Migrants." Wang Qingsong Studio, 2005. www.wangqingsong.com/index.php?option=com_content&view=article&id=96&Itemid=17.

Wu, Hung, ed. *Contemporary Chinese Art: Primary Documents*. New York: Museum of Modern Art, 2010.

Wu, Hung. "Instantaneous Copying and Monumentality: The Historic Logic of Permanence and Impermanence." *Yishu: Journal of Contemporary Chinese Art* 16, no. 3 (2017): 6–25.

Wu Kaming 胡嘉明 and Zhang Jieying 張劼穎. *Feipin shenghuo. Lajichang de jingji, shequn yu kongjian* 廢品生活：垃圾場的經濟、社群與空間 [The Life of Waste: Economy, Community and Space at the Dump]. Hong Kong: Hong Kong University Press, 2016.

Xing Danwen 邢丹文. "*disCONNEXION*: work STATEMENT." danwen.com/web/works/dis/statement.html, accessed December 20, 2019.

Xu Bing 徐冰. *Phoenix*. Hong Kong: Thircuir, 2015.

Xu Yiyang 徐亦揚. "Guangzhou nü shuoshi chengwei gongren weiquan daibiao hou zao kaichu" 廣州女碩士成為工人維權代表後遭開除 [A Female MA Student in Guangzhou Is Sacked after Becoming a Representative of Workers' Rights]. *Dajiyuan* 大紀元 [Epoch Times], July 10, 2018. www.epochtimes.com/gb/18/7/9/n10550038.htm.

Yaeger, Patricia. "Editor's Column: The Death of Nature and the Apotheosis of Trash; or, Rubbish Ecology." *PMLA* 123, no. 2 (2008): 321–39.

Yang Shi 楊時. "Yishujia Zhang Dali: Wo wufa tuoli diceng, guanzhu nongmingong qunti" 藝術家張大力：我無法脫離底層，關注農民工群體 [Artist Zhang Dali: I Can't Extricate Myself from the Lower Rungs of Society and I Care about Migrant Workers].

Zhongguo xinwenwang 中國新聞網 [China News], March 19, 2009. www.chinanews.com/cul/news/2009/03-19/1608769.shtml.
Zhang Dali 張大力. "Zai huati yu zhengyi zhong xunzhao 'zhongzu' mima" 在話題與爭議中尋找「種族」密碼 [Seeking the Key to "Race" in Discussion and Dispute]. *Ku yishu* 庫藝術 [Ku Art], March 31, 2017. chuansong.me/n/1728464852519.

YOMI BRAESTER

Panorama as Method

ABSTRACT Diverse artifacts in contemporary Chinese visual culture—from urban screens to architectural models, art exhibits, and viral media—share a panoramic breadth. This article suggests, however, that we should regard panorama not as a preordained form but as a discursive construct that posits an imaginary vantage point. Panorama as method notes the use of scale, recording of the skyline, and mediation of the cityscape. The article asks what material conditions and ideological circumstances allow for the existence of the images at hand and what brings us to identify them as panoramic. The implications reach far beyond specific artifacts: panorama as method challenges accepted paradigms about the relationship between the modern subject and urban space, including the distinction between cartographic vision and street-level immersion. The article focuses on what may be called the *panoramic imaginary* in contemporary Chinese urbanism: a visual emphasis on expansive space by scaling the built environment up and down, thereby recalibrating social relations and relocating civic engagement to virtual spaces.

KEYWORDS aerial photography, architectural models, painted scrolls, urban planning, urban skyline

This essay has its inception in my investigation of large urban screens in twenty-first-century China, their affinity with painted scrolls, and their use as a spectacle promoting the neoliberal vision of urban planners. Soon my research branched into examining diverse artifacts—from public service displays to architectural models, art exhibits, and viral media. Some commonalities were easy to spot: the images in question sustain public spectacles, use grandiloquent forms, and foreground the symbolism in magnitude. Yet these traits may impart a false sense of coherence. I was wondering if I overemphasized formal attributes and thematic similarities at the expense of pointing out the ideological implications.

Method comes in handy for disrupting formal and thematic inquiry. Insofar as it can be separated from theory, method focuses not on rendering a phenomenon intelligible but on the procedure through which to describe and analyze it. In Sinophone studies, the best-known example is Kuan-Hsing Chen's 陳光興 *Asia as Method*, which takes "the idea of Asia as an imaginary anchoring point" to decenter global history.[1] Chen, however, espouses a narrow definition of method. "Asia as method" challenges colonial power only to affirm the power structure by placing it in the hands of those who speak for Asia, as the new bearers of method. Chen focuses on the subjects of discourse and aims at reconstituting

PRISM: THEORY AND MODERN CHINESE LITERATURE • 16:2 • OCTOBER 2019
DOI 10.1215/25783491-7978507 •

their disenfranchised agency. "Asia as method" questions the site of knowledge rather than the mode of knowledge production. As I see it, method writ large does not stop at validating the objects of study—for instance "Asia"—but rather acknowledges the contingency of such designations and asks why categories such as "Asia" serve us well in our current position. Method insists on the practicalities of inquiry rather than on defining the object of knowledge.

In the case of the images and artifacts I am studying, which span many media, method entails thinking beyond their purportedly objective commonality, namely spectacularity and panoramic breadth. Instead I ask how they have become interlinked in my and others' minds. In other words, what discourse aligns our gaze and these images, grouping them together and making them visible to us?

I therefore turn, when considering urban screens, painted scrolls, architectural models, and other artifacts, to *panorama as method*. Method is divorced from form and medium. Many of the images in question are panoramic, in the sense of affording an expansive view. A few fit the technical definitions of panorama, the proto-cinematic device of a moving, 360-degree, room-sized image.[2] None correspond to the panoramic aspect in analog cameras or the panorama software used in digital photography. When described in Chinese, the word *hongguan* 宏觀 or *daguan* 大觀 (expansive view) is used sometimes. The precise term for panorama, *quanjing* 全景, is mentioned only in some cases, which I point out to be exceptions. Panorama as method does not seek to identify the artifacts as panoramic as an aesthetic terminology. Rather, panorama as method notes the use of scale, recording of the skyline, and mediation of the cityscape. I thereby ask what material conditions and ideological circumstances allow for the existence of these images and what brings me to identify them as panoramic. The implications reach far beyond specific artifacts: panorama as method challenges accepted paradigms about the relationship between the modern subject and urban space, including the well-known distinction between cartographic vision and street-level immersion.

Once the methodological uses of panorama have been established, we can turn our attention back to the artifacts at hand and ask how urban experience has been fashioned by the changing relationship between the human gaze and built environment. Chinese cities have attracted planners, tourists, and happenstance gawkers for the use of urban screens, many of overwhelming sizes. Other impressive displays are also ubiquitous: imposing public artwork, huge architectural edifices dominating the cityscape, and entire districts designed to visually astound the visitor. Technical specifications break records, construction budgets are unprecedented, and government policies target the entire skyline. As metropolises have expanded, their visualization has become more sensitive to scale, whether in monumental edifices or miniatures. Together these structures outline what may be called the *panoramic imaginary* in contemporary Chinese urbanism: a visual emphasis on expansive space by scaling the built environment up and down, thereby recalibrating social relations and relocating civic engagement to virtual spaces. Panorama as method displaces the forms and symbolism associated with panoramic views to expose the constructs created by the panoramic imaginary.

Techniques of the Urban Observer: From Scroll to Screen and Back

In the beginning was the scroll. A genealogy of panoramic imaginary in China—including an inquiry into the production and distribution of images and a phenomenology of their reception—must go back to the traditional scroll and, in particular, the long horizontal paintings used to portray progressions through the city. This painting genre has imbued space with temporal narrative and bridged concerns about urban planning and visual representation. Over the centuries and especially in recent decades, horizontal scrolls have redefined the viewer's vantage point, taking into consideration observation spots such as pavilions and city walls as well as deploying virtual vantage points. Horizontal scrolls have established conventions and norms for which architectural boundary markers, such as gates and memorial arches, should be included; how pathways, arteries, and other urban patterns are to be portrayed; and what elements matter in delineating the skyline.

Painterly interest in panoramic depictions of the city is often traced back to Zhang Zeduan's 張擇端 (1085?–1145?) twelfth-century depiction of the capital Bianjing in *Qingming shanghe tu* 清明上河圖 (Along the River at Qingming Festival). The scroll became a paragon of portraying everyday life in the city and elicited many copies and adaptations. Probably the best-known modern recasting of *Along the River* is *Zhihui de changhe* 智慧的長河 (River of Wisdom), the centerpiece of the China Pavilion at the 2010 Shanghai Expo. Inspired by architectural models (and designed by the leading Chinese firm for such models, Crystal Computer Graphics), *River of Wisdom* digitizes the scroll and animates it. It also blows up the original handheld scroll some twenty-two times, projecting it on a surface 120 meters long and 6 meters high, in a dedicated exhibition space. The digital artwork, an allusion to the Expo's motto, "Better City, Better Life," places the twelfth-century painting in the context of contemporary urbanism. *River of Wisdom* repackages the cityscape as a spectacle that requires the visitor's movement through space, shifting both bodily and ocular position. While retaining the sense of a scene unrolling before the viewer, who is separated from the image by a railing and a simulated river, the artwork also provides an immersive environment. To wit, the visitors almost invariably take out their phones for selfies inside the exhibition space, with the large image filling the background.

River of Wisdom stands at the intersection of two contemporary trends: a glut for jumbo-size high-tech screens, such as the scroll-like display at the opening ceremony of the 2008 Beijing Olympics, and the public display of enlarged scrolls depicting urban life. Much has been written on how so-called urban screens have changed the cityscape.[3] Yet little attention has been given to the remediation of scrolls in traditional painting style into panoramic swaths, whether inked or digitized, taking up entire city blocks or wrapping around large galleries.

A prominent example is Liu Hongkuan's 劉洪寬 (1938–) *Tian qu dan que* 天衢丹闕 (Celestial Roads and Red Pavilions, 2001). At 53 by 0.7 meters, it was celebrated as the first Chinese painting over 50 meters long.[4] It depicts Beijing in the 1930s or 1940s, starting just south of the city gates and continuing along the south-north central axis that traverses the capital from Yongdingmen Gate; next to the Altar of Heaven; through the markets around Qianmen South Road; into the corridor now remodeled as Tiananmen Square; to the Forbidden City and Drum and Bell Towers; and out toward the hills to the north of the city. The scroll features everyday street scenes, including over five thousand human figures. In 2010 it was exhibited at the Beijing Planning Exhibition Hall 北京市規劃展覽館 along with the hall's permanent exhibition of miniature models, maps, and other renderings of the city. The painting employs a bird's-eye view, at a steady height and a constant distance from the central axis. Maintaining the same position, facing northwest, the scroll feels as if the viewer engages in a high-angle tracking shot. The scroll imparts a panoramic feel, not only due to the large area covered and the aerial viewpoint but also because of the extreme detail in which every element is rendered. There is no single focal point, visual or thematic; rather people, buildings, and other landmarks all bring the city to life.

Celestial Roads and Red Pavilions builds on the portrayal of cities in court paintings. Long scrolls depicting emperors' expeditions conclude with a representation of the imperial procession making its way back through the capital. In particular, Wang Hui 王翬 (1632–1717) and others' *Kangxi nanxun tu* 康熙南巡圖 (Emperor Kangxi's Southern Expedition, 1691–93), in twelve scrolls of a total length of 203 meters, and Xu Yang's 徐揚 *Qianlong nanxun tu* 乾隆南巡圖 (Emperor Qianlong's Southern Expedition, 1751), in twelve scrolls measuring together 154.17 meters, rely on similar conventions. The painter zooms in on Beijing's central axis and uses a constant isometric perspective, beginning south of the city gates and following the main thoroughfare all the way north to the palace complex. Wu Hung, in discussing Wang Hui's scroll, notes the appropriation of public space for the use of the emperor, who remains hidden from sight. Wu claims, "This representational mode became obsolete in Chinese art when the country entered the modern era."[5] Indeed, in contrast with Wang Hui's painting, Liu Hongkuan's scroll is populated with common people and stresses the accessibility of public space. In a return to the panoramic urban scroll, which had also become mostly obsolete as a genre, *Celestial Roads and Red Pavilions* emerges from the Chinese representational tradition yet ends up creating an immersive experience, more akin to the architectural models I will discuss later.

Through the specific conditions of its exhibition, *Celestial Roads and Red Pavilions* has made the scroll into part of urban experience. In 2008 a replica of the scroll, blown up to about three times its original size, was hung up on top of a wall that closed off the gentrification project at the Qianmen area in Beijing. Placed on the south-to-north Qianmen East Avenue, it paralleled at close range the central axis depicted in the scroll. Imbuing the area with nostalgia for its past and at the same time looking forward to the completion of the district's renovation, the public display of *Celestial Roads and Red Pavilions* created a layered historical narrative for Beijing's new identity as a space of commodified leisure.[6] The panoramic overview was literally projected upon the city and introduced into public space.

Following the branding of cities for domestic and international consumption in the twenty-first century, urban scrolls have become more widespread and more spectacular. To promote the 2022 Beijing Winter Olympics, Xu Ziwen 徐子文 (1961–) painted the 20.22-meter scroll *Jing Ji dongle tu* 京冀冬樂圖 (Joys of Winter in Beijing and Hebei, 2015). *Jiu Jing huangu tu* 舊京環顧圖 (An Overview of Old Beijing, 1991) by Wang Daguan 王大觀 (1925–1996) shows Beijing in the 1930s; its three scrolls measure in total 220 meters. In October 2011, it was enlarged and digitized as *Lao Beijing dongqilai* 老北京動起來 (Old Beijing Animated) (fig. 1), an exhibition on the grounds of the former Olympic village. As Beijing's response to the Shanghai Expo's *River of Wisdom*, this animated scroll boasted being the longest digital screen in the world, at 3 by 228 meters. *Emperor Qianlong's Southern Expedition*, which inspired both *Celestial Roads and Red Pavilions* and *An Overview of Old Beijing*, was exhibited in April 2017 at the National Museum of China, together with digitized, animated renderings of three of its scrolls, including scroll 12, the one depicting the emperor's procession through Beijing.[7] Traditional painting, especially in supersized digital form, has become part of the contemporary panoramic imaginary. Not only do the scrolls provide the formal foundation for depicting the city, but they also suggest that expansive aerial views represent the ideal of the newly gentrified city.

The contemporary city scrolls adhere to traditional aesthetics, yet they also point to radically new cityscapes and mediascapes. The imperial scrolls accentuate the symbolic order of capital city planning, harking to the ideal layout stipulated by *The Book of Rites* 禮記 (ca. first century). Vista points are located where the symmetrical plan and carefully proportioned buildings are best observed, such as the appropriately named Prospect Hill 景山 at the geometrical center of Beijing's Inner City. In the twenty-first century, the low-lying imperial edifices have been challenged by high-rises and brand-name architecture that introduces distinctive shapes. While the painted scrolls linger nostalgically on the old skyline, current construction aims at disrupting it.

Even as the recent scrolls pay tribute to earlier images, panorama as method requires us to look beyond formal similarities to historical precedents. The hori-

FIGURE 1. *Old Beijing Animated.*

zontal scroll is now also imbued with a neoliberal vision of urbanism. The supersized scrolls uphold an aestheticized mirage of the new city that panorama as method is in a position to demystify and challenge.

Scaling New Heights: Rooftopping Selfies

Large horizontal scrolls, as symptoms of neoliberal urbanism, may be placed next to a very different expression of the panoramic imaginary, namely rooftopping selfies. A new genre of selfies appeared in the early years of the twenty-first century, as part of the phenomenon of roofing or rooftopping—that is, reaching the roofs of skyscrapers (complete or under construction), often gaining illegal access and using no safety equipment. The images recording the ascent are dizzying, often featuring the photographer's legs dangling hundreds of feet above ground, sitting on a ledge level with the tops of the highest landmarks, or balancing on a narrow antenna base while holding a selfie stick with an outstretched arm.[8] Although the photos typically use the standard 9:16 ratio, they capture exceptional breadth, depth, and height. These selfies are emblematic of a new synergy between image making, urban development, and social media.

The trendiness of rooftopping selfies might obscure their importance as an articulation of urbanism. Granted, the photographers' performative defiance of legal restrictions and danger of death place the climbers at the center of attention. The photographers' use of Instagram, YouTube, and live feed foregrounds the chance that any photo might be their last, raising empathy among users of social media. Yet the image of the rooftopper against the backdrop of the built environment also identifies him or her more specifically as a heroic figure who conquers the city. Rooftoppers are entrepreneurs of viral images, vying with the master builders for defining the contemporary skyline. The rooftopper claims the position of an urban subject, taking advantage of—if not outright celebrating—the city's vertical growth and the development of corporate architecture.

Leveraging rooftopping selfies for becoming a social media influencer was explicit in the case of the People's Republic of China's (PRC) most famous high-rise

FIGURE 2. Wu Yongning, selfie.

climber, Wu Yongning 吳永寧 (1991–2017). Wu (fig. 2) gained acclaim by taking precarious photos, often attaining striking and innovative mise-en-scène. In one heart-arresting example, Wu posed at the very edge of a high-rise roof, a slippery stone surface, while standing on a hoverboard.[9] It would have taken not even a step, but only a slight shift of balance, to send him rolling into the abyss. On November 8, 2017, Wu, then twenty-six years old, plummeted to his death while executing his signature performance of hanging from a rooftop by his fingertips. He was filming himself on the sixty-two-story Huayuan Centre in Changsha, allegedly as a commercial publicity stunt, when he slipped. Wu ended up capturing his own death on camera, in a video that became viral.[10] As I was lecturing in 2018 in China about rooftopping, every college student seemed to be familiar with Wu's story. In his life—and even more in his death—Wu became an icon.

Wu Yongning's tragic fall did not put an end to rooftopping in China. China's cities, with their vast choice of record-breaking high-rises, have become favorite destinations for scaling daredevils both domestic and from around the world. The Shanghai Tower, the Goldin Finance 117 in Tianjin, and the Shenzhen Ping An International Finance Centre were climbed time and again and made popular by rooftopping celebrities such as Keow Wee Loong, Angela Nikolau, and Vitaly Raskalov and Vadim Makhorov.[11] The rooftoppers, typically in their twenties, combine photography with other popular pastimes of their generation: international travel, extreme sports, and the pursuit of Internet celebrity status. The "world city" has acquired a new meaning as clickbait rooftoppers have made tours to Dubai, Hong Kong, Toronto, and other sites known for vertical skylines. Although Chinese authorities have discouraged rooftopping, the prominence of PRC high-rises on the global scene, including in social media, fits right into the policy branding China as a world-class capitalist paragon through its modern cityscape.

Rooftopping selfies combine recent developments in two visual mediums. One is photography: the climbers look for new ways to portray the city. Daniel Cheong, a Hong Kong professional photographer, claims that for him, "the goal is to capture the cityscape. . . . The attraction really has nothing to do with the fact that you go to the 100th floor. It is purely for composition."[12] The rooftopping selfie is akin to other genres of self-photography at dangerous heights, such as those described in Winfried Gerling's history of parachuters and aerial divers, culminating in GoPro videos.[13] In particular many rooftop photographers take advantage of the smartphone camera's combination of light weight, ease of use, geolocation service, and online networking. The second medium involved is architecture. Rooftopping reflects the boom in monumental construction. As current urbanism copes with real estate scarcity through ever-rising skyscrapers and outspreading megalopolises, rooftopping exploits the new viewpoints, which in turn allows better vantage points for taking in the enormity of urban sprawl.

Celebrating neoliberal urbanism through rooftop selfies is symptomatic of what I have called the panoramic imaginary. On its face, the images express spatial freedom—yet it is a freedom available only to the few who are in exceptional physical shape, can afford international travel, and whose socioeconomic status allows confrontation with law enforcement agencies. From the rooftopper's privileged viewpoint, the selfies establish an analogy between the climber's mobility, the viewer's ability to scan the expansive landscape, and the city's unhindered expansion. The images gain an implicit symbolic significance: they not only suggest that the latest additions to the skyline provide the city dweller with advantageous positions; the photos also imply that the newly built environment relies on a symbiosis of human and machine. The rooftopping selfies require an intricate apparatus, from the elevators and scaffolding used for access to equipment for sports photography, such as a GoPro or drone. The panoramic view becomes a metaphor for the interconnectedness of vision, mobility, and agency in built environments.

Deploying panorama as a method, by examining Chinese urbanism through a network of panoramic images from painted scrolls to rooftopping selfies, decenters the urban discourse and exposes an unspoken, perhaps unconscious bias favoring policies that prioritize building central business districts while giving a false sense of empowerment to the urban subject.

Panoramic Genealogies: Landscape Painting in the Maoist Period

My reading of rooftopping joins criticism of contemporary photographic and urbanist practices that has often remarked on their connection to consumerism and neoliberal ideology. It is equally important, however, to pay attention to the historical perspective, from the traditional scroll to the medium known as "panorama" and to earlier twentieth-century landscape painting. The following outline for a media archaeology of panoramic forms can serve as a genealogy of the panoramic image and illuminate the gradual emergence of the panoramic imaginary.

Somewhat surprisingly, an ideologically charged precedent to the rooftopping selfie can be found in paintings from the Maoist period (1949–76). To emphasize the sublimity of revolutionary subject matter, people were often portrayed standing above the landscape, in positions of self-control and mastery of the environment.

A case in point is Shi Lu's 石魯 (1991–82) *Zhuanzhan Shanbei* 轉戰陝北 (Fighting in the Northern Shaanxi, 1959). The large, nearly square watercolor (233×216cm.) shows Mao Zedong looking over precipitous terrain (fig. 3). Striking an upright figure that continues the outline of the red, firmly outlined mountains, Mao stands almost precariously at the edge of a cliff. The tension in the painting's *taiji*-like composition is held in place by Mao's stout posture. The painting may be attributed to the tradition of depicting, in poetry and painting, the theme of "climbing high and looking far" 高登望遠 (*gao deng wang yuan*). Yet Shi diverges from earlier conventions, both by featuring none other than Chairman Mao as the subject and by employing an extreme high angle. As Julia Andrews notes, with this painting Shi found his voice: having received a commission from the Museum of Revolutionary History for the PRC's tenth anniversary, Shi aimed for an innovative and striking layout.[14] The result is indeed unusual in that Mao, though clearly the painting's centerpiece, occupies a relatively small part of the composition. He faces away, inviting the viewer to see the landscape along with him, from above.

Mao's unusual and precarious position—alone, dwarfed by the mountains, even if sure of foot—was at the center of controversy, leading to the painting's withdrawal from exhibition. As Shi revealed in 1979, officials were wary of the implications of Mao's horse's strained position. The painting was seen as a criticism of the Great Leap Forward, urging Mao to "rein one's horses at the precipice" (*xuanya lema* 懸崖勒馬).[15] The composition was seen as too perilous.

Shi's painting was followed by more acceptable panoramic views. His work reveals much about the development of panoramic views in modern Chinese painting. Perhaps the most famous derivative of this genre is Zheng Shengtian 鄭勝天 (1938–), Xu Junxuan 徐君萱 (1934–), and Zhou Ruiwen's 周瑞文 (1945–) *Renjian zhengdao shi cangsang: Mao Zhuxi shica dajiangnanbei* 人間正道是滄桑——毛主席視察大江南北 (Man's Whole World Is Mutable, Seas Become Mulberry Fields: Chairman Mao Inspects the South and North of the Yangtze, 1968), which has in turn influenced the composition of many later paintings.[16] A panoramic landscape lies under Mao, who contrary to Shi's painting looms large in the foreground. The bird's-eye view emphasizes the relationship between the scenery far below and the dominating human figure. Such a composition exemplifies the Romanticist and revolutionary imagery that uses panoramic expanse to express human historical agency.

FIGURE 3. Shi Lu, *Fighting in Northern Shaanxi.*

Shi Lu's work reflects also the modernization of Chinese painting associated with the New Nanjing School 新金陵畫派, which includes Fu Baoshi 傅抱石 (1904–65), Qian Songyan 錢松嵒 (1899–1985), and Song Wenzhi 宋文治 (1919–99). These painters integrated linear perspective into bird's-eye compositions, accentuating expansive views. By the 1950s they modified traditional watercolors to fit revolutionary aesthetics. Whether depicting the sun above a sea of clouds (Fu Baoshi and Guan Shanyue 關山月 [1912–2000], *Jiangshan ruci duojiao* 江山如此多嬌 [The Land Is So Rich in Beauty, 1959), a revolutionary site (*Jinggang shan* 井岡山 [Jinggang Mountains], 1965), or a model industrial town (Song Wenzhi, *Yangzi jiangpan Daqing hua* 揚子江畔大慶花 [On the Banks of the Yangzi River, Daqing Blooms], 1975)—these and many other paintings feature revolutionary subject matter, glowing in red amid natural beauty rendered with traditional brush technique. Despite their familiarity with traditional painting, many painters in this genre abandoned the scroll format, which lends itself to horizontal or vertical scanning. The landscape is to be taken in at a single glance.

The panorama as developed in revolutionary painting resists a gradual, contemplative perception of the landscape. Maoist painting accentuates contrasts and often depicts the scenery as literal battleground. A striking example is Shen Jiawei's 沈嘉蔚 (1948–) *Wei women weida Zuguo zhangang* 為我們偉大祖國站崗 (Standing Guard for Our Great Motherland, 1974). This oil painting (also made familiar through poster reprints) shows a guard post up close, just above eye level, with a frozen Manchurian landscape at a dizzying distance below. The post juts out at an angle right above the frozen river, and the characters strike heroic poses as they stand with just a railing to stop them from falling down. Prevailing from up high testifies to the ideological rectitude of the guards, ready to die in the service of the motherland. The painting is based on the painter's experience in the 1970s, adding a self-referential element; the image is a self-portrait of sorts.[17] Like the works discussed above, Shen's oil painting is monumental, at 189×159cm. Standing in front of it, one feels the depth of the Sungari River gorge below. As the artist explains, the painting gives another meaning to the revolutionary aesthetics of "tall, big, and complete" 高大全 (*gao da quan*): originally describing the heroism of human characters, the principle may also apply to the formal composition. The guard post is perched up high, the figures loom large, and the field of vision is endless.[18] If only in retrospect, recent panoramic composition has found anchoring in revolutionary aesthetics.

Standing Guard underlines the importance of vision as a means for mastering the landscape, as two guards wield binoculars. Berry and Farquhar have noted how the revolutionary look, exercised by film stars and modeled in Mao statues, aims beyond what the eye can see and conveys an indomitable spirit.[19] The vista in the revolutionary paintings is conveyed through the eyes of viewers who appear within the frame, thereby establishing the symbolic value of the scenery. More specifically, the topography stands for ideological challenges, to be vanquished by the gaze.

The succession of images of viewing the scenery below, from the landscape paintings of Fu Baoshi, Shi Lu, and Shen Jiawei to the rooftopping selfies, demonstrates a shift in ideological focus. The heroism of Mao and the military guards is replaced in twenty-first-century photography by the adventure of climbers. Whereas revolutionary subjects stand for an everlasting presence, rooftoppers teeter and signal temporary existence. Even in the unlikely case that rooftoppers were aware of the painterly precedents, their images veer far from genteel ink drawings or academic oil painting. Their medium of choice—photography posted online—suggests a carefree coolness. Instead of the socialist motherland in Maoist painting, the rooftopping selfies feature the capitalist global city. The rooftoppers themselves prefer precarity over stability: they are risk-takers. Holding the selfie stick high, they subject themselves willingly to others' gazes, becoming both entrepreneurs and the object of consumption. They are the champions of new urbanism, and the panoramic view celebrates their dominant position in the contemporary city.

The physical insecurity in the images at hand, from revolutionary heroism to rooftopping selfie, resonates with the economic precarity discussed by Margaret Hillenbrand in this special issue. Chen Chen Chen's 陳陳陳 *Bu sha zhi en 2.0* 不殺之恩 2.0 (The Mercy of Not Killing 2.0, 2017) makes the association concrete: a multimedia installation re-creates a performance during which construction workers were hoisted up a water tower and clung to its top with their fingers for two hours (while wearing security harnesses). The resonance with Wu Yongning's rooftopping is chilling: Wu's signature feat involved hanging from rooftops by his fingertips; like Wu, the construction workers regularly risked their lives. Yet the workers in Chen's artwork are driven to their precarious position by financial want, whereas the Maoist heroes and the intrepid rooftoppers are fashioned as masters of their destiny. The vulnerability of the workers and the daring of the rooftoppers mirror each other, yet the former remain invisible, as are the structural and ideological causes of their lack of privilege.

Beyond Dichotomies of Scale: Aerial Views and the Panstereorama

Insofar as we can draw a line from painted scrolls and revolutionary landscapes to rooftopping selfies, it is also because of the connotations of aerial photography. The modern metropolis and the airborne camera have shaped each other, materially and conceptually. Panorama as method, however, questions fundamental paradigms. Urbanist discourse has associated aerial photography with the idea that there are two ways to define the city: either by looking from above or by immersing oneself at street level. Many have suggested that the choice between these two modes of experiencing built environments determines the ability to cope with the ills of urban modernity. A closer look at the ideological appropriation of aerial photography invalidates the dichotomy between airborne vision and immersive experience, as a false dilemma that abets neoliberal policies.

The early stages of aerial photography are well known, starting with photos taken by Nadar (Gaspard-Félix Tournachon) in 1858 from a tethered hot-air balloon. Nadar's photos documented the modernization of Paris under Napoléon III and Georges-Eugène Haussmann. Similar to Haussmann, who regarded his plan as the rationalization of urban space, Nadar conceived aerial photography as an objective, mechanical means of visualization, an improvement upon cartographic practices.[20] Panoramic views were umbilically tied to the technological innovation that enabled high-rises, flight, and aerial photography. The mastery of these media rendered seeing into a measure of human agency in the city. The fascination with devices for high-altitude viewing and imaging has also caught on in China. Fanciful stories about hot-air balloons and flying machines were often featured in *Dianshizhai huabao* 點石齋畫報 (Dianshizhai Pictorial), an illustrated magazine that appeared in Shanghai in 1884–98. The accompanying images associated modernity with the ability to render panoramic vistas.

More recent examples continue to link aerial views with the modern city. It does not necessarily take climbing the outer walls of a high-rise: many landmark structures feature lookouts, from observation decks to selfie-ready windows, designed to frame the visitor. For example, the Beijing CCTV tower (architect, Rem Koolhaas; 2004–12) includes round windows on the floor of the cantilevered structure above, looking straight down from the height of 161 meters. To such urban spectacles one may add the recent craze for transparent suspension bridges and hovering decks. The latest to date, in Huangyagu, Hebei, opened in December 2017; it spans 488 meters over a vertical drop of 218 meters and was touted to mark "the 2.0 era for China's glass-bottomed bridge."[21] Catering to China's booming tourism industry, panoramic views are marketed as both joyrides and architectonic marvels. The common Chinese term for these bridges is *zhandao* 棧道, sometimes translated as "gallery road," referring to planked paths hugging the mountainside (fig. 4). The contrast between the term—associated with ancient, remote sites—and the modern tourist attraction foregrounds the commodification of such destinations through claims to modern technology and spectacular views. Online postings evidence that the glass bridges attract selfie-conscious youngsters.[22] The photos from high-rises and bridges combine the panorama and self-portraiture, in a manner that not only rethinks the relationship between the viewer and the scenery but also generates a material transformation of the built environment to accommodate the photographer and his or her camera eye.

It is tempting to interpret photography from high structures and airborne vehicles as an exponent of distanced abstraction, as opposed to street-level immersion. The distinction between these two modes of observation has become commonplace since Walter Benjamin's juxtaposition of the imperial renovation of Paris as captured by Nadar, on the one hand, and the flaneurs walking the streets on the other. Yet once we regard panorama not as a preordained form of vision but as a discursive construct that posits an imaginary vantage point, aerial photography can no longer be defined by the scenery it affords. What marks aerial photography is not the expansive vista but the very perception that it represents a newly discovered sight; not the technology used for scaling heights but the idea that the view from above is made possible only through a dedicated, modern apparatus.

The function of panorama as a virtual reference is well exemplified in the growing popularity of simulated cityscapes created by architectural maquettes. As it happens, modern scale models have their origin in the impulse to create panoramic views. Soon after people started flying in balloons in the nineteenth century, the adventure was also made into a safer amusement in the form

FIGURE 4. Glass walkway on Tianmen Mountain.

of the so-called panstereorama. Using the technique for warfare dioramas and inspired by panoramas, as large horizontal paintings of cities were called at the time, panstereoramas featured 3-D ("stereo") models of entire cities. These urban reliefs, made of various materials, provided virtual travel to places such as London, Paris, and New York. Paying great attention to topographical and architectural detail, panstereoramas aimed at a comprehensive urban experience.[23] These models, akin to variety shows, differed from maps by paying more attention to the bodily relationship between viewer and the built environment.

The panstereorama further gives the lie to equating the bird's-eye-view with abstract cartography and promoting ground-level exploration, what Michel de Certeau calls "walking in the city"—the only immersive experience.[24] Panoramic views can be just as absorbing and playful as strolling on the street and have indeed been so ever since flying balloons popularized aerial images. Nadar's self-fashioning as a mapmaker notwithstanding, the narrative according to which built environment succumbed to a cartographic impulse ignores the panstereorama as a missing link in the development of aerial imaging. Visualizing the modern city first followed not maps but miniature models, an aerial view that is at the same time somatic and immersive.

Attempts have been made to introduce nuance to the historical account of aerial photography, but without taking into account the panstereorama as a middle ground the discussion tends to fall back onto placing the subject outside the image and privileging either the cartographic or human view. For instance, Paula Amad provides a corrective, finding in aerial photography an example of "the blindspot of western rationality."[25] Amad proceeds, however, to ask how aerial photography relates to cartography, thereby separating human vision and camera eye from the cityscape.

Long before the rooftopping selfies and before camera-ready high-rises and bridges, the panstereorama broke down the barriers between the viewer and the experienced environment. Not only did panoramas visually encompass the visitor within the image; they also recalibrated the size of the represented scenery and brought the cityscape down to scale. Patrick Ellis outlines the process through which the panstereorama repurposed the practices of architectural modeling: by being miniaturized, models introduced a simulated aerial view. Balloonists started describing Earth from above as a "panorama," "model," and "miniature."[26] In other words these aerial photographers conflated the urban experience with the experience of scale models and used panorama as a metaphor. In similar fashion rooftopping selfies, glass-bottom bridge photography, and urban screens have mediated a panoramic imaginary closely linked to architectural models.

Architectural Models: Rescaling the City

The distinction between looking from above and immersing oneself in the city is put in question by panorama as method. Once the panoramic view is understood as a construct in the service of power, the dichotomy is no more than a subterfuge. The miniature model in particular is emblematic of how corporeal engagement with the city is hijacked to idealize the urban experience. Patrick Ellis notes that the panstereorama conveniently ignored the clutter, noise, and crowds of the modern metropolis.[27] As architectural models proliferate and influence the perception of urban dwellers, the simulated environment arguably becomes the norm. The sterile environment of the maquettes sets the ideal for walking in the street. Whether in miniature or in full size, the purportedly immersive environment gives the citizen a semblance of agency while sustaining neoliberal urbanism.

It is in this context that I look at the prolific use of scale models in urban exhibition halls and real estate promotional exhibits: in bridging aerial views and corporeal immersion, maquettes propagate the panoramic imaginary. Replicas and downscaled models of buildings and cities are used in China for publicity and entertainment alike. Much has been written about how entire towns have copied Western architecture and how theme parks of miniature models have gained popularity.[28] I have written elsewhere about the use of maquettes in China's contemporary mediascape. Scale models at urban planning exhibition halls have signaled the government's ability to produce new cityscapes almost instantaneously. Even private projects, such as the Ping An Finance Center 平安國際金融中心 in Shenzhen (China's second-tallest building to date) have become showcases for official urban policy. (In parallel, artists created flawed displays to criticize the notion of readymade utopia.[29]) The models are often placed below the visitors or literally under their feet, recalling the models' provenance in aerial photography and celebrating the planners' control over urban environments.

The panorama, especially when housed in a dedicated exhibition space, creates a spatial exception, a location that enhances the relationship between the citizen and built environment as spectacle. These sites may take various forms, but the ideal underlying them is that of three-dimensional miniature models. It is in this context that we may understand the flourishing of urban planning exhibition halls in China, which feature expansive maquettes of the city—past, present, and future. These exhibition spaces, often designed specifically for the models, offer an experience that is in many ways panoramic.

The architectural maquettes in wide use in China, planned by specialized offices with national and international reach such as Crystal CG and yU+co, integrate panoramic elements both well established and innovative. The models provide detailed renderings of buildings and entire districts, often extending to the urban surroundings even when tasked with representing a single building. Flamboyant aesthetics, in the form of maquettes with inner lighting, slick surfaces, and motorized movement, present the models as spectacles with a high entertainment value. Whereas in Europe and the United States architects have leaned toward conceptual models, in the line of Peter Eisenman and Rem Koolhaas, the Chinese market prefers figural models.[30] The models are often part of multimedia installations, alongside large LCD screens, moving projection surfaces, and viewing decks. Scale works both ways: the model is miniaturized, but the exhibition space imparts an immersive capaciousness. The grandeur of such models preserves the historical flavor of panoramas and panstereoramas.

The logic of scaling down the view and at the same time making the viewer an engaged party is common to rooftopping selfies, socialist-era paintings, high viewing platforms, and architectural models. The vistas are part of an apparatus that invites visitors to take scale at face value: the viewing human is larger than the toy-sized buildings in the background. The city is miniaturized and turned into a stage set. The human viewer takes also the position of presenter, photographer, and film director. The built environment has always been planned for hosting entertainment; the miniaturization implied in panoramic compositions and materialized in maquettes has precipitated a process by which urban structures have become spectacles in their own right. Large urban screens are ubiquitous, and even entire buildings double as digital displays.[31] The cityscape is manipulated, enlarged or shrunk to fit the ideology underlying the new techniques of observation.

By recognizing the panoramic view as an ideological construct, panorama as method redefines the rapport between built environment and artifacts capturing its image. Rather than drawing a mimetic relationship between material edifice and simulation, we are called upon to dismiss all hierarchy between urban plans, architecture, painting, photography, and models. They are all media for articulating urban policy and the underlying ideology. Twenty-first-century urbanism has formed a media ecology expressed by multimedia panoramic views that render the city through transformations of scale.

Although ideology, by definition, remains unseen, sometimes the visual reasoning of power is laid bare through its arbitrary, even absurd workings. Such was the case when the Beijing municipal government took a heavy-handed approach to engineering a skyline befitting its urbanist vision. In November 2017 the municipal government issued an edict requiring that billboards and rooftop signs over three stories high—hundreds existed around town—be taken down to "create a spatially conforming, visually clear, and orderly environment of public space public, getting a step closer toward sorting out the urban skyline" 打造空間協調、視覺晴朗、規范有序的公共空間環境，進一步梳理城市天際線.[32] The campaign resonated with regulations released a decade earlier, in preparation for the Beijing Olympics.[33] In another case a directive issued by the Xi'an municipal government in June 2019 mandated changing the names of neighborhoods and buildings that were too "obsequious to the West" (*chongyang* 崇洋), "feudal" (*fengjian* 封建), or just "strange and unintelligible" (*guaiyi nandong* 怪異難懂). Terms were carefully regulated: "pavilions" (*ge* 閣 or *xuan* 軒) could not be used to refer to structures that were more than seven stories tall.[34] As the urban skyline changes, it cannot hold onto traditional, poetic nomenclature without being subjected to bureaucratic regulation.

The surprise and scorn with which such policies were met evidence a gap between planners' aesthetics and the norms to which residents had gotten accustomed. Redesigning the cityscape foregrounds an underlying tension in the official perception of twenty-first-century urban development. On the one hand, the government fashions itself as the representative of the people, notably in commissioning scrolls portraying everyday life. On the other hand, the authorities undertake grandiose projects, made conspicuous by expansive spaces and monumental architecture. This seeming conflict is, however, easy to resolve when we bear in mind that the panoramic imaginary relies on the ability to scale the built environment up and down at the planners' will.

Coda: Battle Panoramas

Insofar as panorama as method decenters the concept of panoramic vision and demonstrates its ideological deployment, one may ask, what is the role of literal panoramas—larger-than-life images that fit the historical definition of panorama painting—in contemporary Chinese visual culture? The proliferation of battle panoramas provides such a case, and it shows that panoramas narrowly defined are marginal to the urbanist discourse at hand.

In the late twentieth century, a new painting genre rose to prominence in China: the battle panorama. The first was *Gongke Jinzhou* 攻克錦州 (The Attack on Jinzhou, 1989, 124 by 16 meters), commissioned for the Liaoning-Shenyang Campaign Memorial 遼沈戰役紀念館. In 1993 the four-panel panorama *Battle of the Ch'ongch'on River* 清川江畔圍殲戰 (132 by 16 meters) was installed at the Korean War Memorial in Dandong 丹東抗美援朝紀念. These were followed by *Laiwu zhanyi* 萊蕪戰役 (The Laiwu Campaign, 1997, 119.78 by 17 meters); *Chibi zhi zhan* 赤壁之戰 (Battle of Red Cliff, 1999, 135 by 18 meters); *The Assault on Yuncheng* 鄆城攻堅戰 (2000, 126 by 17 meters); and *Jinan zhanyi* 濟南戰役 (The Battle of Jinan, 2004, 120 by 16 meters), all installed in dedicated galleries.[35] Only a relatively small number of such paintings—probably just over twenty—have been produced, because even with a large crew it takes two to four years to complete a single work, and because only well-funded museums can commission such paintings and build the space for them. The subject matter is also of limited appeal: the large scrolls parallel "main melody" (*zhuxuanlü* 主旋律) art—extolling the history of the Communist Party—created in other media. The panoramas toed the official line, both in style (realistic oils) and in choice of theme (major battles), contrasting with the avant-garde forms that grew popular and lucrative in the private art market. For financial, stylistic, and cultural reasons, the heyday of the Chinese battle panorama was short-lived.

The large battle paintings were explicitly referred to as "panoramas" (*quanjinghua* 全景畫), and scholarly discussion of these paintings often placed them in the context of eighteenth- and nineteenth-century Western panoramas and cycloramas. Some of these works stood at the center of conferences organized by the International Panorama Council, hosted in China in 2001 and 2005.[36] Ji Yunhui notes that the Chinese panoramas benefit from the precedent set by earlier panoramas as a tool for educating the masses.[37] And yet it is precisely the way these paintings fit so neatly with the historical paradigm of the panorama that underlines how images of urbanism in twenty-first-century China have little to do with technical definitions. Rather panorama as method displaces historical conventions and stresses plays of scale.

This essay has provided at best a sketch, a mountaintop survey as it were, of the panoramic imaginary. I have not addressed, among other media, the moving image. Cinema and video art have contributed striking exemplars and arguably have proven more resistant to the official urbanist discourse. A more comprehensive study of the relation between built environment, image making, and ideology in twenty-first-century China will need to examine also how other forms have mediated the city.

YOMI BRAESTER is Byron and Alice Lockwood Professor in the Humanities and professor of comparative literature, cinema, and media at the University of Washington in Seattle. He is also the coeditor of *Journal of Chinese Cinemas* and former president of the Association of Chinese and Comparative Literature. Among his books are *Witness Against History: Literature, Film, and Public Discourse in Twentieth-Century China* (2003) and *Painting the City Red: Chinese Cinema and the Urban Contract* (2010), which won the Joseph Levenson Book Prize.

Notes

1 K.-H. Chen, *Asia as Method*, xv.
2 On the 360-degree panorama, see Huhtamo, *Illusions in Motion*.
3 On recent usage of urban screens in China, see Berry, "Screen Cultures and the 'Generic City'"; and Braester, "Traces of the Future." See also McQuire, Martin, and Niederer, *Urban Screens Reader*.
4 *Tian qu dan que*, www.itsfun.com.tw/%E5%A4%A9%E8%A1%A2%E4%B8%B9%E9%97%95/wiki-9775691-2178581.
5 Wu, *Remaking Beijing*, 171.
6 Braester, "Traces of the Future," 24–27.
7 "*Qianlong nanxun tu* 'dong' qilai le?"
8 Doward and Gibbs, "Lure of Tall Buildings." See also "Rooftopping" in Wikipedia.org and urbandictionary.com.
9 See photos at lbc9.com/wu-yongning.
10 Wilson, "Wu Yongning"; Hauser, "Death of Man in Skyscraper Fall."
11 Photos and videos of these climbers and others have gone viral; the four mentioned here maintain personal YouTube and Instagram pages.
12 Hauser, "Death of Man in Skyscraper Fall."
13 Gerling, "Be a Hero."
14 Andrews, *Painters and Politics in the People's Republic of China*, 236–38.
15 Hawks, *Art of Resistance*, 171.
16 On *Man's Whole World Is Mutable*, see Chiu and Zheng, *Art and China's Revolution*, 32–34.
17 On *Standing Guard for Our Great Motherland*, see Chiu and Zheng, *Art and China's Revolution*, 133–47.
18 Chen L., *Geming de shidai*, 402.
19 Berry and Farquhar, *China on Screen*, 116–18.
20 Gandy, "Paris Sewers and the Rationalization of Urban Space"; Castro, "Cinematic Cartographies of Urban Space," 51.

21 Wong, "World's Longest Glass Bridge Opens in Hebei, China."
22 See, for example, Jacobs, "I Visited the Viral, 1,400-Foot Glass Bridge in China."
23 Ellis, "Panstereorama."
24 Certeau, *Practice of Everyday Life*, 91–110; see also Haraway, "Persistence of Vision."
25 Amad, "From God's-Eye to Camera-Eye," 83.
26 Ellis, "Panstereorama," 83.
27 Ibid., 90.
28 See, for example, Bosker, *Original Copies*.
29 Braester, "Architecture of Utopia."
30 Ibid.
31 Papastergiadis et al., "Mega Screens for Mega Cities."
32 See, for example, "Beijing."
33 Broudehoux, *Making and Selling of Post-Mao Beijing*, 164–65.
34 "Yin quming 'da yang guai chong' Xi'an 151 ge xiaoqu he jianzhuwu jiang gengming."
35 Song, "Huihong, yongxuan de wujian."
36 See panoramacouncil.org.
37 Ji, "Quanjinghua meixue yanjiu."

References

Amad, Paula. "From God's-Eye to Camera-Eye: Aerial Photography's Post-humanist and Neo-humanist Visions of the World." *History of Photography* 36, no. 1 (2012): 66–86.

Andrews, Julia. *Painters and Politics in the People's Republic of China, 1949–1979*. Berkeley: University of California Press, 1994.

"Beijing: Shiyu nei wuding guanggao paibian niannei qingli wanbi" 北京：市域內屋頂廣告牌匾年內清理完畢 [Beijing: Clearing the Rooftop Advertisement Plaques within the City Will Be Completed by the End Of the Year]. *Zhonguo xinwen wang* 中國新聞網 [China News], November 2, 2017. www.chinanews.com/sh/2017/11-02/8366184.shtml.

Berry, Chris. "Screen Cultures and the 'Generic City': Public Screens in Cairo and Shanghai." In *Global Cinematic Cities: New Landscapes of Film and Media*, edited by Johan Andersson and Lawrence Webb, 143–56. London and New York: Wallflower, 2016.

Berry, Chris, and Mary Farquhar. *China on Screen: Cinema and Nation*. New York: Columbia University Press, 2006.

Bosker, Angela. *Original Copies: Architectural Mimicry in Contemporary China*. Honolulu: University of Hawai'i Press, 2013.

Braester, Yomi. "The Architecture of Utopia: From Rem Koolhaas's Scale Models to *RMB City*." In *The Spectacle and the City*, edited by Jeroen de Kloet and Lena Scheen, 59–73. Amsterdam: Amsterdam University Press, 2013.

Braester, Yomi. "Traces of the Future: Beijing's Politics of Emergence." In *Ghost Protocol: Development and Displacement in Global China*, edited by Carlos Rojas and Ralph Litzinger, 15–35. Durham, NC: Duke University Press, 2016.

Broudehoux, Anne-Marie. *The Making and Selling of Post-Mao Beijing*. New York and London: Routledge, 2004.

Castro, Teresa. "Cinematic Cartographies of Urban Space and the Descriptive Spectacle of Aerial Views (1898–1948)." In *Cinematic Urban Geographies*, edited by Francois Penz and Richard Koeck, 47–63. New York: Palgrave Macmillan, 2017.

Certeau, Michel de. *The Practice of Everyday Life*. Berkeley: University of California Press, 1984.

Chen, Kuan-Hsing. *Asia as Method: Toward Deimperialization*. Durham, NC: Duke University Press, 2010.

Chen Lüsheng 陳履生. *Geming de shidai: Yan'an yilai de zhuti chuangzuo yanjiu: Zengbuban* 革命的時代：延安以來的主題創作研究——增補版 [Revolutionary Art since the Yan'an Era: Extended Edition]. Beijing: Renmin meishu chubanshe, 2014.

Chiu, Melissa, and Shengtian Zheng. *Art and China's Revolution*. New Haven, CT: Yale University Press, 2008.

Doward, Jamie, and Alice Gibbs. "The Lure of Tall Buildings: A Guide to the Risky but Lucrative World of 'Rooftoppers.'" *Guardian*, February 25, 2017. www.theguardian.com/cities/2017/feb/26/rooftopping-do-you-have-to-be-crazy-to-hand-off-a-skyscraper.

Ellis, Patrick. "The Panstereorama: City Models in the Balloon Era." *Imago Mundi* 70, no. 1 (2018): 79–93.

Gandy, Matthew. "The Paris Sewers and the Rationalization of Urban Space." *Transactions of the Institute of British Geographers* 24, no. 1 (1999): 23–44.

Gerling, Winfried. "Be a Hero: Self-Shoots at the Edge of the Abyss." In *Exploring the Selfie: Historical, Theoretical, and Analytical Approaches to Digital Self-Photography*, edited by Julia Eckel, Jens Ruchatz, and Sabine Wirth, 261–83. London: Palgrave Macmillan, 2018.

Haraway, Donna. "The Persistence of Vision." In *The Visual Culture Reader: Second Edition*, edited by Nicholas Mirzoeff, 677–84. London and New York: Routledge, 2002.

Hauser, Christine. "Death of Man in Skyscraper Fall in China Puts a Spotlight on 'Rooftopping.'" *New York Times*, December 14, 2017. www.nytimes.com/2017/12/14/world/asia/china-daredevil-skyscraper.html.

Hawks, Shelley Drake. *The Art of Resistance: Painting by Candlelight in Mao's China*. Seattle: University of Washington Press, 2017.

Huhtamo, Erkki. *Illusions in Motion: Media Archaeology of the Moving Panorama and Related Spectacles*. Cambridge, MA: MIT Press, 2013.

Jacobs, Harrison. "I Visited the Viral, 1,400-Foot Glass Bridge in China—And It Was a Traveler's Worst Nightmare." *Business Insider*, April 25, 2018. www.businessinsider.com/china-glass-bridge-zhangjiajie-longest-highest-photos-tour-2018-4.

Ji Yunhui 及雲輝 "Quanjinghua meixue yanjiu" 全景畫美學研究 [The Aesthetic Study of Panorama Paintings]. *Wenyi zhengming* 文藝爭鳴 [Literary Contentions], no. 10 (2010): 14–19.

McQuire, Scott, Meredith Martin, and Sabine Niederer, eds. *Urban Screens Reader*. Amsterdam: Institute of Network Cultures, 2009.

Papastergiadis, Nikos, et al. "Mega Screens for Mega Cities." *Theory, Culture and Society* 30, nos. 7–8 (2013): 325–41.

"*Qianlong nanxun tu* 'dong' qilai le?" 《乾隆南巡圖》「動」起來了? [*Emperor Qianlong's Southern Expedition* Animated?]. *Zhihu* 知乎, March 31, 2017. zhuanlan.zhihu.com/p/26128787.

Song Huimin 宋惠民. "Huihong, yongheng de shunjian: Zhongguo quanjinghua de jueqi" 恢弘・永恆的瞬間——中國全景畫的崛起 [A Vast, Eternal Dance Space: The Rise of Chinese Panorama Painting]. *Meishu* 美術 [Art Magazine], no. 12 (2001): 75–79.

Wilson, Samantha. "Wu Yongning: 5 Things to Know about Famed 'Rooftopper' Who Accidentally Fell to His Death." *Hollywoodlife*, December 11, 2017. hollywoodlife.com/2017/12/11/who-is-wu-yongning-facts-rooftopper-daredevil-china-dead.

Wong, Maggie Hiufu. "World's Longest Glass Bridge Opens in Hebei, China." *CNN*, January 4, 2018. www.cnn.com/travel/article/hongyagu-glass-bridge-hebei-china/index.html.

Wu Hung. *Remaking Beijing: Tiananmen Square and the Creation of a Political Space.* Chicago: University of Chicago Press, 2005.
"Yin quming 'da yang guai chong' Xi'an 151 ge xiaoqu he jianzhuwu jiang gengming" 因取名「大洋怪重」西安151個小區和建筑物將更名 [Because Their Names Are "Exaggerated, Westernized, Strange, or Duplicate," 151 Neighborhoods and Buildings in Xi'an Will Change Names]. *Wangyi* 網易 [Netease], June 19, 2019. news.163.com/19/0619/15/EI1UPEMQ0001875P.html.

ROBIN VISSER

Ecology as Method

ABSTRACT In "China as Method," Mizoguchi Yūzō argues that "a world that takes China as method would be a world in which China is a constitutive element." Similarly, a world that takes ecology as method is a world in which humans are a constitutive element, one of "the ten thousand things" (*wanwu* 萬物). In this essay, the author examines distinct ways in which fictional writers imagine relational dynamics between humans, nonhuman animals, regional ecosystems, and the cosmos to theorize ecology as method. Ecology as method works to radically decenter anthropocentric understandings of the cosmos, historicizes regional ecologies in order to illuminate global dynamics, and acknowledges deterritorialization. While mourning loss, it resists sentimentalizing cultural narratives that rationalize the genocide of species as inevitable. This article focuses on three contemporary eco-writers of Inner Mongolia. Mandumai 滿都麥, one of the People's Republic of China's earliest post-Mao eco-writers, romanticizes indigeneity in his Mongolian-language stories (read in this article in Mandarin translation). Mongolian-Han Sinophone writer Guo Xuebo 郭雪波 juxtaposes "grassland logic" against "agrarian logic" in his desert fiction series, illustrating how *agrilogistics* dominates the ecological imagination of the ethnically diverse desert-dwellers. Finally, the article analyzes the best-selling *Wolf Totem* by Beijing-based sent-down youth Jiang Rong 姜戎. Despite attributing desertification to Han ignorance, the novel simultaneously maps the steppes via ecological understandings from *Hanspace* ontology.

KEYWORDS eco-criticism, Inner Mongolia, indigeneity, Sinophone, ontology

Ecology as Method

In "China as Method," Mizoguchi Yūzō argues that "a world that takes China as method would be a world in which China is a constitutive element."[1] Similarly, an ontology that takes ecology as method is one in which humans are a constitutive element, or in early Chinese cosmological parlance, "one of the ten thousand things" (*wanwu* 萬物). Unlike methodologies that privilege imperial cosmologies, ecology as method radically equalizes the organic and inorganic entities comprising the cosmos, seeing each as vital to its existence. Indeed the possibility that humans "are such an overwhelming malignant force that Life itself faces planetary extinction has changed the topical foci of the humanities and humanistic social sciences and the quantitative social sciences and natural sciences."[2] This article illustrates ecology as method by examining how Sinophone eco-fiction from Inner Mongolia, marginalized from a *Hanspace* perspective,[3] conveys relational dynamics between humans, nonhuman animals, regional ecosystems, and the

PRISM: THEORY AND MODERN CHINESE LITERATURE • 16:2 • OCTOBER 2019
DOI 10.1215/25783491-7978515 •

cosmos. Inner Mongolian eco-fiction illuminates this method at national, global, and cosmological scales given the proximity of the Inner Mongolia Autonomous Region (IMAR) to Beijing, the existence of an independent Mongolian nation that complicates understandings of the "indigenist-environmentalist alliance,"[4] and the radical nonattachment inherent in shamanism and Tibetan/Mongolian Buddhism.

One way to illustrate ecology as method is to compare diverse ontologies of similar ecosystems, in this case analyzing fiction set in IMAR by three male writers born just prior to the founding of the People's Republic of China in 1949. Fiction featuring ecosystems north of Beijing and beyond the Great Wall explores complex dynamics between indigenous and nonindigenous knowledge and practices. It presents environmental practices and perspectives of nomadic pastoralism, hunting, and agrarianism, variously informed by Han, Mongolian, and hybrid cosmologies. Mongolian indigene and Communist Party member Mandumai 滿都麥 (1947–) publishes in Mongolian and Mandarin translation. While his eco-fiction is constrained by certain Party norms, it also highlights environmental racism and evokes Buddhist taboos against practices that ravage ecosystems. Mongolian-Han Sinophone writer Guo Xuebo 郭雪波 (1948–) writes philosophically eclectic eco-fiction that reveals fault lines in rights discourses that abstract "nature," "indigeneity," and "ethnicity." Instead he highlights the violence inherent in what philosopher Timothy Morton calls *agrilogistics*. Finally, Beijing political science professor Jiang Rong 姜戎 (1946–) combines Han scientific rationalism with Mongolian eco-centrism in his best-selling 2004 novel *Lang tuteng* 狼圖騰 (Wolf Totem).

In general, eco-fiction by former sent-down youth (*zhiqing* 知青) such as Jiang Rong, who moved from urban centers to ethnically diverse border regions during the Cultural Revolution (1966–1976), appropriates indigenous ecological perspectives to criticize Maoist destruction of the environment and concomitant undermining of neo-Confucian values.[5] These Beijing Westerns produce Hanspace cosmological mappings of "peripheral" ecologies long considered exotic in the Han imagination. While *Wolf Totem* is an intriguing novel that transmits scientific knowledge of grassland ecosystems and admiration of nomadic culture, it exoticizes the ethnic other to legitimate extracting its ecological knowledge, just as Beijing's Go West policies instrumentally commodify the lands, resources, and customs of border societies. Sinophone eco-fiction by indigenous writers, on the other hand, complicates dynamics between Han and non-Han ecological knowledge and practices and the borders created by Hanspace. Guo Xuebo's desert fiction, in particular, unleashes the possibilities of what Morton calls *dark ecology* by radically contextualizing the carbon imaginary of the Anthropocene as mere figure.

As Shuang Shen argues in this special issue, geopolitics is a historical process of bordering. If borders are interfaces connecting or separating disparate entities, ecology as method compares ontologies produced within these entities, exposing each as instrumental and one among many, rather than naturally occurring or inevitable. It problematizes highly anthropocentric understandings of the cosmos, just as sinologists such as Mizoguchi and Takeuchi Yoshimi sought to radically decenter Europe as historically paradigmatic and prescriptive. This method seeks to avoid the trap of Cold War knowledge categories analyzed by Petrus Liu in this issue, whereby works produced by "first-world" ("imperialist") thinkers seemingly transcend both national and disciplinary boundaries, while those produced by the Global South ("indigenes") merely reflect the essence of their societies of origin. Thus while Mizoguchi sought a pluralistic framework to disrupt dyadic East-West paradigms, ecology as method recognizes that Inter-Asia is itself pluralistic. It aims to further the incomplete project of decolonization in Asia, as Kuan-Hsing Chen advocates in *Asia as Method*. Regional knowledge that extends beyond nation and discipline can undermine eco-ontologies informing what Belinda Kong in this issue calls *bio-orientalist necropower*, rationalized by cosmological imaginations of unchanged cultures and outdated modes of thought.

In sum, ecology as method works to identify and destabilize hegemonic ecological ontologies. It understands bordering as a productive, generative process that connects and separates myriad animate and inanimate entities in time and space. Second, it historicizes regional ecologies in order to illuminate global dynamics. For example, it may uncover shared imperialist rationalizations for Chinese and American eco-exceptionalism, such as ideologies of biological determinism and social Darwinism informing the discourse of Chinese ecological civilization and the origins of the US conservation movement.[6] Finally, it acknowledges the reality of radical deterritorialization, tackling climate migration, endangered species, and environmental racism via systemic and territorial ties to the planet versus localities.

Ecologies and Indigeneity in IMAR

It is helpful to provide a brief overview of the environmental history of IMAR and define indigeneity to contextualize the literary works. IMAR, China's third largest province, is 70 percent grassland. Temperate steppes lie across a plateau confluence of dry alpine rain shadows to the west and moist ocean winds to the east, with extreme sensitivity to inter-annual variation in climate and land-usage change.[7] Despite temperate average temperatures, the steppes experience temperature fluctuations of as much as thirty degrees Celsius in a day, combined with harsh winters and punishing summers. For example, in 2001 a steppe winter event caused the worst natural disaster in IMAR recorded history, during which 30 percent of the total herd population died because the forage was impenetrably frozen.[8]

Migration of farmers to the region accelerated in the eighteenth century when the Qing lifted Han migration limits to present-day Inner Mongolia to mitigate starvation. Although Mongol nomads in the southeast of the region had long practiced "casual cultivation" to supplement their livelihood from foraging and hunting, "Han-style cultivation," as official Manchu documents refer to it, restricted mobility vital to herding populations, creating seriously and potentially irreversible environmental damage to herd areas.[9] Due to recent government policies designed to tackle desertification, which Beijing blames on overgrazing, many herders have been required to relocate to cities and encouraged to seek alternative lifestyles. Today the few pastoralists who remain on the grasslands find their livelihood challenged by stocking limits, mining concerns, infrastructure projects, and land-enclosure fences.[10] Pastoralists are usually non-Han, thus tensions over land use implicate the "nationalities question" (*minzu wenti* 民族問題). According to environmental historian Ling Zhang, Beijing has historically viewed the northern grasslands as a "green barrier" protecting the capital: its function within an ecological system is to conserve water, act as a wind barrier, and inhibit shifting sand.[11] Pastoralists, however, view their ecosystem more holistically: rather than merely shielding the nation's capital against sandstorms, grasslands should sustain multispecies life.

Unsurprisingly, diverse geopolitics in the Sinophone world complicate understandings of indigeneity in Chinese-language literatures. Taiwan refers to indigenous (or aboriginal) Austronesian tribal groups as *yuanzhu min* 原住民 (lit., "native inhabitants"), while the People's Republic of China (PRC) term for indigenous is *tuzhu* 土著, meaning native or local, in contrast to outsider or foreigner (especially 'imperialists'). The PRC term *shaoshu minzu* 少數民族 is used to identify indigenous groups, classified as fifty-five "minority nationalities" (or "ethnic minorities," a more recent translation of *minzu* that weakens the term's territorial connotations). Concerned with unifying the nation-state, the PRC sets ideals of national unity (*minzu tuanjie* 民族團結) against national split-ism or secessionism (*minzu fenlie* 民族分裂), a norm that sustains the majority and delegitimizes minority difference.[12] This logic also undermines the legal regime providing the basis for global understandings of indigenous rights. The influential 1981 UN Report on Indigenous Populations (Cobo Report) defines indigenous peoples as those that (1) have a historical continuity with lands subsequently confiscated; (2) consider themselves distinct from dominant societies; (3) wish to continue existing in accord with their own distinct cultures and customs.[13]

While current PRC policy on ethnic minorities is largely in agreement with the Cobo Report, it rejects the claim that indigenous lands were confiscated, and many believe Beijing's ultimate goal is cultural Sinification and the elimination of ethnic differences altogether. The Cobo Report also explicitly contrasts nonindigenous approaches to "the development of land and its effective use" from indigenous approaches that are, "in ecological terms, more rational and sound."[14] This strategic linking of indigeneity to ecological knowledge began in the 1970s, first by associating indigenous communities with their lands, then expanded in the 1980s to incorporate religious practice to mark transnational indigenous identity by endowing specific rights for "indigenous peoples." In the wake of global neoliberalism, however, by the 2000s the original aims of self-determination had transformed into claims for autonomy *within* states. This is one reason that indigenous cosmology became crucial to legal arguments claiming rights to ancestral territories and resources when fighting against eminent domain or corporate interests.[15]

In the PRC, however, the indigenist-environmentalist alliance does not hold sway, partially due to secular rejection of indigenous cosmologies as sacred, but also to different understandings of indigeneity itself. The nation-state of Mongolia notwithstanding, the PRC does not recognize a historic continuity of ethnic Mongols to confiscated lands and ways of life. Many Chinese still refer to the previous Qing territory by its former name of "Outer Mongolia" (Wai Menggu 外蒙古) despite its independence, conceiving it as politically contiguous with "Inner Mongolia" (Nei Menggu 内蒙古). Further, the PRC has adopted neoliberal strategies similar to those of Brazil and South Africa, safeguarding indigenous knowledge from foreigners ("imperialists") by converting it into intellectual property of the indigenous nation-state. Han Chinese that previously viewed Mongols as peripheral to the state now celebrate them as key partners in narratives of the Chinese nation.

Historically, Chinese rarely romanticized nomads, instead considering them a barrier to the expansion of civilization; the Great Wall is a symbol of defense against northern barbarian invasion. According to early China historian and linguist Uffe Bergeton, conceptualizations of non-Zhou groups changed around 600–400 BCE from notions of warfare to proto-anthropological concepts of "civility/civilization" (*wen* 文): the Zhou contrasted the "barbarians" (*yi* 夷) with the "Great ones" (*Xia* 夏) and local "customs" (*su* 俗) with universal "rites" (*li* 禮).[16] The late Ming, early Qing philosopher Wang Fuzhi 王夫之 (1619–92) went further, claiming non-Chinese were not human: "As for barbarians, it is not unmerciful to examine them. It is not unjust to plunder them. It is not unrighteous to cheat them. Why? It is because justice and righteousness, modes of intercourse between men, do not apply to a different species" 夷狄者，殲之不為不仁，奪之不為不義，誘之不為不信。何也？信義者，人與人相於之道，非以施之非人者也.[17]

Yet in the early 2000s, China churned out numerous books and movies celebrating Mongols, especially Genghis Khan, as "The Only Chinese to Defeat the Europeans."[18] In the early 1900s, China also celebrated Mongols in a context of pan-Asian racism, inciting iconoclastic writer Lu Xun's 魯迅 (1881–1936) sarcasm: "When I was a kid, I knew that after 'Pangu created the world' China had the Song dynasty, Yuan dynasty, Ming dynasty, and 'Our Great Qing.' At the age of twenty, I then heard that 'our' Genghis Khan conquered Europe, and it was 'our' most glorious era. Only when I reached twenty-five did I learn that 'our' most glorious era was nothing but when the Mongols conquered China and we were slaves" 幼小時候，我知道中國在「盤古氏開辟天地」之后，有三皇五帝，……宋朝，元朝，明朝，「我大清」。到二十歲，又聽說「我們」的成吉思汗征服歐洲，是「我們」最闊氣的時代。到二十五歲，才知道所謂這「我們」最闊氣的時代，其實是蒙古人征服了中國，我們做了奴才.[19] Lu Xun satirizes Chinese selective historiography and specifically its claims that central Asian Mongols and Manchus ("Our Great Qing") become "Chinese" when it is strategic to incorporate them into the empire. Still, there is no compound nomenclature of Mongolian Chinese, unlike US designations of Asian American or African American. Although Mongols have full citizenry rights in the PRC (unlike, for example, the *zainichi* 在日, the ethnic Koreans who are permanent residents of Japan), the ethnic Mongolian marker retains an ambiguous status in the Chinese nation-state.

Outer Mongolia declared independence four days prior to the founding of the Republic of China in 1911. Sun Yat-sen, as provisional president, adopted the five-color flag to represent the unity of the "republic of five nationalities" (*wuzu gonghe* 五族共和): Han, Manchurians, Mongolians, Tibetans, and Muslims. He advocated equal relations while stressing assimilation into Han (Hua) culture, inherent in the name Zhonghua 中華 of the Republic of China (Zhonghua gongheguo 中華共和國). Later, although many Mongols were farmers, the Chinese Communist Party (CCP) classified them as nomadic pastoralists—using a lower economic designation legitimating class-based paternalism by Han agrarians. Post-Mao Chinese ethnopolitics shifted from evolutionary Marxism to cultural commodification as the entire economy privatized. Twenty-first-century Mongolian culture is interpreted via the pseudo-anthropological notion of "grassland culture," a part of Chinese civilization. In 1998 Mongolia established the International Institute for the Study of Nomadic Civilizations (IISNC) with support from UNESCO. After Chinese academics participated in IISNC projects in 2000–2002, the Inner Mongolia Academy of Social Sciences launched a Grassland Culture Research Project (GCRP). According to Nasan Bayar, dean of the School of Ethnology and Sociology at Inner Mongolia University:

> One can see this action as a response to international academic projects focusing on nomadic peoples, including those on Mongolian history and culture. It is a sensitive field for China, because China's Mongolian population is greater than that of Mongolia proper, and China claims that the cultural centre of Mongolia is in China, arguing that the traditional Mongolian writing system,

> Chinggis Khan's mausoleum, and other forms of Mongolian culture are preserved in China alone.[20]

The first dozen GCRP volumes, published in 2007 and mostly written by ethnic Mongolians, provide evidence of culture on lands depicted in ancient Chinese literature as wild, desolate, and barren. Importantly, the authors almost exclusively compare "grassland culture" to "Yellow River culture" and "central plain culture," despite other scholarship associating nomadic culture with Central Asian or Eurasian cultures. Nicola Di Cosmo, for example, concludes that a nomadic steppe culture emerged in the Mongolian Plateau from the sixth through the fourth century BCE with "the appearance of the Scythian-triad assemblage: weapons, horse gear, and objects decorated in animal style."[21]

Not only does GCRP scholarship subtly reinforce Hanspace cosmologies based in narratives of civilizational superiority dating back to the Warring States period, but it also rationalizes contemporary "go West" policies by associating the spirit of grassland culture with that of neoliberal development. As summarized by Bayar, GCRP characterizes grassland culture as exhibiting four qualities: "the spirit of pioneering and forging ahead ([*kaita jinqu*] 開拓進取), the spirit of freedom and openness ([*ziyou kaifang*] 自由開放), the spirit of heroism and optimism ([*yingxiong leguan*] 英雄樂觀), and the spirit of esteeming integrity and justice ([*chongxin zhongyi*] 崇信重義)."[22] By linking grassland culture with Chinese civilizational values (such as core Confucian values of integrity and justice), researchers imply grasslanders have the potential to be modernized within the framework of Chinese civilization. Unlike hierarchical cosmologies that blatantly assign lower status to minority cultures via center-periphery, civilized-barbarian, or progressive-backward dichotomies, the GCRP celebrates grassland culture yet views it as static. According to Nasan Bayar, the GCRP

> emphasized the geo-body of the Chinese nation state in order to retain the culture within the bounds of China. The aim is thus to prevent the culture of Inner Mongols from being connected with a nomadic civilization that exceeds the bounds of the Chinese nation. Otherwise, the culture of the Inner Mongols risks being considered as a part of culture or civilization of Mongolia, a part of Buddhist civilization in Huntington's perspective, and thus potentially leading to a "clash of civilizations" between Chinese and Buddhists.[23]

The GCRP reifies culture to contain indigenes within the nation-state. It defines grassland culture as encompassing the Mongolian Plateau to Xinjiang to the Tibetan Plateau, thus blurring diverse historical, ecological, religious, and linguistic distinctions between national minorities who were historically hunter-gatherers, slash-and-burn agriculturists, mountain farmers, or pastoralists.

This essay is centrally concerned with proposing ecology as method to acknowledge the impact of the Anthropocene on conceptual frameworks of governance, such that these sorts of examples may be viewed as instances of strategic appropriation of indigenous ecological knowledge by reifying indigenous culture in the service of the nation-state. Recognizing that Foucauldian biopolitics inadequately reveal contemporary mechanisms of power, this essay follows Elizabeth Povinelli's suggestion that late settler liberalism is governed by geontopower, a mode of power that operates through the regulation of the distinction between life and nonlife illustrated by figures such as the desert or the animist.[24] Povinelli argues that prior to the era of the Anthropocene the distinction between life and nonlife was thought to matter, but today we are faced with a posthuman conundrum: "It is certainly the case that the statement 'clearly, *x* humans are more important than *y* rocks' continues to be made, persuade, stop political discourse. But what interests me . . . is the slight hesitation, the pause, the intake of breath that now can interrupt an immediate assent."[25] The "slight hesitation" comes from both environmentalists and capitalists: environmentalists prioritize the integrity of a mountain ecosystem over locals dependent on the mining economy; operators prioritize mineral extraction over miner safety if cost-benefit analyses favor compensation payouts. Although biopolitics has always been subtended by geology, critical awareness of the Anthropocene makes this transparent.

Indigenous cosmologies illustrate ecology as method because they elude the posthuman crisis posed by geontology. Indigenous writers do not tend to hesitate because they readily attribute agency to inorganic mountains, minerals, and sand, informed by belief systems governed by radically non-anthropocentric detachment from human life. While some consider shamanistic beliefs scientifically irrational and even suicidal, critical theory increasingly questions ontological distinctions among biological, geological, and meteorological entities. Given the extreme duress to life in IMAR, it is not surprising that much of IMAR eco-fiction, particularly by indigenous writers, explores Anthropocene themes of nonlife.

Mandumai: From Politically Correct to Cosmologically Buddhist Ecocriticism

The Mongolian-language eco-literature of indigene Mandumai is a case in point. His stories not only level critiques against Han chauvinism despite constraints of political correctness but also ultimately convey the radical nonattachment to life that undergirds Buddhist and Shamanistic philosophies. Born in Chifeng in eastern Inner Mongolia, where he herded sheep until publishing his first story in 1971, Mandumai graduated from the literary studies department of Inner Mongolia University in 1983 and currently lives in south-central Inner Mongolia in Ulanqab. His posts in the CCP and Chinese Writer's Association include vice-director of Ulanqab History and Literature Committee, chair of the Ulanqab Literary and

Art Association, and former chief editor of the now-defunct Mongolian-language journal *Cheleige'er tala zazhi* 敕勒格爾塔拉雜誌 (Spacious Steppe).

The Party's promotion of grassland culture as an attempt to conceptualize indigenous culture within Chinese civilization gave rise to the "Key Works in Grassland Literature Project." In 2015 the Chinese Writers Association published *Junma, canglang, guxiang* 駿馬・蒼狼・故鄉 (Horse, Wolf, Home), a two-volume collection of fifteen of Mandumai's Mongolian eco-stories published in Mandarin translation between 1981 to 2007. In her foreword, Wu Lan, chief editor of the Grassland Literature Project and then propaganda minister of the IMAR Party Standing Committee, wrote: "More than a creative undertaking for Inner Mongolian literature, the project is a contribution of the grassland to literature."[26] Civilization (*wen* 文) offers its imprimatur to (previously denigrated) grassland culture, deeming it a worthy contributor to literature (*wenxue* 文學). This despite the fact that Mandumai had already won multiple Mongolian literary awards throughout his career.

Reifying the grasslands in cultural arts to promote national aims is not new. For example, in 1964 IMAR Party secretary Ulanhu promoted the hugely popular story "Caoyuan yingxiong xiao jiemei" 草原英雄小姐妹 (Heroic Little Sisters of the Grassland), based on a true event (but with strategically altered facts). He published it prominently in the leading IMAR Party newspaper, and two weeks later staged it as a Peking opera by the Inner Mongolia Art Theater. Highly praised by Zhou Enlai, the opera may have inspired the subsequent creation of model operas during the Cultural Revolution.[27] What is new about the twenty-first-century grassland culture initiative is that it does not merely represent nomads as willing participants in the civilizing mission of the "Great ones" (whether a kingdom, an empire, or a nation-state), but it also incorporates nomadic culture into the very fabric of agrarian civilization. This calls to mind the grafting metaphor used by Chen Zhen, protagonist of *Wolf Totem*, who states, "There'd be hope for China if our national character could be rebuilt by cutting away the decaying parts of Confucianism and grafting a wolf totem sapling onto it" 如果中國人能在中國民族精神中剜去儒家的腐朽成分，再在這個精神空虛的樹洞裡，移植進去一棵狼圖騰的精神樹苗.[28] This logic replicates that popular with North American eugenicist conservationists in the late nineteenth century. As Miles Powell argues in *Vanishing America*, "Not only could Indians provide white Americans with cultural values that were free of civilization's corrupting influence, so this argument ran, but they could also offer an infusion of untainted, primitive blood."[29]

Mandumai's stories, however, introduce cosmological complexities into so-called grassland literature that defy evolutionary or civilizational paradigms even when they hew closely to Party norms. His 1981 story "Ruizhao zhiyuan" 瑞兆之源 (Source of Fortune), anthologized in Chinese and Mongolian textbooks, features politically correct themes including the ravages of the Cultural Revolution, kind Mongolian "mothers," and interethnic marital unity between a Mongolian woman and a Han man. Aidebu searches for his lost horses and is aided by long-suffering, widowed Mongolian women from a neighboring village. The story's melodramatic conclusion is that all grassland mothers embody the hardworking, honest, compassionate Mongol national character.[30] Mandumai types Mongolians as compassionate mothers partly out of political exigency: in the post-Mao era, Han male anxiety regarding "masculine" Inner Asians still manifested in culture and realpolitik. For example, Cao Yu's 曹禺 (1910–96) 1978 play *Wang Zhaojun* 王昭君, awarded China's highest national literary award, emasculates the non-Han male (unlike in ancient versions of the tale). Han consort Wang Zhaojun marries Xiongnu prince Huhanye, who swears to be "a good horse" for the Chinese emperor, one that "isn't unruly in eating and moving, and [when] on its back, it does not bolt or run amok."[31] Cao Yu may have been influenced by Wang Fuzhi's notorious claim that the difference between Chinese and Manchurians is like that between a horse and a man whose natures are distinct even if both are white. [32]

Mandumai thus astutely promotes politically correct gender types. Aidebu is easily cowed by Mother Eji. The elderly widow first encounters the young man kneeling to drink from a pond, orders him back on his horse, then demands he follow her, threatening to attack him. He follows meekly, but when she confirms he is not a thief, she laughs at him, and he feels mortified. Such comic relief at the expense of the Mongolian male likely eases Han anxiety about the indigenous other.

Despite capitulating to gender stereotypes, Mandumai still undermines dominant narratives of the "unscientific" or "lazy" nomad destroying the grasslands through overgrazing. The Mongol widows, who stand in for the nationality as a whole, protect the grasslands through their indigenous knowledge. They know lost livestock destroys newly recovered grass, so they rescue livestock at their own expense and lead the animals to graze elsewhere since the survival of all living beings depends on the health and abundance of grass. The ecological mother nurturing a female-gendered nature is a long-standing trope in many societies. Yet as ecofeminist and historian of science Carolyn Merchant points out, "The image of the earth as a living organism and nurturing mother had served as a cultural constraint restricting the actions of human beings. One does not readily slay a mother, dig into her entrails for gold or mutilate her body."[33] Even in the twenty-first century, nomadic communities in the Mongolian People's Republic continue to promote such ideas. Morton Pedersen's anthropological study of a northern Mongolian pastoral community includes a humorous anecdote of a Mongolian woman, bored with the tired metaphors, who insists on singing something other than "those songs about Mother and Nature that we always sing."[34]

While Mandumai sometimes anthropomorphizes animals similar to Han Chinese eco-literature such as the *Shijing* 詩經 (Book of Poetry, ca. 1000–600 BCE),[35]

Tang dynasty prose parables by Han Yu 韓愈 (768–824) and Liu Zongyuan 柳宗元 (773–819), or Xiao Hong's 蕭紅 (1911–42) ecofeminist fiction, he also uses zoomorphism to criticize environmental racism. For example, in "Biye shenchu" 碧野深處 (Deep in the Wilds, 1985), wounded Najide and a wounded gazelle are being stalked by a hungry mother wolf and cub. Najide equates the plight of the gazelle with that of Mongolians. When the (Han-like?) wolf cub lunges, Najide lets out a blood-curdling scream and kills it with his knife. Najide screams again, and the "cowardly" mother wolf runs away. Then, in an almost comic embrace of Deng Era neoliberalism, Najide vows to make it home to install his girlfriend's TV antenna, inspired by the wounded gazelle forging ahead for a better life (1:35).

The anthropocosmic "resonance" (*ganying* 感應)[36] between humans and animals in Mandumai's fiction is influenced by Han cosmologies and didactic literary traditions in Confucianism and Communism; indeed most Chinese literary critics interpret his eco-fiction via such paradigms.[37] Yet it also criticizes secularism by evoking Lamaist taboos against overhunting gazelles (and metaphorically, Mongolians). Party member notwithstanding, Mandumai incorporates legends and motifs from both Buddhism and shamanism in his fiction. In Mongolian cosmology, the sky (*Tengri*) is father, the earth is mother, and each natural element had its own *lus* (spirit master). The devout make offerings and follow rules to coexist with these entities, promoting ecologically sound practices such as limited digging of earth, defiling of rivers, cutting of trees, destroying the roots of grasses, disturbing the nests of birds, or killing of animals. Mongolian Buddhists believe breaking these taboos results in great misfortune to person, family, and community.

The fascinating story "Si'er lang yu lieren" 四耳狼與獵人 (The Four-Eared Wolf and the Hunter, 1997) cautions against flaunting such taboos. Crooked Hand Baladan, who tumbles into a deep ravine when his rifle backfires while shooting a fox, reflects on his life. He and his hunter friends have all incurred disabilities in the process of greedily killing wolves for their pelts and medicinal innards. When his sixth wife (the previous five died in childbirth) releases the wolf cubs he was raising to sell, he viciously beats her. She curses him as a "beast" and leaves with their son (1:203).

The closing scene is ominous. A vulture hovers above the helpless man; it sweeps down to eat the fox he had shot. A pack of male wolves circles menacingly at the top of the ravine. Strangely, a "four-eared" female wolf in heat prohibits the pack from attacking. Baladan recalls how, when one of the wolf cubs had fallen ill, he had rashly grabbed his wife's sewing scissors and sliced through its ears, anxious about losing the three hundred yuan. Chunks of blood fell off as the cub's ears healed. Could this be that same wolf his wife had released into the wild? The female wolf tortures the male wolves, and Baladan, with agonized waiting. He knows they only restrain their attack because she is in heat. Baladan agonizes over hunters' using wolf pelts and hearts for warmth, medicine, vitality.

Awaiting sure death by famished wolves and vultures circling the ravine, Baladan repents of his violence against women and animals. His ruminations call to mind the Buddhist doctrine of the dual nature of reality (Sanskrit: *satya*) as he eventually unites "conventional" (*saṁvṛti*) truth with "ultimate" (*paramārtha*) truth. His meditations situate humans in interspecies relationships where death is not a simple ending but central to the ongoing life of multispecies communities. In his seminal book *Flight Ways*, Thom van Dooren describes vultures as liminal creatures, inhabiting a strange space between life and death. Ultimately this story conveys how the real and metaphorically dead—through the active presence of decaying bodies (the fox, Baladan's friends, his deceased wives) or the absence of their living participation (his ex-wife)—help to shape the world in which all creatures make their lives.

Mandumai's 1987 story "Lao Cangtou" 老蒼頭 (Old White-Hair) also criticizes hunting with unequivocal recourse to Buddhist philosophy. Written in the magical realist style popular with Chinese writers in the 1980s, the parable opens by introducing a venerable old man who ritualistically honors nature by scattering his day's first bowl of milk tea to the "Bayin sangsilei" 巴音桑斯勒 (Rich World). In their youth, Old White-Hair and his Buddhist teacher had been avid hunters for sport, but one day a long-bearded old man appeared as they were about to shoot a deer drinking at a pond. He warned that continued cruelty toward heavenly beings would end their own lives, but if they would protect the Rich World, the grassland's birds and beasts, then Heaven will not only forgive them but also bring blessing and long life. He then disappeared. The Buddhist monk built a temple in the mountains, where he meditated for life. Old White-Hair farmed quietly, proselytizing against hunting, and bringing alms to the monk every few days. One day Old White-Hair goes missing and the villagers find him on the mountain, mutely fasting, but the monk is gone. When the narrator returns to feed Old White-Hair, he and the temple have disappeared without a trace. The reader is left to ponder the significance of the story's disappearing characters, reminiscent of Tsagaan Uvgun (Tibetan: Tsering Nam Tuk; Chinese: *Shoulao* 壽老), lord of nature and bodhisattva of longevity in Mongolian Buddhist mythology.

Framed by disappearances at the beginning (a bearded old man) and end (Old White-Hair, the recluse, the temple), the story evokes the Buddhist doctrine of the dual nature of reality. The doctrine differentiates between "provisional" (*saṁvṛti*) and "ultimate" (*paramārtha*) truth, ultimately meant to unite. As the renowned teacher Śāntarakṣita (705–62) explained, "If one trains for a long time in the union of the two truths, the stage of acceptance (on the path of joining), which is attuned to primordial wisdom, will arise."[38] "Old White-Hair" illustrates this practice, implying the bodhisattvas (the story's disappearing characters) enact ecological harmony and attain enlightenment by unifying dual truths. Mongolian Buddhism emphasizes the interconnectedness of all elements of nature, in both the visible and invisible worlds. Da Lama Bayambajav of Gandan Monastery in Ulaanbaatar explains this by contrasting organic and internal worlds: "Environmental issues and problems in the organic world are due to impurities in the internal or non-organic world. Human greed is unlimited—but the environment is limited—and Buddhist teachings try to regulate this."[39]

Guo Xuebo's Anti-agrarian Ecocriticism

In general, Mandumai's eco-literature engages the reality of nonlife as karmic retribution for nonorganic impurities within humans. In fact, Baladan predicts his grandson will have no game to hunt, because his generation has flaunted the ancestral taboos on overhunting. Species extinction is a given. In other instances, such as when Baladan calmly awaits his death, or when Old White-Hair actively fasts to hasten his transmutability, a radical acceptance of nonlife as inevitable or even desirable is also conveyed. Guo Xuebo's eco-fiction includes these themes but extends them far beyond individuals embracing death, or repenting for species extinction, to the eradication of all life, particularly by the figure of the desert. Both indigenous writers anticipate, as early as the 1980s, the recent evolution in critical inquiry from post-human to post-life queries of a post-extinction world.

Guo Xuebo's Shandong ancestors intermarried with Mongolians in the Horqin Sandy Land, stabilized sand dunes spreading from eastern IMAR to western Jilin and Liaoning provinces. He was born in Hure Banner (Kulun Banner 库伦旗), where he lived alongside Koreans, Manchurians, and Hui. In an interview included in *Desert Wolf*, a translation of his fiction, Guo attributes his intimacy with the desert to indelible childhood experience:

> The first thing I saw when I came into this world was sand. The women in my hometown would spread a layer of dry, comfortable sand on the *kang* when they gave birth. That's probably why I have an affinity with sand. I know the desert all too well. When I was a child, I would run naked after hares on the dunes, dig out edible roots and break off thin branches of willow to make a horse whip; I'd cover myself all over with yellow sand and splash in small pools in the low-lying land—childhood is unforgettable.[40]

Guo was inspired to write by his Mongolian father, a painter and balladeer, and his ecological knowledge of desert sand, vegetation, and animals pervades his stories. After working as editor in a county broadcasting station and scriptwriter for a song-and-dance ensemble, he graduated from the Beijing Central Institute of Drama in 1980 and did research in the Literary Research Institute of the Chinese Academy of Social Sciences, specializing in Mongolian history, culture, and literature. Unlike Mandumai, Guo Xuebo chose to write stories in Mandarin to reach a broader audience. After achieving acclaim for his 1980s series of desert ecological works, he joined the Chinese Writers Association and to date has published more than thirty works, many of which have been translated into Japanese, French, and English. While it is difficult to summarize such a large corpus of ecological writing, his powerful fiction is poignant, penetrating, even haunting.

Guo's earliest stories are particularly noteworthy for their attention to the figure of the desert and their critique of the carbon imaginary of agrilogistics. As a whole, his literary corpus conveys ambivalence toward agrarianism in terms resonant with Timothy Morton's claim that agrilogistics (logistics governing agrarian, versus nomadic or hunter-gatherer, forms of settlement, civilization, and technology) is responsible for the Anthropocene, because it conceptualizes nature as separate from humans.[41] Morton's thesis in *Dark Ecology* is that agrilogistics arose 12,500 years ago at the end of the Ice Age, when a climate shift experienced by hunter-gatherers as a catastrophe pushed humans to find a solution to their fear about where their next meal would come from. Agrilogistics "promises to eliminate fear, anxiety, and contradiction by establishing thin rigid boundaries between human and nonhuman worlds and by reducing existence to sheer quantity."[42] Morton argues that civilization was a long-term collaboration between humans and wheat, humans and rock, humans and soil, out of desperation: "We turned the region into a desert, and had to move west."[43] Civilization, according to Morton, is a form of agrilogistic retreat.

This calls to mind the opening paragraph of "Shahu" 沙狐 (The Sand Fox, 1985), the first story in Guo's desert fiction series. It starts by noting the evolution of the Horqin from grasslands to sandy lands, starting in the Sui and accelerating in the Qing due to agrarian practices.[44] The story then describes the "blind enthusiasm" 盲目而狂熱 of Han migrant farmers during the Great Leap Forward (1957–59), when an army of laborers arrived carrying a banner inscribed "Wrest grain from the desert!" 向沙漠要糧 (87; 85). Despite the fact that settlers from the interior had to relocate after being buried in their tents by a sandstorm, they retained their enthusiasm for opening up and cultivating the desert, rationalizing desperation with civilizational willpower.

The story focuses on Sandy, an ex-convict from the interior, and his teen daughter, Willow, who apply for abandoned sand dunes under the new household contract system in 1980. The story's climax comes when two visitors insist on visiting his dunes with their rifles. Sandy fears they will shoot a sand fox with whom he has a mutually beneficial relationship. The plants he cultivated on the dunes had initially withered because rats ate the roots. Sandy set traps and poison, which instead killed his hens. One day the rats disappeared, and Sandy discovered that a sand fox eats three thousand rats per year. Although Sandy raises

Willow to respect all living beings, telling her not to hurt a single blade of grass or insect because life depends on other life, he aggressively poisons rats and "happily slaughters chickens" 在殺雞的樂趣中 (89; 86–87). The author elaborates in gruesome detail: "He did it in a strange way, breaking the chicken's spine first, twisting its head round to tuck under a wing, then dashing it to the ground so that its legs stretched and went stiff" 他殺雞的辦法很特別，先把雞的脊骨用手折斷，然後把雞腦袋擰過來掖在翅膀下，使勁往地下一摔，雞就蹬腿了 (95; 93).

When the visitors first shoot in the dunes, Sandy does not respond, because he assumes they are shooting his chickens, which he devalues, but when he hears more shots, he jumps as if scalded (like his chickens) (96; 93). He can count the number of hares and pheasants in the dunes after he contracted and planted them, attracting animals and birds. Willow also feels proprietary, protesting to her father that the visitors are shooting *our* hares and pheasants (97; 94). Hierarchical eco-logic notwithstanding, they see the dunes as an interconnected ecosystem. The visitors, on the other hand, dualistically bifurcate nature and culture. One tells Willow that the hares and pheasants are wild, unlike Sandy's chickens and rabbits. By abstracting some animals as wild, the visitors rationalize their rights to them. Father and daughter have more holistic ecological knowledge than the visitors, yet Sandy, a Han farmer who treats domesticated animals and agricultural pests with cruelty, also imports agrarian biases into the Mongolian grasslands.

Guo illustrates how fear is rationalized as civilizational willpower in the 1987 novella *Sand Rites* (the English title of *Damo hun* 大漠魂 [lit. Desert Soul], winner of the Taiwan United Press Literary Prize), in which two Mongolian shamans and lovers survive from the 1940s to the 1980s, only to be decimated by yet another drought. The female shaman retains her spirituality, while the male shaman is portrayed as brutally misogynistic and cruel to animals, children, and the land. When he takes an orphan to plant millet in the desert, he kills their dog who drinks the water, brutally whips their starving bullock, and forces the orphan to walk the plow behind him as he shouldered the yoke in place of the bullock. Only after the shaman promises to adopt him does the child agree, declaring that he hates his adoptive father as the plowshare stabs into the sandy soil (171; 49).

Guo also masterfully executes an ecofeminist critique of agrilogistics in the novella *Shazang* 沙葬 (Sand Burial, 1996), a complex story that features perspectives of sand, nonhuman animals, plant species, Mongolians, and Han as multispecies components of a desert ecosystem. An exiled Han scientist attempts to remediate the ravages of Han agrarian practices adopted by Mongolian pastoralists by creating a green biosphere around a Buddhist temple in the desert. The scientist's viridity model was to plant *xibag* artemisia (*Sha ba ga hao* 沙巴嘎蒿), or Mongolian wormwood, and sand willows, yet sand buries him alive while he is trying to draw the root of a Chinese pea shrub. Whether the story conveys anthropocosmic resonance where the cosmos responds to human actions in kind or the perspectivalism of Daoist or shamanistic cosmologies, a similar fate befalls his friend, the lama. During a deadly sandstorm the lama saves a menagerie of desert birds and animals along with humans, ignoring his nephew's pleas to only give water and oxygen to the humans. His Sinicized nephew, a Party officer, believes in Confucian love with distinctions (prioritizing humans) and Mao's mandate that humans must overcome nature, but the Buddhist insists on protecting all living creatures. He refuses to exit his sand-battered shelter, allowing the sand to bury him alive.

The title of the novella, *Sand Burial*, does not refer only to the desert burial of the "politically incorrect" Han desert plant researcher, forced into reeducation by labor by pulling the harrow to gather vegetation for the profligate burning by village Party elites. Nor does it refer only to the suffocation of the "politically incorrect" Mongolian lama, forced to pull the harrow, painfully kneel during public criticism sessions, and give up his beloved dog, all because he was said to be hiding golden religious statues. Nor does it refer to the imminent sandstorm burial of the scientist's "politically correct" but guilt-stricken ex-wife and the lama's loyal wolf-dog. Instead the Anthropocene suggests that human existence is so malignant that life itself faces planetary extinction. This changes the topical foci. The political camps of the Cultural Revolution, the ecological differences between Buddhism and Han rationalism, the distinctions between human and nonhuman animals, pale in comparison to this stark fact. As Povinelli puts it, "Increasingly not only can critical theorists not demonstrate the superiority of the human to other forms of life—thus the rise of posthumanist politics and theory—but they also struggle to maintain a difference that makes a difference between all forms of Life and the category of Nonlife."[45]

The indeterminate ending of *Sand Burial* means the birds, humans, and nonhuman animals that escape the lama's oxygen-deprived structure during the sandstorm may or may not survive the elements. Yet its message is bleak. Povinelli claims the figure of the desert maintains the distinction between life and nonlife by dramatizing life under threat from the creeping, dessicating sands of nonlife: "The Desert is the space where life was, is not now, but could be if knowledges, techniques, and resources were properly managed . . . the Carbon Imaginary lies at the heart of this figure."[46] Ultimately, *Sand Burial* calls the figure of the desert into question. It indulges the dream of the carbon imaginary—the final scene features hard-won expertise contained in hard-won documents transported by the desert researcher's ex-wife, supported by the wolf-dog through the sandstorm—the desert refusing to definitively kill her off as a third sand burial. Yet, as in Guo's other works, such figures call attention to themselves *as* figures. The desert biosphere is described in such utopian ways it resembles Tao Qian's

陶潛 (365–427) "Taohua yuan ji" 桃花源記 (Peach Blossom Spring), an agrarian fantasy if one ever existed.

Ecological Imperialism in *Wolf Totem*

If Mandumai's fiction critiques environmental racism and Guo Xuebo's fiction sublimates dynamics between indigenous and exogenous knowledge of ecosystems, Jiang Rong's *Wolf Totem* coopts indigenous knowledge to strengthen the center. The semiautobiographical, best-selling novel won the 2007 Man Asia Literary Prize, has been translated into more than thirty languages, and has been adapted to film. Set during the Cultural Revolution, it ostensibly criticizes Han insensitivity to ecological, religious, and cultural diversity, implying ignorance of the fragile ecosystem of the steppe destroys it. Yet detractors have denounced the work as didactic and even fascist. Like his novel, the past of Jiang Rong (pen name of Lü Jiamin) is mysterious and controversial. His father, a doctor of Chinese medicine, was denounced as a "black gang capitalist-roader" and beaten nearly to death during the Cultural Revolution. His mother worked with the CCP underground. Jiang was a Red Guard at Beijing Art Academy middle school before shepherding in IMAR. Imprisoned in 1970 for criticizing Lin Biao, his death sentence was commuted. He was active in the 1978 Beijing Spring, was imprisoned after the 1989 Tiananmen Square protests, and then taught political science in Beijing.[47]

The novel follows the exploits of Chen Zhen and Yang Ke, two sent-down youth from Beijing who develop a deep appreciation of Mongolian culture during their decade-long stay with the nomads. Old Bilgee, his daughter-in-law, and his grandson embody qualities they most admire: experiential knowledge of the grassland ecosystem, courage, and resilience. The major themes center on ethnic difference between Han agrarian and Mongolian grassland philosophy: Han Chinese are "sheeplike," while Mongolians are "wolflike"; Han are secular materialists, while Mongolian Lamaists revere Tengger (Tengri); Han are scientific rationalists, while Mongolians are holistic, if superstitious.

The novel has been critiqued for its allegedly eugenicist views, reinforced by chapter epigraphs (in the Chinese version) offering historical "evidence" of the Mongolian racial character. To be a Mongol, Chen Zhen tells Yang Ke, "all you need is an infusion of wolf blood. Hybrids are always superior creatures."[48] The Han are said to "meekly submit" to a "Dragon King" (versus a Wolf Totem) (33; 23) and greedily kill wolves, dogs, gazelles, marmots, and swans. *Wolf Totem* seemingly criticizes the Han as weak, narrow-minded, cruel, and ignorant. Yet it also attributes the historical agency of Genghis Khan and the Mongols to their wolf mentors (57; 36).

Many Mongol scholars are outraged at the novel's primary trope, the wolf totem, saying nomads are more likely to shoot wolves than worship them. In contrast, Mandumai pointedly identifies the cairn (Mn. *oboo*; Ch. *aobao* 敖包) as the Mongolian totem in a 2013 book of essays on Mongol ecological civilization.[49] Guo criticized *Wolf Totem* after its 2015 adaptation to film:

> Wolves have never been a Mongolian totem, the Mongolian nationality has absolutely no historical records of this! This is a false Mongolian cultural framing by a Han sent-down youth who only lived on the grasslands for three years. Mongolians initially believed in Shamanism and later in Buddhism. Wolves were considered the natural enemies of Mongolians. Wolves don't exhibit "team spirit." They are selfish, greedy, ruthless, and cruel. To preach "wolf spirit" is antihuman, fascist thought.
>
> 狼從來不是蒙古人圖騰。蒙古所有文史中從未記載過狼為圖騰！這是一漢族知青在草原只待三年，生生嫁禍蒙古人的偽文化！蒙古人最早信薩滿後佛教。狼是蒙古人生存天敵，狼並無團隊精神，兩窩狼死磕，狼貪婪自私冷酷殘忍，宣揚狼精神是反人類法西斯思想。[50]

Guo's critique is valid. Jiang juxtaposes accepted Han cultural tropes against fabricated ones, notably Yellow River aphorisms by "the Chinese race" and reverence for the wolf totem by "grasslanders":

> After thousands of years, during which unknown numbers of minor races had died out or were violently displaced, the grasslanders would never question their predatory totem, which would remain their sole icon even after killing seventy or eighty fine horses. Chen was reminded of the sayings "The Yellow River causes a hundred calamities but enriches all it touches"; "When the Yellow River overflows its banks, the people become fish and turtles"; "The Yellow River—cradle of the Chinese race." The Chinese would never deny that the Yellow River was the cradle of the Chinese race or that it was crucial to the survival and development of their race even if it sometimes overflows its banks and swallows up acres of cropland and thousands of lives. The grasslanders' wolf totem deserved to be revered in the same manner.
>
> 草原民族的獸族圖騰，經歷了幾千年不知多少個民族滅亡和更替的劇烈顛簸，依然一以貫之，延續至今，當然不會被眼前這七八十匹駿馬的死亡所動搖。陳陣突然想到：「黃河百害，惟富一套。」「黃河決堤，人或為魚鱉。」「黃河——中華民族的搖籃……」中華民族並沒有因為黃河百害，吞沒了無數農田和千萬生命，而否認黃河是中華民族的母親河。看來「百害」和「母親」可以並存，關鍵在於「百害的母親」是否養育了這個民族的生存和發展。草原民族的狼圖騰，也應該像中華民族的母親河那樣得到尊重。(90–91; 57)

This false equivalency is problematic on several counts. First, a majority writer manipulates historical fact about a minority nationality while the narrative voice presents it as factual: the power differential makes false narratives difficult to contest once propagated in the popular imagination. Second, it both praises and denigrates minority culture as other-than-human hybrid. Finally, the "wolf totem" rationalizes the suffering of indigenes in IMAR due to state development just as the state has long evoked the "Yellow River totem" to normalize the suffering of Chinese peasants. Such evolutionary musings rationalize the annihilation of Mongolian culture in much the same way that white Americans adopted eugenics ideas to romanticize the diminishing populations of Native Americans.

The novel attributes desertification to Han agrarian logic, but the grasslands and Mongol customs become decimated nonetheless, and Old Bilgee's folk wisdom is nostalgically conveyed as inadequate to a scientific era. Indigenous knowledge is instead coopted by Han rationality. Chen Zhen coins the term *grassland logic* (which "intrigues" his Mongol friend) as a hybrid between Mongol eco-centrism and Han science. In fact, the novel's central question is how to save the Han empire. Halfway through the novel Chen Zhen asks what will happen to Beijing if desertification occurs north of the Great Wall (258; 164). The apocalyptic epilogue set in 2002 declares that 80 percent of the Olonbulag pastureland is desert and that China's imperial city is a hazy city of yellow sand (524; 408).

In a Confucian metaphysical cosmology, the solution to a weak center is to energize it from the periphery.[51] As IMAR scholar Nassan Bayar quips, "One Inner Mongolian told me once after reading *Wolf Totem* he realized that the Mongolians had become Viagra for the Chinese!"[52] This raises the question of whether *Wolf Totem*, as Sinologist Wolfgang Kubin has argued, is a fascist novel. In 2017 I conducted a series of interviews with five Inner Mongolian academics who each received their doctorates at prestigious universities in England, Japan, and Taiwan and who specialize in Mongolian sociology, religion, and literature.[53] I asked them about their understanding of the novel and specifically its nationalist implications. One said that *Wolf Totem* promotes Chinese nationalism by encouraging more "wolflike" Mongol aggressiveness. He compared the novel to the 1980s TV drama *Heshang* 河殤 (River Elegy), which he said claims Chinese civilization is too modest and insular but should instead expand outward, like colonizing Westerners. Another commented on the novel's gender politics, claiming only the elder, Bilgee, and his daughter-in-law, Gasmai, were heroic, while the young Mongolian men were less impressive. Another academic liked the novel, seeing it as cathartic for a traumatized author witnessing desertification of the cherished landscape of his youth, even if his understanding of Mongol culture was inauthentic. Yet another claimed it was an Orientalist exaggeration of Mongol eco-consciousness:

> Why was *Wolf Totem* so famous? It was a Han writer writing about Mongolian culture for a Han audience. . . . It emphasized the need for the Han race to

strengthen itself and expand outward, in order to use wolf spirit to overcome domestic and international relations. I felt both proud and very embarrassed.

為什麼《狼圖騰》那麼出名，它是漢族作家寫蒙古族的故事講給漢族聽……一方面是環境保護和人與生態之際和諧的關係的需求，另一方面他是不是要強調一個漢族一定要怎樣強大起來，怎樣往外，用狼的精神去克服目前這個國際國內各種各樣的地位的問題呢？一方面覺得很自豪，又另一方面覺得很不好意思。

While individual opinions of the novel differed, the consensus was that although the novel raises awareness of ecologically responsible Mongolian practices, it ultimately denigrates the culture as inadequate to facing the challenges of the twenty-first century. The Han Chinese, with their scientific rationalism, must adapt Mongolian "grassland logic" to effective ecological solutions and infuse Mongolian "wolflike spirit" into their developmental agendas. Several recommended comparing *Wolf Totem* to eco-literature by Mandumai and Guo Xuebo.

Conclusion

Mongolian nomads may be celebrated in films and narratives of the Chinese nation, but their sacred sites are not honored and their land rights are minimal. Indigenes are elevated to accomplish other aims, such as energizing state nationalism by incorporating peripheral areas into the Chinese nation. In this sense, Jiang Rong's eco-novel is a "Beijing Western" that maps Hanspace cosmologies onto exotic peripheries to rationalize development and inspire Han nationalism based on so-called ecological civilization (*shengtai wenming* 生態文明). One of twelve provinces slated in 2000 for "western development" (*xibu dakaifa* 西部大開發), IMAR has become a site of bioprospecting and mining on unprecedented scales. Chinese researchers understood the severity of IMAR desertification but insisted on implementing "environmentally friendly production" (*huanbao shengchan* 環保生產) throughout the province.[54]

Such absorption of the "indigenous-environmentalist" alliance into the nation-state is occurring on a global scale. Geontopower manifests as governments worldwide safeguard what they deem to be their indigenous knowledge by guarding against biopiracy and bioprospecting from outsiders. Whereas previously Brazil's nationalists viewed Amazonia's indigenous populations as suspicious outsiders, now they are increasingly included in the Brazilian nation and identified as strategic partners in efforts to regulate bioprospecting in the national interest.[55] In 2009 Bolivia approved a constitution that extends rights not only to indigenes but also the earth and, "in seeking to reappropriate control of the nation's resources from foreign corporations, has itself come into conflict with the communities it originally empowered."[56]

The calculus of "humans versus rocks" is increasingly indeterminate. For example, in 2011 a herding activist was run over by a truck while attempting to block a coal transport caravan trespassing on IMAR pastureland. Infuriated cyberactivists called for May 10 to be declared "Herders' Rights Day."[57] The government publicly denounces such atrocities but fails to act. Instead intensified censorship since Xi Jinping's 習近平 (1953–) appointment as president and general secretary of the CCP in 2012 has significantly curbed protests. Zhao Liang 趙亮 (1971–) only managed to produce his apocalyptic environmental film *Beixi moshou* 悲兮魔獸 (Behemoth, 2015) in IMAR through what he calls guerrilla filmmaking. The film depicts once-thriving grasslands ravaged due to intensive coal mining, with miners dying of black lung disease, the most prevalent occupational disease in China. Zhao claims he had to film surreptitiously: "These coal mine owners are so rich you can't bribe them to solve your problems."[58] *Behemoth* is not permitted to be screened in the PRC.

While agrilogistics prevails at present, writers such as Guo Xuebo powerfully unleash the possibilities of dark ecology by conveying indigenous knowledge that acknowledges the carbon imaginary of the desert *as* mere figure. Guo's desert fiction exposes fault lines in the indigene-environmental alliance based on "rights" discourses that abstract "nature" or "indigeneity" or "ethnicity." Instead he foregrounds the violence inherent in agrilogistics. Like *Behemoth*, Guo's most recent novel, *Mengu liya* 蒙古里亞 (Mongoliya, 2014), attempts to broach taboo subjects such as the exploitation of pasturelands by ruthless coal mining firms and self-immolation among ethnic minorities to protest policies aimed at acculturation. It features the narrator's spiritual quest for his shamanic roots; adventures of Henning Haslund-Christensen, born in 1896 to a Danish missionary family in the Chahar grasslands (and author of the anthropological masterpiece *Men and Gods in Mongolia*); and a twenty-first-century Mongol herdsman threatened by desertification and a coal mining company that covets Mongolian pastureland. Translator Bruce Humes suggests it is only because of its carnivalesque tone that the novel avoided censorship.[59]

Mandumai's eco-fiction is contradictory for different reasons. Working within the more narrow confines of political correctness, it both censures and enacts anthropocentrism and environmental racism (self-orientalism). Such contradictions are precisely those sublimated in his stories by the eventual Buddhist unity of provisional and ultimate truth. His moralistic vignettes aim at enlightening readers to regain ecological balance by cultivating virtues of moderation and inner purity, including compassion toward animals and women. At the same time, they contradict their formal (Party) objectives in their bleak portrayal of irreversible extinction and merciless cruelty.

Indigenous writers tend to acknowledge the fact that, in a post-extinction world, distinctions between life and nonlife no longer matter in regimes governed by geontopower. Mandumai's dialectical Buddhism purifies humanity by transmuting it in the face of impending annihilation for ecological sins. Guo Xuebo's radical eco-critique favors no one, but his dark ecology suggests a possible upside: the Anthropocene has a way of leveling distinctions. Jiang Rong's agrarian ontology of biopower, on the other hand, maintains the civilizational illusion that if farmers enervated China into the sick man (of Asia), grafting the wolf-nomad onto the national body can revitalize it by bordering, bioprospecting, and consuming its diverse nationalities, lands, resources, and customs.

ROBIN VISSER is associate professor at the University of North Carolina at Chapel Hill. She is author of *Cities Surround the Countryside: Urban Aesthetics in Postsocialist China* (2010) and numerous translations and articles on Chinese and Taiwanese literature, environmental humanities, urban cultural studies, art, and cinema. She received a 2017–18 National Humanities Center Fellowship for current research on Sinophone eco-literature.

Notes

1 Mizoguchi, "China as Method," 516.
2 Povinelli, *Geontologies*, 13.
3 Bello coins this term in *Across Forest, Steppe, and Mountain*.
4 Alberts coins this expression and historicizes the alliance in *Shamanism, Discourse, Modernity*.
5 I analyze post-Mao eco-fiction by sent-down youth in "Anthropocosmic Resonance." IMAR eco-stories featuring Han sent-down youth include Ma Bo's memoir, *Blood Red Sunset*, and Liu Cixin's science-fiction novel *The Three-Body Problem*.
6 For example, a leading Han eco-critic, Wang Nuo, draws heavily upon Aldo Leopold's ideas in his influential book, *Shengtai piping yu shengtai sixiang*. Yet Miles Powell, in *Vanishing America*, argues Leopold was a white supremacist who adapted Nazi eugenics ideologies to conservation theories.
7 Bello, *Across Forest, Steppe, and Mountain*, 128.
8 Ibid., 129; Shoudu Jingji Maoyi Daxue ketizu, "Xibu dakaifa," 25–26.
9 Bello, *Across Forest, Steppe, and Mountain*, 150.
10 White, "Transforming China's Desert," 8.
11 L. Zhang, *River, the Plain, and the State*, 20.
12 Bulag, *Mongols at China's Edge*, 6.
13 Alberts, *Shamanism, Discourse, Modernity*, 100.
14 UN Report on Indigenous Populations, para. 65, qtd. in Alberts, ibid., 104.
15 Ibid., 99.
16 Bergeton, *Emergence of Civilizational Consciousness*, 163, 201.
17 Wang F., "Han Zhao Di," 1:75.
18 Bulag, *Mongols at China's Edge*, 6.
19 Lu Xun, "Suibian fanfan." Qtd. in Bulag, *Mongols at China's Edge*, 6. Also A. Wang, "Sino-Mongolian Contention," 359.
20 Bayar, "Discourse of Civilization," 449.
21 Di Cosmo, *Ancient China and Its Enemies*, 57.

22 Bayar, "Discourse of Civilization," 451.
23 Ibid, 453.
24 Povinelli, *Geontologies*, 5.
25 Ibid., 9.
26 Wu Lan, "Zhi duzhe," 1:i.
27 Bulag, *Mongols at China's Edge*, 189.
28 Jiang, *Wolf Totem*, 377.
29 Powell, *Vanishing America*, 147.
30 Mandumai, *Junma, canglang, guxiang*, 1:12. Subsequent page references to *Junma, canglang, guxiang* are given parenthetically in the text.
31 Cao Yu, *Wang Zhaojun*, 55.
32 Qtd. in Duara, *Rescuing History from the Nation*, 59.
33 Merchant, *Death of Nature*, 3.
34 Pedersen, *Not Quite Shamans*, 217.
35 Many eco-critics locate the origins of a Han aesthetics of nature in the *Shijing*. See Zeng, *Shengtai meixue daolun*; Chen, *Chinese Environmental Aesthetics*; Thornber, "Environments of Early Chinese"; and Elvin, *Retreat of the Elephants*.
36 Anthropocosmic "resonance" (*ganying* 感應) posits that humans are in a mutually dependent relationship with the world. Confucian resonance theories are one of the three most important ecological cosmologies that still influence Han Chinese today (along with Buddhist compassion and an image of power that radiated from the margins to the center). See Weller, *Discovering Nature*, 23–25; Tu, "Beyond the Enlightenment Mentality"; and Visser, "Anthropocosmic Resonance."
37 For example, Liu Shi claims Mandumai is warning wolves not to behave like humans in "Deep in the Woods," and Guo Peng interprets "The Four-Eared Wolf and the Hunter" via Mencian ideas about compassion for animals. See Ma Mingkui, *Youmu wenming*, 171–72, 181.
38 Śāntarakṣita, *Adornment of the Middle Way*, 304.
39 Chimedsengee et al., *Mongolian Buddhists Protecting Nature*, 15.
40 Ji, "Spring on the Horqin Sandland," 348.
41 Morton, *Dark Ecology*, 23.
42 Ibid., 43.
43 Ibid.
44 Guo, *Desert Wolf*, 86; Guo, *Damo hun*, 84. Subsequent page references are given in text, respectively, to *The Desert Wolf* and *Damo hun*.
45 Povinelli, *Geontologies*, 14.
46 Ibid., 16.
47 "Living with Wolves."
48 Jiang and Goldblatt, *Wolf Totem*, 34; Jiang, *Lang tuteng*, 23. Subsequent page references are given in text, respectively, to *Wolf Totem* and *Lang tuteng*.
49 Mandumai, *Aobao*.
50 Zhang N., "Mengguzu zuojia pi *Lang tuteng*."
51 See Weller, *Discovering Nature*, and Harrell, "Role of the Periphery."
52 Bayar, "Discourse of Civilization," 452.
53 Interview subjects' names have been removed to protect their anonymity. Transcripts of interviews are on file with the author.
54 Li, "Xibu dakaifa."
55 Alberts, *Shamanism, Discourse, Modernity*, 205.

56 Heise, *Imagining Extinction*, 90.

57 Bello, *Across Forest, Steppe, and Mountain*, 266.

58 Qtd. in Qin, "As China Hungers for Coal."

59 Humes, "'Mongol Would-Be Self-Immolator.'"

References

Alberts, Thomas Karl. *Shamanism, Discourse, Modernity*. London: Ashgate, 2015.

Bayar, Nasan. "A Discourse of Civilization/Culture and Nation/Ethnicity from the Perspective of Inner Mongolia, China." *Asian Ethnicity* 15, no. 4 (2014): 439–57.

Bello, David Anthony. *Across Forest, Steppe, and Mountain: Environment, Identity and Empire in Qing China's Borderlands*. New York: Cambridge University Press, 2016.

Bergeton, Uffe. *The Emergence of Civilizational Consciousness in Early China: History Word by Word*. London and New York: Routledge, 2018.

Bulag, Uradyn Erden. *The Mongols at China's Edge: History and the Politics of National Unity*. Lanham, MD: Rowman and Littlefield, 2002.

Cao Yu 曹禺. *Wang Zhaojun*. 王昭君 [Wang Zhaojun]. *Renmin wenxue* 人民文學 [People's Literature], no. 11 (1978): 37–111.

Chen, Kuan-Hsing. *Asia as Method: Towards Deimperliazation*. Durham, NC: Duke University Press, 2010.

Chen, Wangheng. *Chinese Environmental Aesthetics*, translated by Feng Su, edited by Gerald Cipriani. London: Routledge, 2015.

Chimedsengee, Urantsatsral, Amber Cripps, Victoria Finlay, Guido Verboom, Batchuluun Ven Munkhbaatar, and Da Lama Byambajav Khunkhur. *Mongolian Buddhists Protecting Nature: A Handbook on Faiths, Environment and Development*. Bath: Alliance of Religions and Conservation, 2009.

Di Cosmo, Nicola. *Ancient China and Its Enemies: The Rise of Nomadic Power in East Asian History*. Cambridge: Cambridge University Press, 2002.

Duara, Prasenjit. *Rescuing History from the Nation: Questioning Narratives of Modern China*. Chicago: University of Chicago Press, 1995.

Elvin, Mark. *The Retreat of the Elephants: An Environmental History of China*. New Haven: Yale University Press, 2004.

Guo Xuebo 郭雪波. *Damo hun* 大漠魂 [Desert Soul]. Beijing: Zhongguo wenlian chubanshe, 2002.

Guo Xuebo 郭雪波. *The Desert Wolf*, translated by Ma Ruofen. Beijing: Chinese Literature Press, 1996.

Harrell, Steven. "The Role of the Periphery in Chinese Nationalism." In *Imagining China: Regional Division and National Unity*, edited by Shu-min Huang and Cheng-kuang Hsu, 139–43. Nankang, Taiwan: Institute of Ethnology, Academia Sinica, 1999.

Heise, Ursula. *Imagining Extinction: The Cultural Meanings of Endangered Species*. Chicago: University of Chicago Press, 2016.

Humes, Bruce. "'The Mongol Would-Be Self-Immolator,' An Excerpt from Guo Xuebo's 'Moŋgoliya.'" February 1, 2018. bruce-humes.com/archives/12016.

Ji Cheng. "Spring on the Horqin Sandland." In Guo, *Desert Wolf*, 348–54.

Jiang Rong 姜戎. *Lang tuteng* 狼圖騰 [Wolf Totem]. Wuhan: Changjiang wenyi chubanshe, 2004.

Jiang, Rong 姜戎. *Wolf Totem: A Novel*, translated by Howard Goldblatt. New York: Penguin Group, 2009.

Li Xianglan 李香蘭. “Xibu dakaifa yu Nei Menggu huanbao chanye de fazhan.” 西部大開發與內蒙古環保產業的發展 [Western Development and the Development of Environmental Protection Industries in Inner Mongolia]. *Nei Menggu Daxue xuebao* 內蒙古大學學報 [Journal of Inner Mongolia University] 34, no. 5 (2002): 19–24.

Liu Cixin. *The Three-Body Problem*, translated by Ken Liu. New York: Tor Books, 2016.

“Living with Wolves.” *Guardian*, November 22, 2007. theguardian.com/world/2007/nov/22/china.features11.

Lu Xun 魯迅. “Suibian fanfan” 随便翻翻 [A Random Glance]. In *Qiejie ting zawen ji* 且介亭雜文集 [Essays from the Qiejie Pavilion]. Shanghai: Sanxian Shuwu, 1937.

Ma Bo. *Blood Red Sunset: A Memoir of the Chinese Cultural Revolution*, translated by Howard Goldblatt. New York: Penguin Books, 1996.

Ma Mingkui 馬明奎, ed. *Youmu wenming de yousi* 遊牧文明的憂思 [Troubled Thoughts on Nomadic Civilization]. Hohhot: Neimenggu chuban jituan, yuanfang chubanshe, 2013.

Mandumai 滿都麥. *Aobao: Caoyuan shengtai wenming de shouhu shen—Youmu wenhua ganwu lu* 敖包：草原生態文明的守護神——遊牧文化感悟錄 [Cairns: Protector Spirits of Grassland Ecological Civilization—On Nomadic Cultural Sensibilities]. Hulunbuir: Neimenggu chuban jituan, 2013.

Mandumai 滿都麥. *Junma, canglang, guxiang* 駿馬・蒼狼・故鄉 [Horse, Wolf, Home], 2 vols. Beijing: Zuojia chubanshe, 2015.

Merchant, Carolyn. *The Death of Nature: Women, Ecology, and the Scientific Revolution*. New York: HarperCollins, 1980.

Mizoguchi Yūzō. “China as Method.” *Inter-Asia Cultural Studies* 17, no. 4 (2016): 513–18.

Morton, Timothy. *Dark Ecology: For a Logic of Future Coexistence*. New York: Columbia University Press, 2016.

Pedersen, Morton. *Not Quite Shamans: Spirit Worlds and Political Lives in Northern Mongolia*. Ithaca, NY: Cornell University Press, 2011.

Povinelli, Elizabeth A. *Geontologies: A Requiem to Late Liberalism*. Durham, NC: Duke University Press, 2016.

Powell, Miles. *Vanishing America: Species Extinction, Racial Peril, and the Origins of Conservation*. Cambridge, MA: Harvard University Press, 2016.

Qin, Amy. “As China Hungers for Coal, ‘Behemoth’ Studies the Ravages at the Source.” *New York Times*, December 28, 2015. www.nytimes.com/2015/12/29/world/asia/china-film-zhao-liang-inner-mongolia-coal-behemoth.html.

Śāntarakṣita. *The Adornment of the Middle Way: Shantarakshita's Madhyamakalankara with Commentary by Jamgon Mipham*. Boston: Shambhala, 2005.

Shoudu Jingji Maoyi Daxue ketizu 首都經濟貿易大學課題組 [Capital University of Economics and Business Research Group]. “Xibu dakaifa zhong shengtai baohu jianshe ji jinrong zhichi wenti yanjiu—Jing Meng liangdi anli fenxi” 西部大開發中生態保護建設及金融支持問題研究——京蒙兩地案例分析 [Environmental Protection Measures and Financial Support for the Great Western Development: Analysis of Beijing and Inner Mongolia as Two Cases]. *Jingji yanjiu cankao* 經濟研究參考 [Economic Research] 24, no. 8 (2002): 25–33.

Thornber, Karen. “Environments of Early Chinese and Japanese Literatures.” In *A Global History of Literature and the Environment*, edited by John Parham and Louise Westling, 37–51. Cambridge: Cambridge University Press, 2016.

Tu, Weiming. “Beyond the Enlightenment Mentality.” In *Confucianism and Ecology: The Interrelationship of Heaven, Earth, and Humans*, edited by Mary Evelyn Tucker and John

Berthrong, 17–19. Cambridge, MA: Harvard University for the Study of World Religions, 1998.
Van Dooren, Thom. *Flight Ways: Life and Loss at the Edge of Extinction*. New York: Columbia University Press, 2014.
Visser, Robin. "Anthropocosmic Resonance in Post-Mao Chinese Environmental Literature." *Wenyi lilun yanjiu* 文藝理論研究 [Theoretical Studies in Literature and Art] 33, no. 4 (2013): 34–44.
Wang, Anran. "The Sino-Mongolian Contention over the Legacy of Chinggis Khan." *Studies in Ethnicity and Nationalism* 16, no. 3 (2016): 357–77.
Wang Fuzhi 王夫之. "Han Zhao Di" 漢昭帝 [Han Emperor Zhao]. In *Dutong jianlun* 讀通鑒論 [On *Zizhi Tongjian*], *juan* 4, 1:74–76. Beijing: Zhonghua shuju, 1975.
Wang Nuo 王諾. *Shengtai piping yu shengtai sixiang* 生態批評與生態思想 [Ecological Criticism and Ecological Thought]. Beijing: Renmin chubanshe, 2013.
Weller, Robert P. *Discovering Nature: Globalization and Environmental Culture in China and Taiwan*. New York: Cambridge University Press, 2006.
White, Thomas Richard Edward. "Transforming China's Desert: Camels, Pastoralists and the State in the Reconfiguration of Western Inner Mongolia." PhD diss, University of Cambridge, 2016.
Wu Lan 烏蘭. "Zhi duzhe" 致讀者 [To the Reader]. In Mandumai, *Junma, canglang, guxiang* 駿馬・蒼狼・故鄉 [Horse, Wolf, Home], 1:i–ii. Beijing: Zuojia chubanshe, 2015.
Zeng Fanren 曾繁仁. *Shengtai meixue daolun* 生態美學導論 [Introduction to Ecological Aesthetics]. Beijing: Shangwu yinshu guan, 2010.
Zhang, Ling. *The River, the Plain, and the State: An Environmental Drama in Northern Song China, 1048–1128*. Cambridge: Cambridge University Press, 2016.
Zhang Nan 張楠. "Mengguzu zuojia pi *Lang tuteng*: Lang conglai bushi Mengguren tuteng" 蒙古族作家批《狼圖騰》：狼從來不是蒙古人圖騰 [Mongol Author Criticizes *Wolf Totem*: Wolves Have Never Been a Mongol Totem]. *Fenghuang* 鳳凰 [Phoenix], February 25, 2015. js.ifeng.com/humanity/cul/detail_2015_02/25/3582365_0.shtml.

LORRAINE WONG

Cannibalism as Method

ABSTRACT *Tian yu di* 天與地 (When Heaven Burns, 2011), a primetime television series that was screened in Hong Kong from November 2011 to January 2012, tells the story of a young rock band struggling with the memory of having eaten a fellow bandmate in order to survive a mountaineering accident. Cannibalism not only bewildered the mainstream TV audience, but it was also viewed as an allusion to the June Fourth crackdown on the Tiananmen student movement. This essay explores cannibalism as a method that questions the assimilation of Hong Kong into the national body politic of China. Its argument is twofold. First, cannibalism in this drama disrupts the bourgeois consciousness of a healthy subject, exploring a shattered but renewed life that questions the dissolution of food in the making of a healthy subject. Second, by challenging the bourgeois model of a reconciled body, this drama series throws critical light on Hong Kong's coerced "swallowing" of a China excessive in its material aggrandizement, restoring the power of imagination of possible futures not dictated by Hong Kong's increasing integration with China. Finally, this essay suggests that cannibalism, viewed through the Tiananmen legacy, may function as a method to explore modes of relationality between Hong Kong and Mainland China.

KEYWORDS cannibalism, TV drama series, Tiananmen student movement, June Fourth crackdown, Hong Kong–Mainland China integration

Tian yu di 天與地 (When Heaven Burns, 2011) is a primetime television series that was screened in Hong Kong from November 2011 to January 2012. Alternating between 1992 and 2010, *Tian yu di* tells the story of a rock band composed of four good friends—Ka-ming, Angus, Joe, and Ronnie. Having tried without success to make a name for themselves, the four youngsters decide in 1992 to make a mountaineering trip up to the Tianshan 天山 Mountains and bring their musical career to a close by attending the rock festival there. The journey takes an unexpected turn, however, when the group becomes lost in the snow and Ka-ming is severely injured. Desperate, the three remaining bandmates decide to kill Ka-ming and consume his flesh, in hopes that this will enable them to survive until they are rescued. The majority of the drama then focuses on the three surviving bandmates and Ka-ming's former girlfriend, Yan, as they struggle, eighteen years later, to deal with the memory of this traumatic event.

Tian yu di is classified as a *shenju* 神劇 (godly drama series)[1] by netizens, who appreciate the way it tells a story that is different from typical soap operas.

PRISM: THEORY AND MODERN CHINESE LITERATURE • 16:2 • OCTOBER 2019
DOI 10.1215/25783491-7978523 •

The work is also considered to be an allegory of the Tiananmen Square crackdown on June Fourth in 1989. This reading is specific to the generation of Hong Kong people whose sense of Chinese national identity and ethical righteousness materialized in their compassion for the students who sacrificed their lives in the Tiananmen student movement, as well as in their condemnation of what they saw as a cold-blooded regime that shot its own people to death. In the memorials for the Tiananmen student movement held in the run-up to 1997, *xue nongyu shui* 血濃於水 (blood is thicker than water), a slogan that suggests Hong Kong people's blood tie with the student victims, was often held to be the reason for Hong Kong people to remember resolutely this pro-democracy movement and its violent crackdown, as another slogan, *wuwang liusi* 毋忘六四 (never forget June Fourth), suggests. Seen through this Tiananmen legacy, cannibalism in *Tian yu di* can be read as a moral indictment of the self-violation of the Chinese national body; yet its theoretical implications for Hong Kong's subjectivity have yet to be understood. Written and produced in 2009, *Tian yu di* aired on Channel Jade of Television Broadcast Limited (TVB) after a delay of two years. As this drama was not released immediately after it had been completed, its references to union activities, legislature election, black market futures, and conservation campaigns were a bit dated. However, *Tian yu di* helps us understand post-handover Hong Kong precisely because it goes beyond a mere representational relationship to reality and instead explores issues of time, subjectivity, and moral feelings anchored in the Tiananmen legacy.

Under the arrangement between the Chinese and British governments, it was agreed that from 1997 to 2047 Hong Kong would operate under a "one country, two systems" framework with a "high degree of autonomy" 高度自治.[2] This fifty-year period constitutes a historical threshold of uncertainty and restlessness, as Hong Kong is changing its identity from a British colony to a special administrative region (SAR) under the People's Republic of China (PRC). As a cultural text, *Tian yu di* illustrates this threshold experience, where the passing and emergent generations of Hong Kong people are connected via a living continuity of generative immediacy. Drawing upon the music of the 1990s Hong Kong pop-rock band Beyond, *Tian yu di* explores local community resistance in the 2010s, as well as linking this resistance to a reconfigured temporality and subjectivity.

This essay examines how cannibalism in *Tian yu di* breaks away from a binary understanding of the relationship between colonizer and colonized that has carried over from the era of British colonialism to post-handover Hong Kong, as seen in much of the scholarship dedicated to Hong Kong identity across the 1997 threshold.[3] With its metaphors of indigestion, excess, and vomit, cannibalism in this drama disrupts the bourgeois consciousness of a healthy subject, exploring a shattered but renewed life that questions the dissolution of food in the making of a healthy subject. Challenging the bourgeois model of a reconciliation of flesh and soul, cannibalism stages a scenario of Hong Kong's coerced "swallowing" of a China excessive in its material aggrandizement, a scenario that flips the unidirectional, oppressive flow of power from Mainland China to Hong Kong since the handover. As such, cannibalism is not merely a theme or a figure that metaphorizes the absorption of Hong Kong by Mainland China, the feeding off of a *tequ* 特區 (special administrative region) by the *zhongyang* 中央 (central government), or the incorporation of an internal colony by an alienated sovereign power. Instead it restores the power of imagination of possible futures not dictated by Hong Kong's increasing assimilation into China. The following article analyzes how cannibalism offers a method of exploring modes of relationality between Hong Kong and Mainland China along an open-ended historical horizon, a horizon that nevertheless remains from an earlier time of the Tiananmen student movement.

Television, Storytelling, and Hong Kong Subjectivity

Tian yu di was released just as the Hong Kong special administrative region (HKSAR) government was reviewing its broadcasting policy and considering more free-to-air TV licenses in addition to the two licenses held by TVB and Asia Television (ATV). The drama anchors Hong Kong's subjectivity in a site of cultural production, as the public was becoming increasingly aware of how creative and quality TV can cultivate their power to shape society. In its bid for a free-to-air TV transmission license, Hong Kong TV Network Limited (HKTV) steered public opinion to support its cause of media freedom.[4] Ricky Wong, the founder of HKTV, remarked that *Tian yu di* had a novel theme (cannibalism) but fell short of the serious and quality TV programming that Hong Kong people deserved and that HKTV aspired to produce.[5] Central to HKTV's publicity campaign was a heavy investment in producing what Wong claimed to be higher-quality drama than could be found on TVB. This ambition to use television serial dramas to tell stories differently won the support of the middle class and youth, who had become increasingly disenchanted with local television culture. The lure of alternative storytelling drew the middle class and youth back to local television culture, which was tantamount to reclaiming the power to interpret reality from the corporate and governmental ruling class.

HKTV's unsuccessful bid to secure the license led to a public outcry. As Lisa Yuk-ming Leung suggests, the campaign for a diverse TV culture was part of a series of social movements in the decades following the handover in 1997—including the Queen's Pier Preservation Campaign in 2005, the Choi Yuen Village/Anti-Express Rail Movement in 2009, and the Anti-national Education Campaign in 2012, which culminated in the Umbrella Movement in 2014.[6] *Tian yu di* was embedded within these struggles of the local community to shape their way of life and resist corporate and governmental authority.

Walter Benjamin suggests that humanity suffered from a decline of storytelling in the wake of World War I.[7] Post-1997 Hong Kong is not in the same war-torn situation that Benjamin refers to, but the field for stories is similarly sparse, as public attention is increasingly directed to economic growth and political obedience. As Tai-lok Lui reminds us, the HKSAR government primarily assesses the success of Hong Kong's integration into Mainland China on the basis of GDP, retail sales, and tourism—as if this were all a matter of abstract statistics.[8] What aims to facilitate capital flow, talent immigration, and real estate transactions between Mainland China and Hong Kong can end up removing the local community from the fraught ground of history, especially as the Beijing government aims to slot Hong Kong into a national framework. Storytelling serves to counter this disembedding of local livelihood from the messy historical ground of post-1997 Hong Kong.

In *Tian yu di*, storytelling does not belong to Joe, Angus, and Ronnie, who bury their youthful dreams from the 1990s and become silent about how they came into their current positions as a labor unionist, stockbroker, and actuary, respectively. Instead the power of storytelling resides with Yan, who was Kaming's girlfriend and now has a late night radio talk show. On her show, Yan recounts how

> When I was small my grandma liked to take me for tram rides. She liked to tell me what she could see as the tram went from the Western District, over Ngo Keng Bridge to King's Road, and then all the way to Shau Kei Wan. But that is not what I can see now. What was once a harbor strand has become blocks of buildings; what was known as Banyan Boulevard is now covered by billboards. Hasn't this city changed too quickly? When the next generation comes along, will they share our doubts? Nevertheless, we can still take comfort from the unchanged *ding-ding* of the tram. In my memory, my grandma liked watching the tram approach the terminal and then reverse direction. With just a simple change of the destination sign, the tram can get back on track again. I remember clearly how she remarked that the destination of one tram was the starting point of another. Life is the same way.
>
> 細個嘅時候，外婆好鍾意帶我搭電車。響佢口中，由西環去到鵝頸橋，之後轉上英皇道，或者嚟到筲箕灣，沿途嘅一切，都唔係我所見嘅嘢。響佢口中，本來嘅海皮邊，我只見到大厦。所謂嘅榕樹大路，除咗招牌，我一塊葉都見唔到。呢個城市會唔會變得太快咗啲呢？當年我哋嘅疑問，到我哋嘅下一代，會唔會又再出現呢？慶幸嘅係，呢種咁獨特嘅叮叮聲，始終無變。我記得我外婆話佢最鍾意望住架叮叮駛到總站，見到佢調轉頭，換個路牌，就可以重新開行。所以，我好記得佢話過，一班叮叮嘅總站，其實係另一班叮叮嘅起點。同做人無乜分別。[9]

Yan does not learn the truth of how Ka-ming died until eighteen years after the incident in question, though in the interim she had experienced as much pain as the three surviving bandmates. Melancholic yet resourceful, Yan stands her ground and fights for rock music in a society whose way of life is disappearing to make way for ruthless economic development. Just as British colonialism ended and Hong Kong began its new journey under Chinese jurisdiction (like the tram changing its destination sign), Yan and the three bandmates attempt to come to terms with the loss of their youthful dreams and the prospect of an unknown future. Yan serves as a storyteller who offers moral counsel through the medium of radio. Her stories contain a sort of wisdom distilled from experience, which can then be absorbed, reflected upon, and reciprocated by the listeners.

Not without commercial calculation, Ricky Wong strategized the production of a television drama in the belief that socially engaged and thought-provoking works can change the status quo of a monopolistic and hegemonic television culture. Free-to-air TV transmission helps fulfill the wish for storytelling that comes to articulate Hong Kong's emergent subjectivity, even though this fulfillment can also be compromised by the corporate and governmental forces that shape local television culture. In an interview, Chow Yuk Ming 周旭明, the scriptwriter for *Tian yu di*, suggested that television companies and television audiences share the responsibility for the quality of public discourse. He observed that, since the handover of Hong Kong in 1997, the outburst of protests and demonstrations against corporate power and governmental authority has turned reality into something more surreal and unbelievable than what can be seen on TV. Rather than assume that audiences have been duped into surrendering to the mainstream, hegemonic interpretation of reality as a result of the reflection of this reality on television, Chow instead maintains that TV dramas can provoke the audience to think critically (*shenshi* 審視) about the discrepancies between fictional representations and the social realities within which they are embedded.[10] *Tian yu di* reflects the changing television culture at a time when HKTV was aggressively recruiting creative and performative talents from TVB and promoting its alternative drama series, and when the middle class and youth were fighting for the power of telling the stories of Hong Kong.

Telling stories differently on television entails the cultivation of creative talent and thoughtful consumers. Rather than being a neutral medium of representation, television is the surreal post-1997 reality in which it is embedded. It can play a role in changing the reality of which it is simultaneously a representation, which is also why television is heavily censored. According to Leung, despite its failed bid for free-to-air TV transmission license, HKTV has recast a local Hong Kong identity in terms of creativity, freedom, and democracy by showing a commitment to produce dramas about politically sensitive and controversial issues.[11] Such an exercise of creativity, freedom, and democracy often frames Hong Kong as the "last bastion of democracy" in China under the "one country, two systems" framework; and such local identity construction often aims at an indigenous identity that is distinct from the one imposed by outside "colonial" powers—be they the British or Chinese governments.[12] Of course, the fight for democracy is an integral aspect of contemporary Hong Kong, but insofar as democracy has a universal dimension, it has a higher stake in shaping Hong Kong's *subjectivity* than as an ideological stand-in for an indigenous Hong Kong *identity*—the latter being a notion that perpetuates the view of a dichotomy between colonizer and colonized. Positioned in the 2010s television market competition—when more licenses are available for free-to-air TV transmission and its implications for democracy are uncertain—*Tian yu di* is a rich cultural text registering previously uncharted possibilities for Hong Kong subjectivity, especially as this drama explores the problem of how Hong Kong people can give substance to their subjectivity by incorporating—cannibalistically ingesting—the Tiananmen legacy into their core while simultaneously reaffirming the inherent distance of this legacy.

Cannibalistic Imagination and Hong Kong's Anti-Nationalism

According to Chow Yuk Ming, in late spring of 2009 (which was also the twentieth anniversary of the Tiananmen June Fourth crackdown), he had experienced a writer's block in finishing the script for *Tian yu di*. Having attended the annual candlelight vigil in Victoria Park commemorating the crackdown, Chow came to a sudden realization that he could give a "romantic tone" 一種浪漫的調子 to the theme of cannibalism in his story. For Chow and his executive producer, Jonathan Chik Gei-yee 戚其義, cannibalism is an everyday reality that people cannot simply shrug off in self-deception.[13] In fact the theme of cannibalism enabled Chow to break away from conventional local soap opera genres such as family feuds, revenge, and grievances and exercise his freedom as a TV producer to negotiate the boundary between an artwork and a commodity.[14] A few days after Chow's reflections appeared in *Ming Pao*, when the series had only four more episodes to air, Chinese censors ordered TVB's sub-licensees and online video companies in China to remove the series from their sites.

Instead of asking how this drama contravened the censors' code, a more interesting question would be how cannibalism may shed light on Hong Kong's antinationalism. In literary and artistic production, cannibalism may function as a metaphor for a self-destructive society whose members are feeding off one another. The consumption of the other with whom one shares a categorical tie interrogates the boundary between self and other and problematizes the hermeneutic process of discerning identity and alterity.[15] Figured on the threshold between inside and outside, cannibalism distributes cultural and human equivalence by separating those who reduce their own species to food and enter the realm of the inhuman. Writing at a time when China was transforming from an old empire into a modern nation, Lu Xun 魯迅 (1881–1936) problematized nationhood as a means for Chinese people to achieve humanity in the modern world. His writings importantly suggest that the horrific infringement of humanity not only occurs out there in a barbarous, unknown culture but can also happen in one's own national culture. His 1918 short story "Kuangren riji" 狂人日記 (Diary of a Madman) offers a comparative framework with which to understand the figure of cannibalism in *Tian yu di*. In his work Lu Xun blurs the distinction between the literal and metaphorical dimensions of cannibalism—which is to say, between the actual eating of human flesh recorded in Chinese history and the use of cannibalism to comment metaphorically on a self-destructive Chinese tradition. As the madman becomes aware that he is as responsible for the inhumanity of Chinese traditional culture as are his fellow villagers, he attempts to enlighten the villagers and liberate them from their state of primitive eating. Lu Xun, meanwhile, gave his body as a sacrificial offering for national enlightenment at this turn-of-the-century moment when the nation held out the promise of individual freedom from feudal clanship, familial authority, and colonial dominance and was also in the processes of aggressively incorporating individuals into its body politic. For Lu Xun, cannibalism denaturalizes the violence of nourishing a national body; contradictorily, in the hope of national enlightenment, Lu Xun's sacrificial offering also sanctions the violence of such political incorporation.

A cannibalistic national culture finds itself in a vicious circle of self-consumption. As Michel de Certeau suggests, human bodies give life to the law, and the law becomes real through human bodies.[16] In Lu Xun's story, the madman contests how Confucian tradition consumes the bodies of his countrymen and turns their lives into the surface on which the Confucian tradition is inscribed, and he tries to break the circle of the law by gesturing toward an open horizon of history—manifest in his cry to "save the children" (*jiujiu haizi* 救救孩子) at the end of the story.[17] How would the vision of national enlightenment become real if no human body gives it life? What would an embodied vision lead to, if not more repressed bodies? In another turn-of-the-century moment, *Tian yu di* offers a rebellious response to the nation as the law commanding collective embodiment.

Hong Kong's decolonization is premised on antinationalism. Critical scholarship suggests that the 1997 handover marked a change of "colonizers," where the PRC inherited oligarchic governance from the British colonial regime and recast this regressive regime as a postcolonial power bloc in the twenty-first century. This recasting leverages Hong Kong's global connectivity to advance China's national strength and undermine Hong Kong's local distinctiveness.[18] Focusing on the change of colonizers sidesteps the ambivalent political subjecthood of the Hong Kong people under the "one country, two systems" framework. The Basic Law—the mini-constitution of Hong Kong authorized by the Beijing government—lays down the rights and responsibilities of the residents of the HKSAR, comparable to the rights and responsibilities that citizens have in a nation-state. Hong Kong residents, as a matter of legal and institutional arrangement, do not have to fulfill the same obligations to the Chinese nation as other Chinese citizens—including paying taxes and serving in the army. While interest in Hong Kong citizenship is growing within the HKSAR, in China national politics remains dominated by the Chinese Communist Party (CCP), which strategically depoliticizes Hong Kong residents as the constituents of an economic city. Such political seclusion was envisaged in the "one country, two systems" design, with the aim of protecting Hong Kong from interference by the socialist state.[19]

In the 1980s, parallel to the dialogue between the Chinese and British governments about the 1997 handover, a countercurrent was developing as the colonial government introduced direct election into district boards and functional constituency election into the Legislative Council.[20] Hong Kong people sought to optimize the political space by the final decade of colonial rule to establish a democratic system of governance. Amid this trend toward democratization, Hong Kong people expected to "return" to the Mainland as full citizens bearing the political credentials and competencies to contribute to the wider democratization of China.[21] This is clearly shown in the enthusiastic support of Hong Kong people to the Tiananmen student movement in 1989, as well as in the annual commemoration of the June Fourth crackdown on the student movement thereafter. The crackdown increased the local desire for democracy and the growth of political consciousness, while also illustrating the Hong Kong people's dilemma as they negotiate their double identities as residents/citizens of Hong Kong and as Chinese nationals under the "one country, two systems" framework.

In the wake of the June Fourth crackdown, the Beijing government stanched the political and moral passion of Hong Kong for the Tiananmen student movement by suggesting that if Hong Kong people did not intervene in the internal affairs of the Mainland, the Beijing government would reciprocate by not intervening in Hong Kong's local governance. As the saying goes: "well water does not intrude in the river water" (*jingshui bufan heshui* 井水不犯河水). In this way, the Beijing government restricted the space for Hong Kong's political idealism to take root on historical ground and transform into solid political rights, limiting the opportunities for Hong Kong people to put into practice their political credentials and develop these credentials into the substance of Hong Kong subjectivity.

In a post-1997 context, locally oriented protest movements emphasizing self-governance and local community resistance instead of China's democratization have created a new generation of Hong Kong people who differentiate themselves from the "Tiananmen veterans."[22] The Tiananmen student movement, embedded in China's history of socialist nation-building, aimed at comprehensive national reform to fight corruption and to achieve political justice and economic equality, whereas the protest movements in post-1997 Hong Kong, embedded in the growth of political consciousness and local citizenship from the late 1980s, demand universal suffrage and autonomy in local governance, engage critically with economic and welfare policies, and explore local identity.[23] Whether it is mobilizing the Tiananmen legacy to support local community resistance or differentiating local community resistance from this legacy, the Hong Kong people are positioned in a crucial border zone where socialist history, liberal democracy, universal values, and emerging localism are interwoven in shaping change within China. These contact zones are a space where Hong Kong subjectivity emerges. In China, politics is evacuated of its diverse social content under the guise of the "people's" interest that is guaranteed by the authoritarian state. Situated in the contact zones of culture where the local, the national, and the universal intertwine with one another, Hong Kong holds out the possibility of reopening and expanding the political that has been foreclosed in Mainland China.

Cannibalism can be approached as a method that works through the contestation of equivalence and alterity between Hong Kong and Mainland China. In literary and cultural studies, cannibalism is often understood as a trope distinguishing primitive rituals from modern ethics, as a method for comparative, cross-cultural analysis or as a model of hermeneutical process that interrogates the boundary between self and other.[24] It is always inscribed on the thresholds between past and present, inside and outside, human and nonhuman. Yet cannibalism also places these thresholds under erasure by virtue of its status as a fluid space where the material and the semiotic coincide with and interrupt each other. Cannibalism problematizes the referential status of the human body by staging scenarios where the consumption of human flesh can also be something else—either a work of art, a performance, or an allegory that critiques how the powerless arc incorporated into the powerful. The mode of consumption in late capitalism is often understood to be gluttonous, raising the question of whether such metaphoric cannibalism makes us blind to the literal gruesomeness of mutual violation that happens in our time. As Richard King suggests, this contemporary emphasis on the metaphoric nature of cannibalism tends to flatten the power dynamics in late capitalism without advancing cultural critique.[25]

Tian yu di restores the social and moral significance of cannibalism in our time beyond metaphoric operation. There is conflicting evidence as to the precise number of lives lost in the June Fourth crackdown, but *Tian yu di* manages to squeeze out the emotions of an existential loss—be it the loss of Ka-ming as a loyal friend, Wong Ka kui as the talented musician of the rock band Beyond, or an innocent self committed to a utopian dream of freedom. Cannibalism in this drama recasts the Tiananmen legacy as an affective, lived, and everyday experience of loss, an experience that escapes the oppositional structure between a ruthless party-state and the unarmed civilian protesters. As a method, cannibalism not only expands the experiential dimension of the Tiananmen legacy in Hong

Kong, but it also flips over the flow of power from Mainland China to Hong Kong. In 1997 Ackbar Abbas predicted that "one country, two systems" would become one (capitalist) system at different stages of development, where the Chinese government would be relatively inexperienced in handling Hong Kong, as if it were "a gadget from the future."[26] As it turns out, since the handover Hong Kong has been in a defensive position, coping with socioeconomic changes orchestrated by the authoritarian state. Contrary to what was imagined in the pre-1997 period, China's market reform, which integrates socialism and capitalism into an authoritarian structure, has turned the nation into a global economic player determined to recast the world on its terms. China has grown along with the expansion of late capitalism, of which Hong Kong has been a part—shaping itself as that which is other than and more than Hong Kong. Cannibalism evokes the image of Hong Kong being coerced to devour not only its own self but also the other that is more "Hong Kong" in its exercise of capitalism. As such, it unfolds a social tapestry that lacks a preformed identity but calls for active constitution and shaping, like a human body turning into a mass of unidentified elements. Here the issue is not whether cannibalism is a mirror of or a metaphor for reality but how it functions as a method to help frame reality and open new horizons by breaking down preconceived boundaries. Cannibalism works as a method of conceptualization that dislodges dichotomous thinking (concerning indigeneity and colonization) in identity politics and prepares the ground for the formation of Hong Kong subjectivity.

The Tiananmen Legacy and Bourgeois Culture Inside Out

In *Tian yu di*, there is no explicit allusion to the Tiananmen student movement or the ensuing crackdown. However, the Tiananmen legacy enters this drama in ways that demand the audience's full engagement. Chow Yuk Ming, the scriptwriter, commented that "the story is a Hong Kong people's story" 這是個香港人的故事, while "the story of the [Tiananmen] square was a bit far away from us" 廣場上的故事對我們遠了一點.[27] His remark conjoins distance and interiorization and reveals the fraught emergence of Hong Kong subjectivity. As distant as the Tiananmen student movement may have seemed (both ideologically and geographically), in supporting the protesters' calls for democracy the Hong Kong people seek proximity with those protesters while also reaffirming their distance from them. The resulting dialectical relation between distance and interiorization, self and other, China and Hong Kong, allows us to go beyond a superficial reading of *Tian yu di* as an allegorical condemnation of the June Fourth military crackdown.

In China, the memory of the Tiananmen student movement and the June Fourth crackdown is suppressed so that the state's contribution to China's economic miracle and sheer material advancement can be validated; in *Tian yu di*, Ka-ming and his spirit are consumed in order for Joe, Angus, and Ronnie to emerge as members of Hong Kong's middle class during the 1997 period. The consumption of the spiritual by the animalistic bespeaks the fractured subjectivity of the middle class, whose political participation was increasingly important for shaping Hong Kong's future from the mid-1980s and whose hesitancy and vacillation makes it a problematic agent in politics.[28] On one hand, the Tiananmen student movement inspired political activists with middle-class backgrounds, whose belief in the mutual dependence of Hong Kong's autonomy and China's democracy can be traced back to the anticolonial movement in the 1970s.[29] Such radicalism of direct participation in China's politics was eventually obscured by the celebration of liberal democracy associated with party politics and electoral success, as well as by a focus on the Basic Law that was expected to permit the political maneuver of Hong Kong's democratization in a framework prescribed by China.[30] On the other hand, the middle class was skeptical about the viability of a liberal, autonomous, and capitalist Hong Kong after 1997.[31] The spate of community resistance movements led by a diverse group of students and young intellectuals since 2005, along with the contemporaneous financial crises and the devastation related to SARS in 2003, has unsettled the middle class and challenged it to shed its political timidity or its identity as what C. Wright Mills would call "rearguarders."[32] By telling the story of a lost and found youthful dream, *Tian yu di* reveals the socially emergent elements that are breaking out of middle-class values of economic and domestic security.

In *Tian yu di*, Ka-ming, Joe, Angus, and Ronnie, finding themselves at a crossroads in their lives in 1992, decided to disband. Had they had not gone to the Tianshan for the rock festival, they could have all climbed the social ladder and secured professional, administrative, or managerial positions. Rock music would have become nothing more than an amateur pursuit to spice up their monotonous, unimaginative bourgeois lifestyle. This alternative scenario is presented in the final episode, when Yan contemplates what life might have been like if the bandmates had never gone to the Tianshan. In the end, however, each of the three surviving bandmates is faced with a sort of karmic retribution. Joe is killed in an accident in the course of saving a child called Ka-ming from being hit by a car; Ronnie is going blind and is about to lose his actuarial qualification; while Angus remains lonely for the rest of his life. As in classical melodrama, moral adjudication assures the audience of psychological security in the face of capitalism's harsh realities.[33] One might even say that *Tian yu di* perpetuates bourgeois culture and fails to reveal the material and cultural struggles of the downtrodden. For instance, the midlife crises experienced by Joe, Angus, and Ronnie are manifested in their marital tensions, economic insecurity, and health problems, respectively. While this set of anxieties undermines bourgeois comfort, Yan's own bohemianism as an antibourgeois sensibility is somehow compromised by her bourgeois lifestyle and the fact that she drives a nice car.

These two contradictory examples suggest that bourgeois culture is fraught with tensions in *Tian yu di*, as the drama series shakes the middle class out of its complacency. Central to bourgeois culture is a gastronomic concern with nutritious ingredients, tasty meals, smooth digestion, and great recipes, which combines the instrumental reason of efficiency and reproducibility with an organic and beautiful human body.[34] In *Tian yu di*, Yan's ex-husband, Bowman, exemplifies the bourgeois celebration of stylish and pleasurable eating. Throughout the series, bourgeois dining and cannibalistic consumption are presented as opposed modes of incorporation: one mode affirms assimilation, health, and reproduction, while the other operates through indigestion, disgust, and vomit. These two modes of consumption are juxtaposed by means of temporal parallelism, suggestive editing, and innovative camera work.

For instance, early in the story there is a sequence where the specter of cannibalism floats in and out of Joe's, Ronnie's, and Angus's consciousness. As Joe insists on fasting for workers' rights, his interlocutor suddenly changes from a fellow labor union member to the young Joe up from the Tianshan. The younger Joe challenges the contemporary Joe's decision to endure hunger for others, then grabs him and pulls him over to the snowy mountaintop. The audience is taken back to the moment of the bandmates' fateful decision to consume their friend—with Ronnie making the first incision into Ka-ming's flesh and the other two following suit. The camera then cuts to a close-up shot of Ronnie's hands, in the present, slicing salmon for his son as they make sushi in their cozy family kitchen. Their conversation about fine food and good health is followed by a scene where Joe, a vegetarian, is vomiting up some meat he has accidentally eaten. The sequence ends with Angus having dinner with his girlfriend in an upscale restaurant, and with creepy techno music in the background the camera zooms in on a piece of rare steak being sliced up, then cuts to Angus's face as he chews the meat.[35] In this sequence, allusions to cannibalism alternate with scenes of bourgeois dining, thereby disrupting the notion of a subject construed as a member of the tasteful bourgeoisie. Here the biological need to consume food is repackaged within the gastronomic discourse of the middle class, which celebrates coziness, stylishness, and wholesome family life. Ronnie's amnesia can be read as a sublimation of his earlier drive to survive. Conversely Joe's chronic stomachaches and vomiting remind him of his incorporation of Ka-ming, as do the recurring nosebleeds that Angus endures after his boxing exercises.

There is a compelling scene where Joe, Angus, and Ronnie are at a sumptuous dinner, where they have an angry showdown that brings into relief their continual maneuvering from the Tianshan trip to the present moment. Their eating is captured by several close-ups of their faces, after which the camera cuts to them vomiting on a rooftop.[36] Reminiscent of Dada's antidiets arts, the characters' nausea arrests the circulation and reproduction of the ideology, commodity, and identity that maintains the bourgeois hegemony. Indigestion highlights the dysfunctional aspect of physiology as much as it opens up the multilayered, materialistic, and bodily experience that has been repressed in the consciousness of a bourgeois subject.[37] Here cannibalism does not merely suggest a moral condemnation of the June Fourth crackdown; it sets incorporation against assimilation and political subjectivity against the passive consumption and comfort of the middle class. *Tian yu di* raises the corporeal awareness of the local middle class that has long been politically ambivalent. In this drama, cannibalism—as a form of incorporative but undigested consumption—stirs forgotten youthful dreams, transferring the anachronistic elements of a bygone age to the consciousness of rooted-out desires of the contemporary world. In other words, the flipside of cannibalism is anachronism, which shakes the place of a bourgeois subject in time's continuous flow. Ka-ming's spectral presence persists through Ronnie's sudden bursts of involuntary memory, Joe's chronic stomachaches, and Angus's regular nosebleeds, as well as through their vomiting on the roof top. The experiences of the three bandmates—translated from the corporeal to the mental and back again—disturb the individual and collectively ingrained forms of bourgeois consciousness and identity.

In *Tian yu di*, the banal bourgeois subject is awakened to multiple temporalities. Throughout the drama, the worlds of 1992 and 2010 are juxtaposed, as two sets of actors and actresses play the youthful versions and the mature versions of Yan, Ronnie, Joe, and Angus. These two worlds sometimes run parallel with each other, and more intriguingly, the youthful version and the mature version of a character sometimes encounter each other on the same temporal horizon. This temporal interweaving reveals the characters' stream of consciousness, as they are repeatedly exposed to the sudden eruptions of the past. In the first episode, Yan takes shelter in Ka-ming's work tent, where he is wiring telephone lines in a rainstorm. A colonial-era telephone booth and a coin embossed with Queen Elizabeth II arouse a sense of nostalgia but also open a space where the past and the future are brought together. While the mature Yan displays her worldly wisdom to the innocent Ka-ming, Ka-ming dispels Yan's loneliness, cynicism, and melancholia. This is not only a temporal threshold but also one that cuts across dreaming and waking life as two profane areas of experience, whose interweaving becomes a moment of historical revelation. These multiple, dialectical temporalities awaken a subject to the experience of passage and threshold, which goes unrecognized in the bourgeois ideology of progress and growth.

Mourning to Melancholia

Tian yu di is wrapped in a mood of melancholia, which is achieved by the work's strategic use of music and color in suggesting the looming presence of Ka-ming. After Ka-ming's death, the remaining four friends respond to the call of reality by making a variety of compromises. Nevertheless, they continue to feel that they are part of an elusive something—the imaginary plenitude of the youth band eighteen years earlier—and yet simultaneously outside of it. This sense of loss cannot be remedied through *mourning*; instead the four characters fall into the state of *melancholia*, which Sigmund Freud considers to be the pathological counterpart of mourning.[38]

For Joe, Angus, and Ronnie, melancholia is their inability to come to terms with the loss of Ka-ming. Mourning Ka-ming would have let them relinquish their attachment to him and get on with life. However for them mourning is impossible, because they already devoured him. The animalistic aspect of the self—the raw need for survival, no less—led Joe, Angus, and Ronnie to consume Ka-ming, who was not only a fellow human being but also someone who made up the spiritual aspect of their own subjecthood. In other words, Joe, Angus, and Ronnie have eaten a spiritual part of themselves that can never be turned into an external object toward which they could direct their sorrow in mourning. They devoured Ka-ming in order to permit the animalistic side of their subjectivity to live on, but it was also a contradictory way to keep the rock-and-roll spirit by making it disappear. Incorporation here means to let go of the spiritual aspect of subjectivity while at the same time holding onto it. Joe, Angus, and Ronnie are trapped in a boundless sadness, and their inability to mourn also marks the impossibility of a healthy subject—one that is free of attachment to the lost other. Cannibalism plays against the Freudian healthy individual subject and construes an alternative subjectivity.

If melancholia is pathological for the three bandmates, for Yan it becomes the basis for a work of artistic expression. She embodies her attachment to Ka-ming not through devouring him but by exploring a continual expression of Ka-ming in the world. As Ilit Ferber points out, Walter Benjamin views melancholia as a state that gives the lost object a voice, a presence, and an expression in the world. While the lost object is forced into oblivion in mourning, it endures in melancholia and comes to a full rest in a continual unfolding of meanings.[39] Yan tries to circumscribe her loss of Ka-ming within the boundary of a dream, but she repeatedly wakes up to the reality of her loss. Yan periodically plays the recorded audio message that Ka-ming stored in a toy robot, which was a gift he had given her on her birthday eighteen years earlier. Voices and objects have an intimate relation to remembrance: they trigger memories, but cannot replace Ka-ming's absence. Yan tries to accept love from Bowman, who offers her the comforts of domestic bliss. This economic security, however, only makes her more restless and drives her to have an affair with music producer Arthur. Over the preceding eighteen years, Yan has been tormented by a split interiority inscribed with Ka-ming. Whether it be the toy robot, Bowman, or Arthur, no symbolic mediation in the external world will ever be sufficient to replace Ka-ming's absence.

Yan's endless loyalty to Ka-ming seems to reduce her to a placeholder onto which Joe, Angus, and Ronnie project their nostalgic feelings and utopian desires. This position is shared by Dr. Dylan, an older disc jockey who holds onto the spirit of rock and roll, even as his edifying messages sound vacuous. Ka-ming and Dr. Dylan act as a weak link in a society that is consumed by the animalistic instincts of survival. According to Hon Lai Chu 韓麗珠 (1978–), *Tian yu di* is melancholic because the rock-and-roll spirit of independence, antiestablishmentarianism, freedom, love, and fearlessness fails to take root in everyday life.[40] This reading does not explain how melancholia rendered in an aesthetic work can liberate the memory of loss from alienation and nostalgia. In *Tian yu di*, music and storytelling are modes of artistic expression and interventions into reality. What Dr. Dylan fails to achieve, despite his commitment to rock and roll over the decades, is finally realized by Yan through her renewed bond with Joe, Angus, and Ronnie. "The city is dying, you know," Dr. Dylan blurts out to Yan. He is frustrated because Hong Kong has become so homogeneous that the space for diverse meanings and multiple ways of life is disappearing:

> Look around you. What has this city become? People know about money but not the right and the wrong. . . . We all eat the same food, watch the same TV shows, maintain the same political views, and believe in the same life journey from birth to death.
>
> 睇吓我哋呢個城市係咩嘢樣？除咗錢呢個字之外，我哋已經唔識分乜嘢係是非黑白。……鍾意食同一樣嘅嘢，鍾意同一樣嘅電視節目，支持同一種嘅政治立場，信奉一種生老病死做人嘅方式。[41]

Art's restless metamorphosis can interrupt the ideology of progress, continuity, and stability beneath the reduction of life to mere survival. Rather than being an empty placeholder for male desire, erotic or otherwise, Yan is instead a storyteller who anchors the community of experience, as analyzed earlier; she also engages with musical works—not so much to return Ka-ming to life but rather to secure a significance for him that resonates in the world.

Song and Hong Kong Subjectivity

Tian yu di is driven by the gradual unfolding of the song for which Ka-ming composed a tune without finishing the lyrics. The tune is first heard when Ka-ming hums it, as he carries Yan on his motorbike eighteen years earlier; it unfolds as background music rendered on the flute whenever the characters engage in heart-to-heart talks. Long buried in the memories of Joe, Angus, and Yan, the tune is a thread to the past that offers Ronnie a chance to overcome his amnesia. As Yan is telling the story of her grandma taking her for a tram ride, Ronnie tunes into Yan's talk show and tries to remember the tune Ka-ming left behind. Sitting on the curb, Ronnie turns his sudden blurring of vision into a contemplative moment of musical reminiscence. His genetic eye condition gradually compromises his vision, whereas his memory of the past becomes increasingly clear after his reunion with Joe, Angus, and Yan. Ronnie's amnesia and eye disease turn him into a modern-day Tiresias, whose blindness enabled him to retain the past.[42] Ronnie's sight is devoid of memory, but his incipient blindness enables him to remember. Music and sound liberate him from a focus on the visible and open the depth of reminiscence in the innards of human sensitivity. Aside from playing music and telling stories, Yan often carries her microphone on outings to capture the ambient sound of the environment. Sometimes she spends the whole night alone on the beach recording the sound of wildlife, while at other times she immerses herself in the hustle and bustle of the city to record the songs of sparrows. An energized, expanded life opens up when hearing overtakes sight, allowing experience to occur and history to have a fresh start.

Immediately after the sumptuous dinner scene discussed earlier, there is a rooftop scene where Ka-ming's tune runs through the minds and mouths of the three bandmates. As Ronnie starts humming, Angus is drawn to the tune and starts improvising some lyrics, followed by Joe and then back to Ronnie. Together, they finish the lyrics to "Nianshao wuzhi" 年少無知 (Impetuous Youth), then inscribe them on a wall, in the style of rebellious street artists. This style of painting big characters on the wall is reminiscent of the calligraphic graffiti of Tsang Tsou Choi 曾灶財 (1921–2007) in the late colonial period.[43] Evoking nostalgia for the colonial past, the scene more importantly reminds us of the intersection of food and voice. As Deleuze and Guattari observe in their study of Franz Kafka, food and voice both pass through the mouth, and consequently one cannot eat and speak at the same time. Between the materiality of eating and the ideality of speech, there is something that escapes the categorization of the bodily and the semiotic.[44] As the lyrics are coming out of the mouths of the three bandmates and are being painted on the walls, Joe, Angus, and Ronnie are one step closer to the goal of securing meaning. However, this almost successful discovery of meaning does not redeem their friendship. As Joe remarks: "It is just a jamming out to a song. Nothing more" 夾都係夾隻歌啫，無其他嘢.[45] The band is still haunted by the loss of Ka-ming, whose absence is also a most intimate presence. Ronnie, Angus, and Joe have all consumed Ka-ming, who dwells within them as a silent voice of a living truth.

Joe, Angus, and Ronnie finally perform "Impetuous Youth" onstage in the rock festival organized by Yan. To discover the living truth is to become aware of discarded possibilities. As the chorus of "Impetuous Youth" puts it:

> What if we can choose our fate? We can remain unruffled in every step we take at the crossroads.

What if we simply live honestly? Old values are proved not to be dated.
What if we can rehearse our fate? We won't have to accept the cruelty of difficult choices.
Holding onto the thoughts of the past, would I end up living with tyrannical condemnation?

如果，命運能選擇，十字街口你我踏出的每步更瀟灑。如果，活著能坦白，舊日所相信價值今天發現還未老。如果，命運能演習，現實中不致接納一生每步殘酷抉擇。留守，過去的想法，我會否好像這樣生於世上無目的鞭撻?[46]

Since 1997, Hong Kong has entered a historical threshold. On one hand, 2047 marks an open horizon, at which Hong Kong people may finally break free from the "one country, two systems" framework. On the other hand, 2047 also marks the possibility of further integration of Hong Kong with Mainland China. Referring to the three bandmates in the story, the lyrical "we" in "Impetuous Youth" conveys a sense of nostalgia for youthful innocence as well as an involuntary submission to social norms, with a strong sense of resignation and fatalism. In real life, however, "Impetuous Youth" has become a protest song celebrating youthful commitment to justice and freedom. It was first used in this way in the Anti--National Education Movement in 2012 and then again in the Umbrella Movement two years later. The "What if" question in this song energizes Hong Kong youth in their resistance against the status quo. Their desire to take their lives in their own hands outweighs the pessimistic meaning that the lyrics of "Impetuous Youth" seem to suggest.

In real life, Ka-ming's tune connects two generations of dream seekers. The temporal awareness of a crisscrossing continuity is shown in two contrasting revelations. In episode 10, the mature Yan has a sudden epiphany as she is driving, which is captured by a fast intercutting of two consecutive shots: first, a close-up of her surprised face and then a medium shot of the young Yan apologizing to the mature Yan for unexpectedly running into the road. The mature Yan sees the young Yan lead Ka-ming, Joe, Ronnie, and Angus in moving a heavy mattress from the street to their crude studio for use as makeshift soundproofing. In the final episode, the same camerawork presents a comparable scenario; the only difference is that the mature Yan almost hits a young girl who is leading four bandmates transporting a mattress to the same apartment where the protagonists' band practiced their music eighteen years earlier. Following these young people to the apartment, Yan realizes that it is Angus who has prepaid the rent for these young people so that they can embark on their own musical journey. In this scene a snippet of 1992 and its manifestation in 2010 flash through Yan's mind, and this interweaving of 1992 and 2010 also opens up the possibilities of experience in the actual condition of post-1997 Hong Kong. Each struggle for democracy in

Hong Kong marks a step on the way to change the status quo, even and precisely when it fails. Both the Tiananmen student movement and the Umbrella Movement might be considered to be failures (if we relate them to the specific goal of liberal procedural democracy), yet they also bear within them traces of resistance and the leftovers of imagination (outside the official discourse) that might well continue to open possible futures. This helps us understand why, at the end of *Tian yu di*, Yan goes to the Tianshan alone to experience reversible but never redeemable temporality, searching for the possibility of resistance in what might appear to be a failure.

Concluding Remarks

In *Tian yu di*, cannibalism captures something fundamental about Hong Kong's subjectivity in the post-1997 period. Its relevance is more evident now than in 2011, as Hong Kong goes through another round of antigovernment protests dating from the Umbrella Movement of 2014. This time, defying the regressive HKSAR regime under which a controversial extradition bill was introduced and then withdrawn due to escalating tensions, radical protestors advocated *lanchao* 攬炒 (mutual destruction) as a whatever-it-takes strategy or a now-or-never tactic to push through political demands. Whether *lanchao* means destroying Hong Kong's unique and favorable trade relations with the United States or plunging Hong Kong into the unchecked violence that would restage a crackdown similar to that of June Fourth by the PRC is not clear. Irrespective of whether worldwide sanction on the PRC will be warranted, this round of unrest can be seen as a new version of cannibalism that is steeped in realpolitik in its coercive and unscrupulous tendencies.

Alarmingly, realpolitik has become a commonplace in post-1997 Hong Kong politics, which is most pronounced in the separatist-populist movements since the handover. These successive movements have emerged to resist Hong Kong's integration with Mainland China, and they claim to put Hong Kong's interests first and aim for tangible political effects of autonomy and even independence. Not without irony, these separatist-populist forces join forces with the Chinese state in renouncing alternative political visions of Hong Kong's future that fall outside their shared realpolitik agenda of material survival, economic-political calculations, and Machiavellian power struggles.[47] In this political environment, reminiscing about the Tiananmen student movement can shake Hong Kong people's awareness of their own unity defined by realpolitik, challenging them to incorporate a distance into China's democracy that is traveled between the inside and the outside of their imagined unity, beyond the ideological rigidity of total assimilation into or sheer resistance against Mainland China.

Viewed through the lens of the Tiananmen legacy, cannibalism is a method that explores possible modes of relationality between Hong Kong and Mainland

China. In the 1990s "returning to China via democratization" (*minzhu huigui* 民主回歸) opened a horizon for Hong Kong's political future; in the 2010s this vision can empower the Hong Kong people to imagine beyond the predictable futures according to history's determination of victory and failure.

Just as it is impossible for Yan, Joe, Ronnie, and Angus to mourn the loss of Ka-ming so that they can get on with life, it is similarly impossible for Hong Kong people to effectively mourn the Tiananmen student movement so that they can concentrate on their own material survival. Just as *Tian yu di* turns a melancholic invocation of Ka-ming into a song—a work of artistic expression that renders him present and meaningful—so too Hong Kong people can retain the "failure" of the Tiananmen student movement by actualizing and securing its significance in their specific conditions of life.

LORRAINE WONG is lecturer in Chinese studies at the University of Otago. Her research focuses on Chinese script politics and cultures in the global context. Her work appears in *Literature Compass*, *Modern Chinese Literature and Culture*, and *CLEAR*. She is working on a book tentatively entitled "Script and Revolution in China's Long Twentieth Century."

Acknowledgments

An early version of this paper was presented in the research seminar series of the Languages and Cultures Programme at the University of Otago in May 2018. I thank Cecilia Novero, my colleague in German Studies at Otago, for sharing with me her theoretical articulation of the Dada antidiets arts, cannibalism, and the bourgeois hegemony. I also thank the Nordic Institute of Asian Studies for giving me research support at the final stage of writing this essay.

Notes

1 "Godly" does not have a specific religious meaning here. Netizens in Hong Kong use this term to refer to drama series that have distinguished themselves from soap operas by a creative storyline, high visual quality, and thought-provoking content.
2 Article 2, *The Basic Law of the Hong Kong Special Administrative Region of the People's Republic of China*, 2.
3 See Rey Chow's seminal essay, "Between Colonizers," 153; Law, *Collaborative Colonial Power*, 209.
4 Leung, "(Free) TV," 430.
5 Wong, "Cai *Tian yu di* tuoli qunzhong."
6 Leung, "(Free) TV," 422.
7 Benjamin, "Storyteller," 84.
8 Lui, "Missing Page," 403.
9 *Tian yu di*, episode 4, originally aired November 24, 2011. Unless otherwise stated, all translations are my own.
10 Chow Y. M., "Xingqiliu zhuchang."
11 Leung, "(Free) TV," 431–32.

12 Ibid.
13 Chow Y. M., "Lingjiu nian xie *Tian yu di* ji yizhiyilai de qita."
14 Ibid.
15 Bachner, "Cannibal Translations," 147–48; Yue, *Mouth That Begs*, 69; Rojas, "Cannibalism and the Chinese Body Politic."
16 Certeau, *Practice of Everyday Life*, 140.
17 Lu Xun, "Diary of a Madman," 41.
18 R. Chow, "Between Colonizers," 153; Chan, "Delay No More," 330.
19 Lui, "Missing Page," 401.
20 Hung, "Uncertainty in the Enclave," 62–63.
21 Li, "Lun Xianggang ren de liusi shijian lunshu," 17–18.
22 Lagerkvist and Rühlig, "Mobilization of Memory and Tradition," 740.
23 Ibid., 747.
24 See Rojas, "Cannibalism and the Chinese Body Politic"; Bachner, "Cannibal Translations," 171.
25 King, "(Mis)uses of Cannibalism."
26 Abbas, *Hong Kong*, 6.
27 Chow Y. M., "Neidi ershi nianlai shou fengsha gangju."
28 Lui, "Rearguard Politics," 175.
29 Law, "Northbound Colonialism," 231.
30 After the June Fourth crackdown, the Beijing government hardened its stance on Hong Kong's autonomy by indefinitely postponing the direct election of the chief executive and the legislature and by inserting antisubversion laws as Article 23 in the Basic Law. This development explains how the political consciousness emerging before and after the Tiananmen student movement was reduced to electoral politics and constitutional issues under the Basic Law. See Hung, "Uncertainty in the Enclave," 62.
31 Lui, "Rearguard Politics," 175.
32 C. Wright Mills, quoted in ibid., 161–62.
33 Singer, *Melodrama and Modernity*, 137.
34 Novero, *Antidiets of the Avant-Garde*, 57.
35 *Tian yu di*, episode 2, originally aired November 22, 2011.
36 *Tian yu di*, episode 28, originally aired December 30, 2011.
37 Novero, *Antidiets*, 74–78.
38 Freud, "Mourning and Melancholia," 243.
39 Ferber, "Melancholy Philosophy."
40 Han, "Renmen ruhe chidiao ziji."
41 *Tian yu di*, episode 7, originally aired November 29, 2011.
42 Iampolski, *Memory of Tiresias*, 2.
43 Tsang became famous for making complaints about the supposed misappropriation of his land by writing graffiti on the walls of Hong Kong.
44 Deleuze and Guattari, "What Is a Minor Literature?" 20.
45 *Tian yu di*, episode 28, originally aired December 30, 2011.
46 Lam, "Nianshao wuzhi," 303.
47 Hui and Lau make the argument about the shared *realpolitik* practices of Hong Kong's separatist-populist movements and the CCP and its agents in Hong Kong, both of which dismiss local community resistance movements and pan-democratic forces. See Hui and Lau, "'Living in Truth,'" 356. This logic can also apply to how these political forces treat the Tiananmen legacy.

References

Abbas, Ackbar. *Hong Kong: Culture and the Politics of Disappearance*. Hong Kong: Hong Kong University Press, 1997.

Bachner, Andrea. "Cannibal Translations: Cultural Identity and Alterity in Early Modern China and Latin America." *Journal for Early Modern Cultural Studies* 17, no. 2 (2017): 146–74.

The Basic Law of the Hong Kong Special Administrative Region of the People's Republic of China. Hong Kong: Constitutional and Mainland Affairs Bureau, 2017.

Benjamin, Walter. "The Storyteller: Reflections on the Works of Nikolai Leskov." In *Illuminations*, translated by Harry Zohn, edited by Hannah Arendt, 83–110. New York: Schocken Books, 1969.

Certeau, Michel de. *The Practice of Everyday Life*, translated by Steven F. Rendall. Berkeley: University of California Press, 1988.

Chan, Stephen Ching-kiu. "Delay No More: Struggles to Re-imagine Hong Kong (for the Next 30 Years)." *Inter-Asia Cultural Studies* 16, no. 3 (2015): 327–47.

Chow, Rey. "Between Colonizers: Hong Kong's Postcolonial Self-Writing in the 1990s." *Diaspora: A Journal of Transnational Studies* 2, no. 2 (1992): 151–70.

Chow Yuk Ming 周旭明. "Lingjiu nian xie *Tian yu di* ji yizhiyilai de qita" 09年寫《天與地》及一直以來的其他 [Writing *Tian yu di* in 2009 and Other Things since Then]. *Mingbao* 明報 [Ming Pao Daily], December 25, 2011.

Chow Yuk Ming 周旭明. "Neidi ershi nianlai shou fengsha gangju, yinyu liusi *Tian yu di* is dying" 內地二十年來首封殺港劇，隱喻六四《天與地》is dying [Banning a Hong Kong Drama Series for the First Time in Twenty Years, *Tian yu di*, as an Allegory of the June Fourth Incident, Is Dying]. *Pingguo ribao* 蘋果日報 [Apple Daily], December 28, 2011.

Chow Yuk Ming 周旭明. "Xingqiliu zhuchang" 星期六主場 [Saturday Homefield]. November 11, 2013. www.youtube.com/watch?v=wT2yK9ulHPA.

Deleuze, Gilles, and Félix Guattari. "What Is a Minor Literature?" *Mississippi Review* 11, no. 3 (1983): 13–33.

Ferber, Ilit. "Melancholy Philosophy: Freud and Benjamin." *Discourses of Melancholy* 4, no. 1 (2006). journals.openedition.org/erea/413.

Freud, Sigmund. "Mourning and Melancholia." In *The Standard Edition of the Complete Psychological Works of Sigmund Freud*, vol. 14, edited and translated by James Strachey, 243–58. London: Hogarth Press, 1957.

Hon Lai Chu 韓麗珠. "Renmen ruhe chidiao ziji—guanyu tianyudi de yinyu" 人們如何吃掉自己——關於《天與地》的隱喻 [How Do People Eat up Oneself? On Metaphors in *Tian yu di*]. *Mingbao* 明報 [Ming Pao Daily], December 4, 2011.

Hui, Po-Keung, and Kin-Chi Lau. "'Living in Truth' versus *Realpolitik*: Limitations and Potentials of the Umbrella Movement." *Inter-Asia Cultural Studies* 16, no. 3 (2015): 348–66.

Hung, Ho-Fung. "Uncertainty in the Enclave." *New Left Review* 66 (2010): 55–77.

Iampolski, Mikhail. *The Memory of Tiresias: Intertextuality and Film*, translated by Harsha Ram. Berkeley: University of California Press, 1998.

King, C. Richard. "The (Mis)uses of Cannibalism in Contemporary Cultural Critique." *Diacritics* 30, no. 1 (2000): 106–23.

Lagerkvist, Johan, and Tim Rühlig. "The Mobilization of Memory and Tradition: Hong Kong's Umbrella Movement and Beijing's 1989 Tiananmen Movement." *Contemporary*

Chinese Political Economy and Strategic Relations: An International Journal 2, no. 2 (2016): 735–74.
Lam, Riley 林若寧. "Nianshao wuzhi" 年少無知 [Impetuous Youth]. In *Cichang: Hou jiuqi Xianggang liuxing geci lunshu* 詞場：後九七香港流行歌詞論述 [Scene of Lyrics: Discourse of Post-1997 Hong Kong Lyrics], by Liang Weishi 梁偉詩, 299–303. Hong Kong: Infolink, 2016.
Law Wing-sang. *Collaborative Colonial Power: The Making of the Hong Kong Chinese*. Hong Kong: Hong Kong University Press, 2009.
Law Wing-sang. "Northbound Colonialism: A Politics of Post-PC Hong Kong." *positions* 8, no. 1 (2000): 201–33.
Leung, Yuk-ming Lisa. "(Free) TV Cultural Rights and Local Identity: The Struggle of HKTV as a Social Movement." *Inter-Asia Cultural Studies* 16, no. 3 (2015): 422–35.
Li Hanlai 李漢來. "Lun Xianggang ren de liusi shijian lunshu: Shenfen rentong de yanjiu" 論香港人的六四事件論述：身份認同的研究 [A Discussion of Hong Kong People's Discourse of June Fourth: An Analysis of Identity]. PhD diss., Chinese University of Hong Kong, 2002.
Lu Xun. "Diary of a Madman." In *Diary of a Madman and Other Stories*, translated by William A. Lyell, 29–41. Honolulu: University of Hawaii Press, 1990.
Lui, Tai-lok. "A Missing Page in the Grand Plan of 'One Country, Two Systems': Regional Integration and Its Challenges to Post-1997 Hong Kong." *Inter-Asia Cultural Studies* 16, no. 3 (2015): 396–409.
Lui, Tai-lok. "Rearguard Politics: Hong Kong's Middle Class." *Developing Economies* 41, no. 2 (2003): 161–83.
Novero, Cecilia. *Antidiets of the Avant-Garde: From Futurist Cooking to Eat Art*. Minneapolis: University of Minnesota Press, 2010.
Rojas, Carlos. "Cannibalism and the Chinese Body Politic: Hermeneutics and Violence in Cross-Cultural Perception." *Postmodern Culture* 12, no. 3 (2002). dx.doi.org/10.1353/pmc.2002.0025.
Singer, Ben. *Melodrama and Modernity: Early Sensational Cinema and Its Contexts*. New York: Columbia University Press, 2001.
Tian yu di 天與地 [When Heaven Burns]. TVB, 2011.
Wong, Ricky. "Cai *Tian yu di* tuoli qunzhong" 踩《天與地》脫離群眾 [Criticizing *Tian yu di*'s Alienation of the Masses]. *Mingbao* 明報 [Ming Pao Daily], January 7, 2012.
Yue, Gang. *The Mouth That Begs: Hunger, Cannibalism, and the Politics of Eating in Modern China*. Durham, NC: Duke University Press, 1999.

BELINDA KONG

Pandemic as Method

ABSTRACT This essay deploys the concept of pandemic as a set of discursive relations rather than a neutral description of a natural phenomenon, arguing that pandemic discourse is a product of layered histories of power that in turn reproduces myriad forms of imperial and racial power in the new millennium. The essay aims to denaturalize the idea of infectious disease by reframing it as an assemblage of multiple histories of American geopower and biopower from the Cold War to the War on Terror. In particular, Asia and Asian bodies have been targeted by US discourses of infection and biosecurity as frontiers of bioterrorism and the diseased other. A contemporary example of this bio-orientalism can be seen around the 2003 SARS epidemic, in which global discourses projected the source of contagion onto Asia and Asians. Pandemic as method can thus serve as a theoretical pathway for examining cultural concatenations of orientalism and biopower.

KEYWORDS pandemic, orientalism, biosecurity, biopower/biopolitics, SARS

Deimperializing Pandemics

In *Asia as Method*, Kuan-Hsing Chen outlines a paramount task for contemporary intellectuals: to deimperialize, decolonize, and "de-cold war" current conditions of knowledge.[1] Like others before him, Chen grapples with an observed impasse in postcolonial cultural studies, where critical responses to the legacies of empire remain locked in an ongoing critique of the West and hence paradoxically reinstate Western structures of knowledge as de facto frames of reference. The challenge, according to Chen, is "multiplying the objects of identification and constructing alternative frames of reference"[2]—constructing a new practice of thought whereby Asia and the third world can constitute primary conceptual frameworks for their own and each other's identifications and comparisons. For Chen, Asia is perhaps uniquely suited to this method, for its various post–World War II movements of deimperialism, he argues, were interrupted by the Cold War and the rise of US neoimperialism. Asia as site can thus be turned into a matrix of thwarted political histories and uncompleted epistemologies with the potential to catalyze alternative orders of knowledge, serving at once as geopolitical archive and its own internal heterotopias.

In this essay, I propose that pandemic as an object of knowledge bears a similar critical potential as Chen's Asia. Rather than the neutral description of a natural phenomenon, pandemic is treated here as a set of discursive relations,

PRISM: THEORY AND MODERN CHINESE LITERATURE • 16:2 • OCTOBER 2019
DOI 10.1215/25783491-7978531 •

a product of layered histories of power that in turn reproduces myriad forms of biopower in the new millennium. Pandemic discourse traverses multiple spheres of contemporary life, permeating not just national and international public health governance of disease outbreaks but also cultural imaginations of infection and bodies, contact and borders, globalization and otherness.[3] Politically, the framework of pandemic emergency helps grant legitimacy to sovereign and authoritarian applications of power under the sign of biosecurity.[4] Socially and culturally, the fear-inducing trope of planetary contagion works to consolidate and intensify historical forms of racial othering[5]—exemplified, for instance, in a resurgence of biological orientalism toward China and Chinese bodies in the wake of the 2003 SARS epidemic.

This essay proposes two heuristics for pandemic as method. Following Chen, the first deploys the pandemic concept for an archaeology of imperialist knowledge. Rather than simply an archaeology of pandemic discourse, pandemic as archaeology tactically uncovers those moments in this discourse's historical development when biomedicine and biosecurity mutually institutionalized each other. As my analysis accentuates, this has been a bilateral process: even as security regimes have incorporated the logic of infectious disease emergence toward geopolitical ends, so the life sciences have articulated and constituted their microbial objects of knowledge within geopolitical contexts and terms of thought. Since this analysis focuses on a Western and primarily US-driven discourse, it is not an execution of Chen's Asia as method.[6] Instead, it is a critical geopolitics, one that leverages pandemic discourse to denaturalize the idea of infectious disease and reframe it as an assemblage of multiple histories of American geopower and biopower, from the Cold War to the War on Terror. This section, then, may be considered a US-based response to Chen's call for "critical intellectuals in countries that were or are imperialist to undertake a deimperialization movement by reexamining their own imperialist histories and the harmful impacts those histories have had on the world."[7] Insofar as the geopolitical narrative I trace has Asia both near and far as its frequent target—Asia as the site of the communist axis, assorted rogue states, and terrorist insurgency—Asia may be considered the unrecognized geography that has shaped and sustained the territorial imagination of infectious disease knowledge.

The second heuristic deploys pandemic discourse to highlight the theoretical nexus between orientalism and biopolitics. If the geopolitical underpinnings of biomedicine belong to an obscured history, contemporary imaginations of pandemics often explicitly project the site of infectious disease origins onto Asia and Asian bodies. Pandemic can thus serve as one theoretical pathway for examining cultural concatenations of orientalism and biopower. Along this method, Asian sites and bodies can be analyzed as having historically and persistently provided the racialized material for processes theorized as biopolitics—but rarely for these processes' theorizing. This second heuristic I call pandemic as bio-orientalism.

Pandemic Discourse and the Fear Effect

For an exemplary illustration of contemporary pandemic discourse, we can look to the World Health Organization (WHO) and its numerous reports over the past two decades. According to WHO, infectious disease epidemics are "contemporary health catastrophes": not only are they "common occurrences in the world of the 21st century," but "every country on earth has experienced at least one epidemic since the year 2000."[8] Globalization is the "real driving force" behind this crisis, as increased air travel renders the cross-border spread of infectious agents ever more likely and swift.[9] While we cannot undo globalization, we can atone for our past neglect. As the 2000 *WHO Report on Global Surveillance of Epidemic-Prone Infectious Diseases* asserts:

> In the 1970s many experts thought that the fight against infectious diseases was over. In fact, in 1970, the Surgeon-General of the United States of America indicated that it was "time to close the book on infectious diseases, declare the war against pestilence won, and shift national resources to such chronic problems as cancer and heart disease."
>
> Indeed, complacency about the threat of communicable diseases in the 1970s led to less priority for communicable disease surveillance systems. Partly as a result, these systems were not maintained in large parts of the developing world, and this retarded recognition of the magnitude of problems posed by new and re-emerging communicable diseases, and therefore effective action to control them.[10]

On this account, we are currently living out the disastrous health consequences of an earlier generation's biomedical hubris and moral lapse. Not only had experts and laypeople alike been overly smug about the human conquest over microbes, but this misguided belief cost us precious time and "retarded" our biological defense systems, allowing known and unknown microbial dangers to evolve and proliferate in the intervening decades. As the report highlights, "over 20 new pathogens have been discovered since the mid-1970s," HIV prime among them, while numerous other infectious diseases previously thought to be under control, such as malaria, cholera, and tuberculosis, have undergone a troubling resurgence.[11] To optimize surveillance of these disease threats and make up for lost time, we must collect them all under one rubric—as *emerging and reemerging infectious diseases*, or EID, which encompasses not just new infections but also newly virulent old ones. Thus arises the contemporary category of EID as an object of scientific study and global disease governance.

This is the standard narrative of contemporary infectious disease as told in epidemiology textbooks and popular science writings. Tellingly, many of these texts also open with the notorious pronouncement, supposedly made by then-US Surgeon General William H. Stewart, about it being "time to close the book on infectious diseases." The putative year and occasion of his utterance may differ from source to source—from 1970 to 1969 or 1967, from a congressional testimony to a White House visit or a groundbreaking ceremony—but the line is so resonant that it has been cited in countless textbooks, journal and magazine articles, public health documents, and scholarly monographs, by CDC physicians as much as *New Yorker* journalists.[12] Even Stewart's 2008 obituary in the *Lancet* ends with a reference to it.[13] Irrespective of their genre, audience, and level of scientific expertise, these sources are strikingly similar in their interpretation: that Stewart epitomized the medical overconfidence of an earlier era, that his sentiment "captured the hubris of the period,"[14] and that he was profoundly wrong about our coming relationship with infectious diseases. What Stewart proclaimed so "confidently"[15] and "enthusiastically"[16] has turned out, in hindsight, to be "almost laughable naiveté,"[17] and it is the "misfortune of us all," laments one microbiology textbook, that "those wise men [like Stewart] underestimated the adaptability of the multitudinous life forms that share the Earth with us, both infectious agents and predators."[18] In all these instances, Stewart's words are conjured as a point of departure, an easy rhetorical pivot to more sobering warnings about the many microbial threats facing today's interconnected world, weaving a seeming consensus around what might be called a complacency thesis.

This official narrative about the origins of infectious disease underpins contemporary pandemic discourse. Encapsulated by Stewart's eminently quotable line, pandemic discourse puts into circulation a host of themes with subtle yet far-reaching implications regarding the fragility of the globalized world, the precarity of the status quo, the rapid reproduction of invisible enemies, the foolishness of inaction, and the moral properness of fear. With our species life constantly perched on the brink of pandemic calamity, fear is no longer an isolated or temporary emotional state but a baseline of contemporary planetary existence. In recognizing the former surgeon general's benightedness, we are prompted to feel both better and worse, at once more enlightened and more perturbed, more satisfied with our heightened awareness yet more frightened because of it. Enlightenment shifts from an experience of empowered knowledge to a paradoxical one of dread and anticipation. Epiphany makes us afraid—and rightly so, as authorities high and low admonish us. Fear is the proper posture of globalized human life.[19]

Most crucially, pandemic discourse generates this fear effect in order to secure our consent to a range of technologies whose ostensible rationale is to safeguard the survival of our species but that work to consolidate global forms of biopower. According to the dominant narrative, we have ended up in this present state of precarious life not because of anything we did but precisely because we did nothing. This past of collective inaction, with the 1960s to 1980s as a period of planetary surveillance lapse and lost time, makes all the more urgent the present need for biodefense preparations. One supposed lesson of this history is that we cannot trust our own sentiments and judgments, especially our individual and communal feelings of stability and safety, because those feelings have turned out to be perilously deceptive. Instead, for real security in a post-complacency age, we must place our trust in and cede our political agency to strong authority structures that rule for our own good. This discourse casts unguardedness and optimism as near-fatal blunders, contrasted with the embrace of tough countermeasures as responsible and smart action. Brian Massumi would call this regime of affective governance the politics of everyday fear, its operative logic of preemption *ontopower*.[20] In both political and public health arenas, this model of power strategically blurs the distinction between preemptive and actual states of disease emergency so that we are saturated with fear and inculcated into habits of paralysis and compliance.[21] Increasingly normalized, this power now operates under the sign of biosecurity.

Pandemic as Archaeology

The history of this paradigm of pandemic emergency and biosecurity can be retold from the perspective of a critical geopolitics, however. Charting alternative origin stories for this discourse yields three key moments in US geopolitical history: the post-9/11 War on Terror, the late 1980s–90s post–Cold War period, and the 1950s early Cold War era. As Andrew Lakoff and Stephen Collier stress, contemporary biosecurity does not occur solely or even primarily on the terrains of national policy and military defense; it spans multiple domains, constellating government actors and policy experts with health officials and life scientists as well as humanitarian activists in new assemblages of authority and knowledge.[22] By understanding how perceived biological threats such as infectious disease have come to be "problematized," or configured as targets in need of surveillance and intervention, we can better move toward "critical, reflexive knowledge" and an alternative ethics of "living with risks."[23]

The most proximate scene of biosecurity's solidification is the post-9/11 US security state's War on Terror. The extent to which the American government came to coopt the language of disease emergence was illustrated by Donald Rumsfeld's oft-cited speech from a 2002 Department of Defense news briefing in which he observed: "There are known knowns. These are things we know that we know. There are known unknowns. That is to say, there are things that we know we don't know. But there are also unknown unknowns. These are things we don't know we don't know."[24] As Bruce Braun points out, Rumsfeld's logic mimed the contemporary perception of the "virtuality of molecular life": just as biology increasingly gets articulated in terms of virtual networks of unknown and dangerous viruses that "circulate and recombine in novel ways, threatening our bodies and identities," so national security came to be couched in terms of hidden networks of sleeper cells and emerging threats.[25] Melinda Cooper calls this the "biological turn" in US foreign policy after 9/11, but more than a simple rhetorical resonance, she argues that this turn reflected a fundamental philosophical reconceptualization of warfare by the Bush administration. Moving away from the previous geopolitical doctrine of mutual deterrence, the US government strategically "conflate[d] public health, biomedicine, and war" so as to make operative a security agenda of "full-spectrum dominance, counterproliferation, and preemption."[26] The epidemiological tenets of microbial emergence, resistance and counterresistance, and humans' permanent warfare against germs were transferred over and made central to defense policy. Within this new security framework, war became integral to the very conceptualization of life, or as Cooper puts it, "as if permanent war were simply *a fact of life*."[27]

In the reverse direction, national security now propels biological research—including the creation of new infectious diseases. In anticipation of potential bioterrorist attacks, the US government's agency for developing cutting-edge military technology, the Defense Advanced Research Projects Agency (DARPA), has been actively inventing antibiotics and vaccines for not only known pathogens but also ones that do not yet exist. In the name of biodefense, "DARPA finds itself in the paradoxical situation of having first to create novel infectious agents or more virulent forms of existing pathogens in order to then engineer a cure," thus "blurring the difference between defensive and offensive research."[28] For Cooper, this ideological convergence between biomedicine and biosecurity represents the culmination of neoliberalism's politics of life, which entrenches ideas of speculative preemption and catastrophe risk so as to disable a counterpolitics. What we can further emphasize is the real geography that underlies the post-9/11 biosecurity imagination. Despite rather postmodern descriptions of Al-Qaeda as a fluid organization of dispersed and fluctuating networks, the actual targets of US antiterrorism measures remain fixed in Asia and Africa. As in the case of the 2003 Iraq War, Rumsfeld's invocation of "unknown unknowns" served to justify American military invasion of Iraq in the absence of evidence that it was stockpiling weapons of mass destruction. Concurrently, the formulation of a prototerritory of infectious disease emergence took place against the backdrop of this geopolitical theater of war.

Yet the consolidation of the biosecurity position predates 9/11 and can be traced back to the late 1980s and 1990s, as part of the US response to post–Cold War geopolitics after the dissolution of the USSR. As Susan Wright details, up until the 1980s, the American government mostly regarded terrorism as a "second- or third-tier security problem—a problem that happened elsewhere," so that proponents of biological defense remained marginal in national security discussions.[29] With the end of the Cold War, however, the former template of the Soviet threat was replaced by the discourse of hostile third-world "rogue states," and the prospect of nuclear warfare was superseded by the menace of biological and chemical weapons of mass destruction. Before 9/11 gave a concrete context to this logic, the 1995 Aum Shinrikyo attack on the Tokyo subway provided biosecurity advocates within the US government with an early platform. This attack, they warned, represented the "index case" for contemporary acts of bioterrorism: a vital "threshold" had been crossed, a taboo lifted, and henceforth, terrorists of all stripes would follow suit by employing bioweapons on civilians.[30] Bioterrorism, they argued, was "no longer the stuff of science fiction or adventure movies" but "a reality which has already come to pass, and one which, if we do not take appropriate measures, will increasingly threaten us in the future."[31] As Wright recounts, this "alarmist" stance overtook Washington during the 1990s, and the congressional budget for counterterrorism defense soared.

Biological research benefitted directly from this political paradigm shift, as the study of infectious diseases now became a security priority. Significantly, a small cohort of prominent scientists was instrumental in linking infectious disease to biowarfare as coterminous national security threats. These scientists served as key advisers in Washington, organizing research forums and participating on government panels as well as supplying successive White House administrations with numerous reports on bioterrorist scenarios. They presented their views as impartial and nonpartisan extensions of scientific expertise, and their voices carried tremendous weight in determining government policy and budget allocations as well as the direction of scientific research. Two figures in particular stood out. Donald Henderson, the elder statesman of American epidemiology credited with eradicating smallpox in the 1960s and 1970s, was crucial in lending his support to the biosecurity position. At a 1998 CDC-sponsored conference on emerging infectious diseases, for instance, he categorically dismissed the objections of bioterrorism skeptics, and in a report later that year by the Institute of Medicine and the National Research Council, he warned that it would be a "grave mistake" for the government to delay biodefense preparations.[32] In that same year, he was named the founding director of the Johns Hopkins Center for Civilian Biodefense Studies, with an earmarked $1 million in congressional funding.[33] Even more influential than Henderson was Joshua Lederberg, Nobel Prize–winning molecular biologist and scientific adviser since the 1950s for nine consecutive White House administrations. He organized and supervised many of the research panels at the National Academy of Sciences and the Institute of Medicine, and in his reports to the government, he repeatedly forecast the calamitous impact of biowarfare, even handpicking experts specifically to dramatize for politicians apocalyptic scenarios of bioterrorist attacks on American cities. He was the one who identified the 1995 Tokyo subway attack as a "threshold event," claiming that "Aum Shinrikyo has done us a favor by . . . making it obvious that there is a very serious threat; that terrorists would use any means imaginable at their disposal."[34] Again, Asia enters into this history as a strategic site, this time as a "threshold" of biothreat to be held at bay, in a coordinated narrative of bioterrorism. As Wright notes, Lederberg too reaped financial benefit from his political advocacy, as he later became a board member of EluSys Therapeutics, a biotechnology company with a biodefense research focus.[35] The intertwined interests of neoliberal and neoconservative forces with public health became entrenched in this era, even if only a handful of high-profile scientists were directly implicated in this development.

In fact, the basis for the conjunction between biomedicine and biosecurity was set already in the historic 1989 NIAID/NIH Conference on Emerging Viruses held in Washington, DC. This conference was attended by over two hundred American scientists and public health experts, including both Henderson and Lederberg, and it was the forum where the term *emerging viruses* was first coined by the conference's principal organizer, epidemiologist Stephen Morse.[36] In his follow-up landmark edited volume, *Emerging Viruses*, Morse captured the core message of the meeting:

> The problem of emerging viruses is not likely to disappear. If anything, it will increase; episodes of disease emergence are likely to become more frequent. . . . Constructive action has been paralyzed in the past by a combination of apathy and uncertainty. The AIDS epidemic is a powerful reminder of the price of apathy. It is also a demonstration that infectious diseases can still be a major threat to human life. Although we cannot yet predict specific disease outbreaks, and may never be able to, we now understand many of the factors leading to emergence. . . . Part of the question therefore becomes whether people will continue unwittingly to precipitate emerging diseases and suffer the consequences, as has happened throughout history, or will begin to take responsibility for these human actions.[37]

According to Morse, since recent human history has witnessed waves of epidemics culminating in the AIDS crisis, we need to understand outbreaks not as "acts of God" but within a framework of "disease emergence." He therefore coined the phrase *emerging viruses* to designate not just new pathogens but also known ones that are "rapidly expanding their range."[38] As Andrew Lakoff points out, this classification is powerfully "generative," for it unifies under one name an array of illnesses not previously linked. The term converts a "disparate set of disease threats" into a single "imperative" of biodefense preparation.[39] So even if the category of EID seems "self-evident" by our time, it is a "relatively recent invention," by a relatively elite and invested group of microbiologists and epidemiologists.[40]

The 1989 conference laid the conceptual cornerstone for later biosecurity techniques. Nicholas King pinpoints this conference as the catalyzing moment for what he calls an "emerging diseases worldview." Not just a set of scientific explanations or policy proposals, this worldview, he argues, is deeply ideological: it "comes equipped with a moral economy and historical narrative, explaining how and why we find ourselves in the situation that we do now, identifying villains and heroes, ascribing blame for failures and credit for triumph," as well as providing "a consistent, self-contained ontology of epidemic disease" that allows for strategic intervention and management.[41] As King shows, in the decade after the conference, leading scientists and health officials in the United States increasingly conjured pandemic scenarios and tied them directly to national security, helping to formalize and cement the emerging diseases worldview across multiple spheres of knowledge. Endorsing a system of global epidemic surveillance and medical commoditization, this worldview represents a model of capitalist biopower that seeks not only to be omnipresent and omniscient but to profit from sickness everywhere.[42] Indeed, in his edited volume, Morse already strongly promoted global disease surveillance as an "essential first step" for securing national and human health.[43] He cited Henderson's proposal for creating a fleet of international disease surveillance centers modeled on the CDC, as well as global surveillance systems for early detection and rapid tracking of outbreaks, electronic databases for instantaneous accessing of medical information, and the marketization of health commodities such as drugs and vaccines.[44] In fact, given the advent of internet technology and the global pharmaceutical industry, Henderson's blueprint has been not only realized but surpassed. Current systems of syndromic surveillance, which gather real-time data from numerous sources and monitor for patterns of symptoms distributed across populations, now work to "identify potential outbreaks while they are still invisible to healthcare professionals," effectively relocating disease knowledge from physicians and patients to the information systems overseen by national security authorities.[45] In turn, this disease governance template has been exported to the WHO by American CDC officials, and from there it has disseminated into the public health institutions of countries such as China, becoming ever more established on a global scale.[46]

Echoing King's analysis, we can also see a penchant for moral parables in the champions of infectious disease and biosecurity discourse. On their account, in a narrative that has become canonized as scientific lore, Morse and Henderson consistently portray themselves as the longtime underdogs in American public health, the unjustly ignored wise men who were never complacent, the small but marginalized contingent of microbiologists and epidemiologists who valiantly disputed the earlier era's status quo and ultimately came to be vindicated by the microbes' vengeful return. In short, they were the heroes to William Stewart's villain. Ironically, it turns out that Stewart's infamous line about "closing the book on infectious diseases" is itself the stuff of urban legends—one that, as far as the records indicate, originated in this very 1989 conference on emerging viruses, in a personal correspondence between none other than Henderson and Morse.[47] Henderson had apparently heard the remark secondhand, from unnamed people who were in turn recalling a speech from memory years later, and he went on to repeat this anecdote both at the conference and in his essay for Morse's volume.[48] Morse, for his part, footnoted the quotation and attributed it to Henderson in a medical textbook a few years later.[49] Two journalists who attended the conference reported this line in the media, and one of them, Laurie Garrett, further popularized it in her 1994 bestselling book *The Coming Plague*.[50] But Stewart himself never made the alleged statement, and on the contrary, he expressed the opposite view on multiple occasions that "warning flags are still flying in the communicable disease field" and that "we cannot turn our backs on microbiology."[51] That the notion of emerging viruses was bestowed official birth at exactly the same moment as the mythic invention of the Stewart quotation, and by the same group of ascendant scientists, intimates just how essential the fable of a benighted villain is to the founding legitimacy of the infectious disease paradigm, as if the latter must create its own dark prehistory to claim an epochal birthright.

Finally, if we trace the NIAID/NIH 1989 conference and its ideological roots further back, we arrive at the Cold War as another vital scene of pandemic discourse's emergence. Before Morse coined the term *emerging viruses*, microbiologist René Dubos was the first to use *emergence* in the 1950s to describe the behavior of microbes. According to Dubos, microbial evolution was far from stable or linear but radically unpredictable and disruptive, and since humans are locked in an unremitting coevolving ecology with microbes, there can be no final overcoming of them. Cooper sees in Dubos's germ theory "an alternative vision of warfare and a counterphilosophy of disease" that would ultimately culminate in the post-9/11 biosecurity credo of permanent, preemptive, speculative warfare.[52] Along with his protégés, Dubos developed models of disease ecology in these early years of the Cold War.[53] As Lakoff contends, this was the period of the decisive rise of an "ideology of preparedness" in US politics and public health. Toward the end of World War II, some US military strategists argued against demobilization, maintaining that the country needed to remain prepared to respond to new enemy threats such as a nuclear attack. They campaigned for "military and civilian readiness, in peacetime, for an anticipated future war," in effect projecting a state of "permanent mobilization for total war."[54] This preparedness model was transferred over to natural disaster management beginning in the mid-1950s, when defense officials started to treat environmental disasters and modern warfare as bearing "a close affinity."[55] It also led to the founding in 1951 of the CDC's Epidemic Intelligence Service (EIS) by Alexander Langmuir, the father of infectious disease epidemiology and Henderson's mentor. Langmuir advocated an approach of "hypervigilance" against epidemics, of "continued watchfulness" on a global scale, and he proposed a global network of centers that would provide around-the-clock surveillance and early rapid detection for both natural and unnatural outbreaks.[56] Henderson's later template of global disease surveillance was consciously modeled on Langmuir's. As he noted in his essay for Morse's volume, the contemporary issue of infectious disease surveillance is not unprecedented but had been raised "at least once before"—in 1950, at the start of the Korean War, when fears of a biological attack on civilian populations prompted the creation of the EIS.[57] In this essay, Henderson vividly resurrected the Cold War language of permanent total war, writing that "the world is increasingly interdependent, and . . . human health and survival will be challenged, *ad infinitum*, by new and mutant microbes, with unpredictable pathophysiological manifestations."[58]

The 1989 conference, then, had a direct lineage in Cold War epidemiological frameworks, with its presiding scientists pushing for not just a revival but permanent normalization of Cold War biosecurity techniques. Again, this history is anchored in a US geopolitics in which Asia figures repeatedly and strategically as the site of multiple forms of potential biothreat, requiring exceptional modes of power to be mobilized at home. Infectious disease discourse therefore epitomizes the insufficient deimperialization of contemporary conditions of knowledge. So far, I have used pandemic as a prism for a geopolitical archaeology. Now I turn to pandemic as a method for diagnosing contemporary bio-orientalism and tracing it to one particular historical formation.

Pandemic as Bio-orientalism

As a theory of the ways politics captures biological life into its domain—as "power's hold over life," in Michel Foucault's original formulation, "the acquisition of power over man insofar as man is a living being"[59]—biopolitics seems ideally suited as a framework for analyzing the operations of disease governance. Indeed, disease plays a paradigmatic, one might say narratively indispensable, role in Foucault's history of power. Most famously, the plague inaugurated for him projects of disciplinary power, exemplified by mechanisms of panoptic surveillance and control, but this plague template was also preceded by leprosy's "rituals of exclusion." As Foucault underscored, different diseases gave rise to different "ways of exercising power over men" and different "political dream[s]": "The leper was caught up in a practice of rejection, of exile-enclosure . . . those sick of the plague were caught up in a meticulous tactical partitioning . . . the great confinement on the one hand; the correct training on the other. The leper and his separation; the plague and its segmentations."[60] Yet, as epidemics were superseded by endemics, "illnesses that were difficult to eradicate . . . affecting a population" as "something permanent," so too did sovereign and disciplinary power structures give way to a contemporary "'biopolitics' of the human race," represented by a modern "medicine whose main function will now be public hygiene, with institutions to coordinate medical care, centralize information, and normalize knowledge."[61] Later, Foucault would call this last type of power *security*: where sovereignty excludes as in the case of leprosy and discipline quarantines as in the case of plague, security inoculates as with smallpox.[62] Each biopolitical moment has its corresponding disease. Philipp Sarasin calls this recurrent motif a minor "trace of infection" in Foucault's writing,[63] but we can flip the order of priority here and postulate that the history of Western disease governance has been that which underlay the inception of contemporary biopolitical theory.

To be sure, for later theorists, the most telling scenes of biopower will change. For Giorgio Agamben's models of sovereign power and bare life, the intractable historical prototype would be the Nazi death camps; for Achille Mbembe's necropower, slavery and colonialism; and for Brian Massumi's ontopower, the post-9/11 War on Terror. What these subsequent articulations make ever more visible is that biopolitics becomes conceptually relevant not merely when there exists a politicization of *any* life but when the life to be excluded, surveilled, disciplined, detained, stripped bare, subjugated, slain, or preempted entails some form of otherness, whether racial, colonial, or geopolitical. Yet biopolitical theories often take recourse in an abstracted language of space, however real and acknowledged the historical referents, whether it is Foucault's panopticon or "spaces of security";[64] Agamben's "state of exception," "zone of indistinction," or "camp as *nomos*";[65] or Massumi's "prototerritory."[66] Mbembe is perhaps most explicit and steadfast in reversing this intellectual movement from history to theory when he moves instead from imagined geographies back to historically politicized ones. For him, the colony is "the location par excellence" for not just particular variants of biopolitics but also the accumulated operations of it: the colony, as with the plantation system and the apartheid regime, has been a consummate site for the "concatenation of biopower, the state of exception, and the state of siege." And "crucial to this concatenation," he emphasizes, is "race."[67]

Following Mbembe, I would suggest that Asia, akin to the colony, has been the rationale for the concatenation of multiple manifestations of Western biopower; as such, it has occupied a key place in the geopolitical history, if not the conscious theorizing, of biopolitics. As we saw, over the course of the past century, Asia has been variously and strategically cited within US discourses of infectious disease and biosecurity as the threshold of bioterrorism as well as the biological other that justifies preemptive biodefense. A more recent example of the nexus between Asia and global biopolitics centers on the 2003 SARS epidemic. As the new millennium's first pandemic, with its origins in southern

China, SARS incited deep anxieties and fears about the contemporary world and its breakdown of the boundary between first-world health and third-world contagion.[68] The Chinese communist government's initial cover-up of the outbreak at home further fueled age-old orientalist tropes of China as the site of exotic and unhygienic culinary traditions as well as authoritarian secrecy, a lethal combination for global health security.[69] It was partly in the context of these orientalist perceptions that the WHO began to act routinely beyond its jurisdiction in response to SARS, bypassing and sometimes overriding state authorities to issue travel advisories, collecting disease data from nonstate sources, and disseminating this information to other countries without the consent of affected governments. Most controversial among these measures was WHO's unprecedented global travel advisory for Hong Kong and Guangdong, a move calculated not just to safeguard global health but also to pressure the Chinese government into compliance. In 2005, the World Health Assembly would go on to revise the International Health Regulations to formalize these powers for WHO and to grant it additional authority, from everyday surveillance and intelligence gathering to crisis management. David Fidler argues that SARS radically transformed global health governance into a "post-Westphalian" paradigm, which centralizes medical authority and regulatory power on a global scale more than ever before.[70] If for Mbembe colonialism and slavery are the historical forms of life that enact theories of biopolitics, we might say that bio-orientalism similarly haunts global biopolitical history.

Contemporary pandemic discourse further sustains this biopolitical history. In popular culture as much as public health arenas, Asia is frequently depicted as the birthplace of one wave of infectious disease after another. A 2004 issue of *Time* magazine typifies this bio-orientalist pandemic imagination: the cover image shows a giant egg about to be hatched, with a bird's beak poking through a crack in the shell, while the headline poses the ominous question, "Bird Flu: Is Asia hatching the next human pandemic?" As the article goes on to assert, the avian flu was the "latest scourge to emerge from Asia." Barely a year after the containment of SARS, the bird flu was already "spreading with alarming speed through Asia's poultry farms," with outbreaks in South Korea, Japan, Vietnam, and Thailand. Though the virus was not yet virulent among humans, "the great fear of health officials around the world is that the virus could, like SARS, jump the species barrier, mutate into a deadly and highly contagious form and set off a worldwide pandemic." This "next deadly global epidemic" would be what epidemiologists call "a slate wiper," but what endangers the world is not just the virus itself but "dissembling and stalling by local governments [that] have already allowed the pathogen to spread in Asia—not only in birds but also among the men and women who raise them for a living and the kids who gather eggs or simply kick up infected dust in their villages."[71] Given the combination of

Asia's dishonest and corrupt governments, the poor hygiene and general level of medical ignorance of its rural residents, as well as the rapidity of international travel enabled by globalization, Asia stands to jeopardize public health the world over. The expertise of health officials and epidemiologists is summoned, and even the experts, the article declares, are afraid. As Priscilla Wald has demonstrated, cultural narratives of disease outbreaks follow formulaic conventions, one of which is a "geography of disease" where "timeless, brooding Africa or Asia" is imagined as "the birthplace of humanity, civilization, and deadly microbes." Infectious diseases are constructed as third-world problems "leaking" into the global North, in a one-way traffic of emergence.[72] The underlying message of the pandemic orientalist narrative seems to be that, while we may lament the loss of Asian lives to deadly microbes, we should not slacken our vigilance toward Asian bodies precisely because they *may* host those microbes—if not every single body in actuality, then the collective Asian body in potential.

Pandemic bio-orientalism alone, however, does not account for the range of biopolitical theories and practices vis-à-vis Asia. That is to say, an imagined geography of pandemic Asia does not thereby transform actual Asian territories and bodies into spaces of a "terror formation," exceptional violence, or camp life à la Mbembe's colony.[73] For a historical analogue that illuminates alternative orders of biopower over Asian bodies and sites, we can spotlight one particular formation of Asia within the US national polity: Chinatown. As Kay Anderson notes, historically, "Chinatown" has not been a "neutral term" but "one that relied on a range of cultural assumptions held by Europeans about the Chinese as a type . . . it was an evaluative term, ascribed by Europeans no matter how residents of that territory might have defined themselves."[74] Chinatown can thus be productively analyzed along Edward Said's lines as an internal Orient within the United States, and not fortuitously, it has served as the operative site for a wide range of public health biopolitics. We can focus here on one revealing instance: infectious disease governance in San Francisco's Chinatown.

As scholars have long recognized, nineteenth-century American constructions of Chinese racial difference often relied on motifs of Chinese cultural excess, of "disease, contagion, and pollution."[75] San Francisco's Chinatown, as the country's main port of entry for Chinese immigrants and its largest Chinese enclave up until the Chinese Exclusion Act of 1882, was considered by health officials and politicians as "a 'plague spot,' a 'cesspool,' and the source of epidemic disease and ailments,"[76] associated successively with tuberculosis, smallpox, syphilis, leprosy, and plague. For example, as both Susan Craddock and Nayan Shah document, smallpox was progressively attributed to Asians and especially the Chinese over the course of the nineteenth century's closing decades, as four smallpox epidemics broke out in San Francisco. Despite the ambiguous origins and pathways of these epidemics, city health officials increasingly targeted Chinese immigrants as infectious agents and Chinatown as a "cancer spot" and a "laboratory of infection."[77] Ships from Asia with one infected Chinese passenger were quarantined, but while white passengers were simply kept on board, some of them even allowed to go ashore during the quarantine period, Chinese passengers were segregated onto another empty ship at the harbor, "left to suffer their disease imprisoned in the hull of a ship with no medical assistance."[78] Chinatown itself was subjected to a compulsory public health campaign of sanitary cleanup, with teams systematically inspecting and fumigating every household. Some health officials also advocated the building of bigger prisons to incarcerate Chinese residents who failed to comply with health ordinances, while others desired a wholesale ejection of the Chinese population and the decisive expunging of Chinatown.[79] According to one health officer, the 1876 epidemic was so severe because of the "unscrupulous, lying, and treacherous Chinamen," who had a "willful and diabolical disregard of our sanitary laws"; they were, in short, "enemies of our race and people."[80] Within this framework, the Chinese were responsible for smallpox not just as originary biological hosts with unhealthy cultural habits but also as a morally depraved and malicious enemy race intent on destroying America. In the same period, syphilis was another infectious disease often attached to the Chinese race, especially Chinese women, most of whom were regarded as prostitutes. It was considered a "female counterpart to smallpox," with Chinatown as the immoral locale of "stench, decay, and 'oozing slime'" where Chinese sex workers plied their sinister trade.[81] These infectious disease discourses helped fuel anti-Chinese social sentiments and contributed significantly to the passing of a series of federal Chinese exclusion laws by the century's end. Conversely, they also inspired the rise of missionary reform programs by middle-class white women, who with their house-to-house Chinatown visits aimed to "rescue" fallen prostitutes as well as heathen housewives by instructing them in the ways of Christian civilization and cleanliness.[82]

Clearly, the medical and epidemiological racialization of Chinatown and the Chinese in late nineteenth-century San Francisco entailed a host of biopolitical techniques—not merely quarantine but segregation, not merely surveillance but incarceration, not merely expulsion but exclusion, and not merely discipline but conversion. These techniques carried a residue of racial difference, separating out not just all diseased bodies but installing additional divisions between racialized diseased bodies, in a production and reproduction of Chinese otherness. The one-to-one correspondence between diseases and power structures as envisioned by Foucault was saliently confounded in the governance of Chinese bodies, in relation to which even one infectious disease could activate an entire history of Foucauldian biopower. As Shah discerns, "At the turn of the century, 'health' and 'cleanliness' were embraced as integral aspects of American identity; and those who were perceived to be 'unhealthy' such as Chinese men and women, were considered dangerous and inadmissible to the American nation."[83] Aside from consolidations of national domesticity, this period also coincided with the inaugural moment of America as an empire with overseas territories in Asia and the Pacific. In these overlapping contexts, San Francisco's Chinatown may be understood as at once a municipal, national, and imperial terrain, a territorial assemblage at the crossroads of race, nation, and empire. Its discursive construction and biopolitical governance constellated local racial prejudices, nationalist ideologies, and geopolitical ambitions—the very concatenation that constitutes the prehistory of contemporary pandemic bio-orientalism.

Nonetheless, we should not conflate Chinatown's biopolitical order with more extreme historical incarnations of bare life and the medical camp during the same period, such as Hawaii's leper colony on the island of Molokai. In this other colonial annexed space, in the ambiguous geopolitical zone of the US Pacific, the introduction of leprosy was also imputed to Chinese immigrant laborers. Here the disease was called *mai pake*, or "Chinese sickness," since the biomedical establishment at the time identified leprosy as an "essentially Chinese disease," "inherent" to the Chinese race and transmitted by either heredity or sexual contact. In San Francisco, it was treated with procedures of segregated quarantine similar to smallpox cases, though dozens of "Chinese lepers" were eventually deported to Hong Kong, in an early implementation of medical deportation.[84] In Hawaii, however, the majority of those infected were native Hawaiians, leading to an alternative racial discourse of disease susceptibility, with Hawaiians constructed as a hypervulnerable racial population. In addition to biopolitical measures such as those enacted over Chinese bodies in San Francisco, here, leprosy patients became medical subjects along the full spectrum of biopower, in what Neel Ahuja calls a paradigm of "racial engulfment."[85] Within a newly emergent imperialist discourse of "the Hawaiian leper," patients were not simply isolated and quarantined, with their rights suspended in a classic configuration of detention and surveillance. More disturbingly, with the rise of liberal humanist medicine, patients were hailed as self-determining subjects who could volunteer for scientific experimentation in an exercise of their "medical citizenship."[86] The most well-known example involved microbiologist Eduard Arning and a native Hawaiian named Keanu, a convicted murderer and death row inmate. Arning offered Keanu a choice: he could follow through on his sentence of execution by hanging, or he could volunteer for leprosy research. Keanu opted for the latter, and Arning injected him with the bacterium from an infected patient. Keanu eventually developed leprosy in jail and died on Molokai several years later.[87] As Nicholas Turse shows, this episode was not a singular occurrence but part of a wider practice of leprosy research via human experimentation on the island, including instances of other scientists inoculating healthy native Hawaiians with leprosy without the latter's knowledge.[88]

So, as Ahuja rightly concludes, the biopolitical milieu on Molokai cannot be reduced to purely that of either Agamben's sovereign power and camp life or Foucault's disciplinary surveillance or liberal governmentality. Rather, this specific biopolitical matrix strategically confuses sovereignty, discipline, and governmentality, in complex "layerings" of US imperial and racial governance. The semblance of agency and citizenship, in the proffering of a right to be medicalized and experimented on in the name of public health and human security, ultimately reproduced colonial dependency and racial stratification[89]—and, Mbembe might add here, death. At this historical Asia-Pacific site, we can mark the early frontiers of a bio-orientalist necropower.

BELINDA KONG is associate professor of Asian studies and English at Bowdoin College. Her writing and teaching focus on contemporary Asian American and Asian diaspora literatures, with particular attention to China and issues of geopolitics, biopower, and race

Notes

1 Chen, *Asia as Method*, x–xi.
2 Ibid., 1–2.
3 For cultural and literary analyses of the epidemic imagination, see Mayer, "Virus Discourse"; Wald, *Contagious*; Schweitzer, *Going Viral.*
4 For analyses of the connections between national security and infectious disease governance, see Fidler and Gostin, *Biosecurity*; Lakoff and Collier, *Biosecurity Interventions.*
5 For analyses of historical linkages between public health, infectious disease, and the governance of racialized, immigrant, or colonial populations, see Kraut, *Silent Travelers* and "Immigration, Ethnicity"; Craddock, *City of Plagues*; Molina, *Fit to Be Citizens?*; Ahuja, *Bioinsecurities.* For historical analyses of US public health governance of Chinese immigrants more specifically, see Craddock, "Embodying Place"; Shah, *Contagious Divides.*
6 This essay is part of a larger book project on global pandemic discourses on SARS. There I discuss not just US and WHO responses to the outbreak but also the PRC government's; in addition, I spotlight an alternative archive of non-crisis-driven cultural responses to and representations of SARS produced at the epidemic's epicenters, especially China and Hong Kong.
7 Chen, *Asia as Method*, vii.
8 WHO, "Anticipating Epidemics," 1.
9 WHO, *Weekly Epidemiological Record*, 223.
10 WHO, *WHO Report*, 1.
11 Ibid., 1–2.
12 For an example of CDC physicians using Stewart's line to discount its complacency, see Berkelman and Hughes, "Conquest," 426; for an example of a science journalist doing so, see Specter, "Doomsday Strain" and "Risks of Viral Research." A quick Google Books search for the phrase "close the book on infectious diseases" yields over seventeen hundred results, among them medical texts such as *Essentials of Infectious Disease*

Epidemiology, The Encyclopedia of Infectious Diseases, and *Infectious Diseases*. The line has also made its way into a host of anthologies in adjacent medical and public health fields, including *Pandemic Influenza: Emergency Planning and Community Preparedness, Immigrant Medicine, Foundations for Osteopathic Medicine*, and *A Companion to Paleopathology*.

13 Bristol, "William H. Stewart."
14 Gorbach, Bartlett, and Blacklow, *Infectious Diseases*, 108.
15 Buchanan, *Nexus*, 170.
16 Jensen and Jensen, "Microbiologic Considerations," 165.
17 Finger, *Elegy for a Disease*, 13.
18 Winn et al., *Koneman's Color Atlas*, 2.
19 See Margaret Hillenbrand's essay in this issue for an analogous argument about how "the transversal nature of precarity, rather than fostering a natural solidarity, may instead breed fear over fluid social status and the ever-present possibility of a sudden plummet downward," and how this fear of collapsed social distinctions may shape Chinese artists' and viewers' "cruel or disdainful gaze" toward contemporary subalterns such as waste pickers.
20 Massumi, *Politics of Everyday Fear* and *Ontopower*.
21 See Whitehall, "Aesthetic Emergency."
22 Collier and Lakoff, "Problem of Securing Health," 8–9.
23 Ibid., 11–12, 26–28.
24 Qtd. in Braun, "Biopolitics," 18.
25 Ibid., 18–19.
26 Cooper, *Life as Surplus*, 75.
27 Ibid., 98.
28 Ibid., 91.
29 Wright, "Terrorists and Biological Weapons," 66.
30 Joshua Lederberg, qtd. in ibid., 73.
31 Senate Minority Staff Statement, Senate Government Affairs Committee, Permanent Subcommittee on Investigations, "Hearings: Global Proliferation of Weapons of Mass Destruction," March 27, 1996, qtd. in ibid. 78.
32 Ibid., 88, 93.
33 Ibid., 95.
34 Qtd. in ibid., 73.
35 Ibid., 90–91.
36 King, "Security, Disease, Commerce," 766.
37 Morse, "Examining the Origins," 26.
38 Ibid., 10.
39 Lakoff, *Unprepared*, 79.
40 Ibid., 5.
41 King, "Security, Disease, Commerce," 767.
42 Ibid., 776–79.
43 Morse, "Examining the Origins," 21.
44 Henderson, "Surveillance Systems."
45 King, "Networks, Disease," 208–9.
46 For an analysis of the CDC epidemic model in China's health system, see Mason, *Infectious Change*.
47 Spellberg and Taylor-Blake, "On the Exoneration."

48 Henderson, "Surveillance Systems," 283.
49 Morse, "AIDS and Beyond," 23, 41n1.
50 Spellberg and Taylor-Blake, "On the Exoneration," 4.
51 Qtd. in ibid., 2, 4.
52 Cooper, *Life as Surplus*, 78–79.
53 Anderson, "Nowhere to Run, Rabbit."
54 Lakoff, *Unprepared*, 21.
55 Arthur S. Flemming, Director of the Office of Defense Mobilization, qtd. in ibid., 27.
56 Ibid., 80–81.
57 Henderson, "Surveillance Systems," 283–84.
58 Ibid., 283; emphasis added.
59 Foucault, *"Society Must Be Defended,"* 239.
60 Foucault, *Discipline and Punish*, 198.
61 Foucault, *"Society Must Be Defended,"* 243–44.
62 Foucault, *Security, Territory, Population*, 10–11.
63 Sarasin, "Trace of Infection."
64 Foucault, *Security, Territory, Population*, 11, 378–79.
65 Agamben, *Homo Sacer*.
66 Massumi, *Ontopower*, 36–44.
67 Mbembe, "Necropolitics," 24, 22.
68 Hooker, "SARS as a 'Health Scare.'"
69 Zhan, "Civet Cats."
70 Fidler, *SARS*, 23–24.
71 Spaeth, "Revenge of the Birds."
72 Wald, *Contagious*, 44–45.
73 Mbembe, "Necropolitics," 22.
74 Anderson, *Vancouver's Chinatown*, 30.
75 Lee, *Orientals*, 36.
76 Shah, *Contagious Divides*, 1.
77 1880 report by Committee to Investigate Chinatown, qtd. in Craddock, *City of Plagues*, 80.
78 Ibid., 74–75.
79 Ibid., 83–85; Shah, *Contagious Divides*, 57–63.
80 Dr. John Meares, qtd. in Shah, *Contagious Divides*, 1, 60.
81 Craddock, *City of Plagues*, 92.
82 Shah, *Contagious Divides*, 110–19.
83 Ibid., 12.
84 Qtd. in ibid., 99.
85 Ahuja, *Bioinsecurities*, 31.
86 Ibid., 67.
87 Ibid., 66; Turse, "Experimental Dreams," 150–51.
88 Turse, "Experimental Dreams," 139, 151–56.
89 Ahuja, *Bioinsecurities*, 69–70.

References

Agamben, Giorgio. *Homo Sacer: Sovereign Power and Bare Life*, translated by Daniel Heller-Roazen. Stanford, CA: Stanford University Press, 1998.

Ahuja, Neel. *Bioinsecurities: Disease Interventions, Empire, and the Government of Species.* Durham, NC: Duke University Press, 2016.

Anderson, Kay. *Vancouver's Chinatown: Racial Discourse in Canada, 1874–1980.* Kingston: McGill-Queen's University Press, 1992.

Anderson, Warwick. "Nowhere to Run, Rabbit: The Cold-War Calculus of Disease Ecology." *History and Philosophy of the Life Sciences* 39, no. 2 (2017). doi.org/10.1007/s40656-017-0140-7.

Berkelman, Ruth L., and James M. Hughes. "The Conquest of Infectious Diseases: Who Are We Kidding?" *Annals of Internal Medicine* 119, no. 5 (1993): 426–27.

Braun, Bruce. "Biopolitics and the Molecularization of Life." *Cultural Geographies* 14, no. 1 (2007): 6–28.

Bristol, Nellie. "William H. Stuart: Obituary." *Lancet*, no. 372 (2008): 110.

Buchanan, Mark. *Nexus: Small Worlds and the Groundbreaking Theory of Networks.* New York: Norton, 2002.

Chen, Kuan-Hsing. *Asia as Method: Toward Deimperialization.* Durham, NC: Duke University Press, 2010.

Collier, Stephen J., and Andrew Lakoff. "The Problem of Securing Health." In *Biosecurity Interventions: Global Health and Security in Question*, edited by Andrew Lakoff and Stephen J. Collier, 7–32. New York: Columbia University Press, 2008.

Cooper, Melinda. *Life as Surplus: Biotechnology and Capitalism in the Neoliberal Era.* Seattle: University of Washington Press, 2008.

Craddock, Susan. *City of Plagues: Disease, Poverty, and Deviance in San Francisco.* Minneapolis: University of Minnesota Press, 2000.

Craddock, Susan. "Embodying Place: Pathologizing Chinese and Chinatown in Nineteenth-Century San Francisco." *Antipode* 31, no. 4 (1999): 351–71.

Fidler, David P. *SARS: Governance and the Globalization of Disease.* New York: Palgrave Macmillan, 2004.

Fidler, David P., and Lawrence O. Gostin. *Biosecurity in the Global Age: Biological Weapons, Public Health, and the Rule of Law.* Stanford, CA: Stanford University Press, 2008.

Finger, Anne. *Elegy for a Disease: A Personal and Cultural History of Polio.* New York: St. Martin's, 2006.

Foucault, Michel. *Discipline and Punish: The Birth of the Prison*, translated by Alan Sheridan. New York: Vintage, 1995.

Foucault, Michel. *Security, Territory, Population: Lectures at the College de France, 1977–1978*, translated by Graham Burchell. New York: Picador, 2007.

Foucault, Michel. *"Society Must Be Defended": Lectures at the College de France, 1975–1976*, translated by David Macey. New York: Picador, 2003.

Gorbach, Sherwood L., John G. Bartlett, and Neil R. Blacklow, eds. *Infectious Diseases*, 3rd ed. Philadelphia: Lippincott Williams and Wilkins, 2004.

Henderson, Donald A. "Surveillance Systems and Intergovernmental Cooperation." In *Emerging Viruses*, edited by Stephen S. Morse, 283–95. New York: Oxford University Press, 1993.

Hillenbrand, Margaret. "Ragpicking as Method." *Prism: Theory and Modern Chinese Literature* 16, no. 2 (2019): 260–97.

Hooker, Claire. "SARS as a 'Health Scare.'" In *Networked Disease: Emerging Infections in the Global City*, edited by S. Harris Ali and Roger Keil, 123–37. Malden, MA: Wiley-Blackwell, 2008.

Jensen, Lauritz A., and James B. Jensen. "Microbiologic Considerations and Infectious Diseases." In *Foundations for Osteopathic Medicine*, 2nd ed, edited by Robert C. Ward, 165–78. Baltimore: Lippincott Williams and Wilkins, 2002.

King, Nicholas B. "Networks, Disease, and the Utopian Impulse." In *Networked Disease: Emerging Infections in the Global City*, edited by S. Harris Ali and Roger Keil, 201–13. Malden, MA: Wiley-Blackwell, 2008.

King, Nicholas B. "Security, Disease, Commerce: Ideologies of Postcolonial Global Health." *Social Studies of Science* 32, nos. 5–6 (2002): 763–89.

Kraut, Alan M. "Immigration, Ethnicity, and the Pandemic." *Public Health Reports* 125, no. 3 (2010): 123–33.

Kraut, Alan M. *Silent Travelers: Germs, Genes, and the Immigrant Menace*. Baltimore: Johns Hopkins University Press, 1994.

Lakoff, Andrew. *Unprepared: Global Health in a Time of Emergency*. Oakland: University of California Press, 2017.

Lakoff, Andrew, and Stephen J. Collier, eds. *Biosecurity Interventions: Global Health and Security in Question*. New York: Columbia University Press, 2008.

Lee, Robert G. *Orientals: Asian Americans in Popular Culture*. Philadelphia: Temple University Press, 1999.

Mason, Katherine A. *Infectious Change: Reinventing Chinese Public Health after an Epidemic*. Stanford CA: Stanford University Press, 2016.

Massumi, Brian. *Ontopower: War, Powers, and the State of Perception*. Durham, NC: Duke University Press, 2015.

Massumi, Brian, ed. *The Politics of Everyday Fear*. Minneapolis: University of Minnesota Press, 1993.

Mayer, Ruth. "Virus Discourse: The Rhetoric of Threat and Terrorism in the Biothriller." *Cultural Critique*, no. 66 (2007): 1–20.

Mbembe, Achille. "Necropolitics," translated by Libby Meintjes. *Public Culture* 15, no. 1 (2003): 11–40.

Molina, Natalia. *Fit to Be Citizens? Public Health and Race in Los Angeles, 1879–1939*. Berkeley: University of California Press, 2006.

Morse, Stephen S. "AIDS and Beyond: Defining the Rules for Viral Traffic." In *AIDS: The Making of a Chronic Disease*, edited by Elizabeth Fee and Daniel M. Fox, 23–48. Berkeley: University of California Press, 1992.

Morse, Stephen S. "Examining the Origins of Emerging Viruses." In *Emerging Viruses*, edited by Stephen S. Morse, 10–28. New York: Oxford University Press, 1993.

Sarasin, Philipp. "The Trace of Infection in the Work of Michel Foucault," translated by Ahmed Allahwala. In *Networked Disease: Emerging Infections in the Global City*, edited by S. Harris Ali and Roger Keil, 267–80. Malden, MA: Wiley-Blackwell, 2008.

Schweitzer, Dahlia. *Going Viral: Zombies, Viruses, and the End of the World*. New Brunswick, NJ: Rutgers University Press, 2018.

Shah, Nayan. *Contagious Divides: Epidemics and Race in San Francisco's Chinatown*. Berkeley: University of California Press, 2001.

Spaeth, Anthony, et al. "The Revenge of the Birds." *Time*, February 9, 2004, 62–63.

Specter, Michael. "The Doomsday Strain." *New Yorker*, December 20, 2010. www.newyorker.com/magazine/2010/12/20/the-doomsday-strain.

Specter, Michael. "The Risks of Viral Research." *New Yorker*, December 26, 2014. www.newyorker.com/news/daily-comment/risks-viral-research.

Spellberg, Brad, and Bonnie Taylor-Blake. “On the Exoneration of Dr. William H. Stewart: Debunking an Urban Legend.” *Infectious Diseases of Poverty* 2, no. 3 (2013): 1–5.
Turse, Nicholas. “Experimental Dreams, Ethical Nightmares: Leprosy, Isolation, and Human Experimentation in Nineteenth-Century Hawaii.” In *Imagining Our Americas: Toward a Transnational Frame*, edited by Sandhya Shukla and Heidi Tinsman, 138–67. Durham, NC: Duke University Press, 2007.
Wald, Priscilla. *Contagious: Cultures, Carriers, and the Outbreak Narrative*. Durham, NC: Duke University Press, 2008.
Whitehall, Geoffrey. “The Aesthetic Emergency of the Avian Flu.” In *Contagion: Health, Fear, Sovereignty*, edited by Bruce Magnusson and Zahi Zalloua, 71–98. Seattle: University of Washington Press, 2012.
Winn, Washington, Jr., et al. *Koneman's Color Atlas and Textbook of Diagnostic Microbiology*, 6th ed. Baltimore: Lippincott Williams and Wilkins, 2005.
World Health Organization (WHO). “Anticipating Epidemics.” May 2014. www.who.int/csr/disease/anticipating_epidemics.pdf.
World Health Organization (WHO). *Weekly Epidemiological Record*. Geneva: World Health Organization, 2015. www.who.int/wer/2015/wer9020.pdf.
World Health Organization (WHO). *WHO Report on Global Surveillance of Epidemic-Prone Infectious Diseases*. 2000. www.who.int/csr/resources/publications/surveillance/WHO_Report_Infectious_Diseases.pdf?ua=1.
Wright, Susan. “Terrorists and Biological Weapons: Forging the Linkage in the Clinton Administration.” *Politics and the Life Sciences* 25, nos. 1–2 (2007): 57–115.
Zhan, Mei. “Civet Cats, Fried Grasshoppers, and David Beckham's Pajamas: Unruly Bodies after SARS.” *American Anthropologist* 107, no. 1 (2005): 31–42.

SHUANG SHEN

Border as Method

ABSTRACT The current state of Chinese literary studies is undergoing a process of re(b)ordering where the nation-state is no longer seen as the only acceptable framing for Chinese literature, and existing identificatory markers of Chinese literature—locality, language, ethnicity—are subject to radical rethinking. This article proposes a paradigm of border as method for Chinese literary studies, following the lead of Sandro Mezzadra and Brett Neilson's volume by the same title. Border as method refers to a reflexive glance at the cognitive bordering that we as knowledge producers cannot avoid practicing as we set out to define our object of study or outline a polemic or paradigm. It invites questions such as, What sociological facts of compartmentalized space does the study of Chinese literature yield? If we follow the space making capacity of literature, would we take note of other trajectories of connectivity and relationality and produce alternative configurations of literary assemblage? How does the delineated space of Chinese literature engage with the unevenness and differentiation of Asia and the world? This method manifests as a constructionist engagement with Chinese literature and literary history. It also proposes a cultural geography fundamentally different from the conventional center vs. periphery model. In this new mapping, a borderscape defined in terms of a site or locality, a period, or a variety of other ways could become the de facto center that plays a definitive role in shaping the dynamics and critical terms of Chinese literature and culture as a whole.

KEYWORDS border, boundary, Sinophone, Cold War, form

At the center of Kevin Kwan's (1973–) novel *Crazy Rich Asians*, which inspired the Hollywood hit film by the same title, lies a mystery symbolized by a patch of land not locatable on Google Maps. Situated in what looks like a deserted place in the heart of Singapore, Tyersall Park is the residence of the protagonist's grandmother Shang Su Yi, an heiress to a great fortune that traces back to imperial Peking, before the fall of the Qing dynasty. The residence is vigilantly protected by Gurkha guards, supposedly "the deadliest soldiers in the world," its largely permeable boundaries barely separating the estate from "some old section of the Botanic Gardens."[1] The hardly visible borders of Su Yi's estate mirror the boundaries of this upper-crust family, which are vigilantly policed while they are constantly negotiated from both inside and outside the family. The coming into being of the transnational empire of the Shangs and the Youngs—the two families connected by marriage—was an early instance of economic globalization, a history that demonstrates, as anthropologists Sandro Mezzadra and Brett Neilson assert, that

PRISM: THEORY AND MODERN CHINESE LITERATURE • 16:2 • OCTOBER 2019
DOI 10.1215/25783491-7978539 •

borders did not "block or obstruct global passages of people, money, or objects" but became "central devices for their articulation."[2] The family enterprise, which set up its headquarters in Singapore and Malaysia and extended through Southeast Asia and further to Australia, underwent a process of continuous movement that incorporated more and more territory into its orbit, starting with the wealthy Peking banker Shang Loong Ma, who "smartly moved his money to Singapore" before the fall of the Qing and took control of "all the shipping lines from the Dutch East Indies to Siam, and . . . was the mastermind behind uniting the early Hokkien banks in the thirties."[3] Although it is only hinted at in the novel, we can assume that every step of this growth could not have happened without negotiating borders, which, as one character subtly suggests, may have involved the illegal smuggling of opium.

As the novel shows, the transnational capitalism of the "overseas Chinese" old money was forced to confront a Eurocentric world order that posited the West as the progenitor of modernity and the rest of the world as its belated imitators.[4] How the Shangs and the Youngs confronted this world order is shown in the novel's prologue, where Su Yi's daughter-in-law Felicity Young finds herself ejected from the lobby of London's upscale Calthorpe Hotel—an establishment that supposedly has been "owned by the Calthorpe-Cavendish-Gores since the reign of George IV"—when the manager realizes that the Youngs who have booked one of the hotel's luxury suites are in fact Chinese.[5] Using the logic of capitalism to her own advantage, Felicity overcomes the racially inscribed social ordering symbolically represented by the spatial borders of this hotel-cum–private club by taking over its ownership from the British aristocrat Lord Rupert Calthorpe-Cavendish-Gore. Felicity thus stages an act that pits non-Western modernity against its supposedly older and more authentic Western counterpart and insists on the equal status of the two. Through this detail, the novel uses the Chinese tycoon's rise to power to signal a shift in the "pattern of the world" from an East-West configuration to an Asia-centric model.[6]

This new pattern, according to the novel, has the Chinese at its center, since the overseas Chinese know best how to take advantage of their ancestral ties to consolidate their position as the beneficiaries of China's so-called rise in the early twenty-first century. The novel touts Asia's power (indeed the power of the global Chinese) in the new millennium, an age that finds its mirror image in the all--star, mostly Asian real and fictive celebrity guest list at the rich princeling Colin Khoo's wedding, featuring such luminaries as Faye Wong, the "Greta Garbo of Hong Kong," and Tracy Kuan, supposedly the Barbra Streisand of Asia. Yet ironically, while this shift may have upended the Eurocentric old order, it does not fundamentally change its cultural logic. The desire for parity with the West belies an equally strong urge for comparison that upholds the West as the eternal gold standard. The intra-Asian hierarchy is essentially no different from the Eurocentric one. Just as Shang Su Yi's palatial residence in the heart of Singapore resembles "the stately country estates . . . in England, like Chatsworth or Blenheim Palace,"[7] the old-money overseas Chinese treat the nouveau riche from Mainland China and Taiwan with the same disdain to which they themselves have been subjected by those biased Westerners. *Crazy Rich Asians* thus shatters the illusion of a borderless world engendered by neoliberal globalization culminating in the so-called Asian century in brutally honest ways, even as it flaunts the opulence of the "crazy rich" in Asia. It shows that the familiar East-West boundary has not disappeared altogether but has only been internalized, albeit decentralized. In the new world order, borders and boundaries proliferate among global Chinese of different origins, localities, and classes, while Asia once again becomes a new frontier for Asians themselves.

Crazy Rich Asians, both as a cultural production and in terms of the world it depicts, presents a set of provocations for those of us who do Chinese studies. The book's citation of Napoleon Bonaparte's pronouncement "Let China sleep, for when she awakens she will shake the world" can be read as an attempt to name the contemporary moment when the Beijing Consensus threatens to overtake the dominance of Washington consensus. A sense of irony is intended with this citation since the relation of *Crazy Rich Asians* to territorial China—either PRC or ROC—is by no means self-evident. This novel is in a way a story about China's rise without China. More precisely it flaunts a deterritorialized yet no less centered view toward China from the diaspora by focusing on how a specific sector of the ethnic Chinese in Southeast Asia negotiated with a new pattern of intra-Asian and global relationality anchored by China's momentous development in recent decades. Here the diaspora's occlusion should not escape our attention. As Engseng Ho argues, our contemporary understanding of the concept of diaspora follows a "bipolar framework, of old world home and U.S. host," with all the spaces in between "disappeared from the view of diaspora theorists, to be resuscitated as an abstract 'transnationalism' that was now celebrated as the global condition."[8] Although the home of the wealthy Chinese characters at the center of the novel is not the United States (in fact, they sneer at the United States), their diasporic sentiments also follow a bipolar framework. In an act of historical re-narrativization, Asia's crazy rich harken back to China as their ancestral home in a self-serving manner, tracing their fortune to their native place just so that their acquisition of wealth would appear to be not accidental but in fact inevitable. In the meantime, glossed over by the author as well as the characters is how successive generations of wealth seekers of different classes have tackled border regimes, whether of China or of other nation-states, or how they settled in the plurilingual and multiethnic societies in Southeast Asia. This willful negligence is indicative of the novel's erasure of the materialist histories of Chinese migration and Asian modernities. In this novel, the promising inheritor of the Young family fortune, Nick, is blissfully ignorant of how rich the family is, not to mention how it earned its first bucket of gold, claiming, "You know, when there's always been money in your life, it's not something you spend much time thinking about."[9] For sure, *Crazy Rich Asians* is more symptomatic than reflective of the transnational becoming of the ethnic Chinese in Southeast Asia.

Despite its limitations, the novel is still provocative, particularly in terms of its ability to push us to think beyond the conventional China vs. the West paradigm. It depicts a present condition in which the old East-West hierarchy is replaced by but also duplicates itself in a new intra-Asian pattern of differentiation and connectivity, such that it requires us to confront a much more complex geography in Asia and beyond. Would a text like *Crazy Rich Asians* be relevant to Chinese studies, more specifically Chinese literary studies? As we know, the histories of Chinese languages or broadly defined Chinese literature have never abided by the binding of the nation-state. Moreover, recent scholarship has made us more attuned to the unevenness and complexity of the global or regional spread of Chinese language and culture by, first, reexamining the automatic equation of language with ethnicity, the nation-state, or the affective identification as Chinese, and second, imploring us to rethink what used to be taken for granted as the default technology of categorization in the production of Chinese literature as object of knowledge.[10] In this context, to dismiss this novel as irrelevant to Chinese literature because of its linguistic medium (English) or its decentering of territorial China would be unwise and unproductive. Rather, I suggest we use this text to sharpen our critical aptitude to engage with Chinese literature and culture as global history. Kwan's book has inspired me to propose—following the lead of Mezzadra and Neilson's volume by the same title—a paradigm of border as method for Chinese literary studies. A critical engagement with social, historical, geographical, and geopolitical practices of bordering both internal and external to Chinese communities and societies in the world, I argue, could be constructive for literary studies for a number of reasons.

Mezzadra and Neilson's *Border as Method* is primarily focused on the ways in which borders contribute to the formation of uneven labor regimes and social inequalities. How can this anthropological study of the materialist histories of border making shed light on the methods of literary studies? Admittedly Sinophone literature of some localities register sensitivity toward border dynamics more readily than other locations. For instance, engagement with political and geographical borders is a prominent theme in Sinophone literature from Southeast Asia during the Cold War period. In addition, it is hard to imagine geographical and symbolic borders not playing a role in the formation of Hong Kong literature, given its context of a global city of flow and mobility. Yet although the degree of volatility to border dynamics might vary in terms of location, I argue that border as method for literary studies should not be applicable just to those communities with a history of migration and resettlement. Mezzadra and Neilson, along with other border theorists, emphasize the close connections between spatial borders and conceptual boundaries. For them, borders are everywhere. They do not exist only to mark the end of a national territory but can be found "wherever the movement of information, people and things is happening and controlled."[11] To think along the lines of border as method means to consider the intertwining of geographical and cognitive borders, the latter of which are "essential [for] . . . the establishment of taxonomies and conceptual hierarchies that structure the movement of thought."[12] A border's function is not solely as a technology of exclusion. It has a productive aspect manifested in what Mezzadra and Neilson have described as "the strategic role it plays in the fabrication of the world" or Étienne Balibar refers to as the border's "world-configuring function."[13] Thomas Nail also argues that "the border has become the social condition necessary for the emergence of certain dominant social formations, not the other way round."[14]

The current state of Chinese literary studies, as I see it, is undergoing a process of re-b/ordering where the nation-state is no longer seen as the only acceptable framing for Chinese literature, and existing identificatory markers of Chinese literature—locality, language, ethnicity—are being subject to radical rethinking. Sinophone studies as one of the most significant recent polemical initiatives, I believe, plays no small part in engendering this new configuration of knowledge formation and producing new mappings for Chinese literary studies. But Sinophone studies has put in place its own borders that are yet to be critically confronted. It remains a matter of controversy, for instance, whether the term *Sinophone literature* should be reserved for "the Sinitic-language communities and cultures outside China as well as ethnic minority communities and cultures within China where Mandarin is adopted or imposed,"[15] or whether it should also include the Chinese-language culture of Mainland China. At the same time, Sinophone studies' temporal borders need rethinking in the context of the longue durée of continuous movements of Chinese populations and cultures. Without sufficient self-reflection on the bordering of a circumscribed field of study, we risk rendering a specific locality or a particular period into a flat and homogeneous entity, evoked only as a strawman.

One way to avoid this danger, as David Der-wei Wang argues, involves trying to overcome the "dichotomized logic of the Chinese versus the Sinophone" by supplementing the "geopolitical dialectics" of postcolonialism with a consideration of the "historical intricacies of the Sinitic world."[16] Wang believes that Sinophone studies "must not engage merely with the conventional overseas Chinese literature plus ethnic literature on the Mainland. Rather, one must test its power *within* the nation-state of China."[17] While I embrace Wang's argument that Sinophone studies should engage with China from within, my promotion of border as method differs from Wang's, in that I believe we should not turn away from geopolitical dialectics, but on the contrary, we should look more deeply into it, by understanding geopolitics as itself a historical process of bordering with that Sinophone literature intersects through reifying, managing, complicating, and transgressing geographic and symbolic borders that exist inside and outside the texts. We should not only examine the geopolitical history of border making that connects or separates disparate Sinophone locations but also attend to the bordering processes internal to a specific Sinophone community. This mode of thinking would allow us to view this community as a heterogeneous social unit undergoing complex historical processes of self-identification. Border as method thus brings attention to how the geopolitical, the social, and the cultural articulate with each other at all scales, subnational, national, and global.

I understand border as method as primarily a reflexive glance at the cognitive bordering that we as knowledge producers cannot avoid practicing as we set out to define our object of study or outline a polemic or paradigm. This method manifests as a constructionist engagement with Chinese literature and literary history. In addition, "border as method" also proposes a cultural geography fundamentally different from the conventional center and periphery model. In this new mapping, a borderscape, defined in terms of a site or locality (Hong Kong as borderscape, for instance, as suggested by Yiu-Wai Chu's 2017 edited collection *Hong Kong Culture and Society in the New Millennium: Hong Kong as Method*), temporality (the Cold War, for instance, as I will discuss in later sections of this article), or a variety of other ways (for instance, Chinese language itself has been a borderscape since the beginning of the twentieth century), could become the de facto center that plays a definitive role in shaping the dynamics and critical terms of Chinese literature and culture as a whole.

Another takeaway from Mezzadra and Neilson's study is that it is not only illusory but deeply ideological to wish for the elimination of borders. Approaching Chinese literature from the perspective of borders is thus fundamentally different from yearning for what some scholars have called "the world of grand unity" (*datong shijie* 大同世界) of Chinese language or culture.[18] On the contrary, we should use "borders [as] the key to understanding networked connectivity as well as questions of identity, belonging, political conflict, and societal transformation."[19] These issues understood in the context of the continuous processes of reconfiguration and rebordering of the Chinese-language cultural landscape can be taken up as subjects of inquiry for Chinese literary studies. The recent evocation of the Sinophone is but one powerful polemical response to the shifting patterns of power in the Chinese worlds from the Cold War to the contemporary moment. I believe that border as method could enrich as well as give nuance to the Sinophone intervention while insisting on a historical perspective to it. This essay will start with a broad discussion of border theories as they pertain to Chinese literary studies in its current state and proceed to illustrate the significance of border as method for literary studies with a close reading of a short story by the Malaysian Chinese writer Ng Kim Chew 黃錦樹 (1967–).

Border Thinking and Inter-Asian Referencing

In fact, reflecting on *such and such* as method, as this special issue invites us to do, is to put border thinking in action. In a recent iteration of such border thinking, exemplified in the Taiwan scholar Kuan-Hsing Chen's 陳光興 proposal of Asia as method, the goal is to reorient a "West and the rest" framework in the direction of an inter-Asia framing. As Chen puts it, "using the idea of Asia as an imaginary anchoring point, societies in Asia can become each other's points of reference, so that the understanding of the self may be transformed, and subjectivity rebuilt."[20] This formulation, as Chen explicates, comes from the Japanese sinologists Takeuchi Yoshimi 竹内好 (1910–1977) and Mizoguchi Yūzō 溝口雄三 (1932–2010), both of whom reflect on knowledge production in conjunction with their spatial imagining of a world that is scaled by hierarchy and normativity.

Takeuchi's discussion in his essay "Asia as Method" of inter-Asian framework vs. "from the West to Japan" referencing begins with an account of his own first journey to China and proceeds to discuss Rabindranath Tagore's journeys to East Asia. These border-crossing journeys laid the groundwork for his theoretical injunction of Asia as method. For Mizoguchi, on the other hand, "China as method" amounts to a deliberate strategy for countering Japanese sinology's habitual way of thinking that "took the world as the goal and reckoned China's degree of progress (or disparity) using the world as the standard."[21] Conventional sinology in Japan, for Mizoguchi, is a form of cartographic imagination that requires rethinking. Sinologists see "nothing but a conceptualized world, a world of fixed and pre-arranged method." On the contrary, "a world that takes China as method would be a world in which China is a constitutive element. In other words, it would be a pluralistic world in which Europe is also one of the constitutive elements."[22] To move in the direction of recognizing a pluralistic world, the first step, as Mizoguchi proposes, is to resist the reification of the world by pluralizing one's frame of reference and shifting from a dyadic relationship of East vs. West to a more complex, multiaxial inter-Asian framework consisting of the West, Japan, and China.

The reflections on method from Takeuchi and Mizoguchi to Chen foster new understandings of self-formation and subjectivity gained by "'productive inter-referencing' between similar societies" in Asia, according to Meaghan Morris.[23] Asia as method, as Morris sees it, is a habit of thinking "heterotopically, whether from outside *or* inside a rhetorical position of [one's] belonging."[24] This way of thinking illustrates cosmopolitanism in the classical sense, because it is aimed at "a genuinely global creation of universality,"[25] with a goal of "changing the West" as much as the East through "a trans-local vision."[26] In these discussions, Morris views a place (in this case Hong Kong) as constituted in a network of places, "the 'local' . . . [seen as not] a limited patch of space but a mode of *involvement* in the neighbourhoods of thought and practice."[27] These reflections on method concur with Mezzadra and Neilson's proposal to link cartographic practices with knowledge production and pay attention to the "'area form,' as well as the processes of bordering at stake in the materiality of its constitution."[28] The "Asia" in Chen's essay or the "local" in Morris's work are all not fixed or homogeneous entities unriven by differentiation both internally and externally. "In the intellectual history of the twentieth century," Chen cautions us, "the word 'Asia' was in fact loaded with anxieties. . . . Asia as method recognizes the need to keep a critical distance from uninterrogated notions of Asia, just as one has to maintain a critical distance from uninterrogated notions of the nation-state."[29]

Reflecting on the constitution of Asia as an "area form" implies that bordering and identity construction are closely connected with each other. As Balibar argues in "What Is a Border?," "the idea of a simple definition of what constitutes a border is, by definition, absurd: to mark out a border is, precisely, to define a territory, to delimit it, and so to register the identity of that territory, or confer one upon it. Conversely, however, to define or identify in general is nothing other than to trace a border, to assign boundaries or borders."[30] It does not follow from the circularity of border and territoriality that identities are thereby all fictive or unreal; on the contrary, borders are a "strategic claiming of space, place and territory," leading us to focus on the history and context of each articulation of identity.[31] "'*B/ordering*,'" according to van Houtum, Kramsch, and Zierhofer, "as the strategic fabrication and control of a bounded sphere of connectivity, constitutes a reality of (affective) orientation, power and ease, thereby expressing desire for protective distance from the outside world."[32] The crucial issue here thus is not so much that "all identities are constructed" but that we must make room for a discussion of the historical process of identity construction—in the words of van Houtum, Kramsch, and Zierhofer, to understand "*b/order* [as] an active verb."[33]

These contemplations about the border conjoined with the reflections on Asia and method can inspire us to think in more robust terms about literature and space making. As Georg Simmel states, "The boundary is not a spatial fact with sociological effects, but a sociological fact with a spatial form."[34] What sociological "facts" of compartmentalized space does the study of Chinese literature produce and reinforce? If we follow the space-making capacity of literature, would we take note of other trajectories of connectivity and relationality and produce alternative configurations of literary assemblage? How does the delineated space of Chinese literature engage with the unevenness and differentiation of Asia and the world? Situating ourselves at the borderscapes of both China and literature, we would set foot on the same path as Mizoguchi's reflection on method vs. goal in relation to China. Mizoguchi finds it unsatisfactory with a sinology "where the immersion in China becomes its own goal," because it is "entirely predicated on the consumption of privately-held individual goals, it is another type of China-less sinology."[35]

Cold War Bordering and Ng Kim Chew's "The Year I Returned to Malaya"

I want to employ border as method to draw attention to an earlier moment in the twentieth century—the Cold War period, when historical acts of bordering left an indelible imprint on the contemporary cultural polemics in Chinese-speaking societies. In an ongoing larger project, I examine a "Cold War archive" consisting of literary and cultural texts that reflect on this global history in the process of its unfolding or with historical hindsight—in order to rethink how the complex bordering processes at local, national, and global scales impacted the cultural dynamics in Sinophone societies. The Cold War lends itself to the study of borders, because as Balibar argues, this historical event witnessed an overdetermination of borders, which means that "no political border is ever the mere boundary between two states, but is always . . . sanctioned, reduplicated and relativized by other geopolitical divisions."[36] Certain national borders also served as "the super-borders of the blocs," creating "a *de facto* hierarchy among those nations within each bloc," which in turn caused particular national borders to be "strengthened or weakened."[37] Yet, despite the hardening and overdetermination of certain borders, recent scholarship has managed to destabilize to a large extent mainstream Cold War historiography by questioning its periodization and local manifestation in light of the Third World's experience.[38] In light of what has come to be known as new Cold War studies, the question of what is the Cold War for non-Western societies can by no means be taken for granted. Rather, it must be addressed by deeply engaging with local experience, of which cultural imaginary constitutes a significant aspect. The questions of how bordering took place at local and global scales and how literature or culture articulated with local and global borders have to be rethought, rather than assumed to conform to the bipolar logic.

As Heonik Kwon's studies of Vietnam and Korea show, the overdetermined geopolitical division during the Cold War period is subject to translation when it interacts with local lifeworlds on the ground. Although the Sinophone literary sphere was significantly reconfigured and overdetermined by the politics of global Cold War and its local iteration—the Chinese civil war—this literary sphere was anything but static. Xiaojue Wang for one has convincingly shown that China's territorial borders on the northeast and southeast sides in the Cold War period were vital borderscapes that inspired literature written by writers of different backgrounds and political leanings, including both Communist and anti-Communist writers, China-based writers and writers in the diaspora. The entanglement of global and national politics with affective relations rendered these borderscapes into a site of complex overlaying and entanglement, rather than a simple line in the sand that merely divides or connects.[39]

As Petrus Liu argues in this special issue, the Cold War in the Chinese world works as "not just a state of geopolitics but a persistent affective structure, . . . capable of polarizing a wide range of discourses and objects beyond the doctrines of communism and anticommunism."[40] The Cold War's legacy lies in its bordering effect, about which we have yet to come to terms, despite our acquiescence about the existing divisions of different Sinophone localities and competing nationalism overall. While the Cold War as structure of feeling marches on in history, literary analysis is locked mostly in a historicist mode of tracing a specific cultural production's funding source or examining its propagandistic agendas. In other words, we have yet to come up with sophisticated analytical tools that could explain how culture engaged with the Cold War in a critical fashion that takes into account the history's continuous impact on the present. In this respect, the Malaysian Chinese writer Ng Kim Chew's fictional rewritings of the history of Malayan communism offer some useful analytical heuristics that, first, allow us to understand Cold War divisions as historical constructions and, second, implore us to imagine alternative futures beyond the Cold War. I argue that Ng's revisionist literary history manages to force open the Cold War archive and address contemporary concerns only because in an imaginary act, the writer disarticulates cultural boundaries from geopolitical and national borders, imbibing Chinese language and culture with a kind of resilience that allows it to survive the traumatic condition of overdetermining and duplicating borders, which Balibar associates with the Cold War.

Take Ng's story "Nanian wo huidao Malaiya" 那年我回到馬來亞 (The Year I Returned to Malaya) as an example. Intending to come to terms with the history of the Malayan communist movement, Ng's story comes from a collection of short stories titled *Nanyang Renmin Gongheguo beiwanglu* 南洋人民共和國備忘錄 (Memorabilia of the Nanyang People's Republic). Significantly the story constructs an expansive topography of interconnected localities linked by the characters' journeys across several generations. At the beginning, the main character, the son of an erudite Mainland migrant turned local Chinese schoolteacher in Singapore, returns from Taiwan to a fictional nation-state of Malaya. Earlier in the background we are told about the protagonist's exile in Mainland China during the War of Resistance against Japanese invasion; his resettlement in Taiwan; his father's migration to Singapore, presumably in the 1920s or 1930s before the war; and the father's exile in Sumatra, Indonesia, during the war. These individuals' crossings construct a network of places that include Malaysia, Singapore, Taiwan, and Mainland China. In addition, political movements, such as international communism, also reached beyond their immediate localities and helped stitch disparate locations together into transregional imaginaries of different kinds. These regional networks formed prior to the official start of the Cold War constitute a fluid terrain that is later crossed by the Cold War's overdetermined borders. While traveling between these places, the characters engage with the Cold War as a palimpsest, borrowing a term from Petrus Liu, and draw on their prior experience of crossings to challenge or reinforce Cold War ideologies. These border crossers and their acts of crossing are not to be found in a diaspora that Enseng Ho calls an "abstract third space" disembedded from history; rather they play an integral part in the author's reimagination of multiple historical processes in the region.[41]

The story presents a dystopic alternative history loosely based on the real histories of several nations in the Asia Pacific region. For instance, the independent nation-state called Malaya is similar to but divergent from the actual histories of Singapore and Malaysia. The fictional political history of Taiwan in the story is also reversed from its real history. In the course of constructing these alternative historical narratives, Ng decides to hold some historical divisions stable while attempting to interrogate the meanings of other boundaries. The political divisions between the Left and the Right and the ethnic boundaries of Malay vs. Chinese are still the main anchors of this revisionary political canvas, but the outcomes are reversed. In the post–World War II period, as the writer imagines, Taiwan is taken over by Communists from the Mainland. Malaya has turned red and evolved into a People's Republic of Malaya. Debates unfold between the main character's father and Malaya's prime minister, Dr. Chong, around whether the People's Republic of Malaya should become a satellite state of the PRC or retain some independence. The father, himself a polyglot who has married his Malay- and English-speaking Nyonya student, is wary of uncurbed Chinese ethnonationalism and advocates multiculturalism. The British-educated Dr. Chong is pro-China. Other details of this character suggest that he is possibly modeled upon Singapore's founding president, Lee Kuan Yew. Chong eventually wins the battle and places the narrator's father under house arrest. The tension between the protagonist's father and Chong alludes to the entangled relationship between Lee Kuan Yew and the leftist leader Lim Chin Siong. In Singapore history, "Cold Store" refers to a government crackdown on the leftist faction of the People's Action Party that took place in early 1963. In the story, this incident is shown to have been waged by the hardcore Left against the Malays. The Chinese-dominated government of the fictional People's Republic of Malaya, led by Dr. Chong, also organizes a "Great Migration," in which the government expels the Malay population to Indonesia, sending some of the resisters and activists off to Siberia in exchange for the repatriation of the Chinese from Indonesia. Ng's alternative history ends with a Malay people's insurgency in which Singapore is captured and Dr. Chong is killed, an event that sends many Chinese fleeing the country.

What is the story's message? If all it does is reverse the positions of the dominant and the dominated, the historical fates of the Left and the Right, and map those same divisions onto the existing cartographical and ethnic fault lines, then it would not be very useful in enabling a rethinking of history. Fortunately the story is more complex than this. We could argue that the writer takes a liberal position by arguing through this alternative history that prejudice and persecution could originate from any political faction and that both the Left and the Right are not free from ethnocentric tendencies. But a more interesting probability is that the writer makes political faction and ethnic groups interchangeable so as to de-emphasize the fate of any one political or social group but highlight the division itself. The story shows that the most severe form of violence comes from bordering, the history of how heterogeneous communities came to be brutally crossed by new borders, their lifeworlds reordered by the torquing of history—the Cold War, which intervened into postcolonial nation-building and aroused further ethnic strife. In this alternative history in which the outcomes of political struggles are defamiliarized, the effect of bordering as a form of top-down social engineering is shown to disrupt local histories and indigenous ways of living. Discourses of localism and indigeneity have been co-opted by Cold War patterns. For instance, from the perspective of the protagonist who has been charged with handling "minor nationality affairs" 主管少數民族事務 in the fictional Communist Taiwan, we learn:

> The issues of the "mountain folks" are complicated. After the Japanese devils chopped down 80 or 90 percent of the centuries-old forests in the mountains, the traditional economic system sustained by hunting collapsed. In terms of human evolution, the indigenous groups were forced to leap over several stages of civilization and arrive at modernity (with Japanese inflection). My job is to reprogram [their way of life] in the opposite direction, which means holding off development and reverting them back to the age of agriculture (or fishing, in the case of a few offshore islands) and limited hunting, so that traditional way of life can be maintained. Their traditional habit of sharing among the members of community is in fact rather consistent with proletarian ideals. It is a pity that for hundreds of years, imperialist missionaries have penetrated the forests and systematically destroyed their traditional beliefs in the name of medical assistance. Their language has been Romanized, and that transformation has sown the seeds of separatism.
>
> 這些山胞的問題蠻棘手的，日本鬼子砍掉山上八、九成的百年老樹後，他們以狩獵為主的傳統經濟體系就崩潰了。從人類文明史的進程來看，他們一度被強行跳躍好幾個文明階段，直接進入（日式的）現代。我的任務是做反向的調校，把他們限定在農業（或漁業，如少數離島）時代，可以維持有限的狩獵，如此他們的傳統生活方式可以得到一定的保持。他們族群共享的傳統觀念，其實可以很好

的嫁接無產階級理念。只可惜百多年來帝國主義的傳教士深入山林，以醫療為名，有計畫的摧毀他們的傳統信仰。把他們的語言羅馬化，也埋下了分離主義的種籽。[42]

The tone of this passage is ironic. We are led to become deeply suspicious of the evolutionary model of human progress that the fictional Communist regime in Taiwan draws upon even when it tries to reverse of the trajectory of development in the name of preserving traditional ways of life. The destructive force that damaged indigenous communities, the writer implies, does not come from a particular political faction or ethnic group but from the human history of division, segregation, and compartmentalization.

Significantly, in this story the resilient factor that could counter the violent progress of history turns out to be language. In the case of the protagonist's father's migration to Malaya, his Chinese survives this border crossing rather well because it is adaptable and can be shared among people across racial and cultural divides. After he is married to the protagonist's mother, a Peranakan widow, the family becomes increasingly multilingual, using a mix of Mandarin Chinese, Hokkien, Malay, and some English in the intimate setting of the home space. Language in general, not just Chinese, is capable of producing new forms of sociality and intimacy even as the boundaries of the speakers' ethnic identities remain intact. For instance, the sharing of a common language, Malay, between the protagonist's Malayan mother and his Taiwanese wife enables the elderly woman to accept her foreign daughter-in-law as family, even though she has lost all memories about her legal Chinese husband. Multilingualism does not hinder communication but, on the contrary, rekindles lively debates about political, literary, and linguistic issues.

While territorial or geopolitical borders often designate a dualistic division—be it internal vs. external, friend vs. foe—linguistic borders create pathways that engender networks of communication. Language can survive the violent rebordering of the Cold War intertwined with postcolonial nation-building because it belongs to the depth of memory. A language can be kept alive even when official policies declare it to be dead. For instance, when the protagonist's wife, an indigenous woman of the Buyi ethnicity from Taiwan, communicates in Malay with her mother-in-law, this helps to revive the language buried in the depths of her memory and reverses the edict by the People's Republic of Malaya that Malay is an "abandoned vernacular" 被廢棄的語言.[43]

In Ng's story, meanwhile, Chinese is the language of memory as well as history. The father, the story tells us, has purchased a coffin for himself, where he stores many history books. The coffin—a time capsule of a number of ancient civilizations, including Malay, Chinese, Greek, and Roman—also contains the father's lifetime work: a proleptic history titled "Wangguo ji" 亡國紀 (A Chronicle of a Nation's Demise), which is written in Chinese and carved on the inside of the coffin. This history foresees the destruction of the People's Republic of Malaya and the death of Dr. Chong. Applying a long historical perspective to the political currents at present, the writer makes Chinese the privileged medium that preserves the sedimentation of human histories within which the present of the nascent postcolonial state is embedded, but which the state willfully chooses to ignore. Using Chinese as the medium, the protagonist's father performs translation between the past and present, with a utopian aim of finding commonality between ethnic groups whose boundaries are at present tightly policed by the nation-state. How can a language evolve into something beyond the exclusive property of a particular community or group? How can we use language to launch a critique of separatist ethnic nationalisms and divisive political maneuvers? The story emphasizes that language can be a double-edged weapon that needs to be handled carefully. Earlier in the story, the protagonist, as an official in charge of minor nationality affairs, knows clearly that between "cultivating a common language among the different tribes [in Taiwan]" 發展中他們不同族群中間的共同語 and "reinforcing their distinct ethnic identities," 強化他們的族群特性分歧, the latter strategy "makes it much easier to gain control [over these groups]" 保留一定的族群特性方有利於統治.[44] Yet must we choose between "cultivating a common language" and retaining distinct identities? How does a language—a bordered unit in itself—become a gateway to communication rather than a closed door? The story thus can be read as a yearning for an interethnic and interpolitical medium of communication.

Conclusion, or Returning to Literature

Finally, literature, however broadly defined, has its own borders. Ng Kim Chew, in addition to being a prolific creative writer, is also an active literary critic with a contrarian tendency and is obsessed with the borders between literature and social reality. He considers his own stories such as "The Year I Returned to Malaya" to be *Magong shuxie* 馬共書寫 (writings on Malayan communists) to distinguish them from *Magong wenxue* 馬共文學 (Malayan communist literature), the latter of which, for him, falls short in "being descriptive and straightforward, with psychological depictions barely transcending political situations, and consisting mostly of stereotypical portrayals of the 'good' and 'bad' guys" 大量運用白描，直敘，完全不出政治語境的心理描寫——正面反面人物都吻合臉譜程式，都是典型人物.[45] He lambastes "both the nativist literature and literary realism espoused in Taiwan and Malaysia" for "underestimat[ing] the complexity of the domain of representation (the craft of language and literature) to the extent that the impoverishment of language and technique is construed as one of the manifestations of nativism . . . or its unique characteristic."[46] He wonders "whether it is ever possible for literature to change its fate of being hijacked by the state and nationalism . . . and return to being itself?" 文學發展到現在，是否該脫離國家及民族主

義的綁架……回到它自身?[47] Should we interpret Ng's advocacy for literature to "return to being itself" as a retreat to a well-bounded literary space?

Ng's arguments draw our attention to the bordering practices in and of literature itself, particularly when literature is treated not just as an object of knowledge for literary studies but also as an aesthetic form that signals the conjoining of literature with the world. I believe that adopting border as method should not lead to a denial of aesthetic borders. As Johan Schimanski and Stephen Wolfe suggest, we must give equal amount of critical attention to both "the border in the world of the text and the border of the text itself."[48] This means treating intrinsic literary borders "in the ontological sense in which [they] are involved in making or creating worlds."[49] Yet the aesthetic discourse is not self-contained but complexly embedded in and engaged with the geopolitics and the historical transformations in Asia and beyond. The Cold War's divisiveness manifested itself in the aesthetic realm as well when the distinction between modernism and socialist realism, both simplistically defined, was made to accord with geopolitical divisions grafted on to the geography of Sinophone literary sphere. In this context, Ng's adaptive transformation of *Magong wenxue* into *Magong shuxie*, despite his original intention, may very well amount to an unsettling of such well-established aesthetic divisions. His work reminds us that positioning oneself on the borderscape of China and literature as method can allow us to reconnect literature with the sociopolitical world in new and innovative ways while reenergizing the borders both inside and outside literature, so as to rethink history and imagine new ways of being.

SHUANG SHEN is an associate professor of comparative literature and Asian studies at Pennsylvania State University. She is the author of *Cosmopolitan Publics: Anglophone Print Culture in Semicolonial Shanghai* (2009) and coeditor of "China and the Human," a special issue of *Social Text* (2011 and 2012), and "Asian Urbanisms," a special issue of *Verge* (2015). She has published articles and essays in *Comparative Literature, MLQ, Modern China, MCLC, PMLA, Xinmin Weekly* (in Chinese), and *Wanxiang* (in Chinese). She received a Fulbright US Scholar grant and a Chiang Ching-Kuo Foundation Scholar Grant in 2015–2016, a fellowship from the Asia Research Institute in the National University of Singapore in 2015, and a fellowship from the National Humanities Center in 2019–20. She is currently working on a book project that studies trans-Pacific circulation of Sinophone literature during the Cold War period.

Notes

1. Kwan, *Crazy Rich Asians*, 157, 192.
2. Mezzadra and Nielson, *Border as Method*, ix.
3. Kwan, *Crazy Rich Asians*, 306.
4. There have been many debates about whether the term *overseas Chinese* is an accurate description of the ethnic Chinese communities in Southeast Asia and elsewhere in the

world. The term's connotation of a sojourner's identity does not accurately describe the multifarious choices and complex processes of identity formation of the ethnic Chinese. Some scholars have proposed alternative terms, such as *Chinese overseas*. This article retains the conventional usage of *overseas Chinese* while taking note of the term's inadequacy and the controversies around it.

5 Kwan, *Crazy Rich Asians*, 4.
6 Mezzadra and Neilson, *Border as Method*, 41.
7 Kwan, *Crazy Rich Asians*, 158.
8 Ho, "Inter-Asian Concepts for Mobile Societies," 915.
9 Kwan, *Crazy Rich Asians*, 452.
10 Here I refer to the recent scholarship in the field of Sinophone studies, including studies such as *Visuality and Identity: Sinophone Articulations across the Pacific*, *Global Chinese Literature: Critical Essays*, and *Sinophone Studies: A Critical Reader*. For sure, literary scholars and historians of modern China have engaged in trans-local studies of Chinese-language culture even before the invention of the subfield Sinophone studies. But Sinophone studies scholarship has sought to bring more heightened consciousness toward disparate Chinese-language communities and has taken some active steps to engage with these borders.
11 Balibar, "World Borders, Political Borders," 71.
12 Mezzadra and Neilson, *Border as Method*, 16.
13 Ibid., vii; Balibar, "What Is a Border?," 79.
14 Nail, *Theory of the Border*, 4.
15 Shih, Tsai, and Bernards, *Sinophone Studies*, 11.
16 D. D. Wang, "Sinophone Intervention with China," 63.
17 Ibid.
18 The term comes from the title of Liu Denghan's 劉登翰 (1937–) monograph, *Huawen wenxue de datong shijie*.
19 Rumford, "Seeing Like a Border," 68.
20 Chen, *Asia as Method*, 212.
21 Mizoguchi, "China as Method," 516.
22 Ibid.
23 Morris, "Hong Kong Liminal," 15.
24 Ibid., 16.
25 Ibid.
26 Ibid., 15–16.
27 Ibid., 14.
28 Mezzadra and Neilson, *Border as Method*, 47.
29 Chen, *Asia as Method*, 214–15.
30 Balibar, "What Is a Border?," 76.
31 Houtum, Kramsch, and Zierhofer, *B/ordering Space*, 6.
32 Ibid., 3.
33 Ibid., 2.
34 Simmel, "Sociology of Space," 162.
35 Mizoguchi, "China as Method," 516.
36 Balibar, "What Is a Border?," 79.
37 Ibid., 80.
38 Westad, *Global Cold War*; Kwon, *Other Cold War*.
39 See Xiaojue Wang's article "Borders and Borderlands Narratives in Cold War China."

40 P. Liu, "Cold War as Method," TK.

41 See Ho's critique of the notion of diaspora as the concept has been used and popularized in US academe since the early 1990s, in his "Inter-Asian Concepts for Mobile Societies," 915.

42 Ng, "Nanian wo huidao Malaiya," 50–51.

43 Ibid., 52.

44 Ibid., 50.

45 Ng, "Zuihou de zhanyi," 318.

46 Ng, "Minor Sinophone Literature," 17.

47 Ng, "Mahua wenxue de guoji," 228.

48 Schimanski and Wolfe, "Entry Points," 15.

49 Mezzadra and Neilson, *Border as Method, or, The Multiplication of Labor*, 30.

References

Balibar, Étienne. "What Is a Border?" In *Politics and the Other Scene*, translated by Christine Jones, James Swenson, and Chris Turner, 75–86. London: Verso, 2002.

Balibar, Étienne. "World Borders, Political Borders." *PMLA* 117, no. 1 (2002): 71–78.

Chen, Kuan-Hsing. *Asia as Method: Toward Deimperialization*. Durham, NC: Duke University Press, 2010.

Chu, Yiu-Wai, ed. *Hong Kong Culture and Society in the New Millennium: Hong Kong as Method*. Singapore: Springer, 2017.

Ho, Engseng. "Inter-Asian Concepts for Mobile Societies." *Journal of Asian Studies* 76, no. 4 (2017): 907–28.

Kwan, Kevin. *Crazy Rich Asians*. New York: Anchor Books, 2014.

Kwon, Heonik. *The Other Cold War*. New York: Columbia University Press, 2010.

Liu Denghan 劉登翰. *Huawen wenxue de datong shijie* 華文文學的大同世界 [Chinese-Language Literature in the World of Great Unity]. Guangzhou: Huacheng chubanshe, 2012.

Liu, Petrus. "Cold War as Method." *Prism: Theory and Modern Chinese Literature* 16, no. 2 (2020): 408–31.

Mezzadra, Sandro, and Brett Neilson. *Border as Method, or, the Multiplication of Labor*. Durham, NC: Duke University Press, 2013.

Mizoguchi, Yūzō. "China as Method." *Inter-Asia Cultural Studies* 17, no. 4 (2016): 513–18.

Morris, Meaghan. "Hong Kong Liminal: Situation as Method." In Chu, *Hong Kong Culture and Society in the New Millennium*, 3–32.

Nail, Thomas. *Theory of the Border*. Oxford: Oxford University Press, 2016.

Ng Kim Chew 黃錦樹. "Mahua wenxue de guoji: Lun Mahua wenxue yu (guojia) minzuzhuyi" 馬華文學的國籍：論馬華文學與（國家）民族主義 [The Nationality of Chinese Malaysian Literature: On Its Relation with (State) Ethno-nationalism]. In *Huawen xiaowenxue de Malaixiya ge'an* 華文小文學的馬來西亞個案 [Minor Sinophone Literature: The Case of Malaysia], 207–32. Taiwan: Maitian, 2015.

Ng Kim Chew 黃錦樹. "Minor Sinophone Literature: Diasporic Modernity's Incomplete Journey," translated by Andy Rodekohr. In *Global Chinese Literature: Critical Essays*, edited by Jing Tsu and David Der-Wei Wang, 15–28. Leiden: Brill, 2010.

Ng Kim Chew 黃錦樹. "Nanian wo huidao Malaiya" 那年我回到馬來亞 [The Year I Returned to Malaya]. In *Nanyang Renmin Gongheguo beiwanglu* 南洋人民共和國備忘錄 [Memorabilia of the Nanyang People's Republic], 41–62. Taiwan: Lianjing, 2013.

Ng Kim Chew 黃錦樹. "Zuihou de zhanyi—Lun Jin Zhimang de *Ji E*" 最後的戰役——論金枝芒的《飢餓》[The Last Battle: On Jin Zhimang's Novel *Hunger*]. In *Huawen xiaowenxue de Malaixiya ge'an* 華文小文學的馬來西亞個案 [Minor Sinophone Literature: The Case of Malaysia], 315–34. Taiwan: Maitian, 2015.

Rumford, Chris. "Seeing Like a Border: Toward Multiperspectivalism." *Political Geography* 30, no. 2 (2011): 61–69.

Schimanski, Johan, and Stephen Wolfe. "Entry Points: An Introduction." In *Border Poetics De-limited*, edited by Johan Schimanski and Stephen Wolfe, 9–26. Hanover: Wehrhahn, 2007.

Shih, Shu-mei, Chien-hsin Tsai, and Brian Bernards, eds. *Sinophone Studies: A Critical Reader*. New York: Columbia University Press, 2013.

Simmel, Georg. "The Sociology of Space," translated by Mark Ritter and David Frisby. In *Simmel on Culture: Selected Writings,* edited by David Frisby and Mike Featherstone, 137–70. London: Sage, 1997.

Takeuchi, Yoshimi. "Asia as Method." In *What Is Modernity? Writings of Takeuchi Yoshimi*, edited and translated by Richard F. Calichman, 149–65. New York: Columbia University Press, 2005.

van Houtum, Henk, Olivier Kramsch, and Wolfgang Zierhofer, eds. *B/ordering Space*. New York: Routledge, 2005.

Wang, David Der-wei. "Sinophone Intervention with China." In *Texts and Transformations: Essays in Honor of the 75th Birthday of Victor H. Mair*, edited by Haun Saussy, 50–80. Amherst, NY: Cambria, 2018.

Wang, Xiaojue. "Borders and Borderlands Narratives in Cold War China." In *The Oxford Handbook of Modern Chinese Literature*, edited by Carlos Rojas and Andrea Bachner, 334–55. New York: Oxford University Press, 2016.

Westad, Odd Arne. *The Global Cold War: Third World Interventions and the Making of Our Times.* New York: Columbia University Press, 2007.

PETRUS LIU

Cold War as Method

ABSTRACT This essay proposes a reconceptualization of the Cold War as a critical methodology for the study of contemporary Chinese-language cultures and literatures. Arguing that the Cold War is not over but simply transformed, the author redefines it as an enduring "problematic of the present," an emotional structure that continues to shape the contours of literature, academic discourse, and identity formations in ways of which we are not always fully conscious. Hence the Cold War is best understood as a "cultural palimpsest" where the old dilemma of communism versus anticommunism is rewritten into a contemporary idiom of colonialism versus self-determination. After developing the concept of Cold War as method, the second part of the essay offers a concrete example through a critical reading of *Swordsman II*, a 1992 martial arts film adapted from Jin Yong's 1967 novel. While the film has generally been analyzed for its representation of (queer) sexuality, the essay shows that it is the Cultural Revolution and its Cold War legacies that explain the emergence of its main character.

KEYWORDS Cold War, Jin Yong, martial arts cinema, Cultural Revolution, queer sexuality

The Cold War is over, we are told. In an era when we have become accustomed to defining the present against what comes before—postsocialism, poststructuralism, postmodernism, postfeminism, post-contemporary interventions—it seems counterintuitive, if not counterproductive, to even mention the Cold War as an interpretive framework for understanding the contemporary world. Instead of returning to an event that is almost universally regarded as a closed chapter of twentieth-century history, scholars of contemporary Chinese literature are more likely to worry about the fact that our neologisms cannot catch up with just how fast the world is changing. Why the Cold War? Why now? Is the Cold War not that historical period humanity has already surpassed with the worldwide collapse of communism in 1991? Is it not an obsolete term—like its conceptual byproduct, the so-called third world, which has been replaced by analytic categories such as the Global South, center/periphery, and the multitude? Is it useful to think about the Cold War as a relevant framework for *contemporary* Chinese literary and cultural studies?

Certainly, our field has no shortage of outstanding studies of Chinese-language literature, film, music, radio, and newspapers produced between 1946 and 1991 in the PRC, Taiwan, Hong Kong, Malaysia, and Singapore.[1] Very few scholars,

PRISM: THEORY AND MODERN CHINESE LITERATURE • 16:2 • OCTOBER 2019
DOI 10.1215/25783491-7978547 •

however, ever apply the concept of the Cold War to materials produced after 1991. The commonly accepted view is that the Cold War refers to the period of "non-hostile belligerence" between the capitalist Western bloc and the communist Eastern bloc from the period of the Truman Doctrine of 1941 to the collapse of the Soviet Union in 1991. East Asia was involved, but only as the "hot" battleground for a series of proxy wars between the United States and the USSR. With the fall of the Berlin Wall and the dissolution of the USSR, history has decidedly moved into a post–Cold War, "post-ideological" phase. Accordingly, post-1991 Chinese literature is studied in the context of a wide range of periodizing markers such as neoliberalism, post-market-reform, the new world order, New Democracy movements, and the Beijing Consensus, but the Cold War is certainly not among them. As these periodizing markers gain greater currency in modern Chinese literary and cultural studies, the Cold War fades further into the background as an unfashionable topic of historical interest, one that is best discussed by historians and political scientists working in dusty archives. But this bifurcation of Cold War historiography and contemporary Chinese cultural studies is a consequence of a static conceptualization of the Cold War as a *time frame* rather than a *method*. If we accept the temporal definition of the Cold War as the period of geopolitical tension between the United States and the USSR, surely it has very little bearing on the study of today's Asia. If we reconceptualize the Cold War as a method for analyzing contemporary Chinese cultural formations, we open ourselves to a much broader range of interpretative possibilities and analytic tools, which allow us to ask more nuanced questions about affect, embodiment, belongingness, identity, and dystopia in a divided Asia.

Even if we accept the more empirical, commonsense definition of the Cold War as a time frame rather than a contemporary problematic, we must still ask: is the Cold War really over from the point of view of Asia, which is still divided into political states and ideological factions that are derived from the mid-century period?[2] From a Euro-American perspective, the collapse of America's main contender for global supremacy seems to have furnished incontrovertible proof of "the end of history as we know it." In Asia, however, the "division system" between the two Chinas (PRC and ROC) and the two Koreas (North and South) remains unchanged, though recent events since 2018 may have paved the way for a future Korean reunification.[3] In the first part of this essay, I argue that the Cold War is precisely the cultural logic of the present and the most appropriate analytic optic for understanding contemporary Chinese cultures. Our inability to view it as such is the consequence of three interrelated problems and entrenched assumptions: a generalization of imperial history as world history that obscures the agency of Asian subjects and states; a pernicious empiricism that treats the Cold War as a time frame instead of a conceptual problematic; and finally, an intellectual division of labor between disciplinary knowledge and area studies created by the Cold War itself. The future of modern Chinese literary and cultural studies, in my view, depends on our collective effort to dislodge these three assumptions. In the second part of the essay, I offer a reading of *Xiao ao jianghu zhi Dongfang bubai* 笑傲江湖之東方不敗 (Swordsman II: Asia the Invincible), a 1992 martial arts film directed by Ching Siu-tung 程小東 (1953–) and produced by Tsui Hark 徐克 (1950–), using the methodology I am developing in this essay to give the reader a concrete sense of how the Cold War might be retooled for the studies of post-1991 Chinese literatures and cultures. Although the manifest subtext for Ching and Tsui's film is the social anxiety surrounding the impending 1997 handover of Hong Kong, my reading shows that the film's political vocabulary of independence versus unification is derived from Jin Yong's 金庸 (1924–2018) critique of Chinese communism in the novel (1967–69) on which the film is based.[4] This continuity shows that the Cold War is not over but rather simply transformed. However, as my reading of the 1992 film adaptation shows, the Cold War is also an extremely fungible concept. The Cold War is best understood as a kind of cultural palimpsest where the old dilemma of communism versus anticommunism is reconfigured and rewritten into a contemporary idiom of mainland Chinese colonialism versus local self-determination. Because the film adaptation has transformed its ideological referent from the Cultural Revolution to the specter of the reannexation of Hong Kong, the novel's original historical relation to the Cold War becomes an occluded presence, a disavowed trace in the Derridean sense that requires the methodology outlined in this essay to come to view. By developing the Cold War as a reparative reading method that restores such hidden historical relations to view, I also stake a claim for the importance of modern Chinese literary studies and interpretive methods in a field of Cold War studies dominated by the social sciences.

I

Of the three enduring assumptions about the Cold War that are blocking our understanding of its persistence, the generalization of imperial history as world history is perhaps the most deeply entrenched. To begin with, the conventional definition of the Cold War as the period from the beginning of the Truman Doctrine to the dissolution of the USSR naturalizes a Western-centered explanatory framework that completely overlooks the experience and agency of East Asia. The presumption that Cold War studies must begin (and end) with the United States and its Western rivals is part of the imperialist history that organizes our temporal-spatial lifeworlds into the rise and fall of Western empires. As Fredric Jameson observes, the much-touted story about "the end of socialism (for we have now slipped insensibly into that version of received opinion) always seems to exclude China"[5]—and we might add North Korea, Vietnam, Laos, and Cuba to the list. Since political scientists cannot reconcile the rupture thesis with the factual existence of countries that are still officially socialist despite their so-called mixed economies, the euphoric celebration of the worldwide collapse of communism simply ignores East Asia.

While communism and anticommunism are no longer the reigning ideologies that divide China and Taiwan, contemporary cross-strait relations transformed an old vocabulary into an identity politics without reinventing its essence. Indeed, as Kuan-Hsing Chen has argued, decolonization in Asia remains an incomplete project because it was hijacked and derailed by the American installment of a "Cold War structure of feeling."[6] Because the Cold War is not just a state of geopolitics but a persistent affective structure, it is capable of polarizing a wide range of discourses and objects beyond the doctrines of communism and anticommunism. And because the Cold War is a structure of feeling, it does not always have a material, easily detectable presence.

The partition of East Asia into communist and anticommunist zones created nationalities—legal categories, embodied experiences, and subject formations—that persist or even flourish today, despite the dissolution of anticommunism as a doctrine. But while most critics acknowledge the involvement of American, Soviet, and Chinese interests in the creation of the division system on the Korean Peninsula, the explanation of the origins of Taiwan has become much more complicated. If it was once easy to critique US neocolonialism, the Seventh Fleet, and US arms sales as the material conditions that guaranteed a divided Asia, today it is impossible to make that point in reference to Taiwan without appearing to support Chinese imperialism. Increasingly the only politically acceptable view of Taiwan is that it is a separate and distinct entity from any concept of China. Those who understand the division of China and Taiwan as a product of the Cold War are quickly branded as pro-unification Chinese propagandists. While the PRC regards Taiwan as a renegade province and asserts its sovereignty over the island in the name of an anti-imperialist effort to rectify the history of colonial dismemberment, in Taiwan itself an increasing number of citizens see the nation as a victim of multiple colonialisms (Dutch, Spanish, Japanese, and Chinese) currently fighting for its independence from the imperial ambitions of Beijing. Similarly (but for very different reasons), Hong Kong residents are increasingly worried about the "mainlandization" (*daluhua* 大陸化) of the island and its culture. From the 2014 Umbrella Movement to the 2019 anti-ELAB protests, the region's autonomy and its people's civil liberties are repeatedly put into crisis. What we are witnessing is a clash of nationalisms, all of which regard themselves as anti-imperialist movements. This complexity is the reason why we need the concept of Cold War as method, which allows us to explore the hidden context that shapes the contours of literature, art, academic discourse, and political protests in ways that do not always immediately correspond to a legible, binary structure of domination and resistance.

A proper understanding of the Cold War must therefore take seriously the agency of Asian subjects as rational actors instead of reducing them to mere collateral damage, objects of foreign influence and manipulation, proxies, or hapless casualties caught in the crossfire between the superpowers. The marginalization of East Asian agency has produced a de-individuation effect—a construction of Asians as faceless and nameless multitudes in Cold War historiography. Conventionally, scholars interpret the Cold War as the rivalry between the two Western superpowers without acknowledging Asian subjects and states as political actors that have also shaped that history. Seen as the mere recipient of foreign ideologies, Asia is given a complex and turbulent twentieth century in US-based Cold War historiography, but this complexity ultimately turns out to be nothing but collateral damage in a history driven by conflicts within the Western world. In an influential study of postwar politics, for example, historian James Cronin argues that the formation of postwar Japanese culture is a reactive, nationalist effort to discover what is putatively unique in its own tradition to compensate for its integration into "military alliances dominated by the United States, and the mass consumption of American goods, with the inevitable Americanization of taste and popular culture."[7] In other instances, studies of contemporary East Asia characterize its culture industry as a response to the traumatic memory of war—especially the "forgotten war" of Korea—but always place more emphasis on the discontinuities than the commonalities between the Cold War and the present. In these accounts, aesthetic objects in East Asia do not appear as the products or expressions of local history. Rather they are described as reactions or resistance to foreign ideologies.[8]

Our inability to understand East Asian subject formation as anything but a reaction to the interimperial rivalry of foreign powers is the result of a scholarly tendency to underplay the agency of nations and histories outside the Atlantic world. In standard US history textbooks, for example, World War II began with Hitler's invasion of Poland in 1939 and ended in 1945. In reality, the "world" war between the major players began with Japan's invasion of China in 1937 and only later came to involve Europe. Historians typically refuse to recognize that East Asian conflicts were not the ripple effects but, rather, the beginnings of world history. Nor do they believe that the internal politics of East Asia actually made a difference in the course of the war. The denial of East Asian agency works hand in hand with the construction of Asian subjects as indistinguishable drones, mobs, hordes, coolies, or other figures without names, histories, or personalities. If asked, Who did we fight in World War II?, an American of average education would probably respond, "Hitler, Mussolini, and Japan." Unable to attach a name and a face to America's Asian antagonist, the same American might also describe the psychosexual perversions of Hitler in lurid detail. But despite the historical verdicts that Hitler's Holocaust was the ultimate act of barbarism in the entirety of human history, the United States dropped atomic bombs not on Germany but rather on Japan. The implication is that if Nazi Germany was pure evil incarnate, then Japan was beyond good and evil—a mere laboratory for Western experiments. Some historians argue that the decision to drop the bomb on Japan was made because Germany had already surrendered (on May 7, 1945) before the bomb was ready. (The first test bomb, called the Gadget, was detonated on July 16 in New Mexico, before the second and the third were dropped on Japan in August.) However, others believe that the decision was racially motivated. Bruce Cumings argues that a prototype was ready to be deployed on Germany, but American leaders decided not to use it for fear that, if the bomb failed, the Germans could use it to their own advantage, whereas experimenting it on primitive Asians would be strategically safer. In any case, Japan was ready to surrender after the first bomb was dropped on Hiroshima. Since there was absolutely no material explanation for the deployment of the second bomb, Cumings argues that the destruction of Nagasaki reflected a general disregard for Asian lives in comparison to Europeans: "[Hiroshima] was an atrocity on a large scale and therefore a war crime.... Nagasaki is different: If it was gratuitous at best (atomic annihilation as an afterthought), it was therefore genocidal at worst (because it served no clear war purpose)."[9] The trivialization of Asian lives, "subjects without history" who are neither capable of great evil nor deserving of basic human rights, prevents us from seeing East Asia as the true locus of Cold War power struggles.

The second assumption—that the Cold War must be an empirical time frame rather than a mentality that has been internalized by many in the contemporary world—stems from the rupture thesis popularized by Francis Fukuyama.[10] According to Fukuyama, the fall of the Berlin Wall and the collapse of the Soviet Union marked "the end of history" that signaled the triumph of liberal democracies and hence the end of any power struggles between capitalism and communism. Defining *ideology* narrowly as the choice between democracy, communism, and fascism, Fukuyama and his followers proclaim that we now live in a world "free of ideologies." Conservative critics regard the collapse of communism as a powerful vindication of US policy throughout the period.[11] On occasion, the Fukuyama school of thought also appears to reserve the term *ideology* for all alternatives to Western forms of government rather than a choice between them. In this view, democracy is not an ideology but what humanity has always striven to achieve since the times of Plato—a natural, God-given desire for self-governance that was first articulated by the Greeks, dramatically brought to the fore by the French Revolution, and mythically perfected and put into practice by the Americans. Against this concept of democracy, fascism, communism, and oriental despotism appear as interchangeable examples of totalitarianism—unfortunate moments when tyrants rise and the people are either unable to make decisions for themselves or ideologically brainwashed to accept them.[12]

But Fukuyama is right that the Cold War involves the formation and proliferation of ideologies, which is precisely why we need a humanistic discipline such as modern Chinese literary studies to complement the empiricist approaches in Cold War studies. Ideology, as defined by Louis Althusser, is "a representation of the imaginary relationship of individuals to their real conditions of existence."[13] The study of ideologies must begin with the analysis of subjectivities and subject formations, or what Althusser calls interpellation, the process whereby power "hails" individuals into social subjects. Literary studies assumes a privileged role in the study of Cold War subject formations because it lays bare the hidden connections between nodes of knowledge that are obscured by our hopelessly rigid disciplinary fields and by our increasingly reified, privatized existence.

Literary analysis demonstrates that the real difficulty posed by the Cold War in Asia is not merely the question of sovereignty but also the complex range of emotional responses to the legacy and future of the division system. Traditional definitions of postcolonialism based on the historical experiences of South Asia, Latin America, or Africa cannot explain why Hong Kong residents viewed the 1997 handover as Chinese reannexation and the end of human rights and democracy instead of the end of British colonial rule. Similarly a binary vocabulary of domination and resistance, theorized in classic subaltern studies, cannot explain the difference between Taiwanese and Korean responses to Japanese imperialism. While the majority of South Koreans regard the period of Japanese occupation as the derailment of their modernization—frequently depicted in Korean literature as *han* (resentment)—the majority of Taiwanese citizens and leaders characterize the fifty years of Japanese colonialism as a golden age of development that woefully ended with Japan's defeat. With the 1949 arrival of mainlanders, new identities and subject positions were created. In Taiwan, Hokkien-speaking populations who are mostly descendants of Hoklo emigrants from Fujian are now called *benshengren* 本省人 (people from the local province)—meaning people who are considered authentically Taiwanese. By contrast, the émigrés who came to Taiwan in 1949 and their children are called *waishengren* 外省人 (people from the outer provinces)—meaning aliens who cannot be fully assimilated and are marked by their old-fashioned customs and incorrect accents. Although the *bensheng* populations are also Chinese speakers who have migrated from the mainland since the twelfth century, the presence of post-1949 migrants and the Kuomintang (KMT) government are seen as the worst form of Chinese settler colonialism rather than the result of the Cold War in Asia. In addition to the critique of its autocracy and the 228 incident, the chief complaint against the KMT regime is that it was never invested in the infrastructure of the island, which it treated only as a temporary military base to "take back the mainland and rescue our fellow countrymen" (*fangong dalu jiejiu tongbao* 反攻大陸解救同胞, the political slogan of the Chiang Kai-shek administration). In recent years, news reports on almost every earthquake in

Taiwan have characteristically included—in addition to compassionate observations of human casualties—asides about Japanese-era constructions that are still standing tall and proud next to the ruins of KMT-era buildings.

But while some argue that the KMT occupied or colonized Taiwan, it certainly did not do so on its own. Protected by the Seventh Fleet during the Civil War and subsequently by the Sino-American Mutual Defense Treaty, which prevented both Taiwan and China from initiating direct military actions without US interventions, Taiwan from the start has been a product of the Cold War. As Hsiao-ting Lin shows through an examination of recently declassified archives (at Hoover Library and elsewhere), the creation of two Chinas was not, as commonly assumed, a simple result of the Chinese Civil War or a reflection of incompatible ideologies and military interests. Rather it was the cumulative outcome of political compromises, negotiations (between actors who possessed only partial knowledge of the situation), unforeseen circumstances, and ad hoc responses to unexpected turns of events—which is why Lin describes Taiwan as an "accidental state."[14] Today the majority of the 1949 émigré soldiers have either passed away or become socially and politically marginalized, and a significant number of citizens support a name change of the country to Taiwan from its current title the Republic of China. However, given the PRC's staunch opposition to Taiwanese independence, some "deep-green" Taiwanese believe that Taiwan's only hope is to become the fifty-first state of the United States—a movement known as the Club 51 phenomenon.[15] On the other hand, some individuals in both Taiwan and China still believe in the One-China principle, now referred to as the 1992 Consensus. From the perspective of the People's Republic, the One-China policy is a nonnegotiable principle of national sovereignty in response to a history of colonial dismemberment, foreign interferences in its national affairs, and an American strategy of containment that encircled its borders with enemies following the Sino-Soviet split. In other words, China's stance toward Taiwan today is a consequence of its rigidified defense to persistent hostilities from the Cold War in Asia. As Perry Anderson points out, in terms of linguistic, ethnic, or religious differences from the center, in principle both Tibet and Hong Kong have greater claims to independence than Taiwan, and therefore permitting Taiwanese independence could create a domino effect.[16] But what we do not always sufficiently recognize is that Taiwanese, Chinese, and American nationalisms are mutually embedded and interlocked ideologies. The impasse between China and Taiwan (and between the two Koreas) cannot be resolved through a romantic nationalism that has historically created settlements in the Americas or reunified Germany. Instead the present political situation requires a rethinking of the Cold War—one that moves beyond the presuppositions of its conventional historiography as well as a traditional postcolonial analysis of Taiwan as an oppressed nation seeking to liberate itself from its master.

Finally, the third difficulty that Cold War as method seeks to overcome is the division of intellectual labor between the humanities and the social sciences, between discipline and area, and between the study of the West and the study of the rest. In an influential article, Carl Pletsch describes an asymmetrical division of intellectual labor brought about by the Cold War creation of the three-world scheme.[17] Invented by French anthropologists in the 1960s, the three-world scheme divided the planet into three geopolitical categories and created corresponding branches of knowledge that resulted in a chiasmus of area and discipline. Knowledge produced by the first world is institutionally organized by discipline (for example, literature, music, economics, political science, and psychology), but knowledge produced by, for, and about the third world is organized by language and area (China, Japan, the Middle East, Africa, and Latin America). Following the Cold War divide, English became a discipline (literary studies, as opposed to law, economics, or music), but Chinese became an area studies program (the study of China, as opposed to Japan or the Middle East). Pletsch's historical investigation sheds light on many of the perplexing phenomena we find in academia today. For example, an Asian studies department might prioritize hiring a scholar of Buddhism over filling large gaps in Chinese, Japanese, and Korean literary history, but a French department is unlikely to appoint a specialist of Catholicism before it can offer courses on topics such as the eighteenth-century French novel.

This division is clearly troublesome, since works produced by first-world thinkers can transcend both national and disciplinary boundaries, while works produced by the Global South are perceived to reflect the essence of their societies of origin and studied through quantitative and empiricist methodologies. Naoki Sakai traces this division of intellectual labor to a conceptual split between two kinds of subjects of knowledge: *humanitas* and *anthropos*.[18] *Humanitas* refers to humans who are capable of self-reflexivity while embodying particularistic features of a common humanity. By contrast, *anthropos* is reserved for people who participate only in the production of knowledge in the second sense, as particular manifestations of a putatively common human nature. Moreover, as Gavin Walker points out, the selection of an area in area studies is not random but rather a process of enclosure that cannot be understood independently of the historical expansion of capitalist accumulation on a global scale that brings about not only expropriation and dispossession but also commensurabilities.[19] The preference for social scientific methodologies in Asian studies reflects a positivism historically associated with the Cold War task of identifying and gathering information about the enemy, with an emphasis on the discovery of reliable information and transparent communication. In other words, the separation of theoretical and empirical inquiry was politically motivated by the Cold War rather than an organic intellectual development of academic knowledge from within.

II

To develop a more concrete sense of how Cold War as method might shed light on the persistence of history's hold on the present, I turn to Ching Siu-tung and Tsui Hark's *Swordsman II: Asia the Invincible. Swordsman II* is an adaptation of Jin Yong's novel *Xiao ao jianghu* 笑傲江湖 (The Smiling, Proud Wanderer), which was first serialized from 1967 to 1969.[20] The film is considered a milestone in *wuxia* 武俠 cinema for its allegorical import, emotional drama, use of special effects, fluid camera movement, and cinematography.[21] Prior to the *Swordsman* series (the first *Swordsman* film was made in 1990, and the third one was made in 1993), Chinese *wuxia* movies relied on two studio techniques to illustrate superhuman abilities (such as "lightness kung fu"—gravity-defying moves on rooftops, bamboo branches, or lakes). The first technique was based on the trampoline, which combined careful editing and stunt work to create the illusion of flying, gliding, or other highly acrobatic kung fu moves. The second technique is called *wire fu* (wire work and kung fu), which used wires and pulleys to hold actors in midair during a fight scene. The arrival of Tsui Hark on the scene, however, completely revolutionized martial arts cinema and made it appear more modern.[22] Tsui's *Swordsman* movies were among the first ones to employ digital technologies—including computer-aided compositing and generated images—to render superhuman martial arts, which has since then become the industry standard. Combining stylized cinematography with intense action scenes and arresting storytelling, the *Swordsman* series came to be regarded as the beginning of a new chapter in *wuxia* cinema.[23] Thematically the series is also remarkable in that it broke away from the old-fashioned morality tales of revenge, honor, nationalism, and crude kung fu fighting found in earlier martial arts films and shifted to a more complex and visually stunning ecology of human emotions and ethical dilemmas. New Martial Arts Cinema, as works by Tsui and Ching have come to be called, finally moved the genre past a simplistic hero-villain binary commonly seen in socialist propaganda films and the earlier era of kung fu revenge films.

With its modern visual effects and stylized color composition, the *Swordsman* series offers not only bodily spectacles but an invitation to explore the interiority of the human psyche. *Swordsman II* tells the story of Asia the Invincible (Dongfang bubai 東方不敗), a martial arts master who follows the instructions of a "secret scroll" (*miji* 秘笈) called *Kuihua baodian* 葵花寶典 (The Sunflower Manual) and castrates himself to harness its preternatural martial power. Unexpectedly Asia metamorphoses into a woman. As I will discuss more fully in the next section, the episode in Jin Yong's original novel was conceived as a political allegory to demonize Mao, one that employs a homophobic/transphobic perspective to depict how Asia becomes a psychologically damaged and sexually aberrant "neither man nor woman" (*bu nan bu nü* 不男不女) monstrosity as the price he has to pay for his political ambition.[24] Jin Yong tells us that Asia's castration causes him to lose all interest in women and become a homosexual who is willing to play the role of a submissive housewife to a low-ranking but masculine member of his clan.[25] The misogynistic tone is unmistakable, as Jin Yong clearly equates castration with feminization and feminization with social subordination. But the 1992 film performed a stunning cultural coup, turning Asia into one of the most iconic and celebrated queer figures in Chinese-language cinema. Instead of a debased male homosexual, Asia in the film version—portrayed by the talented and scene-stealing actress Brigitte Lin Ching-Hsia 林青霞 (1954–)—is a self-affirming transgender woman who takes much pride in her newfound gender identity as well as her martial powers. Jin Yong reportedly objected to the casting of Lin, as he had meant for Asia to be a source of disgust and revulsion.[26] But as a cultural palimpsest, the story of Asia took on a life of its own, exceeding and transforming Jin Yong's authorial intentions and the political context of its genesis. Indeed the story of Asia has undergone numerous adaptations for both cinema and television, creating a diffused form of collective popular memory that has no singular presence.[27]

Throughout the 1990s, the story of Asia the Invincible has been interpreted by mainstream critics as a film about gender-crossing and homoeroticism, either in a positive or negative sense. For some the film serves as a prime example of homophobia and heterosexism in traditional Chinese culture in that it conflates castration, femininity, and homosexuality. Chou Wah-shan 周華山 (1962–) famously argued that the casting of Lin, a female actress, in the role of Dongfang bubai is a strategic and homophobic move on the part of the producers to heterosexualize a same-sex relationship to make it more palatable to the audience.[28] Clearly the idea that castration can lead to a change in sexual orientation is founded on a cultural perception that homosexuals are somehow comparable to eunuchs, and the conflation of transgender and eunuchs also perpetuates a phallus-centered understanding of the organization of desires and identifications. For other critics, however, this politically incorrect but aesthetically daring film stands as evidence of an irrepressible queer energy in social undercurrents even in the conservative and homophobic 1990s.[29] Both sets of critics note the significance of casting Brigitte Lin, whose successful performance in many crossdressing or androgynous roles before and after this film has earned herself a large queer following.[30] Thanks to Lin's spellbinding performance, Asia the Invincible has become a glamorous, diva-like icon in contemporary queer Chinese cultures.[31] Chinese popular culture is full of vulgar jokes about Asia's "sunflower" techniques (sometimes replacing the word *kuihua* 葵花 [sunflower] with *jiuhua* 菊花 [chrysanthemum], the colloquial term for anus). As a result of the popularity of the character, *Swordsman II* has been exclusively analyzed for its representation of (queer) sexuality. I argue, however, that it is the Cultural Revolution and its Cold War legacies that explain the emergence of the main character and that this context only becomes legible through the concept of Cold War as method.

There are two separate political subtexts for the film: one is the Cultural Revolution, and the other is the 1997 handover of Hong Kong. *Swordsman I* and *II* are adaptations of Jin Yong's 1967 martial arts novel, *Xiao ao jianghu*, which is an allegorical representation of the Cultural Revolution.[32] In Cold War historiography, communism is frequently presented as a distortion of human nature, while capitalism—despite its inequalities and problems—is justified in pragmatic terms as the best of all possible worlds. Following this line of thinking, critics often regard the Cultural Revolution as the most extreme, and catastrophic, outcome of communism's distortion of human nature. In this sense, the critique of the Cultural Revolution cannot be separated from the critique of communism and Cold War politics. Hence Jin Yong's fictional exploration of the Cultural Revolution and its discontents offers an important example of a Chinese intellectual's reading of communism and its effects on traditional Chinese culture during the Cold War.

Written at the height of the Cultural Revolution, *Xiao ao jianghu* is an allegorical novel that depicts the transformation of political differences into personal gains and power struggles. Politics is no longer real or meaningful; rather what is done in the name of ideological causes (unification versus independence) is merely factionalism and personality cults created by power-hungry politicians who have no regard for ordinary people's lives. Jin Yong uses the concept of *jianghu* 江湖, a Chinese idiom that refers to both the world of *wuxia* and the world of politics, to describe a scene of perpetual violence. Violence begets violence, and despair follows. There seems to be no exit from the cycle.

As mentioned above, in the novel Asia the Invincible is a villain, not the protagonist's object of romantic interest. The name Dongfang bubai tacitly alludes to Mao Zedong 毛澤東 (1893–1976), whose given name, Zedong 澤東, could be translated literally as "bringing prosperity to the East," and the film emphasizes this allegorical connection by having Asia always wear a red robe with a symbol of the sun and the moon. The third installment in the series of the films, *Dongfang bubai zhi fengyun zai qi* 東方不敗之風雲再起 (Swordsman III: East Is Red), further exploits the symbolic resonances between the story and Mao's China. In Jin Yong's original novel, Asia the Invincible is the leader of an underground society called the Sun/Moon Sect (*riyue shen jiao* 日月神教), which, like the young Chinese Communist Party, seeks to unify China by ousting opposing clans and ideologies. In response to the rising menace of the Sun/Moon Sect, the major martial arts factions—Shaolin Temple, Wudang, and the schools of the five sacred mountains—form an alliance. They refer to themselves as the "orthodox sects" (*zheng jiao* 正教) and refuse to speak of the Sun/Moon Sect by its real name. Instead all leaders and students of the orthodox sects learn to refer to the Sun/Moon Sect as the demon cult (*mo jiao* 魔教), not unlike the way children in the "free world" were taught during the Cold War to speak of the Chinese Communist Party only as *gongfei* 共匪 (communist bandits) instead of *gongchandang* 共產黨 (communist party). While the world of *jianghu* is thus divided between the orthodox sects and the demon cult, the alliance of orthodox sects itself is plagued by a serious disagreement between the pro-unification camp (those who believe that the only way to stop the advances of the Sun/Moon Sect is to merge into one school) and the pro-independence camp (those who believe that the history, culture, and techniques of each school can be preserved only if they remain separate from one another and that the call for the merger is merely one leader's ruse to increase his personal influence and power within the alliance).

While the choice of Asia as its narrative focus allows the film to derive significant allegorical material from the novel's engagement with Chinese communism, in the original novel Asia is only a minor character. Asia is a usurper who rose to power and ousted the original leader after acquiring special powers from a foreign book titled *The Sunflower Manual*, which is said to come from the West (*xiyu* 西域). If Karl Marx's *Capital* provided the ideological foundation for the Chinese Communist Party, *The Sunflower Manual* proves to be the literal font of Asia's martial powers and political leadership. Asia's actions in the book replicate the most destructive aspects of the Cultural Revolution. He forces young children—reminiscent of the Red Guards—to denounce their parents' political mistakes in public. The same children would cheerfully explain to the world the physical and spiritual benefits of studying and reciting the teachings of the holy master every morning, as if they were carrying a copy of Mao's *Little Red Book*. A boy around ten years old says, "If I spend a day without studying the master's sacred instructions, I lose all appetite and cannot sleep. When I study his sacred instructions, my martial power grows, and I have the energy to defeat our enemies" 一天不讀教主寶訓，就吃不下飯，睡不著覺，讀了教主寶訓，練武有長進，打仗有力氣.[33] The novel's protagonist, Linghu Chong, is a student in the Huashan 華山 Sect. Like his peers, he is raised to fear and distrust the Sun/Moon Sect, but after a chance meeting with the daughter of the deposed leader, Linghu becomes entangled in the internal affairs of the sect and eventually agrees to help the royalists defeat Asia in order to restore the old master to rule. But once the old master resumes leadership, he simply becomes another Asia the Invincible, with the same thirst for power, and uses the same kind of ruthlessness to achieve it. In the end, Linghu realizes that the problem is systemic rather than personal; in choosing one faction over the other, he has only furthered the perpetuation of power, greed, and violence. As the master in the movie says to him regarding his desire to "retire from the *jianghu*" 退出江湖: "Where there are humans, there is *jianghu*. Humanity is *jianghu*" 只要有人的地方就有江湖，人就是江湖. The dream of a peaceful, conflict-free world is not only utopian but naive. Linghu's gradual understanding of this lesson forms the basis of the novel's (and the movie's) sobering political realism.

This thesis is worth careful consideration, for it would be a mistake to simply dismiss *Xiao ao jianghu* as simply Maoist or anti-Maoist, communist or anticommunist. Rather than launching a predictable critique of Mao's China from a liberal point of view, the novel instead tells us precisely the opposite: that the simplistic choices the Cold War forced upon us (between communist and anticommunist ideologies) reduce the complexity of human struggles to a mere matter of political allegiances and identifications without any awareness of systemic mechanisms by which social power reproduces itself. While I argue that it is the Cold War (synecdochically represented by the Cultural Revolution), rather than homophobia, that constitutes the political context for the genesis of Asia the Invincible, in reality the historical relationship between Jin Yong and Maoist politics was extremely complex. What I am characterizing here is therefore not a one-to-one correspondence between the novel's features and Mao's Cultural Revolution, as if it were simply a roman à clef to be decoded as a piece of anti-Maoist propaganda. Rather I am more interested in demonstrating how one cultural logic informs and gives rise to another, and how the Cold War might be more productively understood as a cultural palimpsest that is again and again rewritten from one historical moment to another.

In the initial years of the story's serialization in *Ming Pao* 明報, Jin Yong was widely seen as a right-wing journalist in Hong Kong. On May 6, 1967, massive riots broke out on the streets of Hong Kong, leading to an event dubbed the "Great Proletarian Cultural Revolution of Hong Kong" 香港無產階級文化大革命. Starting with a labor dispute in a factory in San Po Kong, confrontations between the police and picketing workers quickly escalated into violent crises. After the arrest of several workers, procommunist leftists formed the Hong Kong and Kowloon Committee for Anti–Hong Kong British Persecution Struggle. Carrying Mao Zedong's *Little Red Book*, protesters demanded labor rights, equality, the end of British imperialism, and social justice. These large-scale demonstrations against British colonial rule and in support of the Cultural Revolution on the Mainland met with brutal government crackdowns. The leftists then switched to guerrilla tactics and planted bombs around the city. On August 24, Lam Bun 林彬 (1929–67), a famous radio commentator who had sharply criticized the leftists, was burned alive on his way to work. The leftists then announced that their next target was Jin Yong, who had to go into hiding.[34]

The history of Cold War politics is full of contradictory beliefs and mercurial views. Before Jin Yong came to be seen as a traitor to Hong Kong and a sellout to Beijing, he was once called an enemy of socialism, a reputation he garnered from the debates between *Ming Pao*, a newspaper he founded, and the procommunist leftist newspaper *Ta Kung Pao* 大公報. In 1962, Jin Yong published a series of essays criticizing the response of the People's Republic of China to the crisis of refugees from the regime fleeing to Hong Kong—which, he argued, reflected an increasingly rigid dogmatism within the Communist Party that detached it further from the reality and livelihood of the masses. On October 16, 1964, China successfully detonated its first nuclear bomb, an event its foreign minister, Chen Yi 陳毅 (1901–72), described as the pride and glory of all third-world countries in their common struggles against the Soviet Union and the United States. A few days later, Jin Yong published an essay condemning China's entry into the global arms race. He maintained that by choosing atomic bombs (*hezi* 核子) over pants (*kuzi* 褲子), Mao's brand of socialism had shifted its aims from a sustainable livelihood for its citizens to militant nationalism. In response, *Ta Kung Pao* described Jin Yong and his newspaper as "anticommunist and anti-Chinese, follower of England and worshipper of America, betrayer of what the people stand for" 反共反華，親英崇美，背叛民族立場.[35] Although the 1967 Hong Kong leftist riots threatened Jin Yong's life, they did not turn him into a staunch anticommunist writer. Instead, he wrote a novel that explores the ways in which political labels—such as leftist and conservative, communist and anticommunist—divide our world into normative values and fossilized beliefs, often with violent consequences.

As I have been arguing, the figuration of Asia the Invincible is not an instrument of pro- or anticommunist ideologies but an exploration of the mental hold that such labels have over us. After the fall of Asia the Invincible, Linghu Chong is pursued by the leader of the orthodox alliance, Zuo Lengchan (左冷禪, whose name could be rendered literally as "the chan [Zen] Buddhism of Cold [War] leftist [politics]"). Zuo sees Linghu as all that stands in the way of "unifying all of China under one rule"—which is to say, his own. Ultimately Linghu Chong is betrayed by his own teacher, who raised him as his son. We learn, then, that both the demon cult and its opponents in the orthodox sects have dark sides. The object of the novel's critique is therefore neither communism nor anticommunism but dogmatism: the slavish following of inflexible political beliefs. Rather than treating Jin Yong as a leftist, a conservative, a capitalist comprador, or a socialist, it is perhaps more accurate to call him a humanist deeply immersed and invested in China's cultural tradition, something he believes that the proponents of the Cultural Revolution—and their critics—have distorted, destroyed, or else forgotten in their ceaseless power struggles and search for modernity. Linghu Chong is a tragic hero in this sense. He recognizes that the spectrum of human values and actions cannot be reduced to a Manichaean binary of good and evil but is himself unable, at the end of the day, to transcend fossilized ideological binaries.

Manichaeism is the telling metaphor here. The idea that the world can be divided into absolute good and evil, and the various historical religions based on binary principles such as Manichaeism and Zoroastrianism, fascinated Jin Yong and provided rich resources for his craft. In his 1961 novel *Yi tian tu long ji* 倚天屠龍記 (Heavenly Sword, Dragon-Slaying Saber), he uses Manichaeism (*Ming jiao* 明教) as the actual name for an underground society of martial heroes. Set in the final years of Mongol rule in China, the novel is similarly concerned with the internecine struggles between an alliance of orthodox schools and a menacing opponent, the Religion of Light. Like the Sun/Moon Sect, the Religion of Light is also referred to as a demon cult by its enemies. However, the members of the Religion of Light turn out to be the heroes who lead the Han Chinese to throw off the yoke of Mongol rule. Jin Yong's construction of the story reveals the influence of a theory proposed in the 1940s by the Chinese historian Wu Han 吴晗 (1909–69). According to this theory, the leader of the rebellion against the Mongols, Zhu Yuanzhang 朱元璋 (1328–98), chose the name Ming 明 (meaning "light") for his new dynasty to acknowledge the assistance of the Manichees. Jin Yong's novel correctly notes that in medieval China Manichaeism was called the Religion of Light, but otherwise his representation is a confused tangle of elements associated with Persia, Arabs, Nestorianism, Zoroastrianism, and other Middle Eastern content. For example, the Manichees are said to be fire worshippers like Zoroastrians, while in fact they worshipped symbols of the sun and the moon but not fire.[36] The novel discusses the strange ways of the Manichees, including nude burial for deceased members, vegetarianism, and a lineage of virgin female rulers. According to the novel, the word *mani* was changed into the similar-sounding *mo* 魔, the Chinese word for demon, during the Tang dynasty. Here Jin Yong's characteristic blending of fact and fiction adds much flavor to the story. It is safe to assume that the Sun/Moon Sect in the 1967 novel is a code name for the Religion of Light as well, for the Chinese character *ming* 明 is in fact made up of the characters for "sun" 日 and "moon" 月. Ming is also clearly an emotionally evocative character for Jin Yong, who once explained that he named his newspaper *Ming Pao* to emphasize its objective, nonpartisan character and his belief in political transparency. But does Jin Yong mean to suggest that the Communist Party is like the Religion of Light and the Sun/Moon Sect in his novels, "demon cults" that are misunderstood by the people and, indeed, demonized for having revolutionary beliefs? To begin with, we should note that the idea of demon cults occupies an ambivalent place in Jin Yong's universe. In *Yi tian tu long ji*, the demon cult is unambiguously the victim of a witch hunt, persecuted by self-appointed guardians of tradition and morality. In *Xiao ao jianghu*, the demon cult itself is responsible for many atrocities and follows an oppressive and violent doctrine. The shift in Jin Yong's thinking is also discernible in the constructions of the two protagonists. Both characters are invited to join the demon cult, but while the protagonist of the earlier novel readily accepts, Linghu Chong rejects the offer and makes an even more radical choice: he becomes the first male head of a convent of Buddhist nuns, to the outrage and consternation of his peers. In crossing the gender line, Linghu Chong challenges a different kind of ideological divide. The earlier novel subverts social conventions by having its villains turn out to be falsely demonized and grossly misunderstood heroes, but its strategy is still predicated on a binary opposition. The latter, more sophisticated novel dispenses with the language of good and evil altogether.

The 1992 film adaptation inherits the binarism of Cold War thinking that Jin Yong introduces and implicitly criticizes but transforms its object from the Cultural Revolution to the 1997 handover of Hong Kong. In addition to the story of Asia, the film significantly expands on a minor episode in the original novel that is centered on Blue Phoenix, a Miao woman who rules a subsidiary clan of the Sun/Moon Sect. Curiously the movie version turns all members of the Sun/Moon Sect into Miao ethnic minorities. The members of the Sun/Moon Sect are introduced as "women Miaozu" 我們苗族 (literally, "we Miao")—a phrase that is translated as "highlanders" in the English subtitles. Linghu Chong and other members of the orthodox sects become Han Chinese (漢人, translated as "mainlanders" in the English subtitles), who are said to have ruled and oppressed the Miao for centuries. The substitution of ethnic tension for anticommunism in this scene is a clear example of how, under the Cold War in Asia, the sublime object of ideology is radically fungible.

Rather than serving as the embodiment of foreign-influenced dogma, Asia the Invincible becomes the primary object of Linghu Chong's affection and the cause of his crisis in masculinity. The crux of the movie's emotional narrative rests on a misunderstanding and an ambiguity: Linghu Chong meets Asia for the first time when the latter is practicing the art of *The Sunflower Manual* by a lake, and Linghu mistakes him for a woman. Asia is first shocked by the mistake but, in a split second, finds himself amused by it. Being spoken to as a woman overwhelms Asia with a newfound, unspeakable feeling, and he decides to spare Linghu's life. This initial scene of misrecognition is the beginning of Asia's gender transformation, suggesting that it is in and through the eyes of the other that (gender) identity becomes possible. Later Asia acquires a feminine voice from the powers of the manual (or as a result of his castration), puts on full makeup and women's attire, and fully transitions into a woman. She falls in love with Linghu and tricks him into a one-night stand by convincing him to have sex with her concubine who serves as her body double and prosthesis. At the final battle on Black Cliff, Linghu finally realizes that the woman he loves is none other than the dreaded leader of the demon cult. He confronts her, but she seems genuinely puzzled, asking why he wants to interfere in the internal affairs of the Sun/Moon Sect. Then she turns to the old master and says, "The Han Chinese have oppressed us Miao for generations, and today you brought a Han person to Black Cliff to interfere in our internal affairs, how do you face our ancestors?" 漢人世世代代欺辱我們苗族，你現在卻帶了漢人上來黑木崖，來干涉日月神教教內的事，你怎麼對得起諸位列祖列宗?, Asia's response is an apparent non sequitur, which turns Linghu's question of sexuality ("Did I just sleep with a man?") into a question of civil war and national self-determination ("Why did you bring a mainlander into the internal dispute within the Miao tribe?"). The latter question is, of course, at the heart of present political conversations in Taiwan and Hong Kong. As I have argued in the first part of the essay, many commentators in Taiwan do not believe that Taiwan has ever been part of China or shared its culture and identity; hence they do not describe the current cross-strait relations as the result of a civil war. Instead mainstream media and academic discourse treat the presence of *waishengren* in Taiwan as the consequence of a foreign invasion (Chinese settler colonialism and neocolonialism). It is increasingly difficult to decide whether Taiwan's current status was the result of a civil war or foreign colonialism and whether the 1997 handover of Hong Kong marked its liberation from British imperialism or its recolonization by China. This indeterminacy indicates that the Cold War is very much a problematic of the present in Asia. The rhetorical sleight of hand in Asia's response registers this indeterminacy, which provides the real subtext and ideological referent for a question that at first appears to be concerned exclusively with sexuality.

My reading of *Swordsman II: Asia the Invincible* focuses on the rhetorical shift, elision, and slippage between the sexual and the political and particularly the cultural logic of substitutions and displacements. The film's ostensible interest in the sexual narrative requires the cultural logic of the Cold War. Asia the Invincible is the Janus-faced figure and the emotional fulcrum that connects the Cultural Revolution critique and the narrative of Hong Kong's impending doom in 1997—the past and the present of the Cold War in Asia. Through the story of Asia the Invincible, a Cold War framework connects two separate political events—the Cultural Revolution and the 1997 handover of Hong Kong—and imbues them with the same emotional responses and ideological significance. This example shows how the unlikely use of the Cold War as method for the film might yield new insight into its embeddedness in a partially obscured historical conjuncture. In turn, a textured reading of the film also develops a renewed understanding of the Cold War as a multilayered and sometimes contradictory ideology formation.

Conclusion

We can no longer afford to discuss the Cold War as solely the story of the United States and the USSR. But to properly restore to view the agency of Asia in the making of the Cold War, what we need is not a conspiracy theory of secret deals behind closed doors between powerful men and women and their Western allies but an account of the quotidian lives, emotions, and memories of ordinary people and families torn apart by the civil war. Following Kuan-Hsing Chen's work on Asia as method, we can begin to understand that the Cold War is not just a state of geopolitics but a persistent structure of feeling that shapes the emotional landscape of contemporary Chinese culture. Conversely, because the Cold War is a complex psychological phenomenon diffused in everyday life and sustained by the participation of ordinary men and women in Asia, I argue that the study of the Cold War in Asia requires a textual approach to its cultural productions. It is in cultural products such as *Swordsman II* that we find the best tools for understanding the Cold War. History is not a collection of transparent facts but a social text, and a mysterious one at that. The history of the Cold War is full of ideological distortions, literal and figurative displacements, contested emotions, obscured visions, political appropriations, fragmented memories. Reconceived as a cultural palimpsest, the Cold War demands reimagined interpretive paradigms, theoretical approaches, and analytical tools. For modern Chinese literary studies, these goals carry distinct promises and burdens.

PETRUS LIU is associate professor of Chinese and comparative literature and women's, gender, and sexuality studies at Boston University. He is the author of *Stateless Subjects: Chinese Martial Arts and Postcolonial Literature* (2011) and *Queer Marxism in Two Chinas* (2015). He has also coedited several projects, including "Beyond the Strai(gh)ts: Transnationalism and Queer Chinese Politics" (2010), a special issue of the journal *positions*. He is currently completing a manuscript on the problem of alterity in queer theory and Marxism.

Acknowledgments

I am most grateful to Carlos Rojas and the two anonymous reviewers for their critical reading and helpful comments on earlier versions of this essay.

Notes

1 The literature is too vast to cite here, but some representative works include Day and Liem, *Cultures at War*; Fu, "Cold War Politics and Hong Kong Mandarin Cinema"; C. Lee, "Rhythm and the Cold War Imaginary"; S. Lee, "Creating an Anti-Communist Motion Picture Producers' Network in Asia"; Lee and Wong, *Lengzhan yu Xianggang dianying*; and Wang, *Modernity with a Cold War Face*. Several major international conferences held in recent years reflect this trend: "Sights and Sounds of the Cold War in the Sinophone World," Washington University in St. Louis, March 25–26, 2017; "Unlearning Cold War Narratives: Toward Alternative Understandings of the Cold War," National University of Singapore, May 27–28, 2016; "Literature and Cultural Translation in China, Hong Kong, and Taiwan during the Cold War," Lingnan University, March 6–7, 2015; and "Transpacific China in the Cold War," University of Texas at Austin, April 18–19, 2013.

2 Many historians recognize and indeed emphasize that the Cold War in Asia has not ended. See, for example, Kwon, *Other Cold War*, and Westad, *Global Cold War*.

3 See Paik, *Division System in Crisis*, for the concept of the division system.

4 Hong Kong's 1997 handover is well recognized by critics as the "real" referent for this martial arts film set in medieval China. See, for example, Marchetti, "Hong Kong New Wave," 109. For a compelling reading of *Swordsman II* as expressing utopian longings for an unknown and unknowable future beyond 1997, see Chan, "Figures of Hope." For a

brilliant interpretation of Tsui Hark's work as part of a "kung fu cultural imaginary" that denies its own modernity in order to intervene in Hong Kong's anxiety-ridden return to China, see Li, "Kung Fu."

5 Jameson, "Actually Existing Marxism," 15.

6 K.-H. Chen, *Asia as Method.*

7 Cronin, *World the Cold War Made,* 115.

8 The point I am making stems from a broader conversation about the conditions of knowledge production that began with Paul Cohen's call to develop a China-centered alternative to the "impact-response" framework (*Discovering History in China*), the critique of the area studies model in China studies, and the invention of "Asian studies in Asia." Specifically in the context of Cold War studies, many interventionist works have already reconfigured Asia as the protagonist of history. See, among others, J. Chen, *Mao's China and the Cold War*; Hajimu, *Cold War Crucible*; Szonyi, *Cold War Island*; Liu, Szonyi, and Zheng, *Cold War in Asia*; and Jager and Mitter, *Ruptured Histories.*

9 Cumings, *Parallax Visions*, 45.

10 Fukuyama, *End of History.*

11 For an example of this view, see Gaddis, *We Now Know.*

12 In "The Postcolonialism of Cold War Discourse," Pietz argues that while the primary theoretical anchor of Cold War discourse is the specter of totalitarianism, it gained wide acceptance with the general public through a conflation of communism and fascism, despite the fact that communism emerged historically as an antifascist movement. Pietz further shows that this picture of totalitarianism actually derived its vocabulary from an earlier colonialist fantasy about totalitarianism outside of Europe, such as the so-called tribal societies of uncivilized peoples and "oriental despotism."

13 Althusser, "Ideology and Ideological State Apparatuses," 109.

14 H. Lin, *Accidental State.*

15 Political parties in Taiwan are divided into two color-coded blocs. The pan-Green camp supports Taiwanese independence, while the pan-Blue camp favors greater economic linkage with the People's Republic of China. On the Club 51 phenomenon, see K.-H. Chen, *Asia as Method*, 161–73.

16 Anderson, "Stand-Off in Taiwan."

17 Pletsch, "Three Worlds."

18 Sakai, "Dislocation of the West."

19 Walker, "Accumulation of Difference and the Logic of Area."

20 *Xiao ao jianghu* was first serialized in *Ming Pao* 明報 from April 20, 1967, to October 12, 1969. It was also serialized in Singapore's *Shin Min Daily News* (*Xin ming ribao* 新明日報). In 1973 Jin Yong announced that he would "seal his pen" (*fengbi* 封筆) and spend the rest of his career revising his published novels instead of creating new ones, a decision that resulted in multiple editions of all of his works. The editions that appeared after 2000, in particular, feature radical changes. In this essay I cite the most commonly read and historically influential version (usually referred to as *liuxing ban* 流行版 popular edition), published by Yuanliu Press in Taiwan.

21 The film was an enormous success at the box office (grossing 34,460,000 HKD) and became an "instant classic" in Hong Kong cinema. Dou, *Jian xiao jianghu*, 130.

22 On Tsui Hark as a technological innovator of Hong Kong martial arts cinema, see M. Chen, *Zhongguo wuxia dianying shi*, 271; Jia, *Zhongguo wuxia dianying shi*, 103; and Schroeder, *Tsui Hark's Zu.*

23 Teo, *Chinese Martial Arts Cinema*, 164–69.

24 Jin Yong, *Xiao ao jianghu*, 4:1279.

25 Ibid., 3:1255.

26 "徐克透露林青霞敏感易哭 金庸反對她演東方不敗" (Tsui Hark Reveals That the Sensitive Brigitte Lin Cries Often; Jin Yong Objects to the Casting of Lin as Asia the Invincible), 中國新聞網 (China News), July 21, 2008, www.chinanews.com/yl/mxzz/news/2008/07-21/1318813.shtml; "金庸表示不喜歡徐克的《東方不敗》，說他不懂武俠" (Jin Yong Disapproved of Tsui Hark's *Asia the Invincible*, Accusing the Director of Not Understanding *Wuxia*), 娛樂 (Entertainment), November 6, 2018, kknews.cc/entertainment/5zlp43l.html; "為什麼林青霞版的東方不敗是金庸最不喜歡的" (Why Is Brigitte Lin's Version of Asia the Invincible Jin Yong's Least Favorite), 娛樂 (Entertainment) November 5, 2018, kknews.cc/entertainment/xjp4qk9.html.

27 To date, the story has also been adapted for television eight times, with both male and female actors portraying Asia: in 1984 (Hong Kong, Television Broadcast Limited [TVB] 無線電視); 1985 (Taiwan, Taiwan Television Limited [TTV] 臺灣電視公司); 1996 (Hong Kong, TVB); 2000 (Taiwan, China Television Company, Ltd. [CTV] 中國電視公司); 2000 (Singapore, Mediacorp 新傳媒); 2001 (China, China Central Television [CCTV] 中央電視台); 2013 (China, Hunan Satellite TV 湖南衛視); and 2018 (China, Youku 優酷騰訊). Other adaptations, including an earlier film version (1978, Hong Kong, Shaw Brothers), radio shows (e.g., Hong Kong, 1981), a musical (2007, Hong Kong), comics, music, and video games, further consolidate the story's iconic status in Chinese popular culture. On the rise of Asia the Invincible as a "legendary queer icon" in online media, see Zhou, "Dongfang Bubai, Online Fandom, and Gender Politics."

28 Chou, *Tongzhi lun*, 299–302.

29 In Helen Leung's reading, *Swordsman II* is a paradigmatically queer film in multiple senses: "In effect, *Swordsman* 2 has 'queered' three familiar themes in martial arts film. First, it approaches the transformative effect of martial arts on the gendered body as a form of transsexuality. Yet, unlike in the novel, the result from this practice is not portrayed as mutilated monstrosity but instead a perfectly crafted body that is both beautiful and unassailable. Second, the film superimposes two stock relationship types onto its two main characters: the attraction between Dongfang Bubai and the hero Linghu Chong, played by Jet Li, resembles both the free-spirited camaraderie and mutual admiration between men and the heterosexually coded eroticism between the hero and his love interest. Third, when faced with scenes of coy flirtation between the two, the audience is made to see double: their nondiegetic recognition of the stars leads to a sighting of familiar heterosexuality which, within the diegesis, actually signifies the attraction a man feels for a transsexual woman. The film does not allow the audience to 'tell the difference' between the two, thus disturbing the boundaries that are supposed to demarcate heterosexuality categorically from queer attraction." Leung, "Homosexuality and Queer Aesthetics in Chinese Cinema," 522. See also her *Undercurrents*, 71–77, for a powerful reading of the film's transsexual agency.

30 Gina Marchetti characterizes Lin and Maggie Cheung as the female queer icons that are counterparts to Leslie Cheung, and the three as the "queer connections" of Hong Kong New Wave cinema. Marchetti, "Hong Kong New Wave," 109–10. Paul Foster argues that Lin was chosen for the role of Asia "due to her ability to represent a man changed to woman" and that she has "made a career of playing cross-gender roles." Foster, "Kung Fu Industrial Complex," 174.

31 Zhou, "Dongfang Bubai, Online Fandom, and Gender Politics," 111.

32 In the afterword, Jin Yong claims that the novel is not an allusion to the Cultural Revolution but merely an attempt to depict human nature in Chinese society. This disclaimer is unpersuasive and certainly not how the novel has been received by the reading public. Jin Yong, *Xiao ao jianghu*, 4:1682.

33 Ibid., 4:1265.

34 Further information on this story can be found in various biographies and critical studies of Jin Yong. See, for example, Zhang, *Jin Yong yu Ming Pao chuanqi*, 116–49; Sun, *Jin Yong zhuan*, 124–36; and Liu, *Stateless Subjects*, 141–48.

35 *Ta Kung Pao*, October 28, 1964.

36 For a detailed account of the discrepancies between the historical diffusion of Manichaeism into China and Jin Yong's fictional representations, see Lieu, "Fact or Fiction," 62–63, and W. Lin, "Jin Yong bi xia de Mingjiao," 66–67.

References

Althusser, Louis. "Ideology and Ideological State Apparatuses." In *Lenin and Philosophy and Other Essays*, 85–126. New York: Monthly Review Press, 2001.

Anderson, Perry. "Stand-Off in Taiwan." *London Review of Books* 26, no. 11 (2004): 12–17.

Chan, Stephen Ching-kiu. "Figures of Hope and the Filmic Imaginary of Jianghu in Contemporary Hong Kong Cinema." *Cultural Studies* 15, nos. 3–4 (2001): 486–514.

Chen, Jian. *Mao's China and the Cold War*. Chapel Hill: University of North Carolina Press, 2001.

Chen, Kuan-Hsing. *Asia as Method: Toward Deimperialization*. Durham, NC: Duke University Press, 2010.

Chen, Mo 陳墨. *Zhongguo wuxia dianying shi* 中國武俠電影史 [History of Chinese Martial Arts Cinema]. Taipei: Fengyun, 2006.

Ching Siu-tung 程小東, dir. *Xiao ao jianghu zhi Dongfang bubai* 笑傲江湖之東方不敗 [Swordsman II: Asia the Invincible]. Hong Kong: 1992.

Chou Wah-shan 周華山. *Tongzhi lun* 同志論 [On *Tongzhi*]. Hong Kong: Xianggang tongzhi yanjiushe, 1995.

Cohen, Paul A. *Discovering History in China: American Historical Writing on the Recent Chinese Past*. New York: Columbia University Press, 1984.

Cronin, James. *The World the Cold War Made: Order, Chaos, and the Return of History*. London: Routledge, 1996.

Cumings, Bruce. *Parallax Visions: Making Sense of American–East Asian Relations at the End of the Century*. Durham, NC: Duke University Press, 2012.

Day, Tony, and Maya H. T. Liem, eds. *Cultures at War: The Cold War and Cultural Expression in Southeast Asia*. Ithaca, NY: Cornell University Press, 2010.

Dou Xinping 竇欣平. *Jian xiao jianghu: Xu Ke de shijie* 劍嘯江湖：徐克的世界 [The Resounding Sword in *Jianghu*: The World of Tsui Hark]. Beijing: Zhongguo guangbo dianshi chubanshe, 2007.

Foster, Paul B. "The Kung Fu Industrial Complex: Jin Yong's Martial Arts Fiction and Chinese Popular Culture." Unpublished manuscript.

Fukuyama, Francis. *The End of History and the Last Man*. New York: Free Press, 1992.

Fu, Poshek. "Cold War Politics and Hong Kong Mandarin Cinema." In *The Oxford Handbook of Chinese Cinemas*, edited by Carlos Rojas, 116–33. Oxford: Oxford University Press.

Gaddis, John Lewis. *We Now Know: Rethinking Cold War History*. Oxford: Oxford University Press, 1998.

Hajimu, Masuda. *Cold War Crucible: The Korean Conflict and the Postwar World*. Cambridge, MA: Harvard University Press, 2015.
Jager, Sheila Myoshi, and Rana Mitter, eds. *Ruptured Histories: War, Memory, and the Post–Cold War in Asia*. Cambridge, MA: Harvard University Press, 2007.
Jameson, Fredric. "Actually Existing Marxism." In *Marxism beyond Marxism*, edited by Saree Makdisi, Cesare Casarino, and Rebecca Karl, 14–54. London: Routledge, 1996.
Jia Leilei 賈磊磊. *Zhongguo wuxia dianying shi* 中國武俠電影史 [History of Chinese Martial Arts Cinema]. Beijing: Wenhua yishu chubanshe, 2005.
Jin Yong 金庸. *Xiao ao jianghu* 笑傲江湖 [The Smiling, Proud Wanderer]. 4 vols. Taipei: Yuanliu, 1996.
Jin Yong 金庸. *Yi tian tu long ji* 倚天屠龍記 [Heavenly Sword, Dragon-Slaying Saber]. Taipei: Yuanliu, 1996.
Kwon, Heonik. *The Other Cold War*. New York: Columbia University Press, 2010.
Lee, Chris. "Rhythm and the Cold War Imaginary: Listening to John Adams's *Nixon in China*." *differences: A Journal of Feminist Cultural Studies* 22, nos. 2–3 (2011): 190–210.
Lee Pui Tak 李培德 and Wong Ain-ling 黃愛玲, eds. *Lengzhan yu Xianggang dianying* 冷戰與香港電影 [The Cold War and Hong Kong Cinema]. Hong Kong: Hong Kong Film Archive, 2009.
Lee, Sangjoon. "Creating an Anti-Communist Motion Picture Producers' Network in Asia: The Asia Foundation, Asia Pictures, and the Korean Motion Picture Cultural Association." *Historical Journal of Film Radio, and Television* 37, no. 3 (2016): 517–38.
Leung, Helen Hok-Sze. "Homosexuality and Queer Aesthetics in Chinese Cinema." In *A Companion to Chinese Cinema*, edited by Yingjin Zhang, 518–34. Oxford: Blackwell, 2013.
Leung, Helen Hoz-Sze. *Undercurrents: Queer Culture and Postcolonial Hong Kong*. Vancouver: University of British Columbia Press, 2008.
Li, Siu-Leung. "Kung Fu: Negotiating Nationalism and Modernity." *Cultural Studies* 15, nos. 3–4 (2001): 515–42.
Lieu, Samuel. "Fact or Fiction: Ming-chiao (Manichaeism) in Jin Yong's *I-t'ien t'u-lung chi*." In *Proceedings of the International Conference on Jin Yong's Novels*, edited by Lin Lijun, 43–66. Hong Kong: Mingheshe, 2000.
Lin, Hsiao-ting. *Accidental State: Chiang Kai-shek, the United States, and the Making of Taiwan*. Cambridge, MA: Harvard University Press, 2016.
Lin, Wushu 林悟殊. "Jin Yong bi xia de Mingjiao yu lishi de zhenshi" 金庸筆下的明教與歷史的真實 [Jin Yong's Manichaeism versus Historical Reality]. *Lishi xuekan* 歷史月刊 [Historical Monthly], no. 98 (1996): 62–67.
Liu, Hong, Michael Szonyi, and Zheng Yangwen, eds. *The Cold War in Asia: The Battle for Hearts and Minds*. Leiden: Brill, 2010.
Liu, Petrus. *Stateless Subjects: Chinese Martial Arts Literature and Postcolonial History*. Ithaca, NY: Cornell East Asia Series, 2011.
Marchetti, Gina. "The Hong Kong New Wave." In *A Companion to Chinese Cinema*, edited by Yingjin Zhang, 95–117. Oxford: Blackwell, 2013.
Paik, Nak-Chung. *The Division System in Crisis: Essays on Contemporary Korea*. Oakland: University of California Press, 2001.
Pietz, William. "The Postcolonialism of Cold War Discourse." *Social Text*, nos. 19–20 (1988): 55–75.
Pletsch, Carl. "The Three Worlds; or, The Division of Social Scientific Labor, circa 1950–1975." *Comparative Studies in Society and History* 23, no. 4 (1981): 565–90.

Sakai, Naoki. "The Dislocation of the West and the Status of the Humanities." In *Traces I: Specters of the West and the Politics of Translation*, edited by Naoki Sakai and Yukiko Hanawa, 71–91. Hong Kong: Hong Kong University Press, 2002.

Schroeder, Andrew. *Tsui Hark's Zu: Warrior from the Magic Mountain*. Hong Kong: Hong Kong University Press, 2004.

Sun, Yixue 孫宜學. *Jin Yong zhuan: Qian gu wen tan xia sheng meng* 金庸傳：千古文壇俠聖夢 [A Biography of Jin Yong: Dreams of the Everlasting Champion of the Literary World]. Taipei: Fengyun, 2004.

Szonyi, Michael. *Cold War Island: Quemoy on the Front Line*. Cambridge: Cambridge University Press, 2008.

Teo, Stephen. *Chinese Martial Arts Cinema: The Wuxia Tradition*. Edinburgh: Edinburgh University Press, 2009.

Walker, Gavin. "The Accumulation of Difference and the Logic of Area." *positions: asia critique* 27, no. 1 (2019): 67–98.

Wang, Xiaojue. *Modernity with a Cold War Face: Reimagining the Nation in Chinese Literature across the 1949 Divide*. Cambridge, MA: Harvard University Press, 2013.

Westad, Odd Arne. *The Global Cold War: Third World Interventions and the Making of Our Times*. Cambridge: Cambridge University Press, 2007.

Zhang Guiyang 張圭陽 *Jin Yong yu Ming Pao chuanqi* 金庸與明報傳奇 [Jin Yong and *Ming Pao Daily* Legend]. Taipei: Yunchen, 2005.

Zhou, Egret Lulu. "Dongfang Bubai, Online Fandom, and the Gender Politics of a Legendary Queer Icon in Post-Mao China." In *Boys' Love, Cosplay, and Androgynous Idols: Queer Fan Cultures in Mainland China, Hong Kong, and Taiwan*, edited by Maud Lavin, Ling Yang, and Jing Jamie Zhao, 101–27. Hong Kong: Hong Kong University Press, 2017.

LAIKWAN PANG and CHUN-KIT KO

Script as Method

ABSTRACT This essay argues that the two main types of contemporary Chinese scripts, complicated characters (*fantizi* 繁體字) and simplified characters (*jiantizi* 簡體字), are sites of heavy cultural and political contestation. The two script systems witness the internal bifurcation of the Chinese written language, which should not be considered as unified vis-à-vis the diversification of the verbal languages. Supported with many concrete examples, the essay demonstrates the different kinds of political struggles involved in the publication of the same materials in the two different scripts. These cases also illustrate the heavy censorship involved in contemporary PRC literature, and the authors are particularly interested in demonstrating the meanings of the option of *fantizi* publication toward many PRC writers. The two scripts could not be understood as simple variations of the same set of language, but the shifts between them involve actual translations, which in turn would help us gain new insights on the idea of world literature.

KEYWORDS border, censorship, translation, script, world literature

Border is a prominent feature of the post-1949 pan-Chinese culture that no one can brush off easily. Mainland China, Taiwan, Hong Kong, and various diasporic Chinese communities may all use Chinese as their major means of communication, and they may share many overlapping Chinese cultural practices and ways of living, but they are also separated by rigid, politics-based territorial borders, cultivating political and cultural differences. Political borders are often forced onto people, but these top-down operations inevitably encourage the development of different cultures, habits, and ways of thinking, which are practiced and identified by the affected people from the bottom up. We argue that such cultural-political borders are key features defining the vigor and particularities of contemporary Chinese cultural productions. While there are many ways to illuminate this situation, in this essay we focus on the Chinese script, which is manifested in contemporary Chinese communities in two forms: complicated (which some call traditional) characters versus simplified characters. We are aware that there are many other dialects used in the Chinese communities, and some of them also develop their own distinctive scripts, but we focus on these two types because they are most widely used and their tensions most representatively reflect the political tensions inherent within the language.

DOI 10.1215/25783491-7978555

Although the complicated and simplified Chinese writing systems are usually considered versions of the same set of characters, we want to highlight their differences in order to discuss how they represent and manifest the different reading markets and the political economy of the PRC, Hong Kong, and Taiwan. We also want to emphasize the importance of holding onto a mentality of translation instead of the mind-set of convergence to explore the vigor, difficulties, and creativity of post-1949 Chinese cultural productions. Scripts might be the most important, yet most invisible, method used to transmit Chinese literary productions. This essay calls attention to the uniqueness of contemporary Chinese scripts so as to shed a light on the cultural-political particularities of Chinese literary production. Through this study, we also promote the protection—rather than the dissolution—of the cultural differences that are engendered in different geopolitical regions. We advocate translation as an act of worlding.

The internal linguistic diversity of the Chinese language is immense, to the point that *Chinese* should not be understood as referring to a single language with regional dialects but rather as an umbrella term referring to a set of interrelated languages. As Zev Handel observes, "Speakers of Hong Kong Cantonese, Shanghainese, Taiwanese, and Beijing Mandarin cannot understand each other. Linguists therefore speak of Chinese not as a single language but as a family of closely related languages, much as the Romance languages (French, Spanish, Italian, Portuguese, etc.) make up a family of closely related languages."[1] The fact that there are so many different kinds of languages spoken in China makes it problematic to appeal to language to ground claims that China is a unified nation. Although it could be argued that while the spoken dialects differ, the single writing system proves the Chinese people are one, and this essay contends that the two different character systems—complicated characters, or *fantizi* 繁體字, and simplified characters, or *jiantizi* 簡體字—should also be understood as manifestations of a Chinese language that is constantly pluralizing.

Chinese is not only the most widely spoken and written language in the world; it is also the only major language system that currently has two parallel writing systems. Although the pluralism of the Chinese language could be seen as unavoidable, given the language's long history and its vast geographic reach, the current bifurcated writing system is nevertheless clearly the result of contemporary political developments. Simplified characters were designed with an ideological agenda to develop written Chinese language into a modern communicative tool. However, thanks to the non-unified political reality, the continual use of the complicated characters outside the People's Republic of China (PRC) reveals how language is always a political product, but no political control can completely confine the development of language.

From the mid-century period until relatively recently, the two writing systems were mostly independent of one another. There are clear regulations in the PRC that only simplified characters can be used and taught, while complicated characters were used in Taiwan, Hong Kong, and Macau (as well as some diasporic Chinese communities) as a way for those communities to distinguish themselves from the PRC. This situation, however, is changing rapidly, as mainlanders grow more familiar with *fantizi*, and *jiantizi* become more common in Hong Kong, Taiwan, and elsewhere due to the PRC's cultural and economic influence. In these communities, however, *jiantizi* often carries political and cultural connotations of "mainlandization" and therefore tends to be met with considerable anxiety and resistance. We believe that the bifurcated writing system has been undertheorized as a distinctive feature of modern Chinese language and culture. We hope to navigate this dense dynamics of Chinese as a living language and Chinese as a political construct in order to explore the potentiality of the Chinese culture to face a more open world.

With or Without the Characters? A Brief History

Chinese intellectuals have aspired to reform Chinese characters since late Qing. While these intellectuals were primarily concerned with raising literacy rates, they also assumed that the language had to be modernized so that it could carry out the many new duties endowed to the nation. The resulting language reform proposals could be divided into two sets: proposals to render Chinese characters using phonetic transcription and proposals to simplify the characters themselves. Moreover, the first group of advocates was not in agreement over whether the characters should even be retained, while the second group also benefited from accomplishments of the first. These various approaches could be understood as different means to achieve the same—or at least a similar—end of modernization.

Let us first consider the phonetic approach, which included proposals to either maintain or discontinue the use of Chinese characters themselves. Since the late Qing, intellectuals such as Lu Zhuangzhang 盧戇章 (1854–1928), Wang Zhao 王照 (1859–1935), and Lao Naixuan 勞乃宣 (1843–1921) had started to experiment with phoneticizing Chinese characters. Some of these figures were inspired by works of Western missionaries, while others looked up to the success of the Meiji Japanese script reform, but the end they all shared a conviction that Chinese characters were too complicated to learn.[2] These early modern language reformers were convinced that phoneticizing the characters would allow China to catch up with other modern nations, though most of them did not advocate getting rid of the characters altogether.[3] Only a small group of anarchists, such as Wu Jingheng 吳稚暉 (1865–1953) and Li Shizeng 李石曾 (1881–1973), argued that the Chinese characters had to be abolished and be replaced directly with Esperanto.[4]

Entering into the Republican period, these two orientations of the phonetic approach persisted. On one hand, there were intellectuals like Li Jinxi 黎錦熙

(1890–1978), who followed the route of the first group of reformers in advocating the establishment of the *zhuyin zimu* 注音字母 phonetization system as a new educational policy of the Republican government.[5] On the other hand, some other May Fourth intellectuals, such as Chen Duxiu 陳獨秀 (1897–1942) and Qian Xuantong 錢玄同 (1887–1939), took up the radical approach of Chinese anarchists and advocated that Chinese characters should be completely abolished in favor of Esperanto.[6] The establishment of *guoyu luomazi* 國語羅馬字 in the late 1920s could be understood as an interim achievement of this camp.[7] As Lorraine Wong reminds us, before 1949 there had already been many attempts to Latinize Chinese characters based on phonetics, but the existence of many Chinese dialectics became a major challenge.[8] There was a strong urge to get rid of the Chinese characters among some leftists, who contended that the Chinese script contained many ideological and even moral values. As Andrea Bachner points out, Lu Xun 魯迅 (1881–1936) and Hu Yuzhi 胡愈之 (1896–1986) associated Chinese characters with images of death and disease.[9] During his two visits to the Soviet Union, Qu Qiubai 瞿秋白 (1899–1935), leader of the nascent Chinese Communist Party (CCP), was most impressed by Soviet efforts to create writing systems for those ethnic groups who lacked them. Assisted by his fellow Chinese sojourners and some Soviet linguists, Qu experimented with ways to use the Latin alphabet to write Chinese dialects.[10] This writing system, called *xin wenzi* 新文字 (new writing), combined with the *dazhongyu* 大眾語 (common language) also advocated by Qu, enjoyed a considerable degree of influence in the 1930s and was actually used in Yan'an in the early 1940s.[11]

But after the PRC was established in 1949, it called a halt to the attempts to abort the Chinese characters. Instead the *hanyu pinyin* 漢語拼音 romanization system was considered a supplement to—rather than a replacement for—Chinese characters. Although there were still calls to completely phoneticize Chinese,[12] the regime was quick to make it clear that Chinese characters would stay. The new state probably calculated that it was not able to afford to abandon Chinese characters, which might have been perceived as giving up culture altogether. Instead it placed its emphasis on unifying verbal communications first. As Glen Peterson argues, there was a "nation-building imperative that identified national solidarity with linguistic uniformity."[13]

Unwilling to give up characters, the PRC decided to both phoneticize and simplify them, and it was the latter that enjoyed the most official attention.[14] The character simplification movement could be traced back to the efforts of certain late Qing intellectuals,[15] but it was the linguist Qian Xuantong who played a key role in promoting the simplification movement in the 1920s and 1930s. As mentioned above, Qian was committed to the complete abolition of Chinese characters, but he also acknowledged that it would take a long time for that objective to be accomplished. Being a pragmatist, he suggested first simplifying characters for educational purposes, and in a 1920 essay he proposed a few ways to reduce the number of strokes in many characters.[16] In 1922 Qian submitted a proposal to the Ministry of Education advocating the simplification of Chinese characters, though it was ultimately not adopted. He nevertheless continued his efforts, and in the mid-1930s the Ministry of Education finally accepted one of his later proposals.[17] In August 1935, the Ministry of Education announced the first set of 324 *jiantizi*, which was to be used in all primary schools, though the Executive Council aborted the proposal the following year. The *jiantizi* proposal was met with strong oppositions from conservatives on cultural grounds but also on political grounds, given this language reform was proposed primarily by the leftists.[18] The simplification of Chinese characters was again prioritized after 1949. In February 1952, the Zhongguo wenzi gaige yanjiu weiyuanhui 中國文字改革研究委員會 (Research Committee for Chinese Writing Reform) was established under the Education Commission of the State Council and was tasked with studying how to simplify Chinese characters as a national policy.[19] Two years later the unit was reorganized and renamed the Zhongguo wenzi gaige weiyuanhui 中國文字改革委員會 (Committee for Chinese Writing Reform), now placed directly under the State Council. As the new name suggested, the committee was no longer responsible only for research. On the day of its establishment, the committee published *Hanzi jianhua fangan caoan* 漢字簡化方案草案 (Draft of Chinese Characters Simplification Plan).[20] The plan was discussed, trialed, and amended, and the amended *Hanzi jianhua fangan* 漢字簡化方案 (Chinese Characters Simplification Plan) and *Guanyu gongbu hanzi jianhua fangan de jueyi* 關於公佈漢字簡化方案的決議 (Directive Announcing Simplified Chinese Characters) were passed by the State Council and published in *People's Daily* on January 31, 1956.[21]

In the eyes of the new PRC government, the simplification of Chinese characters benefited both the new nation's education and its economy. Before the simplification plan was announced, *People's Daily* published an essay that could be seen as the official statement on this subject:

> Because Chinese characters are so difficult to read, write, and memorize, our nation has therefore wasted much time on public education. It is a huge burden to have to teach children and adults Chinese characters, and it also encumbers our efforts to raise the national literacy level. If we allow Chinese characters to stay the way they are, it would be a major hindrance to improving the people's culture and education, which also would present disadvantages to the development of our industrialization and the national economy.
>
> 由於漢字的難認、難寫、難記，使我國普通教育要在文字的教學方面耗費更多的時間。漢字在兒童教育、成人教育和掃除文盲工作中是一項沉重的負擔。要是保

持漢字的現狀不加改革，就會嚴重地妨礙人民文化教育的普及和提高，對於國家工業化和國民經濟的發展也是十分不利的。[22]

The resulting simplification plan consisted of three separate character lists. The first contained 230 simplified characters that had already been widely tested—such as 罢 for 罷 and 办 for 辦. The second contained 285 characters, including new ones such as 笔 for 筆 and 叹 for 嘆. Finally, the third list contained 54 simplified radicals (the portion of a character that often contains a semantic element), such as 马 for 馬 and 车 for 車.[23] The simplified characters in the first list had already been widely tested and were adopted immediately, while those in the second and third lists were proposed for preliminary consideration, for possible implementation at a later date.[24]

The *People's Daily* essay further specified that "other than the reproduction of ancient books or for specific reasons, original complicated characters should no longer be used" 除翻印古籍和有其他特殊原因的以外，原來的繁體字應該在印刷物上停止使用.[25] In May 1964 the committee published *Jianhuazi zongbiao* 簡化字總表 (General List of Simplified Characters), containing 2,238 characters.[26] The drafting of the *Dierci hanzi jianhua fangan* 第二次漢字簡化方案 (Second Simplification Scheme) also began immediately, though it was aborted during the Cultural Revolution. The Second Simplification Scheme was finally announced in December 1977, but after encountering considerable opposition, the scheme was rescinded in June 1986—finally bringing to an end the decades-long Chinese character simplification movement.[27]

Censored Materials Published outside the PRC

Political censorship continued from the Maoist period to the post-Maoist period, notwithstanding the constantly changing degree of harshness and moving targets of control. There was, and still is, a vigorous self-censorship mechanism in place, and publishers, with or without direct supervision from the party, set up their own editorial committees to control problematic materials before the censorship apparatus actually intervened. Hong Kong critic Leung Man-Tao 梁文道 (1970–) discussed the fact that the PRC does not have any law specifically for book censorship, largely because it allows the government to have the largest degree of flexibility to operate its censorship system.[28] PRC scholar Chen Sihe 陳思和 (1954–) reminds his fellow critics that if they want to study PRC's literary history comprehensively, they should not focus only on published materials, given that there were also many materials that were written but could not be published at the time, and therefore we should read these materials carefully to gain a more comprehensive picture of the corresponding literary landscape.[29] Another scholar, Wang Jinghui 王敬慧, asserts that Mo Yan 莫言 (1955–), the first Chinese citizen to win the Nobel Prize for Literature, actually succeeds in internalizing the rampant and unpredictable PRC censorship by investing in two of his main literary themes: hallucination and paranoia.[30]

In the PRC the political censorship and the character censorship intersect, as censored mainland writers are often able to publish complicated character versions of their works in Hong Kong, Taiwan, and overseas Chinese communities. As mainland political writer Ye Yonglie 葉永烈 (1940–) recounts, by walking on eggshells he was often able to maneuver his writing to circumvent censorship, but there are also times when he could only rely on publishers in Hong Kong and Taiwan:

> Take, for example, my eight-hundred-thousand-word study *The Origin and End of the Anti-Rightists Campaign*. The title of the book already made the whole book a must-ban. I therefore needed to do a roundabout. I bought an ISBN from Qinghai People's Press and asked a separate press to publish the work, and the first printing was for one hundred thousand copies. The book was censored three months afterward, but by that point it had almost sold out. I made some revisions and submitted it for publication, but again it failed to pass the censors. Then I asked another press to publish it with an ISBN I bought from Xinjiang People's Press. It was published, but was banned again. I am still working on the book, and hope to "*yuhui*" 迂迴 it for a third time.
>
> But there were no way for me to "*yuhui*" my three-hundred-thousand-word novel *Mao Zedong Back to the Human World*, and it could only be published in Hong Kong and Taiwan, from which it found its way back to the PRC in the form of pirated copies.
>
> In early 2008, the censor cut one third of my book *The Real North Korea* but permitted the remainder to be published, though upon receiving an "acknowledgement" from the North Korea Embassy, the book was ultimately banned. Recently, I have published the entire manuscript in Hong Kong, thanks to the "One Country Two Systems" arrangement.

如我的八十萬字紀實長篇《反右派始末》，報審時一看書名就被『涮』掉。我只得「迂迴」，交給書商，買了青海人民出版社的書號，一下子就印了十萬冊。出書後三個月遭禁，當時差不多已經售光。此書經過補充、修訂，再度報審，又被『涮』掉。我請另一書商買新疆人民出版社的書號，再度出版，又一次遭禁。眼下我仍在繼續修訂此書，也許還要第三次「迂迴」——這在中國內地是不得已而為之的辦法，港台作家幾乎無法理解。不管出書之後必定遭禁，但是作品畢竟到了廣大讀者手中。

我的三十萬字的長篇政治小說《毛澤東重返人間》，則只能在港台出版，連「迂迴」的餘地都沒有，只能在內地地攤上買到盜版本。

二零零八年初，我的《真實的朝鮮》一書被出版社刪去三分之一，終於得以在內地出版。出版之後由於朝鮮大使館的「照會」，遭禁。最近，我在香港出版了該書三十萬字全文版《解密朝鮮》，算是充份享受了一次「一國兩制」的「優越性」。[31]

Obviously it is not just sensitive political writings that need to find outlets outside the PRC; so do works in literature, history, religious studies, and cultural criticism. There are also a lot of publishers involved, including not only major publishers such as Hong Kong's Oxford University Press and Chinese University Press as well as Taiwan's Rye Field Publishing and Linking Publishing, but also many minor or commercial presses, some of which see the publication of these works as profitable enterprises. In this particular market, we observe how serious scholarship meets reckless sensational writing, revealing the diversity of contemporary Chinese publications.

For a long time, Hong Kong has been viewed as the primary place to publish these works. First, in geographical terms, Hong Kong is closest to the mainland; also, the Cold War structure led to an anticommunist censorship apparatus in Taiwan, Singapore, and Malaysia, where mainland Chinese authors were given extra political attention. This was particularly true in Taiwan, but there were also underground publication venues for escaping censorship, and mainland materials could be published with an altered author's name, title, and contents.[32] In Southeast Asia censorship differed in different countries, but Chinese books were subjected to strict political scrutiny.[33] Comparatively speaking, the political censorship was less severe in colonial Hong Kong, which explains the large number of PRC-censored materials published there. But recently signs have emerged that the PRC government no longer tolerates Hong Kong as the publishing haven for censored materials, as demonstrated by the arrest—both inside and outside the PRC border—of personnel of the Causeway Bay Bookstore and a few other publishers that specialize in this genre.

Those censored works by mainland scholars published in Hong Kong include many genres, among them literature by Eileen Chang 張愛玲 (1920–1995), Xu Xu 徐訏 (1908–1980), as well as works by literary critics such as Cao Juren 曹聚仁 (1900–72). Many of these authors left China in the 1950s, and their works were published when they were already living in Hong Kong.[34] Recently there have been a number of mainland writers who have chosen to publish their works in *fantizi*. The 2015 novel *Rixi* 日熄 (The Day the Sun Died) by Yan Lianke 閻連科 (1958–), winner of 2014 Franz Kafka Prize, was initially published in Taiwan and received the prestigious Hong Kong–based Dream of the Red Chamber Novel Award, but it has never been released in a *jiantizi* edition. In addition, many political titles have also been censored, such as *Guangchang: Ouxiang de shentan* 廣場——偶像的神壇 (The Square: Altar of the Idol), by military critic Liu Yazhou 劉亞洲 (1952–), the son-in-law of former PRC president Li Xiannian 李先念 (1909–1992).[35] This book relates anecdotes of CCP leaders, including Mao

Zedong 毛澤東 (1893–1976), Zhou Enlai 周恩來 (1898–1976), and Jiang Qing 江青 (1914–91). Both the book's title and the last chapter, on the 1976 Tiananmen Incident, reminded people of the later 1989 June Fourth protests and crackdown—thereby ensuring that the book would be banned in the PRC.

Aside from strictly censored materials, some mainland authors choose to first publish *fantizi* versions of their books in Hong Kong or Taiwan and subsequently submit the manuscript to the PRC censors, in order to publish a *jiantizi* version. Ba Jin's 巴金 (1904–2005) *Suixianglu* 隨想錄 (Random Thoughts) is one example of a book published through this process.[36] But heavy editing is often a result, as seen in the case of *Sishou luantan* 四手聯彈 (Piano Duet), cowritten by Zhang Yihe 章詒和 (1942–) and He Weifang 賀衛方 (1960–), which was first published in *fantizi* by Hong Kong's Oxford University Press and was later reprinted in *jiantizi* by Guangxi Normal University Press.[37] In these copublication cases, while the more widely read *jiantizi* version might not reflect the true intentions of the author, the existence of the *fantizi* version serves as a powerful affidavit of the original writing and a protest against censorship.

Cultural and Political Implications

Returning to the *fantizi-jiantizi* debates, most interventions into the debates involve statements of taste, yet strong political positions lurk in the background. In those areas where *fantizi* is used, people tend to show resistance to *jiantizi*. According to a recent survey in Hong Kong, half the city's residents reject the idea of teaching *jiantizi* in primary and secondary schools, and 30 percent resist using *jiantizi* in their everyday lives.[38] In addition to ordinary language users, many Hong Kong and Taiwan scholars, as well as some Western sinologists, also show discomfort with *jiantizi*. Some dismiss the PRC language-simplification policy as one of the CCP's many mistakes. Peng Xiaoming 彭小明, a Chinese dissident living in Germany, argues that there was a link between the language-simplification policy and the Anti-Rightist Campaign.[39] Taiwan scholars like Wang Hsueh-Wen 汪學文 claim that *jiantizi* is contributing to the destruction to Chinese traditional culture.[40] Others challenge *jiantizi* from a linguistic perspective, arguing that this new system creates more problems than it solves. Taiwan's Tu Chung-Kao 杜忠誥 (1948–) points out that the PRC simplification process is unsystematic. In the simplification of the characters 纖, 殲, and 懺, for instance, the component on the right is changed from 韱 to 千, though for a similar character, 讖, which also contains the same component on the right, what is simplified is instead the component on the radical on the left, which is changed from 言 to 讠.[41] Hong Kong column writer Yung-Joek 容若 also points out similar discrepancies in the handling of place-names. For example, Dayu 大庾 county in Jiangxi province is now written as 大余, but the mountain 大庾山 in Guangdong province is still written with the original characters.[42] There are also some who oppose *jiantizi* on aesthetic grounds. For example, Sinologist John Minford states: "I cannot tolerate seeing Tang poetry being written in *jiantizi*. It is just too ugly. Just like seeing a person using all four limbs to crawl, instead of using two legs to walk in grace. I am truly offended, and my feelings are hurt!" 我無法忍受簡體字唐詩，實在太醜！就像看到人用四肢爬行，而不是優雅地用腿行路。很冒犯我，傷害我感受！[43]

Yet not every politician and intellectual in Hong Kong and Taiwan opposes the usage of *jiantizi*. In Hong Kong, support for *jiantizi* is considered by some to be a symbolic support of the PRC. In the early and mid-1980s, when many Hong Kong people welcomed Deng's Open Door Policy, even politicians like Szeto Wah 司徒華, who became a founder of the Democratic Party after 1989, helped promote *jiantizi* in Hong Kong.[44] *Jiantizi* also received the support of pro-CCP politicians like Ng Hong-Mun 吳康民 (1926–), who urged the colonial government to make *jiantizi* the official script in Hong Kong.[45] From a completely different perspective, Hong Kong scholar Lee Fai-ying 李輝英 (1911–91) described those disapproving of the simplification of Chinese characters as "radical conservatives" 特別保守的人.[46] Similarly, in Taiwan, the former chief editor of *China Times* Tsang Yuan-Hou 臧遠侯 expressed support for *jiantizi*,[47] and critic Shen Cheng-Nan 沈政男 believes that *jiantizi* is a more progressive form of written Chinese.[48]

In the PRC, many critics contend that *jiantizi* is a more effective communication tool and will help facilitate China's development into a modern and powerful nation, but there are also some who question the legitimacy of *jiantizi*. Many of these linguistic discussions, however, also carry clear political messages. For example, some who suffered during the 1956 Anti-rightist Campaign were victimized because they challenged *jiantizi*, as a result of which *jiantizi* would inevitably be associated with the brutality of the regime.[49] In the 1980s and 1990s, when PRC intellectuals were submerged in a more liberal atmosphere, some original supporters of *jiantizi* began to confess their skepticism to the simplification project. One prominent example is the philologist Zhou Youguang 周有光 (1906–2017), who wrote in 1985:

> Simplified characters have their advantages, such as clearer rendition on a computer screen. However, there are more disadvantages than advantages. The more the characters are simplified, the more they look alike, making it easier to confuse them. The simplification project results in differences between old and new books, and between books published outside and inside the country, and therefore after learning *jianti* we still need to learn *fanti*.
>
> 簡化有好處，例如在電子電腦的螢幕上顯示出來比較清楚。但是，好處不大，而壞處卻不小。例如，簡化越多，近形越甚，彼此混淆。簡化使新書舊書不同，國內國外不同，學了簡體，還要再學繁體。[50]

At a 1992 "Symposium of Questions about Fantizi," the chief librarian of the Beijing Library, Ren Jiyu 任繼愈 (1916–2009), discussed the relationship between the two systems. He said,

> A very important concept in the *I-Ching* is *qiankun* 乾坤 (heaven and earth). In my *History of Philosophy*, I specified that for this term the character *qian* 乾 cannot be simplified to 干. But in the proofs I still saw that mistake coming up again and again.
>
> 我寫《哲學史》，易經裡常講「乾坤」。我一再注明：「乾」不能簡化，不能寫成「干坤」，一定要寫「乾坤」。但是一次不行，二校以後還是個「干坤」。再說明，再改。[51]

Another presenter, Li Minsheng 李敏生 (1940–), urged that "*fantizi* is always allowed to be used in a wide range of occasions, such as in advertisements or on boards and tablets . . . this is widely known and should be considered natural" 眾所週知，牌匾上使用繁體字從來是廣泛的……關於廣告應用繁體字的問題也是自然的.[52] However, such voices against *jiantizi* are seldom heard nowadays among current PRC academia.

Some writers and artists in the PRC have also commented on *jiantizi* through their artwork. The artist Xu Bing 徐冰 (1955–), for example, pronounces his support for *jiantizi*,[53] but uses *fantizi* as the basis for his *Tianshu* 天書 (A Book from the Sky). If Xu's preference for *fantizi* is subtle, Han Shaogong 韓少功 (1953–) makes a more direct comment in his novel *Maqiao cidian* 馬橋詞典 (Dictionary of Maqiao). Andrea Bachner points out that in the novel a figure named Ma Ming identifies the simplification of the character *shi* 時, meaning "time," to 时 as symptomatic of the political upheaval brought about by the Cultural Revolution.[54] Ma Ming explains that there is a logic inherent in the composition of the original character 時, where the left-hand element 日 (day) corresponds to the character's meaning, while its right-hand element 寺 (pronounced *si*) indicates the character's pronunciation. But when the character is simplified to 时, the right-hand element has a completely different pronunciation (*cun*), thereby destroying the organic sound-meaning unity of the original character. The simplified version no longer links the meaning, pronunciation, and written sign—which, for Ma Ming, signifies the chaos of the present times in the severing of the link between world and word. He concludes, "When time is confused, it must be a time of confusion" 時既已亂，亂時便不遠了.[55]

Public discussions of *jiantizi* and *fantizi* are often ideological, revealing a complicated cultural and political landscape of contemporary Chinese communities. The situation is particularly complex in relation to the ways censorship is contested and offset through the two writing systems. Around the world, translation is used to permit censored materials to be published elsewhere, though these translations usually have little opportunity to reach what would have been the work's original readership. In contrast, the *fantizi* versions of banned materials are now relatively accessible to mainland Chinese readers, who can read the complicated characters with varying degrees of difficulty. Moreover, PRC readers may physically cross the *jiantizi-fantizi* border when they travel, or they may purchase works published in Taiwan and Hong Kong through alternative channels. For these mainland readers, the censored materials, once translated into complicated characters, acquire new meanings and attract new attention, precisely because of the strong ideological significations of the two character types.

Diversification and Unification

Some PRC linguists tried to legitimize the *jiantizi* movement by emphasizing a natural process of language simplification, so that the government-led simplification movement in the PRC would be viewed as natural.[56] We want to question this assumption by exploring a dialectics of language between diversification and unification. The two character systems clearly signify different political environments, but this internal bifurcation structured in modern Chinese language also allows us to understand the potentiality of Chinese literature that is conditioned by and transcends the political environment.

Walter Benjamin's essay "The Task of the Translator" was written precisely to address this dialectic relationship between singularity and plurality in language. Although the essay was Benjamin's introduction to his translation of Charles Baudelaire's *Tableaux Parisiens*, it actually tells readers little about the translation itself and instead is generally considered an independent provocation in its own right. Benjamin emphasizes the artistic and political meanings of translation as a most direct strategy to illustrate the nature of language, suggesting that "the basic error of the translator is that he preserves the state in which his own language happens to be instead of allowing his language to be powerfully affected by the foreign tongue. . . . He must expand and deepen his language by means of the foreign language."[57] Benjamin argues that translation should carry us away from both the original language and the translated language, and that this distancing would then bring us back to the originally singular "pure language," where "language and revelation are one without any tension."[58] According to Benjamin, instead of something that could be achieved, "pure language" is more properly understood as an absolute originating force of language in which meaning is unified with truth.

The most important, and mystical, message of Benjamin's essay involves its emphasis on the dialectical relationship between linguistic diversification and unification. The Tower of Babel metaphorizes how human language, and humanity in general, continues in an ever-diversifying process, and there is no way to return to the unified origin. But meaning could be derived from this metonymical chain only because there was this original moment of pureness, the absolute point of silence from which all meanings originate. On one hand, language diversifies in the natural freedom of linguistic flux, but on the other hand, it is only by piecing together all the fragmented languages that we may observe an original pure language. This is the impossibility of language, but this impossibility also defines all the potentialities of language.

Benjamin argues that translation brings this dialectic to light, and a translator should call attention to and problematize the assumption of equivalence that makes translation possible. It is true that translation "ultimately serves the purpose of expressing the central reciprocal relationship between languages,"[59] but this reciprocal nature does not make languages identical. Translation shows precisely the ways in which languages differ. In general, translation allows us to see the many manifestations already contained in the original, while the translated text would reveal itself as only one such manifestation, "thus making both the original and the translation recognizable as fragments of a great language, just as fragments are part of a vessel."[60] Translation offers a glimpse of the nature of language, and that totality is forever lost. But Benjamin argues that translation points the way to the predestined, hitherto inaccessible, realm of reconciliation and fulfillment of languages.[61] Paul de Man argues that Benjamin did not want to point back to the unity of language but rather sought to emphasize an essential disarticulation that was already present in the original: "The translation belongs not to the life of the original, the original is already dead, but the translation belongs to the afterlife of the original, thus assuming and confirming the death of the original."[62]

We are not trying to simply apply Benjamin's theory to the Chinese language, but we do think his ideas may help us think through the *jiantizi-fantizi* dichotomy. In particular, we could understand the *jiantizi-fantizi* conversion as a form of translation, wherein there is not a simple one-to-one correspondence between the two systems. For example, the character *hou* 后 means "empress," but it could also be the simplified version of the character 後 (behind). The phase *yitianhou* 一天后, accordingly, could mean either "one day later" or "an empress/a diva." Similarly the phase *xiamian* 下面 could be a simplified versions of either 下面 (below) or 下麵 (cooking noodles). Another example is the character *gan* 干, which could be the simplified form of either 幹 (tree trunk, main body, or work) or 乾 (dry), while the same character is also used in traditional Chinese phrases like *ganfan* 干犯 (commit/offend) and *ganshe* 干涉 (meddle with). In another case, the character *e* 恶 means "evil" or "harsh," but it can also be the simplified version of 噁, which means "nasty" or "nausea." We know that there are many heteronyms in Chinese language, but the problem becomes even more acute with *jiantizi*. One could, therefore, describe the relationship between *jiantizi* and *fantizi* as a form of translation, given that different renditions might result in different meanings.

If the simplified versus complicated characters system is inherent in the modern written Chinese language, and if we follow Benjamin's idea that translation points to the direction of the pure language, the Chinese language might be closer to Benjamin's "truth" than we would otherwise assume. We might say that both simplified and complicated characters are fragments of a vessel, and the fact that these pieces correspond to and differ from each other allows us to be more sensitive to the creative potential of the Chinese language. As mentioned above, the most important insight of Benjamin's idea is that the unity is forever lost. Complicated and simplified characters could be understood as stages of the transformation or evolution of the Chinese written language, and neither should be seen as representing the most efficient or accomplished communicative tool, and therefore the end of history. Like de Man, we do not want to read Benjamin's provocation as a religious one claiming that there is a pure language to which we can return, as Benjamin clearly writes that a final solution of the foreignness of languages remains out of reach of humanity.[63] Instead we should take the opposite direction—that is, constantly diversifying languages and producing translations—to infer the "purer" linguistic creation. Pointing out the diversity of the two character systems is not to fetishize differences or contingencies. But we believe that the two systems do point to the same historical process that constantly transforms. This transformative process reveals the historicity of Chinese language in its singularity—or, in other words, the universality of language resides precisely in all its particularities ever produced.

It is true that Benjamin's specific formulation of the pure language must be rendered in his specific ideological context: the fascist violent usurpation of arts and life into its totalitarian politics, to the extent that nothing in the past or the future can escape its ideological control.[64] For Benjamin, it is of utmost importance to reemphasize the radical violence and radical singularity of creation that can resist such fascist appropriation. Although Benjamin was protesting German fascism, we believe that his political and cultural commitment to safeguarding plurality and potentiality offers useful insight into the situation in today's PRC. By highlighting the differences between the two character systems, we may see the Chinese language in a more original and creative light as something that can resist the nationalist/nativist appropriation.

In the research or debates around this bifurcated Chinese character system, many critics reveal a subtle yearning for a unified written language. Many of them, regardless of which system they prefer, describe the parallel usage of the two systems as a phenomenon of *shu butong wen* 書不同文 (not writing the same language). This phrase is derived from a famous line in the Confucian classic *Zhongyong* 中庸 (*Doctrine of the Mean*), which states, "Jin tianxia, shu tong wen, che tong gui, xing tong lun" 今天下，書同文、車同軌、行同倫 (In the current world, we write in the same scripts, carriages are run on the same roads, and we have the same moral system to govern our acts). This line describes the cultural, social, and moral standardization that had allegedly already been achieved by the Eastern Zhou Dynasty (1000s BCE to 700s BCE). Therefore there is clearly a derogatory implication in the usage of the phrase *shu butong wen* to describe the parallel use of *jiantizi* and *fantizi* in modern Chinese communities.

These critics advocate the transformation of *shu butong wen* to *shu tong wen*, underlined by typical nationalist thinking. Some scholars contend that regions using *fantizi*, like Taiwan and Hong Kong, should switch to *jiantizi*,[65] while others advocate establishing *fantizi* as the only official Chinese written system on both sides of the Taiwan Strait. But overall, underlying most of the *shu butong wen* discussion is a concern with political unification. For example, Du Zhonggao writes:

> "Shu butong wen" is a hindrance to the political and economic exchange between the two peoples in the two sides of the Strait. Resuming the usage of complicated Chinese characters (in mainland China) would be the most effective catalyst to realize also the moral unification of Chinese descendants at home and abroad.
>
> 「書不同文」是海峽兩岸進行政經文化交流的無形「絆腳石」，傳統漢字的恢復使用，是海內外華夏子孫同心同德的最大「催化劑」。[66]

Du Zhonggao and Peng Xiaoming both anticipate that, in the future, complicated characters will once again be used by people in mainland China. By then the characters would no longer be called *fantizi* but *zhengtizi* 正體字 (orthodox characters). Peng Xiaoming suggests that the people in the PRC should begin with reading *fantizi*, and gradually *fantizi* will be used in publication and official documents, at which point *jiantizi* will become relegated to nonofficial uses.[67] In Peng Xiaoming's scheme, this unification process would ultimately spread to Japan and Korea:

> We could even suggest the governments and the people in Japan and Korea to abolish their own simplified Chinese characters and resume the same set of complicated Chinese characters, reuniting and singularizing the Chinese-character cultural circle.
>
> 甚至可以建議日、韓兩國也跟我們進一步協調漢字的統一規範，廢止日韓簡體字，逐步建立漢字文化圈的漢字字符集，全面單一化。[68]

Many critics are confident that the tension between *jiantizi* and *fantizi* will ultimately be overcome and argue that either the simplified or the complicated system will eventually become the only official language. But these assumptions are influenced by politics. For these critics, this history of philological confusion will end at the time when one system takes over, offering the promise of a future where the Chinese polity will finally be united once again. Similarly, when Peng proposes a Chinese-character cultural circle, he is not only suggesting a pan-Chinese nationalist project but an East-Asian Sinocentric imperialism, which reveals how easy language attracts and facilitates political investment.

A World Literature with Borders?

We conclude here with a note to demonstrate how this internal bifurcation of Chinese language may point to the possibility of constructing an alternative model of world literature. Recently there has been a recent surge of interest in world literature as a new paradigm for literary studies in the global age. Literary scholars are becoming increasingly aware of the difficulty as well as the importance of comparisons beyond the Eurocentric framework. To respond to the impact of globalization, critics argue that we need to reengage with the possibility of world literature. Readers and writers should find new ways to connect, while scholars also need to break down national and cultural barriers in order to articulate the common.[69] We are also urged to develop a new world literature as one transcending traditional normative concepts such as masterpieces and major writers to allow all kinds of works to appear in our horizon and to supply works of precursors, contemporaries, and successors of canonical writers beyond national and imperial spaces. Literature should be seen as conjunctions instead of fixed texts.[70] In other words, world literature could be understood as a set of new practices of literature production and reception without borders.

Given that the recent discussion of world literature galvanizes forces against Eurocentrism, many Chinese literary scholars have readily taken up the discourse and argued for a world literature that includes more Chinese literature. Wang Ning 王寧 (1955–), for example, calls for a large-scale translation of contemporary Chinese literature into major world languages. As much as China benefited from the translation of Western materials to construct its (alternative) cultural and political modernity one century earlier, Wang claims that translating Chinese literature into Western languages—particularly English—also helps to deconstruct the Eurocentric mode of world literature and reconstruct new world literature.[71] Another PRC-based scholar, Ji Jin 季進 (1965–), also believes that more high-quality translations are needed, which will eventually make the West realize the uniqueness and significance of Chinese literature as an integral part of world literature.[72] However, both Wang and Ji appear to treat Chinese literature as a singular entity that is waiting to be incorporated into—and therefore helps to expand—an English-based category of world literature. As we have mentioned, the contemporary literary canon in mainland China is a result of heavy political intervention. The existence of the strict censorship system in the PRC, which does not allow certain Chinese literary works to be published in China in the first place, raises questions regarding the integrity of Chinese literature as such. Translators and publishers intending to translate contemporary Chinese literatures into English should be highly sensitive to the political factors behind the formation of the canon and should acknowledge an internal translation process already at place: authors have to find creative ways to translate what they want to say into materials the censor approves.

From a different perspective, Pheng Cheah reminds us that a common limitation of world literature scholarship involves a lack of attention to the temporal dimension of the world. He argues that most scholars consider the world only in a spatial framework along a global system of exchange and circulation and that while recent world literature discourse may have introduced new openings that cross national and regional borders, it does not offer an opening of a normative horizon that transcends the present global political-economic framework.[73] With a strong Heideggerian tone, Cheah contends that the only way to challenge the spatialized economic metaphor of the globe is to temporalize the world. He argues that literature opens up the world through its formal structures, by the incalculable gift of time.[74] Literature should be understood as the product of intersubjectivity that resists solidification and constructs an ever-renewing commons. Instead of being objectified into a set of works, world literature should be understood as the power of literature in making the world—that is, its power of "worlding." Cheah's concept of worlding echoes Benjamin's concept of pure language that is always caught in the process of pluralization. This idea of worlding through time also calls attention to the political development in the twentieth century that selectively separates mainland China from other parts of the Chinese world. This is an important element constituting our Chinese literatures, something we should treasure instead of annihilate.

In light of Cheah's call, we would argue that the intersubjectivity inherent in the dual writing system of modern Chinese may demonstrate the worlding potentiality of the Chinese literature. We also agree with David Wang that the concept of worlding may help us understand Chinese literary modernity in the broader sense of *wen* 文 as a vehicle "bringing the world home" and, more important, as an agency that continuously opens up new configurations of the world.[75] We do not believe in a world literature without borders. On the contrary, we contend that there is a need to reconsider the importance of borders as a basic constituent of literature—because borders produce differences, from which communications arise and imaginations are encouraged. Borders, border crossers, and borderland experiences within and among the pan-Chinese communities are important to contemporary Chinese literatures, allowing new and shifting forms of identity to emerge.[76] If we want to understand Chinese literature as world literature, then in addition to advancing more translations from Chinese into English, we should also pay attention to the potentiality and limitation of the inter-translatability of Chinese as a lively language that is being used by more than a billion people every day in different cultural-political zones. Apart from including a wider range of forms and genres into literary history, we should also take script as a manifestation of *wen*, following David Wang's call to allow Chinese literature to enact within the world.[77] We must expand our vision not only with the internal stratification of the Han Chinese scripts but also the many minority languages being used in China. The various languages associated with Chinese, either culturally or geopolitically, demonstrate precisely the vigor of Chinese literature.[78] The Chinese people should therefore be encouraged to embrace their multilingual environments and engage in such translations on a daily basis.

Consider Benjamin's bilingual writing in both German and Hebrew, which demonstrates his commitment to both languages. Like other bilingual writers, Benjamin's constant crossing back and forth between the two languages may be seen as a key source of his inspiration to produce thinking against the mainstream fascism. As Robert Alter argues, Benjamin transposes the Hebrew language he never really learned into a universalist utopian vision of "language as such."[79]

Similarly, while most Chinese may not have the education and ability to understand other Chinese minority languages, at least they have access to the complicated and simplified Chinese characters, which might offer them a kind of translational experience. Many Chinese readers who first approach the script with which they are unfamiliar might share the same experiences: the other script simultaneously is and is not readable, and the process of learning the script with which one is less familiar would bring to the fore many preexisting prejudices and fascinations about the corresponding cultural-political system. The scripts vividly illustrate the intersubjectivity of the other group of Chinese people. Learning, reading, and writing the unfamiliar script is a way to approach this unfamiliar intersubjectivity and to transcend one's horizon. In a way, Chinese language users are blessed with the scripts' internal split, which could help us to locate the alterity contained within this language in order to resist its fossilization and totalization. In this way, this ancient language—with its constant expansion and diversification—could allow its users and writers to experience time, connect with people, and world the world.

PANG LAIKWAN is professor of cultural studies at the Chinese University of Hong Kong. Her books include *The Appearing Demos: Hong Kong during and after the Umbrella Movement* (2020), *The Art of Cloning: Creative Production during China's Cultural Revolution* (2017), *Creativity and Its Discontents: China's Creative Industries and Intellectual Property Rights Offenses* (2012), and *The Distorting Mirror: Visual Modernity in China* (2007).

KO CHUN KIT is a PhD candidate of the Division of Cultural Studies in the Chinese University of Hong Kong. His research interests include the "revolution plus love" novels in 1920s and 1930s and instrumentality and noninstrumentality of play in modern China.

////////////////////////////////

Notes

1 Handel, "Classification of Chinese," 34.
2 Cheng, "Yuyan dengji yu qingmao minchu de hanzi geming," 371–89.
3 Zhou, *Hanzi gaige gailun*, 36.
4 Yasui, *Zhongguo wuzhengfuzhuyi de sixiang jichu*, 151–55.
5 Huang, *Mingguo shiqi yuyab zhengce yanjiu*, 58–62.
6 Cheng, "Yuyan dengji yu qingmao minchu de hanzi geming," 397–99.
7 Huang, *Mingguo shiqi yuyab zhengce yanjiu*, 106–7, 148–58.
8 Wong, "Threshold Nationhood."
9 Bachner, *Beyond Sinology*, 20–24.
10 P. Chen, *Modern Chinese*, 184.
11 Zhao, *Hanzi geming*, 126–225.
12 Lu, *Yuwen changtan*, 95–106.
13 Peterson, *Power of Words*, 107.
14 There were actually two different approaches: reduction of the number of strokes per character (*jiantizi*) and the reduction of the number of characters in common use. Chen, *Modern Chinese*, 148.
15 Zhou, *Hanzi gaige gailun*, 321.
16 Qian, "Jiansheng hanzi bihua di tiyi."
17 Huang, *Mingguo shiqi yuyan zhengce yanjiu*, 106–7, 159–60.
18 Zhao and Baldauf, *Planning Chinese Characters*, 31–38.
19 Wenzi gaige zazhi bianjibu, *Jianguo yilai wenzi gaige gongzuo biannian jishi*, 26–27.
20 Ibid., 54.
21 Ibid., 77–78.
22 Renmin chubanshe, *Zhongguo wenzi gaige de diyibu*, 75–76.
23 A study by Lu Teng-Kuang and Lu Teng-Chao compares the *jiantizi* announced by the Kuomintang in 1935 and those announced by CCP in 1956 and finds that the two sets of characters are quite similar. See Lu and Lu, *Haixia liangan jiantizi yanjiu*, 307–28.
24 Wenzi gaige zazhi bianjibu, *Jianguo yilai wenzi gaige gongzuo biannian jishi*, 78.
25 Renmin chubanshe, *Zhongguo wenzi gaige de diyibu*, 1.
26 Zhao and Baldauf, *Planning Chinese Characters*, 46.
27 Ibid., 51.
28 Leung, "Shenmo shu jiaozuo jinshu?"
29 See Chen S., "Shilun dangdai wenxueshi," and Liu, *Qianzai xiezuo*.
30 J. Wang, "Hallucination and Madness."
31 Ye, "Liushi nian xiezuo de jianxin."
32 See Lin, *Weishu yu jinshu*.
33 Lo, *Xianggang wenhua jiaoyin*, 104–7.
34 Du, *Chonggou wenyi jizhi yu wenyi fanshi*, 30–32.
35 Luo, *Xianggang wenhua manyou*, 41.

36 Ibid.

37 Zhang and He, *Sishou liantan*. See also the comments of the chief editor of Hong Kong's Oxford University Press on the heavy censorship and editing involved in the publication of the *jiantizi* version of the book: Lam, "Sishou liandan he jiucheng ziyou."

38 "Zhongda diaocha."

39 Peng, *Hanzi jianhua debuchangshi*, 64–82.

40 H.-W. Wang, *Lun Zhonggong de wenzi gaige*, 71–86.

41 Tu, *Hanzi yange zhi yanjiu*, 39.

42 Yung, *Zhu zi lu*, 95.

43 "Guangdonghua yueer, fantizi caishi zhen zhongwen."

44 Ching, *Fan jian you zhi*, 71–74.

45 Ng, "Tuixing jiantizi."

46 Lee, *Sanyan liangyu*, 142.

47 Tsang, *Qidai liangan shutongwen*.

48 Shen, "Wusi yundong weijing zhi gong."

49 Peng, *Hanzi jianhua debuchangshi*, 72–82.

50 Zhou, "Wenzi gaige de xinjieduan."

51 "Beijing tushuguan guanzhang Ren Jiyu xiansheng jianghua."

52 Li, "Guanyu fantizi wenti."

53 Xu, "Xu Bing tan jianfanti zhi zheng."

54 Bachner, *Beyond Sinology*, 125–26.

55 Han, *Maqiao Cidian*, 34.

56 Zhou, *Hanzi gaige*, 315–20.

57 Benjamin, "Task of the Translator," 81.

58 Ibid., 82.

59 Ibid., 72.

60 Ibid., 78.

61 Ibid., 75.

62 de Man, *Resistance to Theory*, 85.

63 Benjamin, "Task of the Translator," 75.

64 See Koepnick, *Walter Benjamin and the Aesthetics of Power*, 187–211.

65 Tsang, *Qidai liangan shutongwen*, 23.

66 Tu, *Hanzi yange zhi yanjiu*, 113–114.

67 Peng, *Hanzi jianhua debuchangshi*, 123.

68 Ibid., 129.

69 Pratt, "Comparative Literature and Global Citizenship."

70 Damrosch, "World Literature in a Postcanonical, Hypercanonical Age."

71 N. Wang, "Translating Modernity and Reconstructing World Literature."

72 Ji, "Zuowei shijie wenxue de Zhongguo wenxue."

73 Cheah, *What Is a World?*

74 Ibid., 11.

75 D. D. Wang, "Introduction," xiv.

76 X. Wang, "Borders and Borderlands Narratives in Cold War China."

77 D. D. Wang, "Introduction," v.

78 For the PRC state multilingual and translation policies, see Pang, "'Nature' of Ethnic Tensions."

79 Alter, *Necessary Angels*, 46.

References

Alter, Robert. *Necessary Angels: Tradition and Modernity in Kafka, Benjamin, and Scholem.* Cambridge, MA: Harvard University Press, 1991.

Bachner, Andrea. *Beyond Sinology: Chinese Writing and the Scripts of Culture.* New York: Columbia University Press, 2014.

"Beijing tushuguan guanzhang Ren Jiyu xiansheng jianghua" 北京圖書館館長任繼愈先生講話 [The Speech of Chief Librarian of Beijing Library Ren Jiyu]. *Hanzi wenhua* 漢字文化 [Culture of Chinese Characters], no. 4 (1992): 7.

Benjamin, Walter. "The Task of Translator," translated by Harry Zohn. In *Illuminations*, edited by Hannah Arendt, 69–82. New York: Schocken Books, 1968.

Cheah, Pheng. *What Is a World? On Postcolonial Literature as World Literature.* Durham, NC: Duke University Press, 2016.

Chen, Ping. *Modern Chinese: History and Sociolinguistics.* Cambridge: Cambridge University Press, 1999.

Chen Sihe 陳思和. "Shilun dangdai wenxueshi (1949–1976) de 'qianzai xiezuo'" 試論當代文學史（1949–1976）的「潛在寫作」[An Attempt to Discuss the "Invisible Writings" in Contemporary Literary History (1949–1976)]. *Wenxue pinglun* 文學評論 [Literary Criticism], no. 6 (1999): 104–13.

Cheng Wei 程巍. "Yuyan dengji yu Qing mo Min chu de hanzi geming" 語言等級與清末民初的漢字革命 [Language Hierarchy and the Revolution of Chinese Characters in Late Qing and Early Republican Era]. In *Shijie zhixu yu wenming dengji: Quanqiushi yanjiu de xinlujing* 世界秩序與文明等級：全球史研究的新路徑 [Origins of the Global Order: From the Meridian Lines to the Standard of Civilization], edited by Lydia H. Liu 劉禾, 347–404. Beijing: SDX Joint Publishing, 2016.

Ching Cheung-Fa 程祥徽. *Fan jian you zhi: Hanzi jianhua wu jiang* 繁簡由之：漢字簡化五講 [Not to Enforce Complicated Characters or Simplified Characters: Five Talks on the Simplification of Chinese Characters]. Hong Kong: Sanlian shudian, 1985.

Damrosch, David. "World Literature in a Postcanonical, Hypercanonical Age." In *Comparative Literature in the Age of Globalization*, edited by Haun Saussy, 43–53. Baltimore: Johns Hopkins University Press, 2006.

de Man, Paul. *The Resistance to Theory.* Minneapolis: University of Minnesota Press, 1986.

Du Ying 杜英. *Chonggou wenyi jizhi yu wenyi fanshi: Shanghai, 1949–1956* 重構文藝機制與文藝範式：上海, 1949–1956 [Reconstructing the Literary Mechanism and Literary Paradigm, Shanghai, 1949–1956]. Shanghai: Joint Publishing, 2011.

"Guangdonghua yue'er, fantizi caishi zhen Zhongwen" 廣東話悅耳 繁體字才是真中文 [Cantonese Is Dulcet, Fantizi Is the "True" Chinese]. *Xinbao caijing yuekan* 信報財經月刊 [Hong Kong Economic Journal Monthly], no. 4 (2016): 128.

Han Shaogong 韓少功. *Maqiao cidian* 馬橋詞典 [Dictionary of Maqiao]. Beijing: Zuojia chubanshe, 1996.

Handel, Zev. "The Classification of Chinese: Sinitic (The Chinese Language Family)." In *The Oxford Handbook of Chinese Linguistics*, edited by William S. Y. Wang and Chaofen Sun, 34–44. New York: Oxford University Press, 2015.

Huang Xiaolei 黃曉蕾. *Mingguo shiqi yuyan zhengce yanjiu* 民國時期語言政策研究 [The Study of Language Policy in the Republican Era]. Beijing: Zhongguo shehui kexue chubanshe, 2013.

Ji Jin 季進. "Zuowei shijie wenxue de Zhongguo wenxue—yi dangdai wenxue de yingyi yu chuanbo wei li" 作為世界文學的中國文學——以當代文學的英譯與傳播為例 [Chinese Literature as World Literature—The English Translation and Propagation of

Contemporary Literature as Example]. *Zhongguo bijiao wenxue* 中國比較文學 [Comparative Literature in China], no. 1 (2014): 27–36.
Koepnick, Lutz. *Walter Benjamin and the Aesthetics of Power*. Lincoln: University of Nebraska Press, 1999.
Lam To-Kwan 林道群. "Sishou liandan he jiucheng ziyou" 四手聯彈和九成自由 [Piano Duet and 90 Percent Freedom]. *Pingguo ribao* 蘋果日報 [Apple Daily], March 21, 2010. hk.apple.nextmedia.com/supplement/columnist/art/20100321/13843092.
Lee Fai-ying 李輝英. *Sanyan liangyu* 三言兩語 [In a Few Words]. Hong Kong: Wenxue yanjiushe, 1975.
Leung Man-Tao 梁文道. "Shenmo shu Jiaozuo jinshu? (Zhongguo meiyou jinshu zhi er)" 什麼書叫做禁書？（中國沒有禁書之二）[What Kinds of Books Are Called Censored Books? (China Does Not Have Any Censored Books, II)]. *Pingguo ribao* 蘋果日報 [Apple Daily], February 14, 2016. hk.apple.nextmedia.com/supplement/columnist/4301523/art/20160214/19489951.
Li Minsheng 李敏生. "Guanyu fantizi wenti" 關於繁體字問題 [On the Issue of Complicated Characters]. *Hanzi wenhua* 漢字文化 [Culture of Chinese Characters], no. 4 (1992): 22.
Lin Ching-Chang 林慶彰. *Weishu yu jinshu* 偽書與禁書 [Forged Books and Prohibited Books]. Xinbeishi: Huayi xue shu chubanshe, 2012.
Liu Zhirong 劉志榮. *Qianzai xiezuo, 1949–1976* 潛在寫作, 1949–1976 [Potential Writing, 1949–1976] Shanghai: Fudan daxue chubanshe, 2007.
Lo Zeon 羅隼. *Xianggang wenhua jiaoyin* 香港文化腳印 [Hong Kong Cultural Footprints]. Hong Kong: Cosmos Books, 1994.
Lu Shuxiang 呂叔湘. *Yuwen changtan* 語文常談 [Casual Talks of Language]. Hong Kong: Sanlian shudian, 1982.
Lu Teng-Kuang 路燈光 and Lu Teng-Chao 路燈照. *Haixia liangan jiantizi yanjiu* 海峽兩岸簡體字研究 [The Study of Simplified Characters across the Strait]. Taipei: Taiwan xue sheng shu ju, 1992.
Luo Fu 羅孚. *Xianggang wenhua manyou* 香港文化漫遊 [Hong Kong Cultural Roaming]. Hong Kong: Chunghwa Books, 1993.
Ng Hong-mun 吳康民. "Tuixing jiantizi" 推行簡體字 [Put Simplified Characters into Practice]. *Wenhui bao* 文匯報 [Wen Wei Po], September 2, 1984.
Pang, Laikwan. "The 'Nature' of Ethnic Tensions: *Under the Flaming Mountains* as Xinjiang's First Novel." In *Chinese Shock of the Anthropocene: The Making of Image, Music and Text in the Age of Climate Change*, edited by Kwai-Cheung Lo and Jessica Yeung, 179–201. New York: Palgrave Macmillan, 2019.
Peng Xiaoming 彭小明. *Hanzi jianhua debuchangshi* 漢字簡化得不償失 [Simplifying Chinese Characters Did More Harm than Good]. Hong Kong: Xiafei'er guo ji chuban gongsi, 2007.
Peterson, Glen. *The Power of Words: Literacy and Revolution in South China, 1949–95*. Vancouver: University of British Columbia Press, 1997.
Pratt, Mary Louise. "Comparative Literature and Global Citizenship." In *Comparative Literature in the Age of Multiculturalism*, edited by Charles Bernheimer, 58–65. Baltimore: Johns Hopkins University Press, 1995.
Qian Xuantong 錢玄同. "Jiansheng hanzi bihua di tiyi" 減省漢字筆劃底提議 [The Suggestions of Reducing Chinese Character's Strokes]. *Xin qingnian* 新青年 [New Youth], no. 3 (1920): 111–16.
Renmin chubanshe 人民出版社, ed., *Zhongguo wenzi gaige de diyibu* 中國文字改革的第一步 [The First Step of the Chinese Language Reform]. Beijing: Renmin chubanshe, 1956.

Shen Cheng-Nan 沈政男. "Wusi yundong weijing zhi gong: Jiantizi cai shi jinbu de zhongwen wenzi, dan xuduo Taiwan ren gao bu qingchu zhuangkuang" 五四運動未竟之功：簡體字才是進步的中文文字，但許多台灣人搞不清楚狀況 [The Unfinished Project of the May Fourth: Simplified Characters are Progressive, but Many Taiwanese Don't Know about It]. *Guanjian pinglun wang* 關鍵評論網 [News Lens], May 5, 2016. www.thenewslens.com/article/28856.

Tsang Yuan-Hou 臧遠侯. *Qidai liang'an shutongwen: Ruhe tupo fan jian zhijian de zhang'ai* 期待兩岸書同文：如何突破繁簡之間的障礙 [Anticipating a Common Script across the Strait: How to Break through the Barrier between the Complicated Characters and the Simplified Characters]. Taipei: Shibao wenhua chuban qiye gufen youxian gongsi, 1996.

Tu Chung-Kao 杜忠誥. *Hanzi yange zhi yanjiu* 漢字沿革之研究 [Research on the Historical Development of Chinese Characters]. Taipei: Laogu wenhua shiye gufen youxian gongsi, 2011.

Wang, David Der-wei. "Introduction: Worlding Literary China." In *New Literary History of Modern China*, edited by David Der-wei Wang, i–xxiv. Cambridge, MA: Harvard University Press, 2017.

Wang Hsueh-Wen 汪學文. *Lun Zhonggong de wenzi gaige* 論中共的文字改革 [On the Reform of Characters by the Chinese Communist Party]. Taipei: Liming wenhua shiye gongsi, 1978.

Wang, Jinghui. "Hallucination and Madness: The Impact of Censorship on Mo Yan's Writing." *minnesota review*, no. 82 (2014): 97–110.

Wang, Ning. "Translating Modernity and Reconstructing World Literature." *minnesota review*, no. 79 (2012): 101–12.

Wang, Xiaojue. "Borders and Borderlands Narratives in Cold War China." In *The Oxford Handbook of Modern Chinese Literatures*, edited by Carlos Rojas and Andrea Bachner, 334–55. New York: Oxford University Press, 2016.

Wenzi gaige zazhi bianjibu 文字改革雜誌編輯部 [Editorial Office of *Character Reform* Magazine], ed. *Jianguo yilai wenzi gaige gongzuo biannian jishi* 建國以來文字改革工作編年記事 [Events of the Characters Reform since 1949 in Chronological Order]. Beijing: Wenzi gaige chubanshe, 1985.

Wong, Lorraine. "Threshold Nationhood: Huang Guliu's The Story of Shrimp-Ball, Chinese Latinization, and Topolect Literature." *Modern Chinese Literature and Culture* 30, no. 2 (2018): 223–28.

Xu Bing 徐冰. "Xu Bing tan jianfanti zhi zheng: Lishi shang fantizi yeshi jianhua jieguo" 徐冰談「簡繁體之爭」：歷史上繁體字也是簡化結果 [Xu Bing Said Even Complicated Characters Were the Result of Simplification]. *Fenghuang wang* 鳳凰 [Phoenix], February 7, 2016. culture.ifeng.com/a/20160207/47386351_0.shtml.

Yasui Shinsuke 安井伸介. *Zhongguo wuzhengfuzhuyi de sixiang jichu* 中國無政府主義的思想基礎 [An Inquiry into the Intellectual Structure of Chinese Anarchism]. Taipei: Wunan tushu chuban gufen youxian gongsi, 2013.

Ye Yonglie 葉永烈. "Liushi nian xiezuo de jianxin" 六十年寫作的艱辛 [Sixty Years of Difficult Writing]. *Kaifang zazhi* 開放雜誌 [Open Magazine], no. 10 (2009): 41.

Yung Joek 容若. *Zhu zi lu* 煮字錄 [The Collection of Essays on Writing]. Hong Kong: Ming bao chubanshe, 2002.

Zhang Yihe 章詒和 and He Weifang 賀衛方. *Sishou liantan* 四手聯彈 [Piano Duet]. Hong Kong: Oxford University Press, 2010.

Zhao Liming 趙黎明. *Hanzi geming: Zhongguo xiandai wenhua yu wenxue de qiyuan yujing* 漢字革命：中國現代文化與文學的起源語境 [The Revolution of Chinese Character:

The Original Context of Modern Chinese Culture and Literature]. Beijing: SDX Joint Publishing, 2016.
Zhao, Shouhui, and Richard B. Baldauf Jr. *Planning Chinese Characters: Reaction, Evolution or Revolution?* Dordrecht: Springer, 2008.
"Zhongda diaocha: Yu ban ren fandui zhongxiaoxue jiao jianti" 中大調查：逾半人反對中小學教簡體 [Survey Conducted by CUHK Shows More than 50 Percent of Interviewees Oppose Teaching Jiantizi in Secondary and Primary School]. *Mingbao* 明報 [*Mingpao*], May 4, 2016. news.mingpao.com/pns/dailynews/web_tc/article/20160504/s00011/1462298574751.
Zhou Youguang 周有光. *Hanzi gaige gailun* 漢字改革概論 [Overview of the Chinese Characters Reform]. Beijing: Wenzi gaige chubanshe, 1964.
Zhou Youguang 周有光. "Wenzi gaige de xinjieduan" 文字改革的新階段 [The New Phrase of the Character Reform]. *Wenzi gaige* 文字改革 [Character Reform], no. 5 (1985): 5.

HSIAO-HUNG CHANG
Translated by CARLOS ROJAS

Asia as Counter-method

ABSTRACT By taking the recent legalization of same-sex marriage in Taiwan as a point of departure, this paper attempts to differentiate a "bloc asia" as a virtual aggregate from an "Area Asia" as a concrete geo-historical region in order to theorize the possibility of taking Taiwan or Asia as a counter-method. The paper starts with an examination of Takeuchi Yoshimi's 1960 "Asia as Method" in light of the two possible Asias—Asia as entity and Asia as method—suggested in Koyasu Nobukuni's poststructuralist reinterpretation. It then moves on to the two possible methods as disclosed in Kuan-Hsing Chen's *Asia as Method*—one adopts an "Asian studies in Asia" approach with an inter-referencing system; the other foregrounds a dynamic process of turning and hybridizing that occurs between Western colonial powers and local structures—to warp up the similar differentiation of Area Asia and bloc asia, as well as that of Asia as entity and Asia as method. The second part of the paper focuses on Taiwan's recent "Pikaochiu" incident, which uncannily conflates questions of same-sex marriage rights and ancestral tablet terminology. Instead of regarding it as merely an Internet *kuso*, the paper takes it to demonstrate how out of the old clan patriarchy in East Asia there may emerge new "homophobic" forms that rely not on a proscription of specific sex practices but rather on defending the integrity of the family surname and patrilineage. Yet its potentiality as a rollback against a Euro-American model of marriage, kinship, and family, and simultaneously a reversal against East Asian Confucian values, makes it a bizarre yet challenging case to explicate how Asia could function as a counter-method, a virtual "not yet."

KEYWORDS same sex marriage, Taiwan, Takeuchi Yoshimi, Koyasu Nobukuni, Kuan-Hsing Chen

What does it mean for Taiwan to be the first country in Asia to legalize same-sex marriage?

On May 24, 2017, Taiwan's Constitutional Court issued a ruling known as Judicial Yuan Interpretation No. 748, which affirmed that same-sex couples were guaranteed the right to marry by virtue of the Constitution's Article 22 protecting freedom of marriage and Article 7 protecting the right to equality. The court gave the Legislative Yuan a maximum of two years to bring all relevant laws into compliance. Two years later, on May 17, 2019, the Legislative Yuan passed the Enforcement Act of Judicial Yuan Interpretation No. 748. The act went into effect on May 24—thereby making Taiwan the first country in Asia to legalize same-sex marriage.

From 2001, when the Netherlands became the first country in the world to legalize gay marriage, to May 2019, when Taiwan became the newest one to do so, a total of twenty-seven nations crossed this legal threshold—but until Taiwan,

PRISM: THEORY AND MODERN CHINESE LITERATURE • 16:2 • OCTOBER 2019
DOI 10.1215/25783491-7978563 •

none of these countries had been in Asia.[1] Asia is often regarded as one of the world's most backward regions when it comes to gay rights and marriage equality, and therefore the "first in Asia" status of Taiwan's same-sex marriage law in the eyes of advocates reflected the region's process of opening up to the world. Here, however, we have no interest in advancing an ideological critique or psychoanalytic exploration of the Pride of Taiwan mentality that underlies this sort of *first in Asia* discourse, nor do we want to return yet again to answer questions of why and how Taiwan became the first in Asia. Instead we propose to take the *first in Asia* premise as a point of departure to differentiate a "bloc asia" ("asia" as a virtual aggregate) from an "Area Asia" ("Asia" as a concrete geo-historical region) in order to theorize the possibility of taking Taiwan or Asia as a counter-method.

With respect to the concept of an Area Asia, Taiwan's status as the first in Asia to legalize marriage equality refers to the assumption that Asia functions as an identifiable geographic/historical/political/economic area with distinct boundaries, composed of different nation-states, which manifests an irreducible or nonassimilable heterogeneity at the level of ethnicity, religion, and culture. Here the designation of being first suggests that Taiwan is positioned as more advanced and democratic than other Asian nations and territories. However, if we consider this question from the concept of a bloc asia, then Taiwan's status as the first in Asia to achieve marriage equality might lead to the assertion that Asia itself does not exist—suggesting that the corresponding ranking of first might not even be possible. This concept of a *bloc* refers not to an entity (i.e., a region or nation) that has already been confirmed but rather to a virtual aggregate that remains a mere potentiality and is the contingent product of an intersection of different transhistorical, transregional, transnational, and transcultural forces. By this logic, Asia cannot be determined in advance, nor can it be designated on a map. The concept of bloc asia denotes a virtual aggregate that permits novel forms to unfold—a kind of force to constantly activate the vitality of Asia itself. However, this singularity does not enjoy any sort of prior or superior status—it does not develop in sequential order, nor does it have a claim to the particularity of the universal (with Taiwan being a particular case of the realization of the universal right to global marriage equality). Instead, this singularity lies in the fact that it is impossible to carry out a ranking or a comparison by relying on a shared identity or a common denominator.

Therefore, if the concept of Area Asia treats Asia as an actualized form, the concept of bloc asia instead approaches Asia as a force of virtuality. The former can be assessed based on elements such as historical period, political movement, and legislative form, while the latter is an unpredictable event that is realized through a process of creative folding, unfolding, and refolding. The former highlights a process of differen*c*iation, while the latter instead emphasizes a process of what might be called "differen*t*iation."[2] The reason why elements within the former can be mutually compared is because they involve different actualized forms (for instance, we may compare the appeal of and resistance to same-sex marriage movements in Taiwan and South Korea), while the latter relies on a process of virtual differentiation that does not treat the actualized form "as it is." In other words, Area Asia and bloc asia are not binary opposites, just as the concepts of the actual and the virtual are not mutually opposed either. Instead one continually attempts to find the becoming of bloc asia within Area Asia and to sense the transforming force of virtuality within the aggregate configuration of an actualized form.

The following discussion will use the concepts of *bloc asia* and *Area Asia* to help address two key questions. First, if Area Asia can be differentiated, virtualized, and event-ivized, thereby rendering it into a bloc asia as a creative aggregate, how might we similarly *differentiate*, virtualize, and event-ivize the contemporary critical discourse of Asia as method, such that "Asia" can be thereby transformed from an area into a bloc, and method can be similarly transformed into a counter-method—thereby creating a counter-actualization that marks a return to a force of virtuality? Second, how can we use a nonlinear, nonfixed, noncausal way of thinking to disentangle the singularity that is folded, adhered, and emergent within contemporary Taiwan's marriage equality discourse, together with the transhistorical, transregional, transnational, transcultural forces of virtuality that it brings with it? What kind of virtual aggregate can be used to transpose the Euro-American-led marriage equality discourse into a field that is neither Western nor Chinese, neither ancient nor contemporary, and that cannot be confined to a Eurocentric or universal rights framework, nor can it be reduced to an Asia area or a corresponding ethnonational category?

Asia as Method and as Counter-method

Asia as method is one of the most important discourses to develop within contemporary Asian cultural studies. From Takeuchi Yoshimi's 竹内好 1960 "Asia as Method" to Mizoguchi Yūzō's 溝口雄三 1989 "China as Method," Koyasu Nobukuni's 2000 "Edo as Method," and Kuan-Hsing Chen's 2006 *Asia as Method: Toward Deimperialization*, together with more recent studies such as Leo Ching's "Taiwan as a Method," Yu-lin Lee's "Taiwan as Method," and Stephen Yiu Wai Chu's edited volume *Hong Kong Studies as Method*, the link between the concepts of *Asia* and *method* in each case is based on a line of analysis that relies on a concern with how to convert subjectivity.[3] In this article I turn first to Takeuchi's conceptualization of Asia as method, attempting to foreground how what he calls method could turn out to be a process of "rolling-back" (reversal or strike-back). I then move to the contemporary discourses of Asia as method to demonstrate how the possibility of a virtual Asia as method (the potentiality of rollback) is geo-historically and culturally actualized, while method inevitably lapses into a comparative analysis within the Asia area and between different cultural entities that leads to the regional integration of Asia as the ultimate goal of anticolonialism, anti-Cold War, and anti-imperialism. That is to say, the goal is to fight back on the basis of Area Asia as a site of actual resistance, instead of relying on a bloc asia as virtual rolling-back. Therefore, the counter-method proposed in this article is an attempt both to return to Takeuchi's method as more a potentiality of rolling-back and to link it with Gilles Deleuze's notion of "counter-actualization."[4] In this way, I hope to partially reverse the current overemphasis of anti-imperialism by taking Asia chiefly as an actualized entity and its ultimate integration as the final goal—thus demonstrating the potentiality of rolling-back that is often derided as ahistorical and apolitical might also be a radical mode of resistance and disruption.

Takeuchi's "Asia as Method" was initially presented as a pair of lectures, and on the surface it appears rather easy to understand. Takeuchi describes not only his own maturation and turn toward modern Chinese literature but also what he had learned from figures like John Dewey, Bertrand Russell, and Rabindranath Tagore—namely, that Japan was accustomed to seeing itself solely in terms of its relationship to the West, and only by replacing this sort of Eurocentric approach by inviting a comparative analysis between Japan and China/India would it thereby be possible to gain a new understanding of Japan's own position.[5] Takeuchi noted a key difference between the two types of Asian modernization found in Japan and China, in that ever since the Meiji Restoration of 1868, Japan has adopted Westernization as its primary form of exogenesis, while in China, ever since the May Fourth Movement of 1919, there has been an inverse emphasis on the nation's resistance to foreign aggression as its primary form of endogenesis. As a result, although Japan appeared to join the ranks of modern nations, in reality its feudal structure was never fully eradicated, while China used an elimination of all residual structures in order to obtain a strength from within.[6]

The part of Takeuchi's intervention that proves most obscure and challenging is precisely the section at the end where he alludes to the process of using Asia as method. Here he describes how the cultural values of freedom and equality began to be disseminated to Asia from the West, accompanied by structures of colonialism and imperialism. He notes the paradox whereby although equality might indeed exist in Europe, it cannot exist in Asian and African regions that have been dominated and exploited under European imperialism. Takeuchi observes that although we cannot imagine that Europe can possibly bring about global equality, Asian writers such as Tagore and Lu Xun nevertheless viewed the pursuit of global equality as their duty and obligation. Does this mean that these Asian authors have internalized Western imperialism's value system? Does it mean that equality as a concept originated in Europe is now already universally accepted? It was exactly as he was challenging these premises that Takeuchi proposed a notion of Asia as method:

> The East must re-embrace the West, and it must change the West itself in order to realize the latter's outstanding cultural values on a greater scale. Such a rollback of culture or values would create universality. The East must change the West in order to further elevate the universal values that the West itself produced. This is the main problem facing East-West relations today, and it is at once a political and cultural issue. The Japanese must grasp this idea as well. . . . When this rollback takes place, we must have our own cultural values, even if these values do not already exist in substantive form. Rather, I suspect they are possible as method—which is to say, as the process of the subject's self-formation. I have called this process "Asia as method," though it is impossible to state definitively what precisely this might mean.[7]

Whereas Takeuchi began from a comparative perspective between Japan and China/India, he concluded with a possible rethinking of cultural transformation between the East and the West. This redirection was enacted through a process that he calls *makikaesu* (巻き返す), referring to a sudden release, dynamic reversal, or "rollback" after a buildup of energy.

The reason why this notion of reversal or rollback is even more challenging for me than Takeuchi's other key concepts (such as his concepts of Asianism and overcoming modernity) is because it relies on a dynamic morphogenesis rather than epistemology or ontology. Takeuchi's emphasis lies not in the question of "What is Asia" (including whether Asia is a product of cultural homogenization, essentialization, or heterogenification; whether or not an Asian entity, Asian culture, or Asian values can exist outside of a European or Orientalist epistemology; and whether Asia is the product of a Western imperialist geographic imagination or is a construct of a militaristic Japanese Greater Asia Co-prosperity Sphere, and so forth) but rather in the degree to which Asia and Europe, the East and the West, are mutually constituted and creatively transformed. Earlier transcultural discourses approached the East and the West as two separate and distinct cultural entities and viewed any possible change as always enforced unilaterally by the West's imperial control over a passive and vulnerable East. When Takeuchi claims that the West is re-embraced by the East, he raises the possibility that Asia may roll back, counterattack, and transform European values. However, this is distinct from other earlier claims that Asia can overtake Europe by relying on the superiority or uniqueness of its own cultural values (i.e., claims that weakness can become strength, defeat can become victory, and that the distinctiveness and superiority of Asian culture may be used to challenge European universalism). Instead it constitutes a negation of any concept of a preexisting Asia prior to the rollback process—which is to say, it involves a recognition that even as Asia transforms Europe, it is simultaneously undergoing a transformation in its own right, with everything developing out of this spacing or in-between, thereby resulting in a continual process of creating new universal values (universalism is not the sole preserve of Europe, nor can it transcend the plane of immanence).

It appears, accordingly, that Takeuchi is actually referring to two different Asias. The first refers to Asian countries or cultures as actualized forms, together with the linkages that may be established between them, such as comparisons between the cultural forms of Japan and China/India and attempts to use this sort of comparative approach in place of an earlier framework of Eurocentrism. The second, however, cannot be clearly designated—not because it is particularly difficult to understand or because we lack appropriate language to describe it but rather because it points to a force of virtuality in a process of rollback, and thus it cannot be described, imagined, or predicted beforehand through any actualized form. Therefore any claim that we can finally reach an overwhelmingly victorious cultural counterattack, or that we can unidirectionally return to, revive, remold or modernize traditional Asian culture cannot be regarded as a method that takes only "not yet" as its potentiality of creating new and experimental changes. Takeuchi's lecture contains both of these understandings of Asia—namely, Asia as entity and Asia as method—but this obviously cannot be simply chalked up to a mere fallacy.

The contemporary thinker who has advanced the most incisive analysis of Takeuchi's two Asias is Koyasu Nobukuni, who raises two key points. First, Koyasu contends that Asia as entity is the hypothetical enemy of Asia as method, in that the latter seeks to eliminate the possibility of rendering the former more essential, originary, innate, unitary, and imperial. Koyasu believes the reason Takeuchi proceeded from an *(East) Asia as entity* model to an *(East) Asia as method* one was because he was attempting to avoid any covert imperial discourse: "'East Asia' as actualized entity will demand an organically unified 'East Asia' as its principle of integration and thus become a discourse of empire; this sort of 'East Asia' can only be a substitute for a Chinese or Japanese empire, or it cannot help but be that way."[8] Second, Koyasu proposes a poststructuralist approach, wherein he uses a notion of "outside (the unthought, the virtual) as method" to reinforce Takeuchi's approach. Koyasu points out that the modernization of Asia (China) in Takeuchi's argument takes place in its relational resistance to European (or Japanese) modernity instead of being an autonomous, independent form itself only in opposition to Europe. In other words, there is no Asia independent of European modernity, just as Europe is not able to separate itself from—or even exist independently of—Asia. Instead both Europe and Asia develop within a relationality of domination and resistance, progress and regression.

Obviously, to consider this sort of "relationality" as a kind of method is quite different from the interpretive trend that treats *Asia as method* more as a way of opposing progressive historicism, attacking Eurocentrism, establishing an Asian inter-referencing system, and promoting a notion of *inter-Asia*. This type of discourse has demonstrated a powerful assemblage of resistance and critique, but it might also overemphasize the importance of "opposition as revolt" by taking Asia as actualized forms individually and collectively and focusing less on the potentiality of "reversal or rollback as resistance" enacted by the force of virtuality that could make method a form of counter-actualization. Therefore this approach runs the risk of not being able to extricate itself from the imperial assumptions implicit in the discourse of Asia as entity. With respect to Takeuchi's example regarding concepts of freedom and equality that were developed in Europe, it was only when Asia engages in a reversal or rollback of European values while simultaneously initiating its own reconstruction, only then will it be possible to have a true revolution of "universal" values. Takeuchi reminds us that a cultural reversal functioning as a force of "not yet" or virtuality permits Asia to reverse European values and rewrite its own claims to universality, while at the same time permitting processes of counter-actualization to subvert any determined form of Asian culture. In short, this is precisely what he would call method.

During the subsequent development of the *Asia as method* discourse, however, the possibility of using method as a creative force of virtuality became limited to a set of mutual comparisons and references within an actualized Asia, in order to try to escape Eurocentrism and American imperialism. Of these discourses, the most representative—but also the most challenging—is Kuan-Hsing Chen's 陳光興 book *Asia as Method: Toward Deimperialization*. However, Chen's understanding of Takeuchi's "Asia as Method" seems to be primarily influenced by Mizoguchi Yūzō's explication. In particular, while Takeuchi uses rollback or reversal as method, emphasizing how Asia can re-embrace Europe in a distinct and continuous change, Mizoguchi instead treats Europe, China, and Japan as three separate entities, arguing that "Asia is not the Orient that exists within a European understanding, but rather it is another world independent of—or at least it should be independent of—Europe," in hopes of addressing the predicament whereby Asia or China loses its distinctiveness and declines into a state of "not-Europe." To this end, Mizoguchi proposed a model of *China as method* in place of the earlier (and oppressive) approach of *world as method, China as object*. Mizoguchi's method not only includes an epistemological framework that develops out of pluralistic vision of mutual recognition of subject-object relations, but also, more importantly, it uses an ontological approach to imagine a cultural "base entity," whereby China functions as "another world independent of . . . Europe," and its most powerful metaphor is that of a snake shedding its skin. Mizoguchi explains that this is not a case of a process of "Westernization of a Chinese core" or of a disintegration of "Old China," but rather it involves a process whereby Old China sheds its skin and is reborn—though he adds that "a snake does not, simply by virtue of having shed its skin, thereby cease to be a snake."[9]

Obviously, Mizoguchi's thesis of base entity development and pluralistic perspective subsequently influenced Chen's own concept of an Asia as method that develops out of an "geo-colonial historical materialist" 殖民—地理—歷史唯物論 framework. As Chen summarizes, Mizoguchi argues that

> each geographical space—be it a village, city, region, country, or continent—has its own base-entity and local history, with different depths, forms, and shapes. The methodological questions are: How can these base-entities be analyzed in terms of their internal characteristics? How can we best identify and analyze the interactions between and among different base-entities? It is in light of these questions that Asia as method can advance its inquiry.
>
> 各個地理空間區域，都有其厚度、形式、長相不一的在地史／基體。問題是如何掌握理解這個／這些基體，乃至於基體內部及基體之間的互動關係？一種方法就是通過對照、比較，在這個意義下，亞洲作為一種方法可以充分地展開。[10]

Here *method* is understood as a comparative analysis of Asia within a geographic space with its own distinctive history and foundation, out of which there emerged a field of "Asian studies in Asia." As Chen explains,

> The emerging phenomenon of Asian studies in Asia seems to suggest that the reintegration of Asia requires a different sort of knowledge production. This is necessary to generate self-understanding in relation to neighboring spaces as well as the region as a whole, while at the same time removing the imperative to understand ourselves through the imperialist eye.
>
> 亞洲不同地方該生產出對於鄰近國家乃至於整個亞洲區域，不同於以往的自我認識，不再繼續透過帝國之眼認識自己及鄰居。[11]

This act of inserting "method" into an inter-referencing system centered around Asia (East Asia, the third world)—yielding an Asian turn that results in a process of "leaving [Euro]-America for Asia"—further contributes to the high expectations of a "regional coalition" taken as a global trend. This sort of regionalism can be observed in a variety of transnational institutions as listed in Chen's book including the African Union, the Latin American Integration Association, the European Union, and the Association of Southeast Asian Nations—transnational associations that collectively constitute the most effective means of checking the expansion of American imperialism. Future Asian coalitions—such as a hypothetical Asia Union or Asian Community—are bound to track with the development of inter-Asia connections.

My interpretation of Takeuchi's "method" does not presume to be the only possible one. Moreover, I am not solely interested in questioning, from a historical and cultural perspective, the imperial shadow of Asian integration, together with the difficulties of regional reconciliation. Nor do I wish to simply use a concept of bloc asia to challenge or replace the concept of Area Asia due to the latter's inherent limitations. Instead I am primarily concerned with seeing whether it might be possible—while considering Takeuchi's concept of two Asias—to also discern the two kinds of method that Chen discusses in his *Asia as Method*. The first of these two methods is the previously mentioned *Asian studies in Asia* approach, which uses a process of inter-reference and inter-recognition within and among Asia's local histories or base entities in order to establish an Asian intellectual network and to break away from the dominance of what Chen calls "the imperialist eye." The second, meanwhile, makes a brief appearance in Chen's book when he recalls his previous advocacy of a "new internationalist localism" (*Xin guoji zaidi zhuyi* 新國際在地主義):

> [Internationalist localism] looks for new political possibilities emerging out of the practices and experiences accumulated during encounters between local history and colonial history—that is, the new forms and energies produced by the hybridization brought about by modernization.
>
> 西方殖民機器、意識形態在具體的轉動過程中，與在地既有的結構與意識形態產生碰撞、雜種化過程中產生出的新形式與能量。[12]

What we observe here is not an epistemological or ontological impasse but rather the potentiality of "new forms and energies" generated by a creative process of turning, encountering, and hybridizing that occurs between Western colonial powers and local structures.

If we can manage to avoid jumping too quickly into a comparison of forms created and actualized by local histories or base entities interior to Asia or the third world (which is the emphasis of the first approach), and instead are able to consider what might emerge in the course of these turns, encounters, and hybridizing processes themselves (which is the emphasis of the second approach), perhaps we could better understand why this inter-Asia-referencing method is unable to be defined within the Asian-centered imagination of any "internationalist localism" and also why *Asia as method* and *bloc asia* have world-changing implications (and not merely international or inter-Asian ones), and also why they offer the possibility of rolling back universal values (and not merely against the imperialist eye). While it is important to have Area Asia function as a strategy to successfully challenge Eurocentrism and transgress prescribed national boundaries, bloc asia is no less important in highlighting cultural vitality as its potential strategy of anti-imperialism. Both of these options constitute real battlegrounds of thought and action in a globalized age. In what follows, I will use the case of same-sex marriage equality in Taiwan to disclose the radical potential that may emerge from the folding, unfolding, and refolding of history, gender, and the politics of the aesthetics when method is taken as a counter-actualization method.

Taiwan's Same-Sex Pokémon

Beginning in the 1990s, marriage equality (the contention that same-sex couples should enjoy the same legal marriage rights as heterosexual couples) emerged as one of the key demands of the Euro-American gay rights movement and gradually expanded to the rest of the world, though it was strongly opposed at the same time by many members of the same community as heteronormative and repressive. Pro–same sex marriage advocates in Taiwan followed this global trend by viewing universal human rights as a progressive value and regarded the attainment of same-sex marriage equality as a key indicator of whether or not a nation possessed an advanced democracy. Local opponents rejected this demand as an indication of the strong influx of Euro-American gay culture, arguing that not only did it threaten traditional family structures, but it also marked a deviation from religious belief and morality. Here I do not wish to take a position that has already been severely constrained—namely a simplified choice between support or opposition, conservatism or progressiveness—and instead I would like to map out the force field into which Taiwan is enfolded. I propose that Taiwan's recent "Pikaochiu" incident marks a possible emergence of "new forms and energies" and may function as an entry point into a political *and* historical rethinking of Asia as counter-method.

Where does the new *Pikaochiu* coinage come from? On March 24, 2017, Taiwan's Judicial Yuan convened the Constitutional Court and invited legal professionals to debate the issue of same-sex marriage. Participants included Minister of Justice Chiu Tai-san 邱太三, present in an ex officio capacity, who cited fears that the legalization of same-sex marriage would create chaos with respect to traditional ancestor worship ritual practices. Chiu raised the question of how same-sex spouses should be addressed on funeral memorial tablets, asking, "Should people then write '*kaokao*' ['father-father'] or '*bibi*' ['mother-mother']?" 究竟應該是寫「考考」還是寫「妣妣」? Chiu's comments drew widespread mockery, as people were baffled by his attempt to link debates over same-sex marriage rights with the question of how to address deceased parents on memorial tablets. Chiu's speech was labeled "Pikaochu" by internet users, who then circulated this coinage as a *kuso*. This *Pikaochiu* (or *Bikaoqiu* in the *pinyin* romanization system) neologism was a portmanteau composed of Chiu Tai-san's surname and the funeral tablet terms *kao* 考 and *bi* 妣, to which he alluded in his remarks. The term's humor, meanwhile, lay in the fact that the neologism was a near homonym of the name of the Pokémon character Pikachu, and internet users amused themselves by superimposing a yellow mouse-face over Chiu's head. If the unintended comedic resonance of Pikaochiu's remarks lies in the way he tried to conflate questions of same-sex marriage rights and ancestral tablet terminology, does not Pikaochiu's uncanny familiarity lie precisely in the way he fallaciously treated same-sex marriage rights as a sign of inadequacy or a limit to its universality?

If we return to scene of the Constitutional Court debate where the "kaokao bibi" comments were first made, we may observe that Chiu Tai-san's widely derided remarks were made in a very colloquial manner that related directly to people's everyday lives. He observed that when he was sacrificing to his ancestors, one of his elders raised three questions: If same-sex marriage were to be legalized, should same-sex couples' memorial tablets be inscribed with same-sex binomes such as *kaokao* or *bibi*, should their obituaries refer to them as "daughter-in-law" or "son-in-law," and at weddings should they be referred to as "bride and groom" or as "male person-to-wed and female person-to-be-wed"? On the surface, these questions might appear to be rather random, but in reality they speak to three key operational fields within East Asian Confucian kinship structure: namely, weddings, funerals, and ancestor worship. Also, although on the surface these questions might appear to involve merely changes in terminology, in reality they have the potential to disrupt the entire East Asian Confucian order, which is grounded on a set of hierarchized binary oppositions between inner and outer, near and far, close and distant, superior and subordinate, major and minor.

The question of whether deceased same-sex couples' funeral tablets should use *kaobi* (father-mother) or *kaokao* (father-father) and *bibi* (mother-mother) reflects not only a confusion at the level of terminology but also, and more important, an undermining of traditional hierarchized binary oppositions between *kao* and *bi*, male and female. The question of whether to use the terms *daughter-in-law* and *son-in-law* reflects not only issues of gender and hierarchy but also the problem of who, in same-sex marriage, will represent the patriline, or even which patriline will be represented (this being more relevant for male same-sex couples than for female ones). Similarly the resulting indeterminacy of gendered terms such as *bride* and *groom*, *male person-to-wed* and *female person-to-be-wed*, destabilizes the divide between the Chinse verbs *jia* 嫁 (used to refer to a woman marrying a man) and *qu* 娶 (used to refer to a man marrying a woman) that can easily extend to a parallel set of destabilizations at the level of property, inheritance, kinship, and social affiliation.

As a result of the Pikaochiu incident, a new patriarchal clan-based—rather than merely religion-based—direction opened up within the discursive fields of same-sex marriage advocates (which centered around key concepts such as equality, human rights, democracy, and antidiscrimination) and skeptics (which centered around concepts such as compulsory marriage mechanisms, capitalist private property, and marriage hegemony enforced by the nation-state). The incident brought together a very old patriarchal code and a very contemporary set of equality concepts and subjected them to a process of folding and clashing. In this way, the controversy allows us to observe the specter of a millennia-old patriarchal system that seems to continue to persist in East Asia in the daily lives of ordinary people, together with the never-fading specter of the clan-based kinship structure. In this way, we can observe the limits of the Euro-American-centered same-sex marriage discourse, and how out of the old kinship morality systems, there may emerge new "homophobic" forms that rely not on a proscription of specific sex practices but rather on defending the integrity of the family surname and patriline. My point, however, is not simply that a Euro-American same-sex marriage discourse is too limited or that East Asia has its own cultural difference that cannot be integrated into a Euro-American discourse. Instead I propose to use the oddity of the Pikaochiu incident to observe how in contemporary same-sex marriage discourse, (East) Asia functions as a virtual "not yet." The appearance of Pikaochiu simultaneously revealed a discursive path and social movement strategy that was not explicitly anti-Euro-American (in the sense of opposition) but thoroughly counter-Euro-American (in the sense of rollback). That is to say, this controversy around the topic of Taiwan's same-sex marriage initially appears to replicate a parallel set of tensions between contemporary Euro-American pro-same-sex marriage, anti-same-sex-marriage, and anti-anti-same-sex-marriage positions. At the same time, in this replication process there also arises another religion-like "clan" as foregrounded by Pikaochiu, which is enough to reverse *both* the Euro-American universal demand for marriage equality and the East Asian Confucian emphasis on patriarchal order. The "not yet" with its forces of the virtual endows "Asia as a counter-method" with the potential to generate countless more bizarre discursive paths and previously unheard-of strategies and alliances. Here *not yet* does not mean "has not yet occurred" (in the sense of something that does not exist in the past or present but which might exist in the future). Instead it refers to the creative conditions inherent in using a sexual field as a nonrepresentational space or using Asia as a counter-method—such as the way these strategies permit one to continuously challenge any self-assigned limits within social movement and to continue disrupting the formation of any structurally stable national or cultural hegemony.

Because Pikaochiu has emerged as the resident Pokémon of Taiwan's same-sex marriage movement, the site of its sudden emergence cannot be merely the realm of casual jokes. Instead Pikaochiu raises new points of reflection with respect to the movement's strategy. At a time when everyone's attention is focused on debates over amending the civil code or launching special laws (debates that take as their model the progress Euro-American nations have made with respect to legalizing same-sex marriage), how can we understand the differences in kinship terms found in the three drafts of civil code amendments that have been submitted to the Legislative Yuan? In particular, the amendment drafted by the

Democratic Progressive Party uses an "equal application" approach and does not remove or change any kinship terms such as *husband and wife* or *mother and father*, while the amendments proposed by the Kuomintang and the New Power Party systematically replace all gender-specific terms with gender-neutral ones. The insignificance of kinship terms for the global same-sex marriage movement becomes a critical point of contention in Taiwan as whether or not to pursue a more radical rupture within (East) Asian Confucian culture and patriarchal tradition. In November 2018 all three of Taiwan's "anti-same-sex marriage" referendums passed, thereby creating a major tension between the Constitutional Court's judicial interpretation and the popular referendums. Therefore, when Enforcement Act of Judicial Yuan Interpretation No. 748 was passed by the Legislative Yuan on May 17, 2019, it strategically avoided using the term *same-sex marriage* but nevertheless still incited angry critiques from opposition groups. Meanwhile gay rights groups and their supporters resolved that, after the expiration of the amendment's two-year term, they would once again attempt to enter same-sex marriage into the civil code. However, an even more radical reflection on same-sex marriage involves the way in which, while striving for substantive guarantees and symbolic meaning (i.e., having gays and lesbians—or what in Chinese are called *tongzhi* 同志—be recognized as citizens with rights to equality and freedom), the singularity of same-sex marriage in Taiwan can be foregrounded, together with its potentiality to roll back the alleged universal same-sex marriage rights. Just as within Taiwan's same-sex marriage debates there emerged a parallel proposal to abolish the family and destroy marriage, which successfully linked Chinese anarchist movements from the late nineteenth and early twentieth century with contemporary leftist queer discourse of sexual minority or multitude in Taiwan. However, the question was how to foreground even more prominently the historical and discursive implications of the *cancellation of the surname (patriname)* strand of the *abolish the family and destroy marriage* discourse, and how to connect its critique of feudal patriarchy with the *mother's surname* campaign in the contemporary Taiwan Women's Movement. Furthermore, would it be possible to establish a closer dialogue between the *same sexes cannot marry* (*tongxing buhun* 同性不婚) campaign, which has emerged as the most prominent marriage prohibition movement in the West, and *same surnames cannot marry* (*tongxing buhun* 同姓不婚) postulate, which was a key marriage prohibition in traditional (East) Asia? Between these two discourses, might it be possible to establish a transcultural dialogue linking the homophonic terms *sex* (*xing* 性) and *surname* (*xing* 姓) as discourses and actions that might constitute a political follow-up to the Pikaochiu intervention?

Apart from inviting a set of social, historical, and legal interventions, the Pikaochiu incident also invites us to return to the political implications inherent in the gap between Area Asia and bloc asia and between a notion of Asia as entity and Asia as (counter-)method. If we start from a consideration of Area Asia, we can of course use a global vision of same-sex marriage and exchange it for a focus on Asia or inter-Asia. We can begin with an internal comparison of the differences inherent in an East Asian Confucian cultural system, such as the way colonial Hong Kong was influenced by English sodomy laws, or the way China—during a historical span stretching across the 1911 Xinhai Revolution, the 1949 socialist revolution, and the 1966–76 Cultural Revolution—continually strove to destroy the feudal patriarchal clan system, or the way Christianity circulated to South Korea, where we can find huge cultural and historical contingencies among these East Asian countries in terms of the degree to which they had a historical influence on same-sex marriage advocacy, movement strategy, topic focus, resistance forces, and legal revisions. The concept of (East) Asia that is being used as a base entity here is derived either from what Kuan-Hsing Chen calls an anti-colonial, anti-cold war, and anti-imperial position, from a transposition of a global same-sex marriage perspective into a local East Asian historical perspective or a matrix perspective, from using the specificities of East Asian culture to challenge the cultural specific ideals of universalism and progress that are promoted by a Euro-American imperial system, from using a colonial history or Cold War structure to analyze the local specificities of East Asia's gender politics and its *tongzhi* movement, and so forth and so on.

However, it bears repeating why it is important to preserve, within Area Asia, a concept of bloc asia to serve as a potentiality of virtual creation, and why it is necessary to preserve—within a use of inter-reference as method—a parallel approach that uses "reversal" as method, in order to roll back the power of European imperialism that promotes what it views as universal values to the world and also to reverse any rigid approach of "returning because of reversing"—which is to say, falling back onto a reliance on Asian values as a result of a resistance to Euro-American imperialism, combined with a process of searching for Asian cultural resources, even at the expense of essentializing or defending traditional cultural values (including the general acceptance of patriarchal power), in order to avoid committing the same error of slipping from anti-imperialism into re-imperialism.

The Asia we are using here as counter-method is not an Asia positioned as a non-Europe within a Europe/Asia binary (which is to say, according to a critique of orientalist epistemologies), nor is it an "actual" Asia outside a Europe/Asia binary (which is to say, a trap of cultural ontology and solipsism). Instead it is an Asia that is continually in formation within a historical setting in which Western cultural imperialism is inexorably advancing and Asia is gradually falling back, and under a procession of rolling out and rolling back. The possibility that this Asia may serve as a kind of counter-method for the global same-sex marriage equality movement lies in the possibility that even as it is functioning as a reversal and rollback against a Euro-American model of marriage and family, it simultaneously functions as a reversal and rollback against the persistent specter of East Asian Confucian patriarchal values. Meanwhile this patriarchy is not located within a traditional patriarchal culture, the same way that this East Asia is not located within a concrete historico-geographic area. Rather it is an East Asian clan-based patriarchy that was summoned into existence and reshaped by the contemporary global same-sex marriage discourse. Therefore the point of opposition is not to return to traditional culture and whip a dead horse but rather to return to a field of contemporary discourse and action in order to pursue new strategies, establish new strategic partners (Euro-American LGBTQ and feminists are not necessarily imperialist enemies, while modern and contemporary Asian and third world anti-imperialist thinkers are not necessarily not homophobic), and open up all sorts of new alliances—including both possible and impossible ones. Perhaps the possibility of Asia as method lies precisely in the possibility of a continual opening up of a not-yet Asia and a not-yet method.

HSIAO-HUNG CHANG is Distinguished Professor of Foreign Languages and Literature at National Taiwan University. Her books include *Gender Crossing: Feminist Literary Theory and Criticism* (1995), *Queer Desire: Mapping Gender and Sexuality* (1996), *Sexual Imperialism* (1998), *Queer Family Romance* (2000), *Encountering a Wolf in the Department Store* (2002), *Fake Globalization* (2007), and *Fashioning Modernity* (2016).

CARLOS ROJAS is professor of Chinese cultural studies; gender, sexuality, and feminist studies; and arts of the moving image at Duke University. He is the author, editor, and translator of numerous books, including *Homesickness: Culture, Contagion, and National Transformation* (2015).

Notes

1 Here I am relying on the US Pew Research Center's most recent internet statistics. These twenty-six countries include Germany, Malta, and Australia but not Mexico, where same-sex marriage is only legal in part of the country, or Israel and Armenia, both of which only recognize same-sex marriages that were performed elsewhere.

2 The dual term differen*t*iation/differen*c*iation is chiefly conceptualized by Gilles Deleuze. In *Difference and Repetition*, he states that "we call the determination of the virtual content of an Idea differen*t*iation; we call the actualization of that virtuality into species and distinguished parts differen*c*iation" (207). The distinction between them thus pertains to the difference between the virtual and the actual: differentiation points to the virtual operation of difference; differenciation points to actual differences.

3 Leo Ching's article was first published under the title "Taiwan as a Method" but was subsequently retitled "Taiwan in Modernity/Coloniality: Orphan of Asia and the Colonial Difference" when it was included in the volume *The Creolization of Theory*.

4 The concept of counter-actualization or counter-effectuation is also taken from Deleuze and Guattari. As they state in *What Is Philosophy?*, "The event is actualized or effectuated whenever it is inserted, willy-nilly, into a state of affairs; but it is *counter-effectuated* whenever it is abstracted from states of affairs so as to isolate its concept" (159). The process of counter-actualization thus leads to a kind of purer virtual plane, liberating events and thing from their states of affairs and allowing them renewed access to the virtual.
5 Takeuchi, "Asia as Method," 156–57.
6 Ibid., 159–60.
7 Ibid., 165; translation modified.
8 Koyasu, *Dongya lun*, 105.
9 Mizoguchi, *Ribenren shiyezhong de zhongguoxue*, 37.
10 Chen, *Asia as Method*, 251; Chen, *Qu diguo*, 400.
11 Chen, *Asia as Method*, 2–3; Chen, *Qu diguo*, 4.
12 Chen, *Asia as Method*, 223; Chen, *Qu diguo*, 359.

References

Chen, Kuan-Hsing. *Asia as Method: Toward Deimperialization*. Durham, NC: Duke University Press, 2010.
Chen Kuan-Hsing 陳光興. *Qu diguo: Yazhou zuowei fangfa* 去帝國：亞洲作為方法 [Toward De-imperialization: Asia as Method]. Taipei: Flaneur Culture, 2006.
Ching, Leo. "Taiwan in Modernity/Coloniality: *Orphan of Asia* and the Colonial Difference." In *The Creolization of Theory*, edited by Françoise Lionnet and Shu-mei Shih, 309–31. Durham, NC: Duke University Press, 2010.
Deleuze, Gilles. *Difference and Repetition*, translated by Paul R. Patton. New York: Columbia University Press, 1994.
Deleuze, Gilles, and Félix Guattari. *What Is Philosophy?*, translated by Graham Burchell and Hugh Tomlinson. London: Verso 1994.
Koyasu Nobukuni. *Dongya lun: Riben xiandai sixiang pipan* 東亞論：日本現代思想批判 [East Asia Theory: Critique of Japanese Modern Thought], translated by Zhao Jinghua 趙京華. Changchun: Jilin renmin chubanshe, 2004.
Mizoguchi Yūzō 溝口雄三. *Ribenren shiyezhong de Zhongguo xue* 日本人視野中的中國學 [China as Method], translated by Li Suping 李甦平, Gong Ying 龔穎, and Xu Tao 徐滔. Beijing: Chinese People's University Press, 1996.
Takeuchi, Yoshimi. "Asia as Method." In *What Is Modernity? Writings of Takeuchi Yoshimi*, edited and translated by Richard F. Calichman, 149–65. New York: Columbia University Press, 2005.

Printed and bound by CPI Group (UK) Ltd, Croydon, CR0 4YY

14/04/2025

14656884-0001